EYEWITNESS TRAVEL

BELGIUM
& LUXEMBOURG

W9-BWE-762

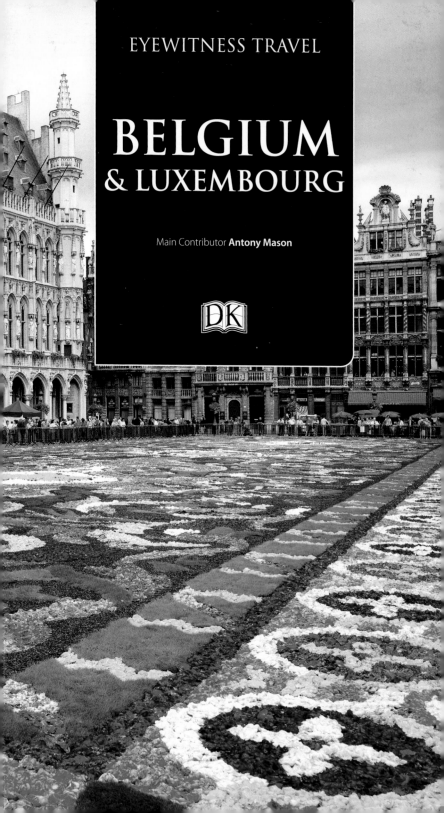

EYEWITNESS TRAVEL

BELGIUM
& LUXEMBOURG

Main Contributor **Antony Mason**

DK

LONDON, NEW YORK,
MELBOURNE, MUNICH AND DELHI
www.dk.com

Managing Editor Aruna Ghose
Senior Editorial Manager Savitha Kumar
Senior Design Manager Priyanka Thakur
Project Editor Sandhya Iyer
Project Designer Stuti Tiwari Bhatia
Editor Shalini Krishan
Designer Namrata Adhwaryu
Senior Cartographic Manager Uma Bhattacharya
Cartographer Jasneet Arora
DTP Designer Azeem Siddique
Senior Picture Research Coordinator Taiyaba Khatoon
Picture Researcher Shweta Andrews

Main Contributor Antony Mason

Photographers
Lynne Mcpeake, Paul Tait

Illustrators
Surat Kumar, Arun Pottirayil, T. Gautam Trivedi

Printed in Malaysia

First American Edition, 2009
17 18 19 20 10 9 8 7 6 5 4 3 2 1

Published in the United States by DK Publishing, 345 Hudson Street, New York 10014

Reprinted with revisions 2011, 2013, 2015, 2017

Copyright © 2009, 2017 Dorling Kindersley Limited, London
A Penguin Random House Company

Published in the UK by Dorling Kindersley Limited.

A catalog record for this book is available from the Library of Congress.

ISSN 1542-1554
ISBN 978-1-4654-5741-7

Floors are referred to throughout in accordance with British usage;
ie the "first floor" is the floor above ground level.

MIX
Paper from
responsible sources
FSC
www.fsc.org FSC™ C018179

Front cover main image: Baroque buildings on the Grand Place, Brussels

 Flowers carpeting the Town Hall at Grand Place, centre of Brussels's Lower Town

Contents

Carvings on a cathedral door depicting the Last Judgement, Antwerp

Introducing Belgium and Luxembourg

Vibrant, colourful costumes at the Pageant of the Golden Tree, Bruges

Vineyards stretching across the wine making commune of Remich, along the banks of River Moselle, Luxembourg

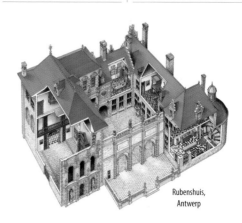

Rubenshuis, Antwerp

HOW TO USE THIS GUIDE

This guide helps you get the most from your visit to Belgium and Luxembourg. It provides detailed practical information and expert recommendations. *Introducing Belgium and Luxembourg* maps the countries and their regions, sets them in historical and cultural context and describes events through the entire year. *Belgium and Luxembourg Region*

by Region is the main sightseeing section. It covers all the important sights, with maps, photographs and illustrations. Information on hotels, restaurants, shops, entertainment and sports is found in *Travellers' Needs*. The *Survival Guide* has advice on everything from travel to medical services, telephones and post offices.

A locator map shows where you are in relation to other European countries.

Belgium and Luxembourg on the Map

The orientation map shows the location of Belgium and Luxembourg in relation to their neighbouring countries. Belgium has been divided into six main sightseeing areas, while Luxembourg has been covered as a whole. These seven sections are dealt with in separate chapters in *Belgium and Luxembourg Region by Region*.

Belgium and Luxembourg Region by Region

Each of the seven regions in this book starts with an introduction and a map. The best places to visit have been numbered on a *Regional Map* at the beginning of each chapter. The key to the map symbols is on the back flap.

1 Brussels
Belgium's capital, dealt with in a separate section, is divided into two sightseeing areas, each with its own chapter. The city centre is shown in detail on the Brussels Street Finder maps on pages 96–101.

All sights are numbered on a map. Detailed information on each sight follows the map's numerical order.

2 Belgium and Luxembourg's Top Sights
These are given two full pages. Historic buildings are dissected to reveal their interiors.

The Visitors' Checklist provides all the practical information needed to plan your visit.

Stars indicate the sights that no visitor should miss.

WESTERN FLANDERS

Charming, fascinating and glorying in the treasures of its historic heritage, Western Flanders is home to vibrant cities such as Bruges and Ghent, and smaller towns such as Oudenaarde, Kortrijk and Veurne. Around them lies a tranquil rural landscape of flat or gently hilly farmland, threaded with rivers and canals. To the north, sandy beaches face out on to the bracing North Sea.

Owing to its location at the crossroads of northern Europe, and to its boundary with the North Sea, Western Flanders has often been thrust into the forefront of historical events. Although a Flemish-speaking land, it was ruled during the Middle Ages by French kings (see part - 2) – a cause of much frustration and strife. Despite this, many of the cities, notably Bruges, Ghent, Ieper, Kortrijk and Veurne, were rich from the cloth trade and industrious with crafts meticulously regulated by their proud guilds. The Golden Age followed in the 15th century, when the dukes of Burgundy took possession and made Bruges the glittering capital of their empire.

However, between 1590 and 1945, Western Flanders was in the doldrums. The economy became largely rural, with small cottage industries such as lace making. The land became a pawn in the big-game politics of Europe,

battered by religious struggles in the 16th century as the Spanish Netherlands disintegrated, then fought over by the Austrians, the French and the English in succeeding centuries. The 20th century brought World War I, which scored a line through Western Flanders, creating a wasteland on either side and demolishing Ieper.

All this changed over the latter half of the 20th century with the rise of Flanders as one of Europe's most prosperous regions. The architectural treasures of the old medieval towns, soldiered and ignored for centuries, but preserved untouched, were restored, and the historic heritage of Flanders has now become one of its greatest assets. Furthermore, Western Flanders has done much to encourage visitors, be it in the great cities, the countryside, on the coast, or on the battlefields of the Western Front.

---

3 Introduction

The landscape, history and character of each region is outlined here, revealing how the area has developed over the centuries and what it offers visitors today.

Each region can be quickly identified by its colour coding. A complete list of colour codes is shown on the inside front cover.

Sights at a Glance lists the chapter's sights by category: castles, abbeys, museums, historic buildings, areas of natural beauty and so on.

Exploring Central Wallonia

The fertile, undulating lowlands of Brabant Wallon are the farmlands setting for the battle-site of Waterloo and for the university of Louvain-la-Neuve. The River Meuse forms a centrepiece, linking Dinant and Namur. It is flanked by the Citadelle of Namur and the châteaux of Annevoie and Freÿr, as well as the abbeys of Floreffe and Maredsous. Crossin roothills in the forested Fagne region, close to the famous Grottes de Hayoune at Petigny. Caves engines puff their way through the Meuse valley between Warenmbourg and Treignes. The hills of the Ardennes begin to rise further to the south and east, where the River Lesse carves a path out of the limestone hills. The spectacular caves of Han-sur-Lesse lie in the far southeast of the region.

Sights at a Glance

Villages, Towns and Cities
- Waterloo *pp182–185*
- Nivelles
- Namur *pp190–197*
- Dinant
- Walcourt
- Rochefort

Churches and Abbeys
- Abbaye de Villers
- Abbaye de Floreffe
- Abbaye de Maredsous
- Basilique St-Materne

Parks
- Jardins d'Annevoie

Castles
- Château de Corroy
- Château de Freÿr
- Château de Spontin
- Château de Lavaux

Areas of Natural Beauty
- Pairi Daiza
- Vallée de la Meuse
- Domaine des Grottes de Han

Museums
- Fondation Folon
- Treignes

Tour
- Vallée
- Citadelle de Namur
- Grottes de Bocq

Getting Around
The main motorway, the E411 (A4), runs southwards across the region, connecting Brussels with Luxembourg. It crosses in the main north-west link (A5) (A15), just north of Namur. The N63 railway network covers all major towns, but fewer areas in the more remote regions, for instance in the area between Ciney and Dinant. A more comprehensive coverage is offered by the bus network of TEC Namur-Luxembourg and TEC Brabant Wallon. Cruises on the River Meuse link Namur and Dinant, for walkers and cyclists, there is the RAVeL Paths. Waremmebourg in the south to Hainguerelles, near Louvain in Flanders. The old routes following the River Meuse, de Dinant and Namur. The GR paths for walkers are concentrated in the south.

Key
- — Motorway
- — Major road
- — Secondary road
- — Minor road
- — Minor railway
- ——— Main railway
- ——— International border
- ——— Provincial border

---

4 Regional Map

This map shows the road network and gives an illustrated overview of the region. All the sights are numbered and there are useful tips on getting around.

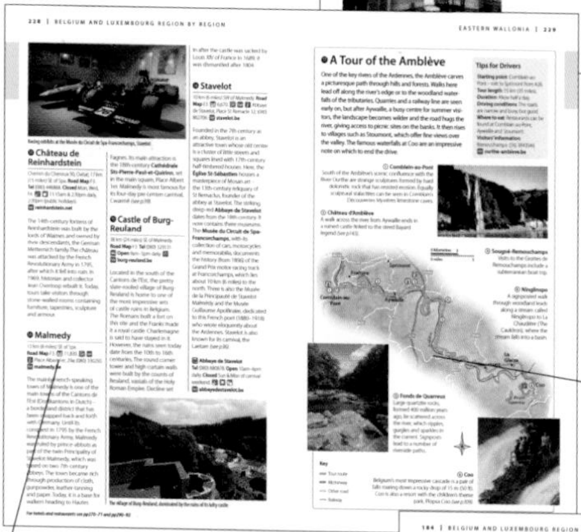

Exploring whilst on the Route du Circuit de Spa-Francorchamps, Ostend

① Château de Reinhardstein

Château-fort Chemin du Cheval, 50 km/ 2.5 miles N of Spa. **Road Map** F3. Tel 080 446 868. **Open** 2pm, Sun & public holidays. 🌐 reinhardstein.net

The 14th-century fortress of Reinhardstein was built by the lords of Waimes and owned for more ages, the counts of Metternich family. The château was attacked by the French Revolutionary Army in 1795, after which it fell into ruin. In 1965 historian and collector Jean Overloop rebuilt it. Today, tours take visitors through the fortress' stone-walled rooms containing furniture, tapestries, sculpture and armour.

② Malmédy

Road Map F3. 🚶 12,000. 🚌 📍 Place Albert 1er, (080 799 668). 🌐 malmedy.be

The main French-speaking town of Wallonia is one of the main towns of the Cantons de l'Est (Eupen is the Germanophone area). The region was part of the Prussian-German territory from 1815 until Belgium reclaimed it in 1919, though briefly occupied by German troops again in WWII. Malmédy resulted by price in attack on all of the twin Principality of Stavelot-Malmédy, which was born in 1661 for many abbeys. The town became rich through protection of cloth, gunpowder, leather-tanning and paper. Today, it is known for walkers heading to Hautes Fens.

For hotels and restaurants in this region see *pp 77 and pp88–89*

In older the castle was sacked by Louis XIV of France in 1689, it was demolished after 1689.

③ Stavelot

18 km/6 miles S of Malmédy. **Road Map** F3. 🚶 6,800. 🚌 📍 Place St-Remacle 32, (080 862 706). 🌐 stavelot.be

Founded in the 7th century as an abbey, Stavelot is an attractive town whose old centre is a cluster of little streets and square-lined with 17th-century half-timbered houses. Here, the **Eglise St-Sébastien** houses a masterpiece of Mosan art, the 13th-century reliquary of St Remacle, founder of the abbey of Stavelot. The striking, deep-red **Abbaye de Stavelot** dates from the 18th century. It now contains three museums. The **Musée du Circuit de Spa-Francorchamps**, with its collection of cars, honours action and memorabilia documenting the history. Room 1840s of the Grand Prix motor racing track at Francorchamps, which lies about 9 km (6 miles) to the north. There is also the **Musée de la Principauté de Stavelot-Malmédy** and the **Musée Guillaume Apollinaire**, dedicated to the French poet (1880–1918) who wrote eloquently about the Ardennes. Stavelot is also known for its carnival, the **Laetare**, best known for its colourful gilles.

🔵 **Abbaye de Stavelot**
Tel 080 880 878. **Open** 9am–5pm Mon–Fri, 10am–6pm Sat & Sun. 🌐 abbayedestavelot.be

---

◆ A Tour of the Amblève

One of the key rivers of the Ardennes, the Amblève carves a picturesque path through hills and forests. Walks here lead off along the river's edge or to the woodland waterfalls of the tributaries. Quaint and a railway line are seen early on, but after Aywaille, a busy centre for summer visitors, the landscape becomes wilder and the road hugs the river, giving access to picnic sites on the banks. It then rises to villages such as Stoumont, which glitter the views over the valley. The famous waterfalls at Coo are an impressive note on which to end the drive.

① **Castellón-sur-Pont**
South of the Nonbélais scenic confluence with the River Ourthe are groups of summer former log-boat elements, rock that has restored decode houses, typically in abrupt dark brown and whitewashed.

② **Château D'Amblève**
A walk across the river from Aywaille is a ruined castle linked to the semi-legend legend (see p143).

③ **Fonds de Quarreux**
Large quartzite rocks, formed half million years ago over past. Are in the river, their edges ripples, gentler and growlers in the river's course.

④ **Tongriel-Remouchamps**
Visits on the Grottes de Remouchamps include a subterranean boat trip.

⑤ **Nonbheron**
A signposted walk through woodland leads along the stream called Ninglinspo to a rock formation called the Bains de Diane (Diana's Bath), where the stream falls into a basin.

⑥ **Coo**
Belgium's most impressive cascade is part of a falls making down a rocky drop of 15 m (50 ft). Coo is also a resort with the children's theme park, Plopsa Coo (see p208).

Tips for Drivers
Starting point: Comblain-au-Pont, 24 km (15 miles) S of Liège.
Tour length: 50 km (31 miles).
Duration: About half a day.
Driving conditions: The roads are clear but winding.
Where to eat: Restaurants can be found at Comblain-au-Pont, Aywaille and Stoumont.

Key
- ━━ Tour route
- ━━ Other roads
- ━━ Railway

For hotels and restaurants in this region see *pp 77 and pp88–89*

---

5 Detailed information

All important places to visit are described individually. Addresses, telephone numbers, opening hours and information on admission charges and wheelchair access is also provided.

Driving tours explore areas of exceptional interest in the region.

The information block provides the details needed to visit each sight. Map references locate the sights on the road map on the inside back cover.

◆ Street-by-Street: Tournai

One of Belgium's oldest urban centres, Tournai has origins dating back to 400 BC. A Roman city, it became the focus of early Christian activity, beginning with St Piat's efforts in the 3rd century AD. Clovis I (AD 465–511), King of the Franks and founder of the Merovingian dynasty and the French royal line, was perhaps born here. The much-venerated St Eleutherius was his first bishop. Although badly damaged by German bombing in World War II, Tournai's long history is written into the city centre. The awe-inspiring Cathédrale Notre-Dame, the soaring belfry and the impressive Grand-Place are surrounded by old cobbled streets which provide a constantly changing view of the city skyline.

Cathédrale Notre-Dame
The colossal and magnificent cathedral is enriched with a wealth of detail, including two of ornate sculpture at the exterior and an elaborately carved 16th-century rood screen inside.

Cathédrale Notre-Dame's Treasury
One of the most precious collections in Belgium, the church's treasury includes the reliquary shrine of St Eleutherius, completed in 1247, which is panelled in the lovely fine-Gothic Rayonnant.

Eglise St-Jacques
This 13th-century church is on the route to Santiago de Compostela in Spain.

The River Schelt
Known here as the Escaut, the river gave Tournai vital navigable access to the sea, making it a trading hub on the Middle Ages.

VISITORS' CHECKLIST
Practical Information
Road Map B3.
🚶 69,000. 🚌 📍 Place Paul-Emile Janson 1, (069 222 045). Grand-Place Vieux Marché-aux-Poteries. **Open** daily.
Cathédrale **Open** daily.
Musée de la Tapisserie **Open** 9:30am–noon & 2–5:30pm Tue–Sun.
Beffroi **Open** Apr–Oct: 10am–1pm & 2–6:30pm Tue–Sun.

Grand-Place
The town square is bordered by numerous 13th-century façades and the cathedral's tower-tours in the east. On the western side, the Halle-des-Draps (Clothmakers' Hall, built in 1610) has a gabled façade. A statue of Christine de Lalaing stands at the centre of the square.

Eglise St-Quentin
This grey-stone columns and moulding gives this 12th-century church a tranquil austerity. It was restored in the 1960s, following wartime damage. In general it houses a statue of Notre-Dame de la Treille in 1740.

The Musée de la Tapisserie
celebrates Tournai's tradition of tapestry weaving.

The Belfry
Begun in the 12th century, but dating mainly from the 14th century, the belfry in Tournai is the oldest in Belgium, and among the navigable access to the sea. Climbing to the top of the 72-step staircase visitors to the top leads to views to the top, where a parapet offers excellent views.

---

6 Street-by-Street Map

This gives a bird's-eye view of the key area in each chapter.

A suggested route for a walk is shown in red.

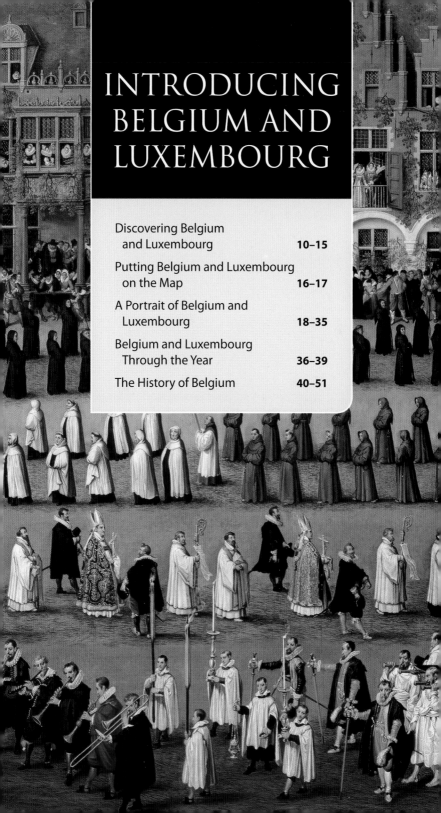

INTRODUCING BELGIUM AND LUXEMBOURG

DISCOVERING BELGIUM AND LUXEMBOURG

The following itineraries have been designed to take in as many of Belgium and Luxembourg's highlights as possible, while keeping long-distance travel manageable. The first itinerary outlined here is a two-day tour of Belgium's capital, Brussels, which takes in the main attractions of the city. This is followed by a week-long tour of the whole of Belgium that covers many of the country's must-see sights, with stopovers at cities and areas of great natural beauty. Additional suggestions are provided for those who want to extend their trip to 10 days. Finally, there is a superb 14-day tour of both Belgium and Luxembourg, which includes all the sights of the one-week tour and more. Pick, combine and follow your favourite tours, or dip in and out and be inspired.

A Week in Belgium

- Appreciate the architectural splendour of **Brussels**.
- Explore picture-postcard perfect **Bruges**.
- Taste Belgium's best fries in **Ghent**.
- Remember the fallen on the battlefields of the **Ardennes**.
- Visit the impenetrable **Château-Fort de Bouillon** of crusader knight Godefroid de Bouillon.
- Discover the industrial heritage of **Western Wallonia**.

Key

━━ A Week in Belgium

━━ Two Weeks in Belgium and Luxembourg

Graslei Embankment, Ghent
Lined with well-preserved guildhouses – some of which date from the 12th century – the Graslei Embankment is one of Ghent's most beautiful streets. An amble along this street in the evening makes for a memorable experience.

0 miles   30

0 kilometres   30

◄ Detail from *The Triumph of the Archduchess Isabella*, painted in 1616 by Denys van Alsloot (1570–1628)

Citadelle *(p209)* and the majestic Collegiale Notre-Dame *(p209)*. Later, check out the Grotte la Merveilleuse *(p209)*, one of the country's best caves for stalactites. Visit the **Château de Vêves** *(p211)* next, before heading to the **Domaine des Grottes de Han** *(p215)*, the most celebrated of the Ardennes cave systems. Within the same complex is the Reserve d'Animaux Sauvages *(p215)*, an excellent safari park.

Day 8: Bouillon to Luxembourg City

Start at the stunning **Château-Fort de Bouillon** *(pp236–7)*, once owned by legendary crusader Godefroid de Bouillon. Then, drive on to **Luxembourg City** *(pp244–9)* and spend the rest of the day exploring the picturesque Old Town on foot. Be sure not to miss the splendid Palais Grand-Ducal *(p244)*.

Day 9: Around Luxembourg

Drive north to **Echternach** *(p255)*, which makes a good base for a tour of the **Petite Suisse Luxembourgeoise** *(p254)*. Stroll around the park soaking in its landscape characterized by steep valleys, gushing streams and dramatic rock formations. Then, move on to the pretty little town of **Vianden** *(p255)* to explore the towering Château de Vianden *(p255)*, complete with original Gothic towers. End the day in **Esch-sur-Sûre** *(p257)*, a small town famed for its setting on a loop of the eponymous River Sure.

> **To extend your trip...**
> Spend a day exploring the vineyards and wine cellars of **Moselle Valley** *(pp252–3)*, a short drive east of Luxembourg City.

Day 10: Bastogne to Liège

Bastogne *(p234)* is the perfect base for exploring the hills and valleys of the Ardennes, which were once the site of the Ardennes Offensive *(p235)*. Visit the many museums and monuments devoted to the battle, particularly the Bastogne War

Baroque portico of the Rubenshuis, crested with a splendid frieze, Antwerp

Museum *(p234)* and Mardasson Hill. From here, it is an easy drive north to **Liège** *(pp220–23)*, home to two fine museums, the Musée Grand Curtius *(p221)* and the Musée de la Vie Wallone *(p220)*.

Day 11: Central & Eastern Flanders

Start your day at the **Bokrijk Openluchtmuseum** *(p171)* for an insight into life in pre-industrial rural Flanders. From here, head to **Leuven** *(pp164–5)*. Amble around its cobblestoned central square, the Oude Markt *(p164)*, one of Belgium's prettiest. Wrap up the day with a visit to the elaborate Stadhuis *(p164)*.

Day 12: Antwerp

Once a busy industrial port and now a centre of high-end fashion design, **Antwerp** *(pp148–59)* offers many attractions. Begin

Equestrian statue of William II at Place Guillaume II in the Old Town, Luxembourg City

with a visit to the Grote Markt *(p148)*, before moving on to the striking **Rubenshuis** *(pp154–5)*, once the home and studio of Paul Rubens. Enjoy lunch in one of the cafés at the lovely Groenplaats *(p151)*. Spend the afternoon exploring **Koninklijk Museum** *(pp156–7)* that houses a fine collection of works by Flemish painters from the 15th century to the present day.

Day 13: Ghent

Drive north to **Ghent** *(pp134–9)* and dedicate a full day to this amazing city, once the largest and richest in Europe. Soak in its rich history at the Design Museum Gent *(p137)*; be sure to reserve a good couple of hours for exploration. Later, take a walk down the Graslei and Korenlei *(p137)* embankments, lined with fabulous townhouses. While around central Poeljemarkt, visit the Stadhuis *(p136)*, the 12th-century St Baafskathedral *(p136)* and the Belfort *(p136)*.

Day 14: Brussels

Begin at the **Place Royale** *(p68)*, where some of the finest palaces in Europe can be seen. The **Palais Royal** *(p68)* boasts a striking Throne Room (open for a few weeks in summer only). Set aside plenty of time to see the treasures of the **Musées Royaux des Beaux-Arts** *(pp72–7)*. After lunch, take a walk around the **Grand Place** *(pp60–61)*, which is fittingly the country's finest public square.

Putting Belgium and Luxembourg on the Map

With an area of 30,530 sq km (11,788 sq miles) and a population of about 11 million, Belgium is a small country, bordered by France, Germany, the Netherlands and the North Sea. Its biggest port, Antwerp, lies on an estuary separated from the rest of the coast by a segment of the southern Netherlands. The Grand Duchy of Luxembourg is landlocked, bordered by Germany, France and Belgium. Less than one-tenth the size of Belgium, Luxembourg is one of the smallest independent nations in Europe. Both countries have a rich historical heritage and highly developed economies. They are also among the founding members of the European Union and home to many of its institutions.

0 kilometres 25

0 miles 25

North Sea

Harwich → Hoek van Holland

Vlissingen

↑ Hull

Knokke-Heist

Zeebrugge

Oostende

Bruges

Maldegem

Zelzate

St-Niklaas

Dover, Ramsgate →

Dunkerque

Veurne

IJzer

Diksmuide

Roeselare

Ypres

Menen

Kortrijk

Ghent

Dendermonde

Scheldt

Aalst

Leie

Oudenaarde

Geraardsbergen

Halle

FRANCE

Roubaix

Escaut

Lille

Lille ✈

Tournai

Ath

Mons

Binche

Béthune

Lens

Douai

Arras

Valenciennes

Key

— Motorway

— Major road

— Railway

— International border

— Regional border

The Language Map of Belgium

Belgium has three official languages: French, Dutch and German. Dutch is spoken in Flanders, the northern half of the country. In the past, the people of Flanders were said to speak Flemish, but this term is now used to refer to the many dialects of Dutch used within Flanders. French is used in Wallonia, the southern half of the country, as well as in Brussels, which lies wholly within Flanders and is officially bilingual. German speakers form a small community in the east, in the Province of Liège. From an administrative point of view, the linguistic borders are precisely drawn, but in reality they are more fluid, creating considerable antagonism where communities using one language are governed by authorities operating in another. This language divide has become more deeply entrenched over recent decades and is a thorny political issue.

Key

Bilingual (French and Dutch)

Dutch

French

German

Hirson

For keys to symbols *see back flap*

A PORTRAIT OF BELGIUM AND LUXEMBOURG

Tied together by a shared and complex history, Belgium and Luxembourg are two of the most prosperous countries in western Europe. This is manifest in their rich cultural traditions, the fine art and architecture of the towns, the high quality of cuisine and the genuine warmth with which visitors are welcomed.

Both countries are small. The Kingdom of Belgium, with its capital at Brussels, has a population of some 11 million. More than 90 per cent of the citizens live in urban centres, leaving relatively uninhabited the large areas of farmland in the north as well as the wilder Ardennes in the south. The Ardennes spill over into the Grand Duchy of Luxembourg. This tiny yet independent country has a population of just 512,000. Its capital, Luxembourg City, has about 95,000 inhabitants.

The histories of both countries are closely linked. They are both fairly young nations, in that they became fully independent only in the 1830s. For centuries before this, they were ruled by a succession of foreign powers: Romans, Franks, French, Spanish, Burgundians, Austrians and the Dutch. They have been fought over ceaselessly, and suffered particularly in the 20th century during the two World Wars.

This bruising history at the hands of their neighbours made Belgium and Luxembourg avid supporters of the European Union (EU) from the start. Today, both Brussels and Luxembourg City play host to many of the EU's major institutions. Along with Strasbourg in France, they are effectively capitals of the EU.

Remnants of medieval walls surrounding the Old Town of Luxembourg City

◀ A group of brightly costumed men rehearse for the Ommegang pageant in Brussels

The medieval château of Bourscheid, nestling in the remote forests of Luxembourg's Ardennes

Land and Nature

Belgium has the reputation of being a flat country. However, without ever being mountainous, much of the land is, in fact, hilly. This is also the case in Luxembourg, whose capital is perched spectacularly on a rocky escarpment.

Broadly speaking, the landscape of Belgium and Luxembourg can be divided into three distinct zones. The northwest of Belgium is fairly flat and low-lying. However, the land rises in the central band on either side of Brussels. To the west, the area around Oudenaarde is hilly enough to have earned the name, the Flemish Ardennes. To the east of Brussels, productive farmlands cover the hills of the Hageland in Flemish Brabant and the Haspengouw (Hesbaye in French) in southern Limburg. The climate is mild and the land well watered; grapes grown in this area make high-quality Belgian wine.

The third zone is the Ardennes, which covers southeastern Belgium and northern parts of Luxembourg. Once dismissed as remote and under-developed, the Ardennes is now a magnet for people who cherish natural beauty. Much of the land-scape rests on limestone karst, riddled with spectacular rock formations and caves.

These wilder regions are home to a rich diversity of wildlife that includes eagle owls, black grouse and wild boar. The coastal region of Belgium is on the migratory routes of egrets, spoonbills and storks. Both nations readily appreciate their natural heritage and are wary of the threats posed by uncontrolled development. This sensitivity is reinforced through numerous parks and nature reserves.

A flock of gulls sharing the beach with walkers along the North Sea coast

People and Society

Belgium and Luxembourg have three official languages, reflecting their geographical position on the borderlands of three major linguistic groups. Luxembourg has German and French, as well as Lëtzerburgesch, a language of the German family. Many of its people are genuinely trilingual, and switch easily between the three languages.

Belgium is divided into two main linguistic regions. In the north is Flanders, with 59 per cent of the population. The people, known as the Flemish, speak Dutch. In the south is Wallonia, which holds 31 per cent of the population; people here speak French. Apart from these, there is a small German-speaking community in the border region of the east.

The Dutch-French language divide has existed more or less since Roman and Frankish times, in other words for 1,500 years. In spite of their differences, the Flemish and French-speaking communities have remained in geographical proximity, bonded by their religion, Catholicism. This circumstance is a result of the religious strife of the 16th century, when Protestants moved north to what is today the Netherlands; the Catholics stayed back in modern-day Belgium. Luxembourg is likewise predominantly Catholic.

Religion is still a significant presence; churches are very much a part of the landscape and most traditional rites of passage, including baptisms, weddings and funerals, are conducted through the church. Many of the carnivals, so prevalent in the calendar of events, are religious in origin, and some, such as the Procession of the Penitents at Veurne, are impressive displays of devotion. However, religion does not generally play an overt role, and society is basically secular.

High-stepping participants in medieval costume enlivening the Pageant of the Golden Tree in Bruges

Dutch road signage in Belgium

Across the linguistic divides, Belgians and Luxembourgers share similar goals – to achieve comfortable lifestyles through education, hard work and enterprise. Their prosperity is reflected in international rankings of the total national wealth generated per head of population (Gross Domestic Product per capita); Belgium is 16th on the list while Luxembourg is first. Such wealth has attracted workers from all over the world. Many come from EU countries; some in Belgium have links with its colonial past in Africa, especially the Congo; others come from Muslim countries of the Mediterranean, notably Turkey and Morocco. Luxembourg's immigrants, mainly from Europe, account for 37 per cent of the total population.

Outdoor café culture, enjoyed in every town throughout the region

Modern façade of the European Parliament in Brussels, looming above a statue of industrialist John Cockerill

Government and Politics

Belgium is a federal constitutional monarchy and King Philippe is the head of state. Politically, Dutch-speaking Flanders and French-speaking Wallonia have each been given their own regional governments, which has, to some degree, satisfied the desire for autonomy. However, it has also reinforced the divisions. There is an overarching federal government, based in Brussels, but intercommunal strains in recent years have resulted in unstable national governments composed of precarious and complex coalitions.

The resentment attached to Belgium's linguistic divide has a long history, dating back to the Middle Ages, when Flanders was ruled by a French-speaking elite. When Belgium began to industrialize, French-speaking Wallonia became the centre of production for coal, steel and manufactured goods. The Flemish fell victim to economic, social and cultural discrimination. This situation

has been reversed in recent times. As the economy shifted towards light industries, financial services and international trade, Flanders prospered and Wallonia drifted into the doldrums. Politically, Flanders became more assertive, achieving ever greater degrees of self-rule. However, new resentments grew in these changed circumstances.

Luxembourg is also a constitutional monarchy. The head of state is the grand duke, who has genuine authority over an elected government. The grand ducal family has strong dynastic ties to Belgium – the mother of Grand Duke Henri, the present incumbent, was Princess Joséphine-Charlotte of Belgium, the aunt of King Philippe. However, it would be a mistake to think that Luxembourg lives in Belgium's slipstream. Small it may be, but Luxembourg is an utterly independent country with its own distinct culture and identity.

The Economy

Belgium has a mixed economy of manufacturing, agriculture, trade, financial services and knowledge-based industries such as pharmaceuticals, biotechnology and information and communication technology. Its old traditional industries, such as steel and chemicals, are now mainly in the hands of multinational companies. The prime exports are foodstuffs, textiles, iron and steel, cars and plastics. Antwerp in Flanders is a world leader in the trade and processing

The old docks at Antwerp, Belgium's most important port-city

Palatial office of the international steel giant Arcelor Mittal in Luxembourg City

of raw diamonds. Belgium also benefits financially from being the primary centre of EU administration. Tourism is a key sector as well, with its main focus on Brussels and the Flemish cities of Antwerp, Bruges and Ghent.

Luxembourg's largest industry used to be the production of high-quality steel. These days, financial services, banking and insurance, are the main income earners. The country also houses numerous major international Internet companies.

Diamonds
from Antwerp

Art and Sport

Historically, Belgium is known for having produced some of the finest art and architecture in Europe. This includes the pioneering oil painting of Jan van Eyck and his contemporaries, Rubens's spectacular Baroque canvases, Victor Horta's Art Nouveau style, as well as the Surrealism of René Magritte and Paul Delvaux. Like its neighbour, Luxembourg also has an outstanding art scene, boosted by the opening of the prestigious Musée d'Art Modern Grand-Duc Jean (MUDAM) in 2006. Similar dynamism has been shown in ballet and film, and also in fashion, where Antwerp-based designers in particular number

among the industry's most respected names. In the world of books, the Belgian authors Georges Simenon, creator of Inspector Maigret, and Hergé, creator of Tintin, rank among the world's top-selling authors.

Both Belgium and Luxembourg produce talented sportsmen, who acquit themselves well at the Olympics, especially in the fields of judo, high jump and athletics. Belgium has produced outstanding tennis players, notably world champions Kim Clijsters and Justine Henin. Both countries excel in professional cycling, with 22 winners of the Tour de France between them. This includes Belgian Eddy Merckx, considered the greatest professional cyclist ever.

Belgium's champion cyclist Eddy Merckx leading the race at Vincennes, 21 July 1974

Landscape and Wildlife

Belgium has a misleading reputation for being a flat country. This is only true of the northwest, where polders of drained coastal marshes form large expanses of rich green pastures. The central band of the country features undulating farmland, while to the southeast, the terrain rises progressively into the dramatic hills and scenic forests of the Ardennes. The rivers Sambre and Meuse slice through central Belgium, forming a natural northern boundary to the Ardennes. Belgium's wildlife reflects this diversity in landscape with a full cross-section of North European flora and fauna, from deer, wild boar and eagle owls in the Ardennes to the huge flocks of migratory birds that visit the coast.

Limestone caves at Han-sur-Lesse in the Belgian Ardennes

The Coast

Along Belgium's North Sea shore, sandy beaches slope gently to the sea, creating a long tidal reach. Resorts now line the coast, protected by high dykes, but the old dune landscapes at the eastern and western ends have been preserved as wildlife sanctuaries.

The pink-footed goose (*Anser brachyrhynchus*) is among the seasonal visitors to the coast, overwintering to the south of its breeding grounds in the Arctic.

Sea lavender (*Limonium vulgare*) dapples the dune landscapes with mauve when it flowers in summer.

The grey seal (*Halichoerus grypus*) lives in the North Sea, and occasionally comes ashore.

Rich Farmlands and Polders

Just inland from the coast, fertile arable land, interspersed with woodland, rises towards a central band. Grain, sugarbeet, vegetables and fruit are grown here. The Pajottenland, Hageland and Haspengouw regions pride themselves on their agricultural produce.

The red squirrel (*Sciurus vulgaris*) is seen around the woodlands, where it nests in conifer trees.

Rosebay willowherb, or fireweed (*Epilobium angustifolium*), is a tough perennial that lends colour to the fringes of farmland.

The brown hare (*Lepus europaeus*) likes open country, farmland and orchards. Living alone or in pairs, it feeds on grasses and twigs and raises its young above ground.

Depleting Wildlife

It is estimated that between a third and a half of Belgium's animal species are threatened with extinction. Twelve mammals are listed as either Endangered, Vulnerable or Near Threatened by the International Union for Conservation of Nature and Natural Resources (IUCN). As ever, the main causes of threat are loss of habitat, climate change, the arrival of exotic predators and pollution or other human activities that cause disturbance. The red squirrel and European otter *(Lutra lutra)* are on the Near Threatened list, as is the European beaver *(Castor fiber)*. The garden dormouse *(Eliomys quercinus)* is listed as Vulnerable, along with four species of bat. But the most

Bechstein's bat
(Myotis bechsteinii)

The beluga whale
(D. leucas)

threatened are the Cetaceans (whales, porpoises and dolphins) in the North Sea. The harbour porpoise *(Phocoena phocoena)*, sperm whale *(Physeter macrocephalus)* and beluga or white whale *(Delphinapterus leucas)* are all Vulnerable, while the northern right whale *(Eubalaena glacialis)* is Endangered.

Forested Ardennes

The Ardennes cover most of southeastern Belgium and the Oesling area of Luxembourg. Rivers thread through forested hills, with pockets of farmland in the valleys and pastures on open upland. To the south, the land drops away into the rural, wooded Gaume region.

The Moors

Much of eastern Belgium is covered by heath and moorland. Large parts of the Kempen (or Campine) region in the north are sandy heathlands of heather and pine woods. The wildest moors are the Hautes Fagnes in the upper Ardennes, east of Liège.

The western honey buzzard *(Pernis apivorus)* arrives in these forests during summer to breed. The bird's name derives from its habit of eating the larvae from wasp and hornet nests.

The European hedgehog *(Erinaceus europaeus)* is an adaptable, mainly nocturnal mammal found in heathland.

Honey mushroom *(Armillaria mellae)* is a forest fungus that lives on the roots of trees.

Harebells *(Campanula rotundifolia)* are delicate bell-shaped flowers that grow wild on the moors.

Roe deer *(Capreolus capreolus)* are shy, solitary deer that live in forests and pasture, eating grasses and shoots. The males grow small antlers each year.

The little bustard *(Tetrax tetrax)* is a migratory bird that breeds on heaths. The male has a flamboyant mating display.

Belgian Artists

Belgian art rose to the fore when the region came under Burgundian rule in the 15th century. Renaissance painters produced strong works in oil, characterized by intricate detail and lifelike, unidealized portraiture. Trade and artistic links with Italy provided a rich, mutual exchange of painting techniques in the perennial quest to capture visual reality. In contrast, during the 20th century, Belgium's second golden artistic age moved away from these goals, abandoning reality for Surrealism in the work of artists such as René Magritte. Brussels's Musées Royaux des Beaux-Arts *(see pp72–7)*, the Rubenshuis *(see pp154–5)* in Antwerp and the museums around St-Martens-Latem *(see p140)* are fine examples of the respect Belgium shows to its artists' works, homes and contexts.

Portrait of Laurent Froimont by Rogier van der Weyden

The Flemish Primitives

Art in Brussels and Flanders first attracted European attention at the end of the Middle Ages. **Jan van Eyck** (c.1395–1441) is believed to be responsible for the major revolution in Flemish art. Widely credited as the pioneer of oil painting, van Eyck was the first artist to mix colour pigments for wood and canvas and to use the oil medium to fix longer-lasting glazes. As works could now be rendered more permanent, these innovations spread the Renaissance fashion for panel paintings. However, van Eyck was more than just a practical innovator, and can be seen as the forefather of the Flemish Primitive school, with his lively depictions of human existence in an animated manner. Van Eyck is also responsible, with his brother, for the striking polyptych altarpiece *Adoration of the Mystic Lamb*, displayed in St-Baafskathedraal *(see p136)* in Ghent.

The trademarks of the Flemish Primitives are a lifelike vitality, enhanced by realism in portraiture, texture of clothes and furnishings and a clarity of light. A highly expressive interpreter of the style was the town painter of Brussels, **Rogier van der Weyden** (c.1400–64), known in French as Rogier de la Pasture. He combined van Eyck's light and realism in paintings of great religious intensity such as *Lamentation (see p76)*. His work was extremely influential across Europe. **Dirk Bouts** (1415–75) applied the style to his own meticulous, if static, compositions. With his studies of bustling 15th-century Bruges, **Hans Memling** (c.1430–94) is considered the last Flemish Primitive. Moving into the 16th century, landscape artist **Joachim Patinir** (c.1480–1524) produced the first European industrial scenes.

The Brueghel Dynasty

In the early years of the 16th century, Belgian art was strongly influenced by the Italians. Trained in Rome, **Jan Gossaert** (c.1478–1532) brought mythological themes to the art commissioned by the ruling dukes of Brabant. However, it was the prolific Brueghel family who exercised the most influence on Flemish art throughout the 16th and 17th centuries. **Pieter Brueghel the Elder** (c.1525–69), one of the greatest Flemish artists, settled in Brussels in 1563. His earthy rustic landscapes of village life, peopled with comic peasants, are a social study of medieval life and remain his best-known work. **Pieter Brueghel the Younger** (1564–1636) produced religious works such as *The Enrolment of Bethlehem* (1610). In contrast, **Jan Brueghel the Elder** (1568–1625) painted floral still-lifes with such a smooth and detailed technique that he earned the nickname Velvet Brueghel. His son, **Jan Brueghel the Younger** (1601–78) also became a court painter in Brussels and a landscape artist of note.

The Fall of Icarus by Pieter Brueghel the Elder

Self Portrait by Rubens, one of many done by the artist

The Antwerp Artists

In the 17th century, the main centre of Belgian art moved from Brussels, the social capital, to Antwerp, in the heart of Flanders. This shift was largely influenced by **Pieter Paul Rubens** (1577–1640), who lived in Antwerp. Rubens was one of the first Flemish artists to become known throughout Europe and in Russia. A court painter, he also served as a roving diplomat abroad. Trained in Italy, he brought a unique dynamism and swagger to painting, which chimed well with the Baroque tastes of the Counter-Reformation.

Chief assistant in Rubens's busy studio was **Anthony van Dyck** (1599–1641), the second Antwerp artist to gain European renown through his court portraiture. Another associate, **Jacob Jordaens** (1593–1678), is best known for his joyous scenes of feasting, while **David Teniers II** (1610–90) found fame with pictures of Flemish life and founded the Royal Academy of Fine Art in Antwerp.

The European Influence

The influence of Rubens was so great that little innovation took place in the Flemish art scene over the 18th century. In the early years of the 19th century, Belgian art was largely dominated by the influence of other European schools. The artist **François-Joseph**

Navez (1787–1869) introduced Neo-Classicism to Flemish art. Brussels-based **Antoine Wiertz** (1806–65) was considered a Romantic, but is also known for producing melodramatic works, such as the *Inhumation Précipitée* (c.1830). Realism took off with **Constantin Meunier** (1831–1905), a noted sculptor of muscular coal miners and factory workers in bronze. **Fernand Khnopff** (1858–1921) was a leading exponent of Belgian Symbolism, notable for his portraits of menacing and ambiguous women. Also on a journey from Naturalism to Expressionism was **James Ensor** (1860–1949), who often used eerie skeletons in his work, in a manner reminiscent of the 15th-century Netherlandish painter, Hieronymous Bosch. Between 1884 and 1894, the artists' cooperative **Les XX (Les Vingt)** brought together painters, designers and sculptors who reinvigorated the Brussels art scene with exhibitions of famous foreign and avant-garde painters.

Surrealism

The 20th century began with the emergence of Fauvism, as reflected in the charming portraits of **Rik Wouters** (1882–1916), filled with bright counter-intuitive colour.

Surrealism arrived in Brussels in the mid-1920s, dominated from the start by **René Magritte** (1898–1967), who defined his disorientating Surrealism as "[restoring] the familiar to the strange". More ostentatious and emotional, **Paul Delvaux** (1897–1994) produced haunting, dreamlike scenes of skeletons, trams and nudes. In 1948, the **COBRA Movement** promoted abstract art, which gave way in the 1960s to conceptual art, led by installationist **Marcel Broodthaers** (1924–76), who used daily objects, such as a casserole dish of mussels, for his own interpretation.

In recent years, Belgian art has witnessed a resurgence, and a number of artists have made their mark on the international scene, notably **Panamarenko** (b. 1940), **Luc Tuymans** (b.1958) and **Wim Delvoye** (b.1965).

Sculpture by Rik Wouters

Underground Art

Some 58 Brussels metro stations have been decorated with a combination of murals, sculptures and architecture by 54 Belgian artists. Only the most devoted visitor to the city is likely to see them all, but there are several notable works worth seeking out.

Belgian artist Pol Bury, a noted member of the avant-garde COBRA Movement

Anneessens was decorated by the Belgian COBRA artists, Dotremont and Alechinsky. In the **Bourse**, Surrealist Paul Delvaux's *Nos Vieux Trams Bruxellois* is still on show with *Moving Ceiling*, a series of 75 tubes that move in the breeze, by sculptor Pol Bury. At **Horta** station, Art Nouveau wrought-iron work from Victor Horta's now destroyed People's Palace is displayed, and **Stockel** is a tribute to Hergé and his boy hero, Tintin (*see pp28–9*).

Belgian Comic Strip Art

Belgian comic strip art is as much a part of Belgian culture as chocolates and beer. The seeds of this great passion were sown when the US comic strip *Little Nemo* was published in French in 1908 to huge popular acclaim in Belgium. The country's reputation for producing some of the best comic strip art in Europe was established after World War II. Before the war, Europe was awash with American comics, but the Nazis halted the supply. Local artists took over, and found that there was a large audience who preferred homegrown comic heroes. This explosion in comic strip art was led by perhaps the most famous Belgian creation ever, Tintin, who, with his dog Snowy, is as recognizable across Europe as Mickey Mouse.

Hergé, the creator of one of the world's most loved comic characters, Tintin

Hergé and Tintin

Tintin's creator, Hergé, was born Georges Remi in Brussels in 1907. He began using his pen name (a phonetic spelling of his initials in reverse) in 1924. At the age of 15, his drawings were published in the *Boy Scout Journal*. He became the protégé of the priest, Abbot Norbert Wallez – who also managed the Catholic journal *Le XXe Siècle* – and was made responsible for the children's supplement, *Le petit Vingtième*. Eager to invent an original comic, Hergé came up with the character of Tintin the reporter, who first appeared in *Tintin au Pays des Soviets* on 10 January 1929. Over the next 10 years, the character developed and grew in popularity. Book-length stories began to appear from 1930.

During the Nazi occupation in the 1940s, *Tintin* continued to be published, with political references carefully omitted, in the approved paper, *Le Soir*. This led to Hergé being accused of collaboration at the end of the war. He was called in for question-ing but was released the same day without charge. His innocence was amply demonstrated by his work before and during the war, as he expressed a strong sense of justice in stories such as *King Ottakar's Sceptre*, where a fascist army attempts to control a central European state. Hergé took great care in researching his books. For the 1934 *Le Lotus Bleu*, which was set in China, he wrote, "I star-ted… showing a real interest in the people and countries I was sending Tintin off to, concerned by a sense of honesty to my readers."

Cover of the *Spirou*

Statue of Tintin and Snowy

Post-War Boom

Belgium's oldest comic strip journal, *Spirou*, was launched in April 1938 and, along with the weekly *Journal de Tintin*, which began in 1946, became a hothouse for the artistic talent that was to flourish during the postwar years. Artists such as Morris, Jijé, Peyo and Roba worked on the journal. In 1947, Morris (1923–2001) introduced the cowboy parody *Lucky Luke*, which went on to feature in live-action films and US television cartoons. Marc Sleen, another celebrated Belgian cartoonist, was the creator of the popular character *Nibbs* (or *Nero*). During the 1960s, the idea of the comic strip being the "ninth art" (after the seventh

Comic Strip Characters

Some of the world's most loved comic strip characters originated in Belgium. *Tintin* is the most famous, but *Lucky Luke* the cowboy, *Suske en Wiske* the cheeky children and *The Smurfs* have been published worldwide. Modern artists such as Schuiten continue to break new ground.

Tintin by Hergé

Lucky Luke by Morris

and eighth – film and television) expanded to include adult themes in the form of the comic-strip graphic novel.

Peyo and The Smurfs

Best known for *The Smurfs*, Peyo (1928–92) was also a member of the team behind the *Spirou* journal that published his poetic medieval series *Johan et Pirlouit* in 1952. *The Smurfs* appeared as characters here – tiny blue people whose humorous foibles soon eclipsed any interest in the strip's main characters. Reacting to their popularity, Peyo created a strip solely about them. Set in the Smurf village, these stories were infused with satirical social comment. *The Smurfs* went on to become a craze between 1983 and 1985, and were featured in advertizing and merchandizing of every type. They spawned a feature-length film, television cartoons and popular music, and had several hit records.

Modern cover by Marvano

Willy Vandersteen

While the artists of *Spirou* and *Tintin* filled the French-language journals, Willy Vandersteen (1913–90) dominated the Dutch market. His popular creation, *Suske en Wiske* has been translated into English, appearing as *Bob and Bobette* in the UK and as *Willy and Wanda* in the US. The main characters are a pair of "ordinary" kids between 10 and 14 years of age who have extraordinary adventures all over the world, and also travel back and forth in time. Today, Vandersteen's books sell in their millions.

Comic Strip Art Today

Comic strips, known as *beeldverhaal* or *bandes dessinées*, continue to be published in Belgium in all their forms. In newspapers, children's comics and graphic novels the "ninth art" remains one of the country's biggest exports. The high standards and imaginative scope of a new generation of artists, such as Schuiten or Marvano, have fed growing consumer demand for comic books. Both French and Dutch publishers issue over 22 million comic books a year. Belgian cartoons are sold in more than 30 countries.

Larger-than-life cartoon by Frank Pé adorning a Brussels building

Street Art

There are about 50 comic strip mural paintings decorating the sides of buildings in Brussels, most of them in the city centre. This outdoor exhibition is known as the Comic Strip Route and is organized by the Belgian Centre for Comic Strip Art, or the Centre Belge de la Bande Dessineé *(see p66)*, and by the city of Brussels. Begun in 1991 as a tribute to Belgium's talent for comic strip art, this street art project continues to grow. A free map of the route is available from tourist information offices, as well as from the comic museum itself.

Contemporary comic strip artists at work in their studio

Suske en Wiske by Vandersteen

The Smurfs by Peyo

A contemporary cartoon strip by Schuiten

Belgian Tapestry and Lace

For over six centuries, Belgian tapestry and lace have been highly prized luxury crafts. Originating in Flanders in the 12th century, tapestry has since been handmade in the centres of Tournai, Brussels, Oudenaarde and Mechelen. The lace trade was practised from the 16th century onwards in all Belgian provinces. Bruges and Brussels in particular were renowned for their delicate work. The makers of this finery often had aristocratic patrons, as grand tapestries and intricate lace were status symbols of the nobility and staple exports throughout Europe from the 15th to the 18th century. Today, Belgium remains home to the very best tapestry and lace studios in the world.

Tapestry weavers numbered over 50,000 in Flanders from 1450 to 1550. With the dukes of Burgundy as patrons, hangings grew more elaborate.

Tapestry designs involve the weaver and artist working closely together. Painters, including Rubens, produced drawings for sets of six or more tapestries illustrating grand themes.

The texture of the weave was the finest ever achieved – often 5 threads to a cm (12 per inch).

Tapestry

By 1200, the town of Tournai and nearby Arras (now in France) were known as centres of weaving across Europe. Prized by the nobility, tapestries were portable and could be moved with the court as rulers travelled over their estates. As trade grew, techniques were refined. Real gold and silver were threaded into the fine wool, again increasing the value. Blending Italian idealism with Flemish realism, Bernard van Orley (1492–1542) revolutionized tapestry designs, as in The Battle of Pavia, *the first of a series. Flemish weavers were eventually lured across Europe, and this transfer of skill led to the success of the Gobelins factory in Paris that finally stole Flanders's crown in the late 1700s.*

Weavers working today in Mechelen and Tournai still use medieval techniques to produce contemporary tapestry, woven to modern designs.

Lace trade rose to the fore during the early Renaissance. Emperor Charles V decreed that lace-making should be a compulsory skill for girls in convents and béguinages *(see p65)* throughout Flanders. Lace became fashionable on collars and cuffs for both sexes. Trade reached a peak in the 18th century.

The Battle of Pavia (1525) is an example of the complex themes that were popular for tapestry series.

Lace-makers, creating intricate work by hand, are traditionally women. Although their numbers are dwindling, many craftswomen still work in Bruges and Brussels, the centres of bobbin lace.

The Victorian fashion for lace triggered a revival of the craft after its decline in the austere Neo-Classical period. Although men no longer wore it, the use of lace as a ladies' accessory and in soft furnishing led to its renewed popularity.

Belgian lace is bought today mainly as a souvenir. Despite competition from the machine-made lace of other countries, the quality here still remains as fine as it was in the Renaissance.

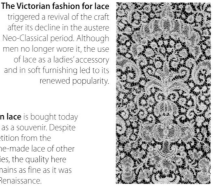

Architecture

Throughout its history, Belgium's international bonds have linked it to the changing trends of European architecture. It was first influenced by Romans, then by the Christian Church and later by styles from across trans-European trade routes. Belgian architecture mirrored trends in Italy and France, moving from Romanesque through Gothic to Baroque and Neo-Classical. However, it always added its own distinctive touches, as seen in the robust muscularity of Scheldt Gothic, in the graceful Brabant Gothic and in the Flamboyant Gothic of town halls. In the 1890s, Belgian architects pioneered the Art Nouveau style.

St-Romboutskathedraal in Mechelen is a masterpiece of Brabant Gothic. After three centuries, work ceased suddenly in 1546, leaving the tower unfinished.

St-Niklaaskerk in Ghent *(see pp136–7)* was built between the 13th and 15th centuries in the austere and elegant Scheldt (or Scaldian) Gothic.

1000	1100	1200	1300	1400
Romanesque			Gothic	
1000	1100	1200	1300	1400

The Collégiale Ste-Gertrude (built 1046) at Nivelles is in the Romanesque style called Ottonian, with the high, turreted Westbau *(see p203)* forming a second transept.

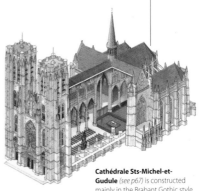

Cathédrale Sts-Michel-et-Gudule *(see p67)* is constructed mainly in the Brabant Gothic style of the 14th and 15th centuries.

The Stadhuis in Leuven *(see p164)* was built between 1439 and 1463 and is the most magnificent example of a secular Flamboyant Gothic building in Belgium. Its façades are encrusted with elaborate stonework of lace-like intricacy, and hundreds of fine statues and carvings.

Antwerp's Stadhuis (built 1561–4), shows how Renaissance architecture was adapted with creative swagger to produce a Flemish Renaissance style. This is seen particularly in the crest of its centrepiece, with sculpture and gilding adding flair to the Classical columns and pediment.

Maison St Cyr (see p79), a private mansion in Brussels, is an extravagant example of Art Nouveau architecture. Designed by the 25-year-old architect Gustave Strauven and completed in 1903, its swirling ironwork is characteristic of this "new art" that made no reference to any architectural style that had come before it.

The Grand Place in Brussels (see p60–61) is lined with guildhouses that were rebuilt after 1695 in the Baroque manner. This style was an exuberant elaboration of Renaissance forms.

St-Carolus Borromeuskerk in Antwerp was the first Baroque church in Belgium.

1500	1600	1700	1800	1900
Renaissance	Baroque	Neo-Classical	Eclectic	Art Nouveau
1500	1600	1700	1800	1900

Kasteel Ooidonk, built in 1595 as a grand country residence in Flemish Renaissance style, shows Spanish influence in its bulb-shaped spires.

The St-Servaasbasiliek at Grimbergen, built between 1660 and 1725, is one of the great Baroque churches of Belgium, a bold, triumphant expression of the Counter-Reformation.

The 14th-century belfry of Tournai, with a carillon of 43 bells

The Oude Griffie in Bruges was built in Renaissance style over 1534–7. Its rectangular windows and Classical columns represented a complete break from the pointed arches of the Gothic style.

Belfries

A symbol of civic pride, the town belfry was used in medieval times to sound an alarm bell as well as to mark the passing of hours. Belfries are built with spiral staircases that lead up through strong rooms where the city charters were kept, and then to the bell lofts and lookout positions. Belgium's belfries are UNESCO World Heritage Sites.

The Théatre Royale de la Monnaie in Brussels, was built in Neo-Classical style in 1819 and resembles a Greek temple.

Castles and Châteaux

Belgium has the distinction of having more castles in a given area than any other country in Europe. Luxembourg might come a close second. These castles range from romantic medieval ruins and stern fortresses built for defence, to the 19th-century fantasy palaces of the super-rich. Today, many of the grander châteaux remain in private hands. However, there are plenty that admit visitors on a regular basis, providing a fascinating opportunity to explore the secular architecture of both countries' often tumultuous past from the inside.

Vianden castle (see p255) rising above the forested hills of Luxembourg

Medieval Castles

Throughout the medieval period, Viking invasions and constant squabbles between rival duchies made it essential for ruling nobles to protect their interests with robust fortresses. The castles that survived have undergone numerous transformations, but still bear witness to the age of the siege-ladder and catapult.

Corner towers protecting the castle's flanks

Exposed causeway crossing the moat to the front gate

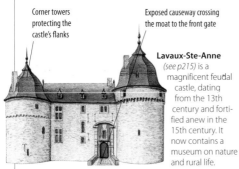

Lavaux-Ste-Anne (see p215) is a magnificent feudal castle, dating from the 13th century and fortified anew in the 15th century. It now contains a museum on nature and rural life.

Kasteel van Beersel (see p168), built in the 14th century, has a moat and three towers facing an inner courtyard. It was partly destroyed in 1489, but reconstructed in the 20th century.

Renaissance Chateaux

After the arrival of gunpowder and cannons in the 14th century, medieval fortifications gradually became less effective. During the relatively more stable rule of the Spanish Netherlands in the late 16th century, rich aristrocrats felt confident enough to build grand châteaux with large windows. However, they still kept an eye on the defences.

Kasteel Ooidonk (see p141), dating from the late 16th century, shows influences from the Italian Renaissance. This is overlaid by the distinctive Hispano-Flemish style of the Spanish Netherlands, as seen in the exotic roof.

Château de Jehay (see p224), another 16th-century fortress, features turrets and a moat. The castle was brought up to date in style during the 18th century, but the interior shows traces of the Renaissance trend towards private, aristocratic life.

17th-Century Fortresses

Armies in this era often adapted medieval castles for defence against powerful artillery. A key figure was the French military architect Marquis de Vauban, who travelled through the Low Countries with Louis XIV's forces. He upgraded the castles of Namur and Bouillon, which had military roles into the 20th century.

Château-Fort de Bouillon *(see pp236–7)*, on a rock by the River Semois, was the stronghold of the crusader Godefroid de Bouillon. Vauban's work can be seen in the inner courtyards and defensive wall positions.

The Citadelle de Namur *(see p206)* was built on a hilltop site used since Neolithic times. It was fortified by the Romans and rebuilt in succeeding centuries.

18th-Century Chateaux

Belgium suffered during the wars of the Spanish and Austrian empires, but châteaux reflected less the imperatives of defence and more the status and taste of their owners. The main stylistic influence was French, but only Château Beloeil *(see p190)* begins to match the grandeur of Versailles.

Château d'Attre *(see p189)*, built 1752, has preserved its original interior, a rare achievement as wars, economic fluctuations and modernization have left few others intact.

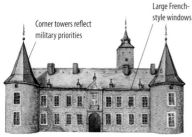

Corner towers reflect military priorities

Large French-style windows

Alden Biesen *(see p172)* was owned by the German Order of the Teutonic Knights. The grim exterior expresses their military heritage, while luxurious rooms match their reputation for extravagance.

Annevoie's famous gardens *(see p208)*, with their fountains and waterfalls, reflect the 18th-century taste for artistically landscaped nature around grand houses.

19th-Century Neo-Medievalism

Wealthy aristocrats and newly-rich industrialists built fantasy castles, as they sought to combine modern comforts with romanticized notions of past grandeur. Sometimes they converted medieval castles such as Gaasbeek *(see p169)*, often with some of the most lavish interiors.

Romantic roofline of decorative turrets

Large windows with river views

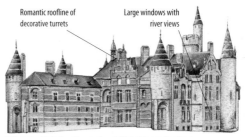

19th-century Kasteel van Bornem *(see p160)*, built in a medieval style

BELGIUM AND LUXEMBOURG THROUGH THE YEAR

Come rain or shine, Belgium has a robust calendar of public events. Some of these are historical parades with centuries of tradition behind them and many are connected to religion, marking saints' days and other Christian festivals. Armies of volunteers turn out in historic costumes and haul vast caricature giants that represent biblical or mythological figures around the streets.

New celebrations, particularly music festivals, are also promoted with vigour and become quickly established. The summer months in particular, are thick with outdoor concerts performed on stages erected in town squares. The events are held in the same spirit of public fun that the Flemish artist Brueghel captured in his paintings almost 500 years ago.

Spring

There may be a chill in the air even as snowdrops and daffodils emerge, and the odd brisk snap can freeze canals, pleasing skaters. Crisp sunny days are ideal for visitors to explore the cities on foot and sample delicious Easter treats.

March
Bal du Rat Mort *(Sat, early Mar)*, Oostende. The Dead Rat Ball, a fancy-dress event, named after a Montmartre cabaret in Paris, has been held for over a century.
Mid-Lenten Carnival *(4th Sun of Lent)*, Stavelot. The Laetare Procession has the traditional Blancs-Moussis (White-Clad) revellers in hooded robes and long red noses.
Easter *(variable)*, nationwide. Children hunt for hidden Easter eggs brought, according to folklore, from Rome by the church bells.

The Holy Blood relic, carried through Bruges by two prelates

April
Serres Royales *(variable)*, Laeken. The greenhouses of the royal palace are open to the public for 12 days.
Ronde van Vlaanderen *(early Apr)*, Flanders. One of the five Monuments of European professional cycling.
Gentse Floraliën *(late Apr, 2021)*, Ghent. This vast garden festival fills halls every five years in Ghent, the heart of the horti-culture industry.

May
Hanswijk Processie *(Sun prior to Ascension Day)*, Mechelen. Costumed parades accompany a revered 1,000-year-old statue of the Virgin Mary.
Processie van het Heilig Bloed *(Ascension Day)*, Mechelen. An 800-year-old pageant celebrating the Holy Blood relic.
Kattefeest *(2018, 2021)*, Ypres. In the Midde Ages, cats were thrown off the cloth-hall tower. This is re-enacted once in three years with cloth cats.
Kites International *(early May)*,

A riot of blossoms welcoming the spring season at Serres Royales

Ostend. Demonstrations by kite masters from all over Europe take place at this annual event.
Jazz Marathon *(weekend, late May)*, Brussels. Jazz fills the city's squares and cafés.

Summer

With longer days and warmer weather, summer has always been the most favourable time for pageants and processions. These months are busy with a variety of excellent outdoor music festivals.

June
Festival van Vlaanderen *(Jun–Dec)*, Flanders. The region showcases its high-quality music and dance.
Ducasse de Mons *(Trinity Sun)*, Mons. Dating from 1380, it displays the reliquary shrine of St Waudru of Mons in the Procession of the Golden Chariot. It culminates in the Battle of Lumeçon between St George and the Dragon.
Les Journées des Quatre

Average Daily Hours of Sunshine

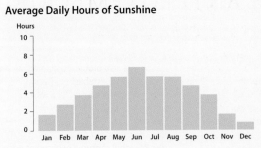

Climate
Belgium and Luxembourg have a fairly temperate northern European climate. Although not often freezing, winters are chilly and a heavy coat is required. Summers can be pleasantly warm though a jersey might still be needed in the evenings. Rainwear is always a necessity.

Cortèges (2nd weekend), Tournai. Folkloric giants take to the streets in four traditional parades.

Battle of Waterloo re-enactments (variable), Waterloo. A major re-enactment marks the anniversary of the battle every five years, but smaller events take place around 18 June every year.

Couleur Café Festival (Jun) in Brussels offers the best in world music.

July

Ommegang (1st Tue–Thu), Brussels. Said to date from 1549, this grand ommegang (walk-around) involves 1,400 participants dressed as stilt-walkers, Renaissance nobles, guildsmen, soldiers, flag-throwers, musicians and acrobats. All parade through the Grand Place before the nobility seated on a rostrum.

Rock Werchter (1st weekend), near Leuven. This four-day outdoor rock festival has gained international fame and attracts a line-up of top acts.

Zevenjaarlijkse Kroningsfeesten (early July, 2023), Tongeren. The Seven-yearly Crowning Festival has a procession of 4,000 costumed people, crowning a 15th-century statue of the Virgin.

Guldensporendag (11 July), Flanders. The anniversary of the Battle of the Golden Spurs in 1302 is a Flemish holiday, marked by a variety of events.

Cactusfestival (2nd weekend), Bruges. Minnewater Park's respected rock festival attracts some big names.

Dour Festival (Thu–Sun, mid-Jul), near Mons. A 20-year-old rock festival with an eclectic set of programmes.

Gentsefeesten (3rd week), Ghent. A ten-day party, mixing street theatre and acrobatics with music concerts.

Moods! (late Jul–early Aug), Bruges. Rock and pop concerts take place in bars, cafés and the two main squares.

Foire du Midi (mid-Jul–mid-Aug), Brussels. Fairground rides and shooting galleries fill the Boulevard du Midi, along with food stands welcoming the shellfish season.

(caption at left of image) Dynamic performance at the Gentsefeesten

Boetprocessie (last Sun), Veurne. The Procession of the Penitents is a solemn affair, and follows a 450-year-old folkloric tradition (see p127).

August

Meyboom (9 Aug), Brussels. Giant figures are joyously paraded to witness the planting of a meyboom (may tree).

Tapis de Fleurs (mid-Aug), Brussels. In even-numbered years, the Grand Place is carpeted in colourful flowers for four days.

Praalstoet van de Gouden Boom (late Aug, 2017, 2022), Bruges. The Pageant of the Golden Tree is held every five years in 15th-century costume, evoking the city's golden age.

Reiefeest (21–31 Aug), Bruges. Theatrical scenes are performed every three years by the River Reie to celebrate the city's history.

Ducasse (4th Fri–Mon), Ath. This procession has folkloric figures such as Monsieur and Madame Gouyasse (Goliath) and includes Belgium's most celebrated parade of giants.

Millions of flowers in intricate designs at the spectacular Tapis de Fleurs

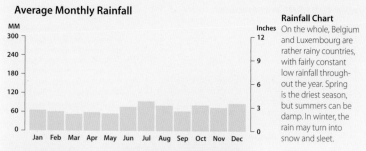

Average Monthly Rainfall

MM
300
240
180
120
60
0
Jan Feb Mar Apr May Jun Jul Aug Sep Oct Nov Dec

Inches
12
9
6
3
0

Rainfall Chart
On the whole, Belgium and Luxembourg are rather rainy countries, with fairly constant low rainfall throughout the year. Spring is the driest season, but summers can be damp. In winter, the rain may turn into snow and sleet.

Cars battling for advantage at the Belgian Grand Prix

Autumn

September can be pleasantly warm, but with a hint of chill in the air. As the crisp days become shorter, restaurants serve warming game dishes.

September
Grand Prix of Belgium
(1st Sun), Spa-Francorchamps. Formula One racing returned to this popular circuit in 2007 after a gap of four years.
Grande Procession *(2nd Sun)*, Tournai. A costumed procession, first held in 1092 after the passing of a plague, accompanies St Eleutherius's reliquary and other church treasures through the city.
Journées du Patrimoine/ Open Monumentendagen *(2nd or 3rd week)*, nationwide. The annual Heritage Days are a rare chance to explore many private historic buildings.
Fêtes de Wallonie *(3rd weekend)*, Namur. Wallonia's role in the 1830 revolution *(see pp48–9)* is celebrated with

events such as a battle of *échasseurs (stilt-walkers)* in 17th-century costumes.

October
Flanders Film Festival *(variable)*, Ghent. This 12-day international festival is respected for its range of films and focus on film music.

Winter

The Christmas markets that start in early December bring a glow of good cheer, but carnival parades, the most exuberant public celebrations, are the real showpieces.

November
Toussaint/Allerheiligendag *(1 Nov)*, nationwide. All Saints' Day, or the Day of the Dead, is when family graves are decorated with flowers.
Kaarsensprocessie *(Sun after 1 Nov)*, Scherpenheuvel. A solemn candlelit procession is the culminating point of the pilgrimage season at the renowned Marian shrine in

Scherpenheuvel *(see p166)*.
St Verhaegen Day *(20 Nov)*, Brussels. Students celebrate "Saint" Pierre-Théodore Verhaegen – founder of the original city university – with madcap antics, often on public transport.

December
Feast of St Nicholas *(6 Dec)*, nationwide. The 4th-century Bishop of Myra, St Nicholas, parades with Zwarte Peter, or Père Fouettard, who threatens to whip naughty children. It is a day of gift-giving and eating *speculoos*, traditional spiced biscuits.

January
Driekoningendag/Fête des Rois *(6 Jan)*, nationwide. Epiphany celebrates the visit of the Three Kings to Christ's nativity. The recipient of a trinket baked into an almond cake gets a paper crown.
Ronsense Bommelfeesten *(Sat after 6 Jan)*, Ronse. This

The traditional Christmas market held in Brussels's Grand Place

Average Monthly Temperature

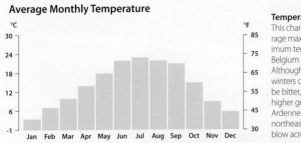

Temperature Chart
This chart gives the average maximum and minimum temperatures for Belgium and Luxembourg. Although generally mild, winters can sometimes be bitter, especially on higher ground in the Ardennes and when northeasterly winds blow across the plains.

"festival of fools" centres on a parade of knockabout characters called Bommels.

February
Carnival (*Thu–Shrove Tue*), nationwide. The weekend before Lent is marked by parades in many cities. Eupen celebrates the arrival of His Madness, Prince of Carnival, and Rosenmontag (Rose Monday). Masked folkloric figures called *haguètes* grab onlookers with huge pincers in Malmedy, while Aalst has satirical floats followed by Voil Jeannetten (Dirty Jennies) in male drag. The best-known carnival, at Binche, is a sea of parading *gilles*, or bizarrely costumed jesters (*see p194*).
Krakelingenstoet (*last Sun*), Geraardsbergen. A costumed parade is followed by throwing *krakelingen* (ring-shaped pastries) into the crowd, recalling a 14th-century event.

Public Holidays

New Year's Day (1 Jan)
Easter Sunday (variable)
Easter Monday (variable)
Labour Day (1 May)
Ascension Day (variable)
Whit Sunday (variable)
Whit Monday (variable)
Luxembourg's National Day (23 Jun)
Belgian National Day (21 Jul)
Assumption Day (15 Aug)
All Saints' Day (1 Nov)
Armistice Day (11 Nov)
Christmas (25 Dec)

Participants at the Sprangprëssessioun, Echternach's dancing parade

Luxembourg Through the Year

Liichtmesdag (*2 Feb*), nationwide. In medieval times, the poor asked for food on St Blasius's day. Today, children with lanterns carry on the tradition by begging for treats.
Carnival (*Sun before Shrove Tue*), nationwide. Parades take place in many towns. Diekirch's has donkeys, the town's mascot, while at Remich, *stréimännchen* (straw guys) are set alight and cast into the Moselle.
Buergsonndeg (*Sun after Shrove Tue*), nationwide. In an ancient tradition of *buergbrennen* (bonfire burning), fires are lit on hilltops to drive out winter.
Éimaischen (*Easter Mon*), Nospelt and Luxembourg City. Pottery is a key feature at this folk fair. Visitors take back *péckvillchen*, or bird-shaped cuckoo-whistles.
Octave (*late Apr*), Luxembourg City. Pilgrims parade to the cathedral in honour of a statue of Maria Consolatrix Afflictorum.
Sprangprëssessioun (*Whit Tue*), Echternach. Ranks of dancers spring past the tomb of St Willibrord, the founder of the abbey here.
National Holiday (*23 Jun*), nationwide. Municipal functions and parties mark the birthday of the Grand Duke of Luxembourg.
International Festival of Music (*May–Jun*), Echternach. A notable festival of classical and jazz music, drawing top names.
Open-air Festival of Theatre and Music (*weekends in Jul*), Wiltz. This offers a varied programme of opera, music and dance in an outdoor theatre (*see p302*).
Schueberfouer (*Aug/Sep*), Luxembourg City. This modern descendant of a medieval shepherds' market is known for serving traditional food and drink.
Grape and Wine Festival (*2nd weekend in Sep*), Grevenmacher. Held as thanksgiving for the grape harvest, the merrymaking starts with the coronation of the Queen of Grapes and culminates in floats offering free wine.

THE HISTORY OF BELGIUM

Both a young country and a very old one, Belgium won independence for the first time in 1830, but owes its name to Gallic tribes who confronted the Romans in 58 BC. Its location on the crossroads of northern Europe made it both a hub of international trade and the battlefield for contending nations. Today, its position has brought new benefits, at the heart of the European Union.

When Julius Caesar set out to conquer the Gauls of western Europe in 58 BC, he encountered a fierce group of tribes there, known as the Belgae. Roman victory in the region led to the establishment of the province of Gallia Belgica. Following the collapse of the Roman Empire in the 5th century, the Germanic Franks came to power here, initially making Tournai, in modern-day Wallonia, their capital. The Frankish ruler Clovis I established the Merovingian dynasty (AD 481–751), whose empire soon encompassed all of Gaul. During this time, Christianity was spread across the land by missionaries such as the French saint Eligius in Flanders. The Merovingians were followed by the Carolingian dynasty (751–987), which produced one of the most important figures of the Middle Ages – Charlemagne, who extended his borders to cover most of western Europe and was crowned by the pope as Emperor of the West. After Charlemagne's death, the empire was divided up among his grandsons, and the province of Belgium was split along the River Scheldt.

Louis the German, as King of East Francia, took the southern portion called Lotharingia (Lorraine). This included the Walha (later, the Walloons) – Romanized Celts who occupied the Meuse valley. Charles the Bald, King of West Francia, took the western portion, which encompassed a large chunk of Flanders. The French claim to Flanders would haunt the region for the next 600 years.

Flourishing Trade

From about 1100 onwards, a number of fortified trading cities developed on inland waterways. Flanders became the focus of the cloth trade, weaving high-quality wool imported from England into valuable textiles and tapestries. By the late medieval period (14th century), trade routes led to France, Germany and Spain, and over the Alps to Renaissance Italy. Belgian towns such as Brussels, Ghent, Ypres, Antwerp and Bruges became famous for their wealth and luxury. Their elaborate town halls, belfries and market squares were physical symbols of their wealth, pride and sense of independence.

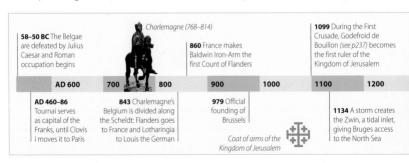

58–50 BC The Belgae are defeated by Julius Caesar and Roman occupation begins

Charlemagne (768–814)

860 France makes Baldwin Iron-Arm the first Count of Flanders

1099 During the First Crusade, Godefroid de Bouillon (*see p237*) becomes the first ruler of the Kingdom of Jerusalem

| AD 600 | 700 | 800 | 900 | 1000 | 1100 | 1200 |

AD 460–86 Tournai serves as capital of the Franks, until Clovis I moves it to Paris

843 Charlemagne's Belgium is divided along the Scheldt: Flanders goes to France and Lotharingia to Louis the German

979 Official founding of Brussels

Coat of arms of the Kingdom of Jerusalem

1134 A storm creates the Zwin, a tidal inlet, giving Bruges access to the North Sea

◀ Charles the Bold (1433–77) in *Rules and Ordinances of the Order of the Golden Fleece*, a 15th-century vellum

A 19th-century painting of the Battle of the Golden Spurs

The Craftsmen's Rebellion

France held sway over its northeastern territory through the counts of Flanders and an aristocracy loyal to the French crown. The trading cities, run by guilds and wealthy merchants, tussled endlessly for the right to control their interests, and won varying degrees of autonomy through the award of precious town charters.

The late 13th and early 14th centuries witnessed a series of rebellions by the craftsmen of Bruges, Brussels and Ghent, against the tyranny of the French lords. On the morning of 18 May 1302, Flemish rebels in Bruges – led by Pieter de Coninck, a weaver, and Jan Breydel, a butcher – slaughtered their French oppressors in an organized uprising that became known euphemistically as the Bruges Matins. Encouraged by this, Flemish troops, armed only with lances and spears, took on and defeated the might of the French cavalry at Groeninge, near Kortrijk, on 11 July. This victory became known as the Battle of the Golden Spurs, after the French spurs that were exhibited in triumph in the Kortrijk cathedral. However, the French took their revenge with a crushing victory at the Battle of Cassel, just south of Dunkirk in present-day France, in 1328.

These tensions continued throughout the Hundred Years' War between England and France. In 1338, it was Ghent's turn to rebel, with a vain attempt to make Edward the Black Prince (son of Edward III of England) the Count of Flanders. The revolt descended into anarchy in 1345 and the new Count of Flanders, Louis de Male (r.1346–84), reasserted French control.

The House of Burgundy

The Duchy of Burgundy had been a major force in European politics since AD 843, and its dukes had close links to the French throne. In 1369, Philip, Duke of Burgundy, married Margaret, daughter of Louis de Male. When the latter died in 1384, the House of Burgundy took over the title of Count of Flanders, along with a patchwork of possessions in the Low Countries. The dukes of Burgundy gradually consolidated

Duke Philip the Good of Burgundy and his court, a miniature painted by Rogier van der Weyden in 1447

Brass effigy of Edward the Black Prince (1330–76)

1302 The Bruges Matins revolt is followed by the Battle of the Golden Spurs – Flemish forces defeat French cavalry

1328 France reasserts control over Flanders after the Battle of Cassel

1300   **1325**   **1350**   **1375**

Breydel and Coninck, leaders of the Bruges Matins revolt

1338 Flemish towns become allied to England in the Hundred Years' War

1337 Start of the Hundred Years' War between England and France

1384 On the death of Louis de Male, his Flemish possessions pass to his son-in-law, the Duke of Burgundy

their rule in the Low Countries, adding Limburg in 1396 and the Duchy of Brabant (which included Brussels) in 1404. Under Philip the Good (r.1419–67), Flanders entered a golden age. Philip was the richest man in Europe and his court was one of the most fashionable and celebrated of the time.

In 1429, Bruges became the capital of Burgundy. For over a century, it had been an important trading city, with a population similar to that of London and Paris. It had a resident international community, with Italian bankers as well as merchants from England, Scotland, Spain, Germany, Genoa and Venice. Paintings by the city's artists, including those by Jan van Eyck and Hans Memling, bear witness to the extraordinary riches of the well-to-do classes in clothing, jewellery and furnishings.

Ruling from his Prinsenhof palace, Philip the Good created the idealistic Order of the Golden Fleece (a reference to the wool trade). This order of chivalry was dedicated to St Andrew and brought many of the kings and leading nobles of Europe to Bruges to iron out their disputes. In 1441, Philip the Good acquired the Duchy of Luxembourg. The only gap that now remained in the Burgundian possessions was the central band of territory along the River Meuse, belonging to the Bishopric of Liège, which included Dinant and Tongeren. Yet, even here, Philip managed to exert control by installing his protégé Louis of Bourbon as prince-bishop.

Death of Charles the Bold depicted by Eugene Delacroix in 1831

The Turning Point

Philip's son and successor, Charles (r.1467–77) used strong-arm tactics that earned him the sobriquets Charles the Bold and Charles the Rash. He captured Dinant in 1466 and Liège in 1468. That same year, he was married for the third time, to Margaret of York, sister of Edward IV of England. Their wedding celebration in Bruges was one of the most spectacular feasts of medieval Europe.

However, Charles overreached himself. In his bid to conquer all of Lorraine, he was defeated and killed at the Battle of Nancy, and, as a result, lost the Burgundian holdings in France.

His only direct heir was his daughter, 20-year-old Mary, who now became ruler of the remaining Burgundian territories in the Low Countries. Louis XI of France hoped to marry his son to Mary of Burgundy, but her stepmother, Margaret of York, had other plans. In 1477, Mary was married to the Habsburg Archduke Maximilian of Austria, son of the Holy Roman Emperor.

Mary of Burgundy (1457–82)

Philip the Good and Isabella

1430 Philip the Good marries Isabella of Portugal, his third wife

1468 Charles the Bold, Duke of Burgundy, seizes Liège

1477 Death of Charles the Bold; his daughter Mary marries Maximilian of Austria

1400	1425	1450	1475

1419 Philip the Good succeeds as Duke of Burgundy

1425 Foundation of the University of Leuven

Tomb of Charles the Bold in Bruges's cathedral

The Habsburg Dynasty

Mary of Burgundy had two children before she died, leaving Maximilian and the Habsburg dynasty the rulers of Burgundy. Maximilian began to raise taxes and tried to reduce privileges that had been granted by Mary to secure the support of the cities. By 1488, Flanders was in revolt.

Maximillian of Austria with Mary and their family, painted in 1516

Bruges made the critical error of holding Maximilian prisoner in a house in the main square. Maximilian exacted his revenge on the city by transferring power to Ghent. At this time, Antwerp also began to rise as a leading commercial centre. In 1494, Maximilian passed his rule of the Low Countries to his son, Philip the Handsome. Philip married Joanna of Castile two years later, and their first son, Charles, was born in Ghent in 1500. While his parents ruled in Spain, Charles was raised by his aunt, Empress Margaret of Austria, who acted as Regent of the Low Countries and moved the capital to Mechelen.

Spanish Rule

In 1516, Charles inherited the Spanish throne and in 1519, he became the Holy Roman Emperor as Charles V. He was now master of a major empire that spanned much of Europe, and also included new overseas possessions in the Americas and East Asia. Nevertheless, he considered Flanders – under the governorship of his sister, Mary – his real home. The Low Countries prospered with land reclamation, canal-building and the expansion of industries producing pottery, glass, tapestry and linen. In 1529, Charles V

forced François I of France to surrender his claim to Flanders. This was the result of a series of battles – mainly for the control of Italy – including that of Pavia in which François I was captured. However, Charles's empire was costly to run, and in 1539, Ghent rose up against heavy taxation and conscription. Charles brutally crushed this rebellion in his native city, forcing its leaders to parade before him in only shirts, with a noose around their necks. *Stroppendragers* (noose-bearers) is still a nickname for the people of Ghent. Meanwhile, the Reformation, begun by Martin Luther in Germany, had started to arouse serious religious conflict. Its ideas took rapid hold in the Low Countries and by the 1520s, Protestant converts in the region were being

Tapestry depicting the Battle of Pavia in 1525 between Francis I of France and the Hapsburg emperor Charles V

The Triumph of the Archduchess Isabella, by Dennis van Alsloot, detailing a procession through Brussels in 1615

burnt at the stake. Charles V abdicated in 1555. In doing so, he fractured the empire's unity, leaving the Holy Roman Empire to his brother Ferdinand and all other dominions, which included the Low Countries, to his devoutly Catholic son, Philip II of Spain. Philip's persecution of Protestants finally sparked the Revolt of the Netherlands (the Eighty Years' War), led by the House of Orange. Protestant rebel leaders were mockingly labelled *gueux* or *geuzen* (beggars), but the "sea beggars" started an effective campaign of naval raids that disrupted shipping. Protestant iconoclasts made their mark by smashing and vandalizing church decorations that offended their sense of spiritual purity. A wealth of medieval sculptures, paintings and treasures were destroyed during this time.

The Duke of Alba, Governor of the Netherlands, responded with a campaign of harsh retribution, in which he was assisted by the much feared Inquisition. Some 8,000 death sentences were issued; among the victims were two conciliatory negotiators, the counts Hornes and Egmont, who were executed

Philip II (1527–98), an oil on canvas painted by Rubens in 1628

in Brussels's Grand Place in 1568. Protestant forces gained ground in the 1570s, until troops loyal to Spain and led by the Duke of Parma regained control over 1578–85. Philip's ambition to crush Protestantism was only curbed when the English defeated the Spanish Armada in 1588.

The Counter-Reformation

In 1598, Philip's daughter, Isabella, and her husband, the Archduke Albert, became rulers of the Spanish Netherlands. Their war on Protestants caused tens of thousands to flee north across the Scheldt estuary to the United Provinces of the Netherlands, which had declared independence from Spain in 1585. The Low Countries had essentially split along this religious divide. Peace intervened briefly after 1609 as, launched by the Council of Trent, the Counter-Reformation turned the tide for Catholicism. Isabella and Albert oversaw a glorious rise in the prosperity of the Spanish Netherlands. This was reflected in the dynamism and swagger of the work of their court painter Rubens, and his fellow artists in Antwerp.

Fernando Alvarez, Duke of Alba (1507–82)

1567 The Duke of Alba sets up the Council of Troubles to eradicate Protestantism and dissent

1598 Isabella and Albert are installed as rulers of the Netherlands and run a strong anti-Protestant regime

1601–04 Archduke Albert lays siege to Oostende to oust the *geuzen*

1560

1580

1600

1568–1648 The Eighty Years' War

1577 Birth of Peter Paul Rubens

Detail from Rubens's Raising of the Cross

1610–11 Rubens, back from Italy, launches his career in Antwerp with *Raising of the Cross* for the cathedral

The armies of Louis XIV of France bombarding Brussels's city centre in 1695

Invasion of the Sun King

The 17th century was a time of great religious and political stuggle for Europe. The Thirty Years' War divided the land along Catholic and Protestant lines. In addition, Spain was engaged in the Revolt of the Netherlands. Under the Peace of Münster, which ended both these wars, Philip IV of Spain finally recognized the independence of the United Provinces. The Spanish Netherlands now consisted of a region more-or-less similar to modern Belgium and Luxembourg. However, under this treaty, the United Provinces gained control of the mouth of the River Scheldt, and Antwerp lost its access to the sea – a disaster for the city that was not rectified until Napoleon overturned the ruling 150 years later.

Ratification of the Treaty of Münster, which ended the war between the United Provinces and Spain

More trouble lay ahead. Following his marriage to Maria Theresa, daughter of Philip IV of Spain, Louis XIV of France (the Sun King) felt he had a claim over the Spanish Netherlands. After Philip IV died in 1665, Louis launched the War of Devolution (1667–8), winning Tournai, Kortrijk and Charleroi. He took Bouillon in 1678, Luxembourg in 1684 and Namur in 1692; all were subsequently fortified by his ingenious military architect, the Marquis de Vauban. However, when Namur was retaken in 1695, the piqued Sun King moved his army to Brussels. On 13 August 1695, the French bombarded Brussels from a hill outside the city, destroying the Grand Place.

Austrian Succession

Subsequent decades were further dogged by war as Austria and England sought to stave off French ambitions. When Philip of Anjou, grandson of Louis XIV, succeeded to the Spanish throne in 1700, it looked as if the combined threat of Spain and France would overwhelm the rest of Europe. Emperor Leopold I of Austria, together with England and many German states, declared war on France. The resulting War of the Spanish Succession raged across Europe for 14 years. Campaigns led by the Duke of Marlborough

Louis XIV, the Sun King

1648 The Thirty Years' War ends and the Peace of Münster recognizes the independence of the United Provinces

1667 Louis XIV of France launches a war to claim the Spanish Nertherlands

| 1620 | 1640 | 1660 | 1680 | 1700 |

1618 Beginning of the Thirty Years' War in western Europe

1660 Work begins on the Baroque abbey church of Grimbergen

1695 French bombardment of Brussels destroys the Grand Place

Altar at Grimbergen abbey church

scored famous victories at Ramillies (north of Namur) and Oudenaarde, which pushed France out of the Spanish Netherlands. Under the 1713 Treaty of Utrecht, it was ceded to Austria.

Emperor Charles VI ruled Austria after Leopold, but failed to produce a male heir. His death resulted in another eight years of war, the War of the Austrian Succession, to resolve whether his daughter Maria Theresa should inherit the crown. The Austrian Netherlands (as they now were) were also drawn into the war. French troops took Tournai, Oudenaarde, Bruges, Dendermonde and Ghent in 1745, and most of the country the following year. With the Treaty of Aix-la-Chapelle (Aachen), the French withdrew from the southern Netherlands, and Maria Theresa's rule was finally acknowledged.

The Treaty of Utrecht that ended the War of the Spanish Succession

Boom and Revolt

In 1744, Empress Maria Theresa installed her sister Maria Anna of Habsburg and her husband Charles of Lorraine as joint governors of the Austrian Netherlands. Maria Anna died in childbirth the same year, but Charles remained governor until his death in 1780. His rule was a period of revival – under the influence of the Enlightenment, Charles's court attracted intellectuals and artists, and Brussels became the most glamorous city in Europe. Industry boomed with the construction of new roads and waterways. Brussels was transformed as the Place Royale and Parc de Bruxelles were laid out in a fashionable Neo-Classical style, which also spread to other cities. However, this prosperity did not filter down to the masses. The people lived in crowded, unsanitary conditions and unemployment was rife. During this time, lace became the industry of the downtrodden.

The Austrian Netherlands were essentially conservative and Catholic. When Joseph II (r.1780–90) succeeded Maria Theresa, he enforced a series of liberal reforms including freedom of religion. Monasteries closed, education was secularized and administration was increasingly based in Vienna. These measures stoked up deep resentment in the citizens. In 1787, a conservative rebellion, led by the Brussels lawyer Henri van der Noot, escalated into the Brabançon Revolt (1787–90). The French Revolution of 1789 further inspired a mood of insurrection. A battle at Turnhout put the Austrians to flight, although the revolt was crushed by Austrian troops dispatched by Joseph's successor, Leopold II. This episode offered a brief taste of independence, but Belgium had to endure further decades of foreign intervention before that could be achieved.

Maria Theresa of Austria (1717–80)

A silver thaler depicting Maria Theresa

1713 The Treaty of Utrecht marks the beginning of Austrian rule in the Netherlands

1740–48 The succession of Maria Theresa to the throne causes the War of Austrian Succession

1782–4 Under Austrian reforms, medieval walls in Bruges are demolished

1720   **1740**   **1760**   **1780**

1719 François Anneessens, a guildmaster in Brussels, leads a revolt against Austrian taxes in Brussels and is beheaded

1745 French troops led by Louis XV invade the Austrian Netherlands

1744 Charles of Lorraine takes up his post as Governor of the Austrian Netherlands

1790 The Republic of United Belgium, formed by the Barbançon Revolt, is crushed by the Austrians

Charles of Lorraine

The Fight for Independence

Belgium was again occupied by foreign powers between 1794 and 1830 – first, by the French Republican Army at war against Austria, then, after Napoleon's defeat at Waterloo in 1815, by the Dutch. French radical reforms included the abolition of the guild system and fairer taxation laws. Although French rule was unpopular, their liberal ideas were to influence the Belgian drive for independence. In 1815, William I of Orange was appointed King of the Netherlands (which included Belgium) by the Congress of Vienna. His autocratic style, together with a series of anti-Catholic measures, bred discontent, especially in Brussels and among the French-speaking Walloons in the south. The south was also angered when William refused to introduce tariffs to protect their trade – it was the last straw. The uprising of 1830 began in Brussels.

King William I of Orange
William's rule as King of the Netherlands after 1815 was unpopular.

A Cultural Revolution in Brussels
The French drove forward a programme of modernization in Brussels. The 16th-century city walls were demolished and replaced by tree-lined boulevards.

Liberals joined workers already protesting in the square outside. All were prepared to die for the cause.

The Battle of Waterloo
Napoleon's attempt to reconquer Europe ended at Waterloo on 18 June 1815. A Prussian army came to Wellington's aid, and by evening Napoleon faced his final defeat. This led to Dutch rule over Belgium.

Agricultural Workers
Harsh weather in the winter of 1829 caused hardship for both farmers and agricultural labourers, who also joined the protest.

The Revolution in Industry
Taxes, unemployment and social divisions under Dutch rule all contributed to the mood of the rebellion that erupted in 1830.

Le Théâtre de la Monnaie
On 25 August 1830, the patriotic song, *L'Amour Sacré de la Patrie*, from French composer Daniel Auber's opera *La Muette de Portici*, goaded the audience into revolt.

Belgian Revolution

The revolution of 1830 was ignited by a radical opera at the Brussels opera house, when the liberal audience rushed out into the street to join a workers' demonstration, raising the Brabant flag. Gustave Wappers (1803–74) brought the drama of Romanticism to his depiction of the Belgian Revolution with the painting, Day in September 1830. Troops were sent by William I to quash the rebels, but the Belgian soldiers deserted and the Dutch were able to retake Brussels. Sporadic fighting rumbled on until 1832. William finally accepted the new borders in 1839.

The initial list of demands asked for administrative independence from the Dutch and for freedom of the press.

Late September of 1830 saw days of costly streetfighting in Brussels, as the rebels defended the city against Dutch troops.

King of Belgium, Léopold I
The crowning of German prince, Léopold of Saxe-Coburg, in Brussels in 1831 finally established Belgium's independence.

1799 Napoleon Bonaparte rules France

William I of Orange

1815 Battle of Waterloo: Napoleon is defeated by an army led by the Duke of Wellington

1830 Rebellion begins at the Théâtre de la Monnaie in Brussels

1800	1810	1820	1830

1792 In the French Revolutionary war against Austria, France invades the Austrian Netherlands

1815 Belgium, allied with Holland under the United Kingdom of the Netherlands, is ruled by William I of Orange; Brussels becomes the second capital

1831 State of Belgium formed on 21 July; Treaty of London grants independence

1835 First continental railway built from Brussels to Mechelen

Consolidating the New State

In Belgium's early days as an independent nation, Brussels was a haven for free-thinkers such as the libertarian poet Baudelaire, and a refuge for exiles such as Karl Marx and Victor Hugo. In 1799, steam power was brought to the textile industry at Verviers, in Eastern Wallonia, and Belgium began following in the tracks of Britain. It was now industrializing fast. Continental Europe's first railway line opened in 1835 between Brussels and Mechelen and by 1870, there were four main railway stations in Brussels that exported goods all over Europe. By this time, the focus of industrial development was Wallonia, with its coal mines and iron industries. This reinforced the age-old supremacy of French-speaking Belgians. Dutch-speaking Flanders remained largely rural, impoverished and increasingly resentful of the imposition of French by the ruling elite – French was the language of administration, education, law and intellectual life.

The long reign of Belgium's second monarch, Léopold II (r.1865–1909), spanned the rapid development of Belgium. He was praised for his vision, but was also associated with the social deprivation that came with industrialization. Equally controversial was his acquisition of the Congo in Africa and the abuses of colonial power that were played out there.

The German Occupations

Like much of Europe, Belgium was enjoying a *belle époque* before the calamities of the 20th century began to unfold. In the summer of 1914, it was invaded by the German army. Although Belgium had been created as a neutral country, some of the bloodiest battles of World War I were staged on its soil. The front line followed a southward path through the marginally higher land around Ypres (Ieper). The opposing armies dug in and suffered years of brutal trench warfare in a stalemate that cost nearly a million lives. Today, the peaceful agricultural land on either side of the salient is spattered with military cemeteries filled with the foreign soldiers who came here to contest the Western Front.

While the Belgian army, led by King Albert I (r.1909–34), put up a spirited resistance from their last stronghold in De Panne in the far northwest, most of the rest of the country remained under occupation – often brutal and vindictive – until the last day of the war, 11 November 1918. The 1919 Treaty of Versailles granted Belgium control of Eupen-Malmedy, the German-speaking area in the east.

In 1940, neutral Belgium was invaded again by the Germans under Hitler. Many Belgians took part in a courageous resistance

Engraving of the interior of a 19th-century forge near Huy in eastern Belgium

1840

1847 Opening of continental Europe's first shopping mall, the Galéries St-Hubert, in Brussels

The Belgian Congo

1884 Léopold II is granted sovereignty over the Congo

1875

1871 The River Senne in Brussels is covered over, and new suburbs are built to cope with the growing population

1893–5 Victor Horta builds the first Art Nouveau house in Brussels

1910

1898 The Flemish language is given equal status to French in law

1914–18 World War I; Germany occupies Belgium

1939–44 World War II; Germany again occupies Belgium

International Status

The latter half of the 20th century was marked by the ongoing language debate between the Flemish and the French-speaking Walloons. Between 1970 and 1994, the constitution of Belgium was redrawn, creating a federal state with three separate regions – the Flemish north, the Walloon south and bilingual Brussels.

Like most of Europe, Belgium went from economic boom in the 1960s to recession and retrenchment in the 1970s and 80s, and renewed growth in the 1990s. This latter period saw a rise in the prosperity of Flanders, while Wallonia declined – a reversal of fortune that reinforced the language divide.

German troops raising the flag of the Third Reich at the Royal Castle at Laeken, near Brussels

movement; the fate of many others was to be forcibly shipped to Germany as labourers. The Nazis also exploited the disaffection of Flemish nationalists, recruiting volunteers to serve their army or operate the notorious concentration camp at Breendonk, near Antwerp. Belgium was liberated by the Allies in September 1944, but the Germans mounted a last-ditch attempt to break the advance by punching a hole through the Ardennes of Luxembourg and southern Belgium in the Battle of the Bulge.

Belgium entered an uneasy peace. King Léopold III (r.1934–51) was at the focus of the contention – he had surrendered in 1940 and was moved to Germany until the end of the war. Rumours, still disputed, that he had collaborated with the Nazis led to his abdication in 1951, in favour of his son, Baudouin (r.1951–93).

Throughout these decades, Brussels's stature at the heart of Europe was consolidated. In 1958, the city became the headquarters for the European Economic Community (EEC), later the European Union (EU). In 1967, NATO also moved to Brussels.

In 2010 , talks began to try to achieve an agreement on the division of power between French and Dutch-speaking areas. After an unsettled period, a coalition government was formed in 2014, with the French-speaking liberal Reform Movement party, headed by Charles Michel, joining three Flemish-speaking parties.

Flags of member states in front of the EU headquarters in Brussels

	1962 The Belgian Congo is granted independence	1989 Brussels is officially a bilingual city	2001 Crown Prince Philippe and Princess Mathilde have a daughter and heir, Elisabeth
1951 Baudouin succeeds Léopold III	1967 Brussels is the new NATO headquarters		2002 The euro becomes legal tender	2014 Charles Michel appointed prime minister

1945   **1980**   **2013**

| 1958 Formation of the EEC, with Belgium as a founder member; Exposition Universelle et Internationale in Brussels, with the Atomium as the star attraction | 1993 King Baudouin dies; Albert II succeeds | 2013 Abdication of Albert II in favour of his son, Philippe | 2016 In March, Islamic State suicide bombers attack Brussels's Zaventem airport and Maalbeek metro station |

Baudouin

BELGIUM AND LUXEMBOURG REGION BY REGION

Belgium and Luxembourg at a Glance

Essentially, Belgium is divided into two halves – Dutch-speaking Flanders in the north and French-speaking Wallonia in the south. Situated wholly within Flanders is the country's capital Brussels, a separate administrative region with a large French-speaking population. Landlocked but independent, the Grand Duchy of Luxembourg is Belgium's southeastern neighbour. Most big Belgian cities are located in Flanders and the northern part of Wallonia. The hilly landscape of the Ardennes covers much of the southern and eastern parts of Wallonia as well as Luxembourg. Here the landscape is more sparsely populated, and cherished for its unspoilt natural beauty.

Brussels *(see pp56–101)* has a glorious centrepiece in its Grand Place, which is fronted by its ornate Flemish-Renaissance guildhouses.

Oostende *(see p126)*, clustered around a busy marina and fishing port, is the largest resort-town on the Belgian coast. Home of the maverick late-19th-century artist James Ensor, it also has a notable museum of modern art.

Oostende
Bruges
Ghent
WEST AND EAST FLANDERS
(See pp108–43)
Aalst
Ypres
Kortrijk
BRUSSELS
(See pp56–101)
Tournai
WESTERN WALLONIA
(See pp180–95)
Mons
Charler

0 kilometres 25

0 miles 25

Tournai *(see pp184–8)* is the oldest cathedral-city in Belgium. It is justly famous for the splendid Gothic and Romanesque Cathédrale Notre-Dame, originally the seat of the city's first bishop, St Eleutherius, in the 5th century.

◀ Colourful, square houses as seen from above in Bruges

Antwerp (see pp148–59) is Belgium's second biggest city, a major European port and an industrial hub. However, its historic centre gives little indication of this. Its primary landmark is the magnificent Gothic Onze-Lieve-Vrouwekathedraal, whose dainty spire soars above the stump of its uncompleted twin.

The River Semois (see pp232–3) snakes through the Belgian provinces of Luxembourg and Namur, past a charmed landscape of forested hills. Walkers, canoeists and motorists come to enjoy the tranquillity and the breathtakingly spectacular views.

Antwerp
Geel

ANTWERP, FLEMISH BRABANT AND LIMBURG
(See pp144–73)

Hasselt

Leuven

Waterloo

Liège
Verviers

Namur

EASTERN WALLONIA
(See pp216–37)

CENTRAL WALLONIA
(See pp196–215)

Marche-en-Famenne

Dinant

Bastogne

Neufchâteau

GRAND DUCHY OF LUXEMBOURG
(See pp238–57)

Arlon

Luxembourg City

Waterloo (see pp200–201) has been preserved as a battlefield site since the defeat of Napoleon in 1815. The man-made hill of the Butte du Lion is its central landmark.

Luxembourg City (see pp244–9) has a refined elegance befitting the capital of the Grand Duchy. This is exemplified by the large central square named Place Guillaume II, with its equestrian statue of the grand duke of the 1840s, William II.

BRUSSELS

The capital of Belgium, and effectively the capital of the European Union, Brussels has always been a hub of trade and politics. Yet, despite its international prominence, the city retains an intimate, human scale, with a web of medieval streets centring upon the superb Grand Place. Brussels's glorious architecture and gilded spires rise over high-fashion boutiques and quaint, time-warped taverns and cafés.

The origin of Brussels lies in the Frankish settlement known as Bruocsella (Village in the Marshes) and a castle built in AD 977. From these beginnings, it became a massively fortified power base for the ruling dukes of Brabant and Burgundy and evolved into a sophisticated city.

From the 12th century onwards, commerce was the engine of growth. The trading centre around the Grand Place was in the Lower Town. In contrast, the palaces of the dukes and nobles stood aloof on the crest of a hill in the Upper Town – a division between the rulers and the ruled that is still detectable in the architecture today. Because French was the language of the elite classes, it became that of the city, which is a French-speaking bubble surrounded by the Dutch-speaking province of Vlaams-Brabant. Officially, if not in practice, Brussels is a bilingual city and all the street names are in both French and Dutch. The city remained the capital as the Spanish Netherlands gave way to the Neo-Classical era of the Austrian Netherlands. During the 19th century, it underwent rapid expansion as a result of which the elegant Quartier Léopold developed in the Upper Town. Today, this zone of orderly avenues and green spaces is home to institutions of the EU. Punctuated with modern buildings, it busies itself with the governmental bureaucracy so readily attached to Brussels's name.

With an urban area of 160 sq km (60 sq miles) and a population of one million, Brussels juggles its great historical legacy and its role in the modern world by offering the best of both heritage and urban prosperity. And true to a city that has the Manneken-Pis as its mascot, a ripple of good cheer is never far from the surface.

The Palais Royal, seat of the royal family in Brussels and centrepiece of the Upper Town

◀ Café life in the Lower Town, beneath a comic-strip mural and the spire of the Hôtel de Ville

Exploring Brussels

The division of Brussels into Lower Town and Upper Town reflects the lie of the land. With the Grand Place at its focus, the Lower Town is the floodplain of the River Senne, which now runs underground. To the east, the land rises to reach the Place Royale, site of the Musée des Instruments de Musique and Musées Royaux des Beaux Arts. A ridge runs all the way from the Palais de Justice, past Notre-Dame du Sablon and Rue Royal to just north of the Centre Belge de la Bande Dessinée. This shape traces the former line of the 14th-century city walls. Further east, the Upper Town becomes more residential and dedicated to running the businesses of the European Union.

The triumphal arches at the Parc du Cinquantenaire

Sights at a Glance

Buildings and Monuments

- ❷ Hôtel de Ville
- ❸ Maison du Roi
- ❺ La Bourse
- ❻ Mannekin-Pis
- ❼ Halles St-Géry
- ⓯ Éditions Jacques Brel
- ⓲ Palais Royal
- ㉑ Palais de Charles de Lorraine
- ㉗ Palais de Justice
- ㉘ Porte de Hal
- ㉝ European Parliament

Museums, Galleries and Theatres

- ❶ Musée du Costume et de la Dentelle
- ❿ Théâtre Marionnettes de Toone
- ⓬ Galeries St-Hubert
- ⓭ Centre Belge de la Bande Dessinée
- ⓳ BELvue Museum and the Coudenberg
- ⓴ Musée des Instruments de Musique

- ㉒ *Musées Royaux des Beaux-Arts de Belgique pp72–77*
- ㉙ Musée Charlier
- ㉚ Musée du Jouet
- ㉞ Musée Wiertz
- ㉟ Institut Royal des Sciences Naturelles

Churches

- ❹ Église St-Nicholas
- ❽ Église Ste-Catherine
- ❾ Église St-Jean-Baptiste-au-Béguinage
- ⓮ Cathédrale Sts-Michel-et-Gudule
- ⓱ Église St-Jacques-sur-Coudenberg
- ㉔ Notre-Dame du Sablon
- ㉖ Notre-Dame de la Chapelle

Parks

- ㉛ *Parc du Cinquantenaire pp80–81*

Streets and Squares

- ⓫ Rue des Bouchers
- ⓰ Place Royale
- ㉓ Place du Grand Sablon
- ㉕ Place du Petit Sablon
- ㉜ Quartier Européen

For hotels and restaurants see p266 and pp280–83

Brussels's Grand Place aglow with a flamboyant carpet of flowers

Getting Around

The distances between the main sights of the Lower Town and the western part of the Upper Town are never great, and are easily walkable in sturdy shoes. However, to reach the eastern parts of the Upper Town, it makes sense to use public transport. This comprises an integrated system of bus, tram, underground tram (premetro) and metro lines. Taxis can be hired from designated taxi ranks. As Brussels is officially bilingual, the names of all the streets and stations on this map are given in both French and Dutch.

Key

▦ Major sights

▨ Minor sights

For keys to symbols *see back flap*

The Grand Place

The geographical, historical and commercial heart of the city, the Grand Place is the first port of call for most visitors to Brussels. The square remains the civic centre centuries after its creation, and offers the finest example of Belgium's ornate 17th-century architecture in one area. Open-air markets took place around this site as early as the 11th century, although Brussels's town hall, the Hôtel de Ville, was built only by the end of the 15th century. City traders further added guildhouses in a medley of styles. In 1695, the French destroyed all but the town hall and two guild façades over three days of cannon fire. Urged to rebuild in styles approved by the Town Council, the guilds produced the harmonious unity of Flemish Baroque buildings that is seen here today.

The Grand Place and Baroque guildhalls

The Maison du Roi was first built in 1536 and redesigned in 1873. Once used to host guests of the monarchy, it now has the Musée de la Ville de Bruxelles, which includes paintings, tapestries and the many tiny outfits of the Manneken-Pis.

① Northeast Corner

② Maison Du Roi

The Hôtel de Ville *(see p62)* occupies the entire southwest side of the square. Still a functioning civic building, Brussels's town hall is the architectural masterpiece of the Grand Place.

Gilded statue of St Michael killing the devil.

The spire was built by Jan van Ruysbroeck in 1449. It stands 96-m (315-ft) high and is a little crooked.

Everard 't Serclaes was murdered defending Brussels in 1388. Touching the arm of his statue is said to bring luck.

⑤ Everard 't Serclaes

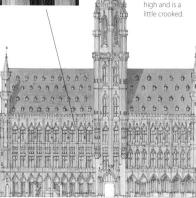
⑥ Hôtel De Ville

Le Pigeon was home to Victor Hugo, the exiled French novelist who chose this house as his Belgian residence in 1852. Some of the most complimentary comments about Brussels emerged later from his pen.

La Maison des Ducs de Brabant is a group of six guildhouses. Designed by the Controller of Public Works, Guillaume de Bruyn, the group looks like an Italian Baroque palazzo.

Locator Map
See Brussels Street Finder, Map 2

Stone busts of the ducal line along the façade gave this group of houses their name.

③ Le Pigeon

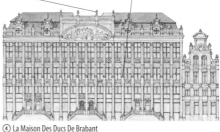
④ La Maison Des Ducs De Brabant

Le Renard (The Fox) was built in 1699 as the guildhouse of the haberdashers by the Flemish architects Marc de Vos and van Nerum. Façade details show St Nicolas, the patron saint of merchants, and cherubs, playing with ribbons.

La Maison des Boulangers, also known as Le Roi d'Espagne, was a showpiece built by the guild of bakers. The 1697 octagonal copper dome is topped by a golden figure blowing a trumpet.

Le Cornet displays the Italianate Flemish style. This boatmen's guildhouse (1697) is most notable for its gable, which is in the form of a 17th-century frigate's bow.

Le Roy d'Espagne now houses the Grand Place's finest bar *(see p94)*, with a popular terrace from which to drink in the splendours of the square. The gilt bust over the entrance represents St Aubert, the patron saint of bakers. There is a vast bust of Charles II of Spain on the second level of the façade.

⑦ Le Renard, Le Cornet And Le Roi D'espagne

❶ Musée du Costume et de la Dentelle

Rue de la Violette 12, 1000 BRU.
City Map 2 D3. **Tel** (02) 2134450.
🚌 29, 38, 46, 48, 63, 71, 86, 95.
Ⓜ Bourse, Gare Centrale. 🚋 3, 4,
31, 32. **Open** 10am–5pm Tue–Sun.
Closed Mon & public holidays. 🚹
🚹 🛈 on request, call (02) 2794355.
🌐 museeducostumeetdela
dentelle.be

Located within two gabled
18th-century houses is a museum
focusing on one of Brussels's
most successful exports – lace.
The intricate skill employed by
Belgian lacemakers has played
a vital economic role in the city
since the 17th century, and the
collection explains the history
of this delicate craft. The second
floor houses a small, carefully
stored collection of antique lace,
demonstrating the various
schools of lacemaking from
France, Flanders and Italy. The
museum also displays temporary
exhibitions on contemporary
textiles and fashion.

❷ Hôtel de Ville

Grand Place, 1000 BRU.
City Map 2 D3. **Tel** (02) 2792343. 🚌 29,
38, 46, 48, 63, 71, 86, 95. Ⓜ Bourse, De
Brouckère, Gare Centrale. 🚋 3, 4, 31,
32, 55, 81. **Closed** election days. 🚹
🛈 Apr–Sep: 3:15pm Tue & Wed,
10:45am & 12:15pm Sun; Oct–Mar:
3:15pm Tue & Wed (English); also
offered in French and Dutch. 🚹
🌐 visitbrussels.be

With its delicate spire soaring to
a gilded statue of St Michael at a
height of 96 m (315 ft), Brussels'
town hall is a city landmark, and
one of the gems of the Grand

Intricate carving on the towering spire and façade of the Maison du Roi

Place. It was built between
1402 and 1455, with the
spire designed by Jan van
Ruysbroeck. During the French
bombardment of 1695 *(see p46)*,
most of the building was
demolished, but the spire
survived, in spite of being
the target of French cannons.
The town hall was rebuilt along
Neo-Classical lines and the
grand public rooms are a
mixture of the 18th-century
palatial and 19th-century Neo-
Gothic styles. The exterior, with
its ranks of statues, dates mainly
from the 19th century.

The building is still used as a
town hall and for civic functions.
Highlights include the fine
18th-century tapestries of
the **Alderman's Room**, the
elaborate **Council Chamber**
and the Neo-Gothic **Wedding
Room**. Paintings show the River
Senne flowing sluggishly
through the city, before it was
covered over in the interests
of public health in the 1860s.

❸ Maison du Roi

Grand Place, 1000 BRU. **City Map** 2
D3. **Tel** (02) 2794350. 🚌 29, 38, 46, 47,
48, 60, 63, 65, 66, 71, 95. Ⓜ Bourse, De
Brouckère, Gare Centrale. 🚋 3, 4, 31,
32. **Open** 10am–5pm Tue–Sun (to
8pm Thu). 🚹 🛈 🌐 brussels.be

Standing on the Grand Place
opposite the Hôtel de Ville, the
Maison du Roi (literally, King's
House, as the site was once
the residence of the Spanish
monarchs) is another successful
venture in the 19th-century
Neo-Gothic style. Built in the
1870s, it was based on etchings
of a 16th-century predecessor
that had served as the Royal
Court of Assizes. It now houses
the **Musée de la Ville de
Bruxelles** (Museum of the City
of Brussels), which includes a
fine collection of the historic
crafts made in the city such as
tapestry, retables (intricately
carved and decorated altarpieces), silverware and
porcelain, as well as paintings
and sculptures. There is also
a good section on the history
and development of Brussels,
brought alive by scale models,
paintings and artifacts. However,
this museum's most famous
attraction is the splendid
collection of outfits made for
the Manneken-Pis *(see p64)*. On
view is a large selection of the
815 carefully tailored costumes
– national, historical, military,
tradesmen's clothing and even
a sub-aqua wetsuit – each one

Luxurious furnishings in the Wedding Room at the Hôtel de Ville

For hotels and restaurants see p266 and pp280–83

Luxurious Lace

Lace (*dentelle* in French, *kant* in Dutch) has always been a luxury product, as it is a hugely labour-intensive accessory. Belgian lace has had a high reputation since the bobbin lace technique was introduced from Italy in the 17th century. Patterns are created by manipulating dozens of threads, each attached to a wooden bobbin, around pins embedded in a cushion. Lace has been used for clothes, shawls and church vestments, as well as table and bed linen. Historically, it was made by women of all social classes – by the nobility as a pastime, by nuns and béguines in convents, and by ill-paid cottage workers exploited by unscrupulous middle-men. During the 19th-century love-affair with lace, there were perhaps 50,000 lace-makers in Belgium. Despite competition from machine-made lace, handmade Belgian lace is still produced and carries a certificate of provenance.

A display of delicately patterned lace

donated by a visiting dignitary since the tradition began some three centuries ago.

❹ Église St-Nicolas

Rue au Beurre 1, 1000 BRU. **City Map** 2 D2. **Tel** (02) 5138022. 🚌 29, 38, 46, 47, 63, 65, 66, 71, 86, 88, 95. Ⓜ Bourse, De Brouckère. 🚊 3, 4, 31, 32. **Open** 8am–6:30pm Mon–Fri, 9am–6pm Sat, 9am–7:30pm Sun & public holidays. **Closed** during services.

A market church was built on this site at the end of the 12th century, but, like much of the Lower Town, it was damaged in the 1695 French bombardment. A cannon ball lodged itself into an interior pillar and in 1714, the bell tower finally collapsed. Several restoration projects were planned but none came to fruition until 1956, when the west side of the building was given a new Gothic-style façade.

Dedicated to St Nicolas, the patron saint of merchants, this low-lit atmospheric church is known for its choir stalls, dating from 1381, which depict the story of St Nicolas on medallions. The unusual angle of the chapel is reportedly to avoid the flow of an old stream.

❺ La Bourse

Palais de la Bourse, 1000 BRU. **City Map** 1 C2. **Tel** (02) 5091373. 🚌 46, 48, 86, 95. Ⓜ Bourse. 🚊 3, 4, 31, 32. **Closed** No longer open to the public. Bruxella 1238: (02) 2794355. **Open** 1st Wed of month; can be visited by appointment at other times. 📷 ♿ obligatory, 10:15am (English), 11:15am (French), 2pm (Dutch).

Brussels's Stock Exchange, La Bourse, is one of the city's most impressive buildings, and it dominates the square of the same name. Designed in Palladian style by architect Léon Suys, the building was constructed between 1867 and 1873. Among its most notable features are the ornate carv-ings on each façade. The great French sculptor, Auguste Rodin (1840–1917), is rumoured to have crafted four caryatids inside, as well as the statues representing Africa and Asia in allegorical groups on the roof. Beneath the colonnade are two beautifully detailed winged figures representing good and evil which were carved by Flemish sculptor Jacques de Haen (1831–1900). Once the scene of frantic trading, La Bourse today houses the offices of Euronext, the owners of the Belgian Stock Exchange, and all financial activity is now via computers.

Allegorical statues crowning the roof line of La Bourse

On its northern side are some archaeological remains from medieval Brussels, exhibited at **Bruxella 1238**. Discovered unexpectedly during roadworks in 1998, these include the remains of a 13th-century Franciscan convent, a church and the grave of Duke John I of Brabant who was buried here in 1294.

A small museum has been built on the site, where interested visitors can see the relics of social and religious life in 13th-century Brussels on display. To protect the remains from degradation, the area is accessible only by guided tours, starting from the Musée de la Ville de Bruxelles in the Maison du Roi.

Simple Gothic shapes on the restored side of the Église St-Nicolas

❻ Manneken-Pis

Corner of Rue de l'Etuve and Rue du Chêne, 1000 BRU. **City Map** 1 C3.
🚌 27, 29, 38, 46, 48, 63, 86, 95.
Ⓜ Bourse, Gare Centrale.
🚊 3, 4, 31, 32.

An unlikely attraction, this tiny statue of a young boy, barely 61 cm (2 ft) high, relieving himself into a small pool is as much a part of Brussels as the Trevi Fountain is of Rome.

The current statue of Manneken Pis by Jérôme Duquesnoy the Elder has been in place since 1619. However, there is evidence to suggest that a stone fountain depicting the same figure stood there before it, possibly as early as 1451.

The charm of this famous statue comes from the many rumours and fables behind it. One theory claims that in the 12th century, the son of a duke was

Brussels's iconic Manneken-Pis

caught urinating against a tree in the midst of a battle and was thus commemorated in bronze as a symbol of military courage. The inspiration for the statue has been revealed as Cupid.

In its long history, the statuette has been the victim of several thefts. A particularly violent theft in 1965 left the statue broken in two pieces, leaving just the ankles and feet remaining. The missing body of the statue reappeared a year later when it was found in a canal.

In the year 1698, the govenor of the Netherlands, Maximilian Emmanuel, brought a gift to the city in the form of a blue woollen coat for the statue. This is a tradition that continues today with visiting heads of state donating miniature versions of their national costume. The little boy has a collection of over 800 outfits which are housed in the Musée de la Ville de Bruxelles, where 100 are on display at any one time. Among the collection is a miniature Samurai, Santa Claus and Elvis suit.

Busy restaurants and cafés on the square outside Halles St-Géry

❼ Halles St-Géry

Place St-Géry 23, 1000 BRU.
City Map 1 C2. 🚌 46, 48, 86, 95.
Ⓜ Bourse. 🚊 3, 4, 31, 32.

In many ways, St-Géry can be considered the birthplace of Brussels. In the 6th century, a chapel was built here supposedly by St Géry, the Bishop of Cambrai at the time. The chapel was located on an island in the marshes of the River Senne, which now flows underground through the city. In AD 977, a fortress took over the site, marking the real foundation of Brussels.

In 1881, a covered meat market was built here in the Neo-Renaissance style. Its glass and intricate ironwork were renovated in 1985, and the hall now serves as a cultural centre with special focus on the city's heritage and environment.

❽ Église Ste-Catherine

Place Ste-Catherine 50, 1000 BRU.
City Map 1 C2. **Tel** (02) 5133481.
🚌 47, 88. Ⓜ Ste-Catherine, De Brouckère. 🚊 3, 4, 31, 32.
Open 8am–5:30pm Mon–Sat, 10am–1:30pm Sun. ♿ on request.

The first church to occupy this site was built in the 15th century. All that remains of it today is a Baroque tower dating from 1629. The present church was redesigned in a variety of styles between 1854 and 1859 by Joseph Poelaert, architect of

the monumental Palais de Justice (see p71). Notable features of the interior include a lovely 14th-century stone statue of the Black Madonna as well as a painted wooden statue of St Catherine, complete with the wheel on which she was martyred. To the east of the church is the stone **Tour Noire** (Black Tower), a remnant of the city's 12th-century defensive walls.

Place Ste-Catherine was laid out as a square in front of the church in 1870, when the canal basin originally on this site was filled in. This used to be the city's main fish market, and is still the best spot to indulge in Brussels's famous seafood, but prices here are generally high. Once situated at the end of the canal link to the North Sea, the **Quai aux Briques** (Brick Quay) and **Quai au Bois à Brûler** (Firewood Quay) flank the square and recall the area's trading past.

Spacious vaulted interior of the serene Église Ste-Catherine

❾ Église St-Jean-Baptiste-au-Béguinage

Place du Béguinage, 1000 BRU.
City Map 1 C1. **Tel** (02) 2178742.
🚌 47, 88. Ⓜ Ste-Catherine.
Open 10am– 5pm Tue–Sat, 10am–8pm Sun. ♿

This stone-clad church was consecrated in 1676 around the country's largest béguine community, which had been established since 1250. Fields and orchards around the site

The Béguine Movement

The béguine lifestyle swept across western Europe during the 13th century. The order is believed to have begun among widows of the Crusaders who resorted to a pious life of sisterhood on the death of their husbands. Single women opted for a secluded existence devoted to charitable deeds, but not bound by strict religious vows.

They were free to leave at any time, for instance to marry. Many béguine convents disappeared during the Protestant Reformation, but begijnhofs (béguinages) continued to thrive in Flanders. These areas generally consisted of a church, a courtyard, communal rooms and homes for the women. Brussels once had a community of over 1,200 béguines, but the movement dissolved as female emancipation spread during the early 1800s. The sites of a number of béguinages have

Portrait of a béguine at prayer in a Brussels béguinage

survived, including those in Bruges (see p117), Ghent (see p139), Leuven (see p165) and Aarschot (see p166).

contained cottages and houses for up to 1,200 béguine women. These were members of a lay religious order who took up charitable work and enclosed living after failed marriages or during widowhood. In medieval times, the béguines here ran a laundry, hospital and windmill for the people of the city. Still a popular place of worship, the church is notable for its Flemish Baroque details from the 17th century, including the onion-shaped turrets and ornamental walls. The unusually wide aisles give it a light, airy feeling inside. The nave, which is also Baroque, is decorated with ornate cherubs, angels and scrolls, while the confessionals are carved with allegorical figures and saints. The apse contains a striking statue of St John the Baptist, and the 1757 pulpit, a fine example of Baroque woodcarving, depicts St Dominic trampling a heretic underfoot.

❿ Théâtre Marionnettes de Toone

Impasse Ste-Pétronille, 66 Rue du Marché-aux-Herbes, 1000 BRU. **City Map** 2 D2. **Tel** (02) 5117137. 🚌 29, 38, 46, 48, 63, 71, 86, 95. Ⓜ Bourse, Gare Centrale. 🚋 3, 4, 31, 32. **Open** pub: noon–midnight; theatre: 8:30pm Thu–Sat, 4pm Sat; museum: performance intervals. 📞 📷 on request, call (02) 2172753. 🅆 **toone.be**

During the period of the Spanish Netherlands (see pp44–5), all theatres were shut down to prevent satirical performances targeting the country's Spanish rulers. This gave rise to a fashion for puppet shows, as the actors' vicious dialogues were more easily forgiveable when they came from inanimate dolls. In 1830, Antoine Toone opened his own puppet theatre and it has been run by Toones ever since – the present owner is the eighth generation Toone. The classics are enacted today by wooden marionnettes in the local Bruxellois dialect, and occasionally in French, Dutch, English or German.

Harlequin puppet

The puppet theatre and museum occupy the top two floors of the building, while the ground floor is a popular pub. The museum displays retired marionnettes, some dating to the 19th century.

Baroque façade of Église St-Jean-Baptiste-au-Béguinage

⓫ Rue des Bouchers

City Map 2 D2. 🚌 29, 38, 46, 47, 48, 63, 66, 71, 86, 88, 95. Ⓜ De Brouckère, Bourse, Gare Centrale. 🚋 3, 4, 31, 32.

Like many streets in this area of the city, Rue des Bouchers retains its medieval name, evoking the time when this meandering, cobblestoned street was home to the butcher's trade. Aware of its historic importance and heeding the concerns of the public, the city council declared this area the **Ilot Sacré** (Sacred Islet) in 1960, restoring surviving buildings and forbidding the further alteration or destruction of architectural façades. Hence, Rue des Bouchers abounds in 17th-century stepped gables and decorated doorways.

Today, this pedestrianized thoroughfare is best known for its plethora of cafés and restaurants, which are mainly aimed at tourists. Many types of cuisines are on offer here, including Chinese, Greek, Italian and Indian. The most impressive sights are the lavish pavement displays of seafood, piled high on mounds of ice and lit by a romantic amber glow from the lamps. However, these displays are only permitted in winter due to city health regulations.

At the end of the street, at the Impasse de la Fidélité, is an acknowledgement of sexual equality. Erected in 1987, **Jeanneke-Pis** is a coy, yet cheeky, female version of her "brother", the more famous Manneken-Pis *(see p64)*.

The 19th-century Galéries St-Hubert, with its soaring domed glass roof

⓬ Galéries St-Hubert

Rue des Bouchers, 1000 BRU. **City Map** 2 D2. 🚌 38, 71. 🚋 3, 4, 25, 31, 32, 94. Ⓜ Gare Centrale. ♿

Sixteen years after ascending the throne as the first king of Belgium, Léopold I inaugurated the opening of these grand arcades in 1847. St-Hubert has the distinction of being the first shopping arcade in continental Europe, and one of the most elegant. Designed in Neo-Renaissance style by Belgian architect Jean-Pierre Cluysenaer, its vaulted glass roof covers three sections – Galerie du Roi, Galerie de la Reine and Galerie des Princes – which house a range of luxury shops and cafés. The ornate interior and expensive goods on sale made the galleries a fashionable meeting place for 19th-century society, including

the resident literati – Victor Hugo and Alexandre Dumas have attended lectures here. The arcades remain a popular venue, with their shops, a cinema, theatre and restaurants.

⓭ Centre Belge de la Bande Dessinée

20 Rue des Sables, 1000 BRU. **City Map** 2 E2. **Tel** (02) 2191980. 🚌 29, 38, 46, 47, 61, 63, 66, 71, 86, 88. Ⓜ Botanique, De Brouckère, Rogier. 🚋 3, 4, 31, 32, 92, 94. **Open** 10am– 6pm Tue–Sun. 🎫 ♿ 🛍 💻 🅿 📷 🌐 **comicscenter.net**

Affectionately known by its initials as *cébébédé*, this museum for comic strip art pays tribute to the Belgian passion for *bandes dessinées* (comic strips) and to many internationally acclaimed comic strip artists from both Belgium and abroad.

Arranged over three levels, the collection is housed in a classic Art Nouveau building originally designed in 1903 by Victor Horta *(see p84)* as Les Magasins Wauquez, an enormous fabric warehouse. Saved from demolition in the 1980s, it reopened in 1989 as an impressive museum and archive centre dedicated to the comic strip, which is often referred to as the "ninth art" *(see pp28–9)*.

One of the most popular permanent exhibitions is a tour of engaging comic strip heroes such as Hergé's *Tintin*, arguably the most well-known Belgian comic character. The tour also includes *The Smurfs*, which first appeared in the *Spirou* journal in 1958 and went on to have its own television show and hit records. Other displays detail the stages of putting together a comic strip, from initial ideas and rough pencil sketches through to final publication. Major exhibitions featuring the work of famous cartoonists and studios are regularly held. The museum also houses some 6,000 original plates, displayed in rotation, as well as an archive of photographs, biographies and other artifacts.

Lively Rue des Bouchers, lined with restaurants and cafés

The exquisitely proportioned Cathédrale-Sts-Michel-et-Gudule

⓮ Cathédrale Sts-Michel-et-Gudule

Parvis Ste-Gudule, 1000 BRU.
City Map 2 E2. **Tel** (02) 2178345.
🚌 27, 29, 38, 63, 65, 66. Ⓜ Gare
Centrale, Parc. 🚋 92, 93. **Open** 7am–
6pm Mon–Fri, 8am–3:30pm Sat (until
2pm Sun). 🅿 to crypt. 🛗 services
throughout the day. 🛗 on request.
🆆 cathedralestmichel.be

Although it is the national
church of Belgium, Cathédrale
Sts-Michel-et-Gudule was
granted cathedral status only
in 1962. It was built with a sandy
limestone brought from local
quarries and is one of the finest
surviving examples of Brabant
Gothic architecture.

There has been a church on
the site of the cathedral since
at least the 11th century. Work
began on the Gothic cathedral
in 1226 under Henry I, Duke of
Brabant, and was finally completed 300 years later at the
beginning of the 16th century,
under the reign of Charles V.
It was dedicated to the city's
patron saints, archangel Michael
and a local 8th-century pious
woman, St Gudule.

Owing to ransackings by
Protestant iconoclasts in 1579
and thefts by French Revolutionists
in 1793, the interior of the
cathedral is far less rich than
it was in medieval times. It
nonetheless contains some fine
stained glass, such as the **Last
Judgement Window**, dating
from 1528, on the west front of
the cathedral, facing the altar.

The transept windows, designed
by Bernard van Orley (c.1490–
1541), date from 1538 and
represent the region's rulers.
Also of particular interest is
the beautiful and original
Grenzing organ.

The flamboyantly carved
Baroque Pulpit in the central
aisle depicts Adam and Eve's
expulsion from Paradise. This
pulpit, by the Antwerp-born
sculptor Hendrik Verbruggen,
was built in 1699, although it
was not installed till 1776.

⓯ Éditions Jacques Brel

Place de la Vieille Halle aux Blés 11,
1000 BRU. **City Map** 1 C3.
Tel (02) 5111020. 🚌 29, 38, 48, 60, 63,
65, 66, 71, 95, 96. Ⓜ Gare Centrale.
Open 10am–6pm Tue–Fri, noon–6pm
Sat & Sun; performances on the hour.
🚻 🛗 🆆 jacquesbrel.be

Established in 1980 by Jacques
Brel's daughter, France Brel,
the Éditions Jacques Brel aims
to give visitors a sense of the
world inhabited by this great
singer-songwriter. It achieves
this through a changing series
of film presentations, which
includes footage from his
mesmerizing farewell concert
at Olympia, Paris, in 1966.
Other installations evoke the
conditions of his life over the
course of nearly 50 years.

The foundation also serves
as an archive and research
centre. It maintains an
impressive collection of
articles, manuscripts, slides,
playbills and other artifacts
associated with Brel's life and
work. In addition, it contains
several hours of audio and video
documentation from some of
Brel's public performances.

Jacques Brel

One of the most celebrated and cherished of all Belgians, Jacques
Brel (1929–78) rose to stardom in the 1950s, when his evocative,
touching and witty songs first came to the attention of the public in

Jacques Brel, Belgium's well-loved
singer-songwriter, in 1965

Paris. Brel wrote and performed
countless songs – about love,
ageing, drinking, the risible
bourgeoisie, hopeless dreams,
Belgium – many of which are
still adored and much played
today. These include "Ne Me
Quitte Pas" and "Le Plats Pays",
also known as "Mijn Vlakke
Land". Brel performed with total
commitment, singing in both
French and Dutch. Although his
passion is clear in recordings,
fans claim that he was even
better in live shows, at the end
of which he would be famously
awash in perspiration. In 1966,
Brel announced that he would
be giving up performing at
concerts and had decided to
devote himself to films and to composing music for the stage. This
promising future was cut short by lung cancer and Brel was buried in
French Polynesia, where he had spent his final years.

⑯ Place Royale

Rue Royale. **City Map** 2 E4. 🚌 27, 29, 34, 38, 54, 63, 64, 65, 66, 71, 80, 95. Ⓜ Trone, Parc. 🚋 92, 93.

The influence of Charles de Lorraine is still keenly felt in the Place Royale. As Governor of the Austrian Netherlands from 1741 to 1780, he redeveloped the site which was then occupied by the ruins of the great, late-medieval **Coudenberg Palace** that had been destroyed by fire in 1731. The ruins of the palace were demolished and the entire site was rebuilt as two squares along Neo-Classical lines reminiscent of Vienna, a city that Charles de Lorraine greatly admired.

In 1995, excavations in the area uncovered ruins of the 15th-century **Aula Magna**, the Great Hall of the former palace. The hall was part of an extension of the palace started under the dukes of Brabant in the early 13th century and further developed by the dukes of Burgundy, in particular by Philip the Good. It was in this room that the Habsburg emperor Charles V abdicated in favour of his son, Philip II. The ruins can now be seen as part of the BELvue museum.

Although criss-crossed by tramlines and traffic, the Place Royale maintains a feeling of dignity with its tall, elegant, buildings set symmetrically around a cobbled square. The equestrian statue in the centre, erected by King Leopold I in 1848, depicts the 11th-century knight Godefroid de Bouillon, a leader of the First Crusade.

⑰ Église St-Jacques-sur-Coudenberg

Place Royale, 1000 BRU. **City Map** 2 E4. **Tel** (02) 5117836. 🚌 27, 29, 34, 38, 54, 63, 64, 65, 66, 71, 80, 95. Ⓜ Trone, Parc. 🚋 92, 93. **Open** noon–2pm Mon; noon–5:45pm Tue–Fri; 1–6pm Sat; 8:30am–6:45pm Sun.

Dedicated to the apostle St James, the pretty St-Jacques-sur-Coudenberg is the latest in a series of churches to have occupied this site. There has been a chapel here since the

Glittering chandeliers in the vast Throne Room of the Palais Royal

12th century, when it served pilgrims en route to the saint's shrine at Santiago de Compostela in Spain. When the Coudenberg Palace was built in the 12th century, it became the ducal chapel. The chapel suffered over the years: it was ransacked during the conflict between Catholics and Protestants in 1579, and was so badly damaged in the 1731 fire that it had to be demolished. The present church was built in Neo-Classical style and was consecrated in 1787. During the French Revolution, it served as a Temple of Reason and Law, returning to the Catholic Church in 1802. The interior is elegant, with large paintings by Jan Portaels (1818–95). The church still has royal connections, and the choir has a direct link to the palace.

The 19th-century cupola of Église St-Jacques-sur-Coudenberg

⑱ Palais Royal

Place des Palais, 1000 BRU. **City Map** 2 E4. **Tel** (02) 5512020. 🚌 27, 29, 34, 38, 54, 63, 64, 65, 66, 71, 80, 95. Ⓜ Trone, Gare Centrale, Parc. 🚋 92, 93. **Open** mid-July–mid-Sep: 9:30am–5pm Mon–Fri. **Closed** 21 July.

The official residence of the Belgian monarchy in central Brussels, the Palais Royal is located close to the site of the old Coudenberg Palace. Its construction began in the 1820s, linking two 18th-century side wings. Most of the exterior was completed during the reign of Léopold II (1835–1909) and in the 20th century, the palace underwent interior improvements and restoration of its older sections.

The huge **Throne Room**, decorated in grand style with large pilastered columns and wall-mounted chandeliers, is one of Brussels's original state rooms. Beyond this, the **Long Gallery** displays late 19th-century ceiling paintings representing dawn, day and dusk. The **Small White Room**, a gilt chamber with late 18th-century Rococo furnishings, features rows of 19th-century royal portraits, while the **Pilasters Room** contains the original portrait of King Leopold I made in 1846. The **Hall of Mirrors**, similar in its grand effect to the mirrored chamber at Versailles, features a ceiling that has been decorated in green beetle and wing designs by sculptor Jan Fabre.

⓳ BELvue Museum and the Coudenberg

Place des Palais 7, 1000 BRU.
City Map 2 E4. **Tel** (02) 5004554. 🚌 27, 29, 34, 38, 54, 63, 64, 65, 66, 71, 80, 95. Ⓜ Trone, Parc, Porte de Namur. 🚊 92, 93. **Open** 9:30am–5pm Tue–Fri, 10am–6pm Sat & Sun. **Closed** 25 Dec, 1 Jan. 🅿 ♿ ✎ 📷 🅆 **belvue.be**

With its collection of paintings, documents and other royal memorabilia, the BELvue Museum charts the history of the Belgian monarchy from independence in 1830 to the present day. The museum is housed in the former Hôtel Bellevue, an 18th-century Neo-Classical building.

Belgian history, starting with the 1830 uprising, is displayed here through 1,500 unique historical documents, film fragments, photos and objects. An underground archaeological site and museum, the Coudenberg, is located in the grounds of the BELvue Museum.

The broad and elegant Neo-Classical façade of BELvue Museum

⓴ Musée des Instruments de Musique

Rue Montagne de la Cour 2, 1000 BRU. **City Map** 2 E4. **Tel** (02) 5450130. 🚌 27, 29, 38, 63, 65, 66, 71, 95. Ⓜ Gare Centrale, Parc. 🚊 92, 93. **Open** 9:30am–5pm Tue–Fri, 10am–5pm Sat & Sun. 🅿 📷 ♿ ✎ 📷 🅆 **mim.be**

Once a department store, the building known as Old England is a striking showpiece of Art Nouveau architecture. Architect Paul Saintenoy gave full rein to his imagination when he designed these shop premises for the Old England company in 1899. The façade is made entirely of glass and elaborate wrought iron. There is a domed gazebo on the roof, and a turret to one side. Surprisingly, it was only in the 1990s that a listed buildings policy was adopted in Brussels, which has secured treasures such as this. In 2000, it became the new Musée des Instruments de Musique (MIM).

The collection of the MIM began in the 19th century when the state bought 80 ancient and exotic instruments. The collection was doubled in 1876 when King Léopold II donated a gift of 97 Indian musical instruments presented to him by a maharaja. A museum displaying all of these artifacts opened in 1877, and by 1924 it boasted 3,300 pieces and was recognized as a leader in its field. Today, the collection contains more than 6,000 items and includes many fine examples of wind, string and keyboard instruments from medieval times to the present. Visitors to the museum are provided with headphones which allow them to hear the sounds produced by many of the instruments on display. Among the chief attractions are prototype instruments by Adolphe Sax, Belgian inventor of the saxophone (*see p209*); mini violins favoured by street musicians; a violin-maker's studio; and a superb group of mechanical instruments,

Unique marble floor in the state room, Palais de Charles de Lorraine

The dome of Old England, home to the MIM

including the componium, a 19th-century barrel organ that composes its own music as it plays. There is also a restaurant on the top floor with fine views over Brussels.

㉑ Palais de Charles de Lorraine

Place du Musée 1, 1000 BRU.
City Map 2 D4. **Tel** (02) 5195372. 🚌 27, 29, 38, 63, 65, 66, 71, 95. Ⓜ Gare Centrale, Parc. 🚊 92, 93. **Open** 10am–5pm first Sat in month. **Closed** last week in Dec. 📷 for details call (02) 5195311.

Set behind a Neo-Classical façade are the few surviving rooms of the palace of Charles de Lorraine, Governor of the Austrian Netherlands and a keen patron of the arts. Few original features remain, as the palace was ransacked by marauding French troops in 1794. The bas-reliefs at the top of the stairway, representing earth, air, fire and water, reflect Charles de Lorraine's interest in alchemy. Most spectacular of all the original features is the 28-point star, set in the floor of the circular state room. Each of the points is made from a different type of Belgian marble, taken from his personal mineral collection. Belgian marble was a much sought-after material used to construct St Peter's Basilica in Rome. The rooms contain a range of 18th-century furnishings and exhibits representing intellectual life during the Enlightenment. The palace also houses the royal library.

㉒ Musées Royaux des Beaux-Arts de Belgique

See pp72–7.

㉓ Place du Grand Sablon

Rue des Sablons, 1000 BRU.
City Map 2 D4. 🚌 27, 38, 48, 71, 95. Ⓜ Gare Centrale, Louise, Parc. 🚊 92, 93, 94, 97. 🛍 Sat & Sun.

Situated on the slope of the escarpment that divides Brussels in two, the Place du Grand Sablon is like a stepping stone between the upper and lower halves of the city. The square's name derives from the French *sable* (sand), as this old route to the city centre once passed through some sandy marshes.

Today, the picture is very different. This area, roughly triangular in shape, stretches uphill from a 1751 fountain at its base to the Gothic church of Notre-Dame du Sablon. The square is surrounded by town houses, with some Art Nouveau façades. This is a chic, wealthy and busy part of Brussels, with upmarket antiques dealers, fashionable restaurants and trendy bars, which really come into their own in warm weather when people sit outside. It is a good place in which to soak up the city's atmosphere. **Wittamer**, the well-known chocolate shop and pâtisserie is at No. 12 and has a tearoom on the first floor. The area near the church hosts a lively, if expensive, antiques market every weekend.

Just north of the Place du Grand Sablon, at Rue Sainte Anne 32, the small **Museum of Erotics and Mythology** houses a private collection of paintings, sculptures, Greco-Roman antiquities and other curiosities.

㉔ Notre-Dame du Sablon

Rue de la Regence 38, 1000 BRU.
City Map 2 D4. **Tel** (02) 2130065. 🚌 27, 38, 48, 71, 95. Ⓜ Gare Centrale, Louise, Parc. 🚊 92, 93, 94, 97.
Open 9am–6:30pm daily.
🎧 on request. ♿

Along with the Cathédrale Sts-Michel-et-Gudule *(see p67)*, this lovely church is one of the finest surviving examples of Brabant-Gothic architecture in Belgium today.

A church was first erected here when the guild of crossbow-men was granted permission to build a chapel to Our Lady on this sandy hill. Legend has it that a young girl in Antwerp had a vision of the Virgin Mary, who instructed the girl to take her statue to Brussels. The girl carried the statue by boat down the River Senne and gave it to the crossbowmen's chapel in the city. The chapel rapidly became a place of pilgrimage. The statue was destroyed in 1565 and all that remains of the incident are two carvings of the original

Rich stained glass at
Notre-Dame du Sablon

pilgrimage tale, showing the young girl in a boat.

The first attempts to enlarge this church took place around 1400 but, due to lack of funds, the work was not completed until 1550. The interior is simple and beautifully proportioned, with interconnecting side chapels and an impressive pulpit dating from 1697. Of particular interest are the 11 magnificent stained-glass windows, each 14-m (45-ft) high, which dominate the inside of the church. When the building is lit, the windows shine into the night like welcoming beacons. Also of interest is the **Tour et Taxis Family Chapel**, built for a German family that once lived near the Place du Petit Sablon. In 1517, the family commissioned a series of tapestries to commemorate the church's legend. Most of them were stolen in the 1790s by the French Revolutionary Army, but some of the remaining examples now hang in the Musées Royaux d'Art et d'Histoire in the Parc du Cinquantenaire *(see pp80–81)*.

㉕ Place du Petit Sablon

Rue de la Regence, 1000 BRU.
City Map 2 D4. 🚌 27, 38, 48, 71, 95. Ⓜ Gare Centrale, Louise, Parc. 🚊 92, 93, 94, 97.

These pretty, formal gardens were laid out in 1890 and form a charming spot. On top of the railings that enclose the gardens are 44 bronze statuettes by Art Nouveau designer Paul Hankar (1859–1901). Each of the figures represents a different medieval city guild. Located at the back of the gardens is a fountain built to commemorate the counts Egmont and Hornes, who pleaded against the introduction of the Spanish Inquisition by King Philip II, and were beheaded in 1568. On either side of the fountain are 12 statues

Chocolates on display at Brussels's famous Wittamer pâtisserie on Place du Grand Sablon

Statues of Count Egmont and Count Hornes at the Place du Petit Sablon

of 15th- and 16th-century figures, including those of Renaissance artist Bernard van Orley and the Flemish map-maker Gerhard Mercator, whose 16th-century projection of the world is the basis of most modern maps.

㉖ Notre-Dame de la Chapelle

Place de la Chapelle 1, 1000 BRU. **City Map** 1 C4. **Tel** (02) 5383087. 27, 48, 95. M Gare Centrale, Anneessens. 3, 4, 31, 32. **Open** 9am–7pm daily. 4pm Sat, 8pm Sun. Flea Market: Place du Jeu de Balle. **Open** mornings daily.

In 1134, Duke Godefroid I decided to build a chapel outside the city's walls. This quickly became a market church, serving the many craftsmen who lived nearby. By 1210, it had become so popular that it was made the parish church. In 1250, it became truly famous when a donation of five pieces of the True Cross turned the church into a pilgrimage site.

The majority of the original Romanesque church was destroyed by fire in 1405. When rebuilding began in 1421, it was in a Gothic style typical of 15th-century Brabant architecture. The Baroque bell tower was added after the French bombardment in 1695 (see p46). Monstrous gargoyles peer down from the exterior walls, while inside, a chapel and plaque commemorate

the 16th-century Belgian artist Pieter Brueghel the Elder (see p26) who lived in **Rue Haute** nearby, and is buried here.

Rue Haute leads through the traditionally working-class and independent-minded district known as **Les Marolles**. The area was home to craftsmen and weavers, and street names such as Rue des Brodeurs (Embroiderers' Street) and Rue des Charpentiers (Carpenters' Street) reflect the district's artisanal history.

Today, the area is known for its fine **Flea Market** in the Place du Jeu de Balle, with the biggest and best markets held on Sundays. These sell almost anything from junk to pre-war collector's items.

㉗ Palais de Justice

Place Poelaert 1, 1000 BRU. **City Map** 1 C5. **Tel** (02) 5086578. 34. M Louise. 91, 92, 93, 94. **Open** 8am–5pm Mon–Fri. **Closed** Jul & public holidays. on request.

Dominating the Brussels skyline, the Palais de Justice can be seen from almost any vantage point in the city. Of all the ambitious projects of King Leopold II, this was perhaps the grandest. It occupies an area larger than St Peter's Basilica in Rome, and was one of the world's most impressive 19th-century buildings. It was built between 1866 and 1883 by Belgian architect Joseph Poelaert who

found inspiration for it in the designs of Classical temples built for the Egyptian pharoahs. Unfortunately, Poelaert died in 1879 while it was still under construction. The Palais de Justice is still home to the city's law courts.

㉘ Porte de Hal

Boulevard du Midi, 1000 BRU. **City Map** 1 B5. **Tel** (02) 5341518. 27, 48. M Porte de Hal. 3, 55, 90. **Open** 9.30am–5pm Tue–Fri, 10am–5pm Sat & Sun. kmkg-mrah.be

This impressive bastion is the only surviving gate from the 14th-century medieval city walls that once surrounded Brussels, and is a vivid indicator of their colossal scale. The walls were pulled down in the 18th century, but their pentagon-shaped path is now occupied by the inner ring road and so is still clearly visible on maps. The Porte de Hal (the gate on the road towards Halle or Hal) survived because it was used as a prison. It was heavily restored in the 1860s when medieval heritage was once again cherished. Under the direction of the Musées Royaux d'Art et d'Histoire (see p81), it now presents a permanent collection of armour and weapons, a historical account of the guilds of Brussels and some temporary exhibitions. There is also a walkway on the ramparts which offers fine views.

The imposing bulk of Porte de Hal, evoking Brussels's medieval past

㉒ Musées Royaux des Beaux-Arts de Belgique: Musée Old Masters

Officially known as the Musées Royaux des Beaux-Arts de Belgique, the Musée Old Masters, Musée Fin de Siècle and Musée Magritte are Brussels's premier art museums. The buildings cover two eras, *ancien* (15th to 18th century) and *moderne* (19th century to present day), as well as René Magritte's works from the early 1900s to 1967. The Musée Old Masters opened in 1887 and has the finest collection of Flemish art in the world. Housed in a Neo-Classical building, designed by fashionable architect Alphonse Balat between 1874 and 1880, the collection was put together in the late 18th century, when it was made up of paintings looted by the French Revolutionary Army. Many more were recovered from France after 1815, and the Musée Old Masters is now the largest of the museums and is famed for holding the finest collection of Flemish art in the world, with Old Masters such as van Dyck and Rubens very well represented.

Façade of Museum Corinthian columns and busts of Flemish painters adorn the entrance.

Ground level

The Census at Bethlehem (1610)
Pieter Brueghel the Younger (c.1564–1636) produced a version of this subject, some 40 years after the original by his father. Both works are in the collection, showing the progression to the son's smoother style.

Main Entrance

Entrance to the Museum Shop

★ **The Annunciation** (1406–07)
The Master of Flémalle, Robert Campin (c.1375–1444) depicted Archangel Gabriel announcing the imminent birth of the Messiah in a contemporary setting. The everyday objects offer a homely contrast to the momentous nature of the event.

Upper level

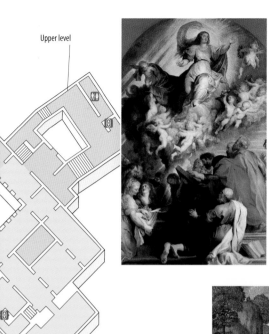

VISITORS' CHECKLIST

Practical Information
Rue de la Régence 3, 1000 BRU.
City Map 2 D4. **Tel** (02) 5083211.
Open 10am–5pm Tue–Fri, 11am–
6pm Sat & Sun. 🎨 🏛 ♿ ✏ 📷
🏠 🌐 **fine-arts-museum.be**

Transport
🚌 27, 29, 38, 63, 65, 66, 71.
Ⓜ Gare Centrale. 🚊 92, 93.

★ *The Assumption of the Virgin*
(1610) Pieter Paul Rubens (1577–
1640) was the leading exponent of
Baroque art in Europe, combining
Flemish precision with Italian flair.
In *The Assumption of the Virgin*, he
suppressed background colours to
emphasize the Virgin's blue robes.

*Madonna with Saint Anne and a
Franciscan Donor* (1470) Hugo van
der Goes (c.1430–82) was
commissioned to paint this symbolic
work by the monk shown on the right,
for his personal devotional use.

To Musée Magritte
➡

Lower level

Interior of the Main Hall
Lit from above by a glass roof, the Main
Hall provides an impressive gateway to
the collections, as well as a generous
space to exhibit paintings and a rotating
selection of sculptures.

Auditorium

Key

☐ 15th–16th century
☐ 17th–18th century
☐ Temporary exhibition
▨ Non-exhibition space

Gallery Guide

*The gallery is divided up into two different eras of
art, as shown in the key. Two large auditoriums
on the ground and lower levels are used for
occasional lectures as well as presentations.
Visitors can enter the Musée Magritte and from
there, the Musée Fin de Siècle, via the escalator
behind the museum's restaurant. Due to ongoing
renovation work, gallery layouts may change.*

Musées Royaux des Beaux-Arts: Musée Magritte and Musée Fin de Siècle

The Musée Magritte gives unprecedented insight into the life and works of one of Belgium's most celebrated painters, René Magritte, a major exponent of Surrealism. Stretching over five floors, the museum occupies a refurbished Neo-Classical building on the Place Royale. Next to it is the Musée Fin de Siècle, laid out in the 1980s over three storeys and six spiralling levels, all ingeniously sunk into the ground to avoid obscuring the 18th-century Place du Musée. This museum showcases European and international art from the end of the 19th century and the beginning of the 20th century. A D-shaped lightwell allows visitors to view the exhibits by natural light, in spite of the building's location underground.

Level 4

Level 3

Level 2

Level 1

Level -1

To Musée Old Masters ↖

To Musée Fin de Siècle

Level -2

Portrait of Baron Francis Delbeke (1917)
Antwerp-born Jules Schmalzigaug (1882–1917) was one of the most original and gifted artists of his generation. He was involved in the Italian Futurist movement in Rome between 1912 and 1914, and his work became increasingly abstract. He moved to the neutral Netherlands at the advent of World War I, where, depressed, he took his own life at the age of 35.

★ ***The Domain of Arnheim*** (1962)
Magritte's painting of an eagle-mountain rearing over a small bird's nest, precariously perched on a wall, is an unsettling image that teases the viewer for an explanation. The title is from a short story by Edgar Allan Poe (1809–49).

La Seine à la Grande-Jatte (1888)
It was in this painting that Georges Seurat first applied his pointilism technique on a large scale; colour dots are juxtaposed and optically fuse in the viewer's eye.

Key

- ☐ Musée Fin de Siècle: 19th–20th century
- ☐ Musée Magritte: 1898–1929
- ☐ Musée Magritte: 1930–1950
- ☐ Musée Magritte: 1951–1967
- ☐ Musée Magritte: multimedia area
- ☐ Temporary exhibitions
- ☐ Non-exhibition space

Level -4

★ ***Woman in a Blue Dress in Front of a Mirror*** (1914)
Brussels-born Rik Wouters (1882–1916) was a sculptor and Fauvist painter whose fascination with the effects of colours led him to experiment with innovative spatula painting and other new techniques.

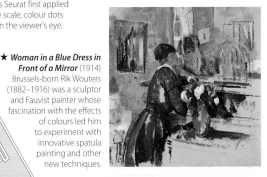

Level -3

Level -6

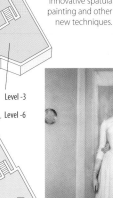

Portrait de Marguerite Knopff (1887)
An austere representation of the artist's sister by the famed Symbolist Fernand Khnopff (1858–1921), captures his interest in the mysterious nature of the human soul. Khnopff's sister was a subject of several of his early paintings.

Level -5

Level -8

Level -7

Gallery Guide

Access to the museums is available through the main ticket hall of Musées Royaux des Beaux-Arts de Belgique. The Musée Magritte is arranged in chronological order. The lowest underground level is a multimedia area, showing Magritte's films. From here, stairs lead down to the uppermost level of the Musée Fin de Siècle, which has been set aside for temporary exhibitions. The area shaded in green is the permanent collection, which displays work from the end of the 19th and start of the 20th century.

Exploring the Musées Royaux des Beaux-Arts de Belgique

The several museums that make up the Musées Royaux des Beaux-Arts de Belgique contain works of many artistic styles, from the religious paintings of the 15th-century Flemish Primitives to the Pop Art and Minimalism of the 1960s and 1970s. All are very well set out, guiding the visitor easily through the full collection or directly to a specific art era. Each section is highly accessible, with the two main museums divided into different sections, each relating to the art of a particular century.

Vase of Flowers (1704) by Dutch still-life painter Rachel Ruysch

Musée Old Masters

The Musée Old Masters exhibits works dating from the 15th to the 18th centuries. In the first few rooms are works by the renowned school of Flemish Primitives *(see pp106–107)*. As is the case with most art from the Middle Ages, the paintings are chiefly religious in nature and depict biblical scenes and details from the lives of saints. Many of these show deeds of horrific torture, martyrdom and violence, attended by the perplexing nonchalance of the elegantly attired bystanders. A typical example is the diptych *The Justice of Emperor Otto III* (c.1460) by Dirk Bouts, which includes a gory beheading (a famous miscarriage of justice in the 12th century) and an execution by burning at the stake. At the same time, the detail is exquisite and provides a fascinating window on the textiles, architecture and faces of the 15th century. Also on display are works such as

Lamentation by Rogier van der Weyden, city painter to Brussels during the mid-15th century, and *The Martyrdom of Saint Sebastian* by the famed Bruges artist Hans Memling (c.1433–94).

Another unique aspect of the section is the extensive collection of paintings by the Brueghels, father and son. Both were renowned for their scenes of peasant life. On display are *The Fall of Icarus* (1558) by Brueghel the Elder and *The Struggle between Carnival and Lent* (c.1559) by his son, Pieter.

In the following rooms are works from the 17th and 18th centuries. A highlight of this section is the world-famous collection of paintings by Baroque artist Pieter Paul Rubens (1557–1640), which affords a fine overview of the artist's work. As well as key examples of his religious works, there are some excellent portraits, such as *Hélène Fourment*, of his young wife. Of special interest are the sketches made in preparation for Rubens's

larger works, including *Four Negro Heads*, for his iconic *Adoration of the Magi* (1624).

Other works of note in this section are the paintings by Old Masters such as van Dyck's *Portrait of a Genoese Lady with her Daughter* from the 1620s and *Three Children with Goatcart* by Frans Hals, the famous portrait painter. Representatives of the later Flemish schools include Jacob Jordaens *(see p107)* and his depiction of myths such as *Pan and Syrinx* (c.1645) and *Satyr and Peasant*. Baroque and Flemish art are all well represented in the museums.

Also on display are some small sculptures that were studies of larger works by Laurent Delvaux, a leading sculptor of the 18th century. Most notably, *Hercules and Erymanthian Boar* is a study for the sculpture by the staircase in the Palais de Charles de Lorraine *(see p69)*. Works of the Italian, Spanish and French schools are also represented, notably the Classical landscape painter Claude Le Lorrain's poetic scene of *Aeneas Hunting the Stag on the Coast of Libya* (1672). Other works on show include *Vase of Flowers* (1704) by Dutch artist Rachel Ruysch, who specialized in still-life paintings of flowers and fruits.

Musée Fin de Siècle

The Musée Fin de Siècle showcases European and international art from the end of the 19th century to the beginning of the 20th century. The collection focuses

Lamentation (c.1441) by Rogier van der Weyden

For hotels and restaurants see p266 and pp280–83

on the combined efforts of various well-established art institutions in Belgium, exploring social topics expressed through decorative arts, literature and music, with influences from Theatre Royal de la Monnaie and the Bibliothèque royale de Belgique.

The collection of work covers 31 different European art academies who, in 1868, collectively created the Société Libre des Beaux-Arts, introducing modernism and the avant-garde to Belgium.

This counterculture art movement pioneered the revolt against materialism and a consequent move towards illustrating landscapes and social ideas as central themes of artwork. The exhibition includes Belgian national literature, the rediscovery of the Primitives, Impressionism, Symbolism and Art Nouveau. Artists in the collection include Khnopff, Seurat, Spilliaert, Gauguin, de Vlaminick and van de Velde, who was also the main founder of the Art Nouveau movement.

There is an excellent range of Symbolist art, including the disturbing classic *Des Caresses* by Fernand Khnopff (1858–1921), which shows an androgynous figure nuzzling a human head on a cheetah's body.

Work by artists such as Henri Evenepoel (1872–99) show a distinctive post-Impressionist style as in *The Orange Market in Blidah* (1898). There are also bizarre paintings by proto-Expressionist James Ensor (1860–1949), including his 1892 work *Singular Masks*.

The highlight of the exhibition and also the main draw to

The Orange Market in Blidah (1898) by Henri Evenepoel

the museum is the extraordinarily vast Gillion Crowet Collection of Art Nouveau paintings and objects, given to the Musées Royaux de Beaux-Arts by the Brussels-Capital Region.

Musée Magritte

The works of the Belgian Surrealist movement have long proved a popular highlight of the Musées Royaux des Beaux-Art's collection. The art of René Magritte in particular has created an extraordinary public fascination since the increase in his popularity in the 1960s. To reflect public demand, and to afford the best possible display, his work is now housed in this separate section of the museum.

Born the son of a wealthy manufacturer in Lessines (see p189), Magritte entered the Brussels Academie des Beaux-Arts in 1916. A former poster and advertisement designer, he created visually striking work, frequently displaying a juxtaposition of

familiar objects in unusual, sometimes unsettling, combinations and contexts. Many of the artist's best-known paintings are shown here in an impressively comprehensive collection of 200 works. These cover everything from large-scale canvases to magazine covers, advertising posters and wallpaper designs, including *L'Empire des Lumières* (1954) and *La Voleuse* (1928). They are also laid out chronologically, so it's possible to see his remarkable rapid development as an artist.

Of particular note are the paintings that date from Magritte's self-titled "Cavernous" period of 1927–30, which reflect both the macabre and the erotic. At this time, while living in Paris, Magritte painted roughly a canvas a day. He then moved back to Brussels, where he lived for the rest of his life. Powerful, arresting paintings on display from this latter period include the eerie *Domain of Arnheim (see p74)* and the melancholic *Saveur des Larmes* (1948).

Des Caresses (1896) by the symbolist artist, Fernand Khnopff

Musée Charlier, home to one of Brussels's most fascinating collections of art and furnishings

㉙ Musée Charlier

Avenue des Arts 16, 1210 BRU. **City Map** 2 F2. **Tel** (02) 2202691. 🚌 22, 65, 66. Ⓜ Madou, Arts-Loi. 🚋 29, 63. **Open** noon–5pm Mon–Thu, 10am–1pm Fri. 🅿 ♿ French and Dutch only. Ⓦ **charliermuseum.be**

This museum was once home to the wealthy collector and patron of arts, Henri Van Cutsem. In 1890, he asked the young architect Victor Horta *(see p84)* to redesign his house as an exhibition space for his extensive collection. When Van Cutsem passed away, his friend, the sculptor Guillaume Charlier, installed his own art collection in the house.

Charlier commissioned Horta to build another museum to house the Van Cutsem collection – the Musée des Beaux-Arts in Tournai *(see p188)*, in western Belgium. After Charlier's death, the house was made into a museum in 1928.

The Musée Charlier contains paintings by several artists, including portraits by Antoine Wiertz, early landscapes by Boulenger, Vogels and Khnopff, still lifes by Ensor and other Realist and Impressionist works. The collection holds sculptures by Charlier, as well as glassware, silverware and porcelain. It also has a unique Asian room with Chinese furniture and wallpaper on display. The museum houses tapestries too – some from the Paris studios of Aubusson – set along the staircases and first floor and the elegant displays of furniture in Louis XV and Louis XVI styles, located on the first floor.

㉚ Musée du Jouet

Rue de l'Association 24, 1000 BRU. **City Map** 2 F2. **Tel** (02) 2196168. 🚌 29, 61, 63, 65, 66. Ⓜ Botanique, Madou. 🚋 92, 93. **Open** 10am–noon & 2–6pm daily. 🅿 ▢ ♿ Ⓦ **museedujouet.eu**

This well-established toy museum, housed in a 19th-century *maison de maître* (urban mansion), will delight visitors of all ages. It contains some 25,000 artifacts, dating from 1850 onwards. Adults will enjoy the nostalgic thrill of seeing the toys of their youth as well as the lead soldiers, model engines, dolls, rocking horses and wooden jigsaws of earlier generations. Hands-on exhibits have been designed to amuse younger visitors.

㉛ Parc du Cinquantenaire

See pp80–81.

㉜ Quartier Européen

City Map 3 B3. 🚌 12, 21, 22, 27, 36, 60, 64, 79. Ⓜ Maalbeek, Schuman.

The area at the top of the Rue de la Loi and around the Schuman roundabout is where the main buildings of the European Union's administration are found.

The most recognizable of all the European Union seats is the cross-shaped **Berlaymont** building, a vast four-pointed building that was completed in 1967 and has since become an iconic symbol of the EU's growing power. It is the headquarters of the European Commission, whose workers are, in effect, civil servants of the EU. The Council of Ministers, which comprises representatives of member-states' governments, now meets in the sprawling pink granite block across the road

Distinctive Art Nouveau curlicues and flourishes on the Maison St-Cyr

from the Berlaymont. This building is known as **Justus Lipsius**, after a 16th-century Flemish philosopher.

Further down the road from the Justus Lipsius building is **Résidence Palace**, a luxury 1920s housing complex that boasted a theatre, pool and roof garden. The International Press Centre is currently based in the palace.

This whole area is naturally full of life and bustle during the day, but much quieter in the evenings; it can feel almost deserted on weekends. Pleasant at any time is the proximity of a number of the city's wonderful green spaces, which include the Parc du Cinquantenaire and **Parc Léopold**. The verdant Square Ambiorix, to the north, contains the **Maison St-Cyr** at No. 11 – the most extravagant of all Art Nouveau houses in Brussels, built in 1903 by architect Gustave Strauven.

㉝ European Parliament

Rue Wiertz 43, 1047 BRU. **City Map** 3 A4. ⊟ 21, 22, 27, 34, 38, 54, 60, 80, 95. Ⓜ Maelbeek, Schuman. 🖺 Book via website: 10am, 11am, 2pm & 3pm Mon–Thu, 10am & 11am Fri. 🖼 Ⓦ **europarl.europa.eu**

This vast, modern steel and glass complex, situated just behind the Quartier Léopold train station, is one of the three homes of the European Parliament, the elected body of the European Union. Its permanent seat is located in Strasbourg, France, where the plenary sessions are held once a month. Luxembourg is the administrative centre, and the committee meetings are held in Brussels.

A gleaming state-of-the-art building completed in 1997, it has many admirers, not least the parliamentary workers and Members of the European Parliament (MEPs). However, it also has critics – the huge domed structure containing a hemicycle that seats 700-plus MEPs has been dubbed *le caprice des dieux* – the whim of the gods – referring both to the shape of

The European Parliament building behind the trees of Parc Léopold

the building, which is similar to a cheese of the same name, and to its lofty aspirations. Many also regret that to make room for the new complex, a large part of the Quartier Léopold that stood here has been lost.

㉞ Musée Wiertz

Rue Vautier 62, 1050 BRU. **City Map** 3 A4. **Tel** (02) 6481718. ⊟ 12, 21, 22, 27, 34, 36, 38, 44, 59, 60, 80, 95. Ⓜ Maelbeek, Schuman, Trone. **Open** 10am–noon & 12:45–4:45pm Tue–Sun. **Closed** some public hols. Ⓦ **fine-arts-museum.be**

The 160 works, including oil paintings, drawings and sculptures that form the main body of Antoine Wiertz's (1806–65) artistic output are housed in Musée Wiertz. The collection fills a studio built for the immensely popular Wiertz by the Belgian state, where he lived and worked from 1850 until his

Awe-inspiring paintings in the huge studio space of the Musée Wiertz

death, when the studio became a museum.

The enormous main room contains Wiertz's largest paintings. Many of them depict biblical and Homeric scenes, some of which are in the style of Rubens, while others bear witness to his macabre imagination. Also on display are his sculptures and death mask. The last of the six rooms contains his more gruesome efforts, with titles as fearsome as their content. These include *Madness*, *Hunger and Crime* and *Premature Burial*.

㉟ Institut Royal des Sciences Naturelles

Rue Vautier 29, 1000 BRU. **City Map** 3 A4. **Tel** (02) 6274238. ⊟ 12, 21, 22, 27, 34, 36, 38, 54, 59, 60, 64, 79, 80, 95. Ⓜ Maelbeek, Schuman, Trône. **Open** 9:30am–5pm Tue–Fri, 10am–6pm Sat & Sun. 🖼 🖼 🖼 🖼 🖼 Ⓦ **naturalsciences.be**

Established in 1846, the Institut Royal des Sciences Naturelles is best known for its collection of iguanadon skeletons which date from 250 million years ago. Discovered in 1870 at Bernissart near Mons (*see p193*), they were among the first complete dinosaur skeletons ever to be reassembled, providing a major contribution to paleontology. The museum contains educational displays on natural history, and a gallery on evolution was added in 2009 to mark the 200th birth anniversary of Charles Darwin.

⑪ Parc du Cinquantenaire

The finest of King Leopold II's grand projects, the Parc and Palais du Cinquantenaire were built for the Golden Jubilee celebrations of Belgian independence in 1880. The park was laid out on land used for military training. The palace, at its entrance, was to comprise a triumphal arch and two large exhibition areas, but by the time of the 1880 Art and Industry Expo, only the two side exhibition areas had been completed. Funds were eventually found and work continued for 50 years. Before being converted into museums, the large halls on either side of the archway held trade fairs, the last of which was in 1935. The halls have also been used for horse races and to house homing pigeons. During World War II, the grounds of the park were used to grow vegetables to feed the people of Brussels.

★ **Musée Royal de l'Armée et d'Histoire Militaire**
The museum exhibits cover Belgium's military history with over 200 years of militaria, including historic aircraft.

Centrepiece Giant Archway
Originally conceived as a gateway into the city of Brussels, the triumphal arch was completed only in 1905.

KEY

① **Pavillon Horta**

② **The Grand Mosque** was built as the Egypt pavilion for the Expo in 1880. It became a mosque in 1978.

③ **Underpass**

④ **The park** is popular with Brussels's eurocrats and families at lunchtimes and weekends.

0 metres   100
0 yards   100

Tree-lined Avenue
Many of the plantations of elms and plane trees that make up the forested walks date from 1880.

For hotels and restaurants see p266 and pp280–83

Central Archway
The arch is crowned by the sculpture of *Brabant Raising the National Flag*, while riding a quadriga.

VISITORS' CHECKLIST

Practical Information
Ave de Tervuren, 1040 BRU.
City Map 3 C3.
Autoworld: (02) 7364165. **Open**
Apr–Sep: 10am–6pm Sat & Sun;
Oct–Mar: 10am–5pm Tue–Fri.
Grand Mosque: (02) 735
2173. **Open** 9am–4pm Mon–Thu.

Transport
12, 21, 22, 27, 36, 60, 61, 79, 80.
81, 83. Schuman, Mérode.

Autoworld
Set in the south wing of the palace, Autoworld has one of the best collections of automobiles in the world. There are some 300 cars, including an 1886 motor, a 1924 Model-T Ford and American limousine of the 1950s.

★ **Cinquantenaire Museum**
Belgian architect Bordiau's plans for these two exhibition halls, later permanent showcases, were partly modelled on London's Victorian museums. The use of iron and glass in their construction was inspired by the Crystal Palace.

Cinquantenaire Museum
Parc du Cinquantenaire 10.
Tel (02) 741 7211. **Open** 9:30am–5pm
Tue–Fri, 10am– 5pm Sat, Sun & public
holidays. **Closed** 1 May, 1 and 11 Nov.
**kmkg-mrah.be/
cinquantenarie-museum**

Part of the Musées Royaux d'Art et d'Histoire, the Cinquantenaire Museum has occupied its present site since the early 1900s and is one of the biggest museums in Belgium. The historic building was erected by former Belgian King Léopold II. A wealth of artifacts, from prehistoric times through antiquity and European applied arts, to a vast collection of non-European art, are on display.

The four main collections of the museum are: Antiquity, including Egyptian sarcophagi and Greek vases; National Archaeology from prehistory to the Merovingian period 751 AD; European Decorative Arts from Romanesque art of the Middle Ages to 20th-century Art Deco; and Non-European Civilizations, which includes sections on Byzantium, China and the Indian subcontinent, South-East Asia, Oceania and the Islamic world as well as the pre-Columbian civilizations of the Americas.

There are decorative arts from all ages, with silverware, glass-ware, porcelain and a fine collection of tapestries. Religious sculptures and stained glass are displayed around a courtyard in the style of church cloisters. The use of iron and glass was inspired by London's Crystal Palace.

Musée Royal de l'Armée et d'Histoire Militaire
Parc du Cinquantenaire 3.
Tel (02) 7377833. **Open** 9am–5pm
Tue–Sun. **Closed** 1 May, 1 Nov, 25 &
26 Dec. **klm-mra.be/D7t**

Together with the section on aviation, the displays cover the Belgian army and its history from the late 1700s onwards, including weapons, uniforms, decorations and paintings. There is a section covering the 1830 struggle for independence (*see pp48–9*). Two other sections showcase the history of the World Wars and the Resistance (*see pp50–51*).

GREATER BRUSSELS

Central Brussels is bound by a heart-shaped ring-road called the Petite Ceinture (Small Belt), which follows the path of the old medieval city walls. Beyond this lie 19 suburbs which form the Bruxelles-Capitale region. Many of these suburbs are residential, but a handful contain treasures of Brussels's history. For fans of early 20th-century architecture, the districts of St-Gilles and Ixelles offer striking Art Nouveau buildings, such as the Musée Horta. To the west lies the suburb of

Anderlecht and the charming house where the Renaissance humanist Erasmus lived. In Koekelberg is the huge dome of the Basilique Nationale du Sacré-Coeur. To the north, Heysel offers attractions such as the Atomium, originally built in 1958, whose modernity contrasts with the historical city centre. To the east, the Musée Royal de l'Afrique Centrale reflects Belgium's colonial past in the Congo, while Musée du Transport Urbain takes visitors on a journey through Brussels's past.

Sights at a Glance

Buildings and Monuments
7 Erasmus House
8 Begijnhof van Anderlecht
9 Basilique Nationale du Sacré-Coeur
12 The Atomium

Museums
1 Musée Horta
2 Musée d'Ixelles
3 Musée Constantin Meunier
4 Musée David et Alice van Buuren
6 Musée Bruxellois de la Gueuze
10 René Magritte Museum

14 Musée du Transport Urbain Bruxellois
15 Musée Royal de l'Afrique Centrale

Tours
5 Art Nouveau Tour

Parks and Gardens
11 Bruparck
13 Domaine de Laeken

Key
- Brussels city centre
- Motorway
- Main road
- Minor road
- Railway

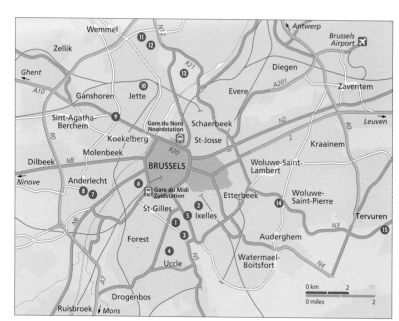

The elegant, light-filled living room showcasing Horta's characteristic style

❶ Musée Horta

Rue Américaine 25, St-Gilles, 1060 BRU. **Road Map** B4. **Tel** (02) 5430 490. 🚌 54. Ⓜ Albert, Louise. 🚊 33, 51, 81, 83, 92, 93, 94, 97. **Open** 2–5:30pm Tue–Sun. 🅿 Ⓦ **hortamuseum.be**

Belgian architect Victor Horta (1861–1947) is considered by many to be the father of Art Nouveau architecture. Horta's prodigious skill lay not only in his grand, overall vision but in his equal talent as an interior designer. He had a huge impact on the architecture of Brussels in his day *(see p86)*, although many of his buildings no longer exist. This museum, the most complete exploration of the Art Nouveau style, is housed in his restored family home and studio. These two delightful buildings were designed by Horta between 1898 and 1901.

The airy interior of the house displays Horta's trademark architectural style, using iron, glass and curves, while retaining a functional approach. The details of his work are best seen in the living room, where sculpted bannister ends and finely made door handles echo forms found in nature. The splendid central staircase is decorated with curved wrought iron, and the stairs are enhanced by mirrors, which bring natural light into the house. In the dining room, white enamel tiles line the walls, rising to an ornate ceiling decorated with the scrolled metalwork used in other rooms. This harmonious blend of colour and materials is characteristic of Horta's work and part of the enduring appeal of Art Nouveau.

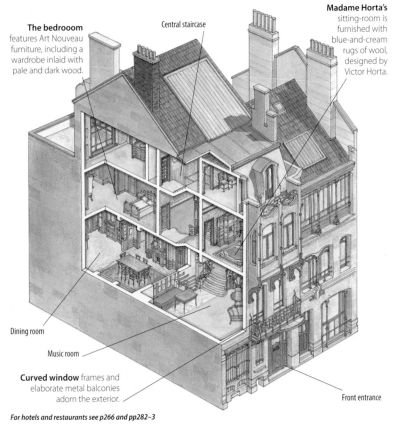

The bedrooom features Art Nouveau furniture, including a wardrobe inlaid with pale and dark wood.

Central staircase

Madame Horta's sitting-room is furnished with blue-and-cream rugs of wool, designed by Victor Horta.

Dining room

Music room

Curved window frames and elaborate metal balconies adorn the exterior.

Front entrance

Wouters's *La Vierge Folle* in the Musée d'Ixelles

❷ Musée d'Ixelles

Rue Jean van Volsem 71, Ixelles, 1050 BRU. **Road Map** B4. **Tel** (02) 5156422. 🚋 38, 54, 59, 60, 71, 95. Ⓜ Porte de Namur. 🚌 81, 83. **Open** 9:30am–5pm Tue–Sun. 🚻 📷 Ⓦ museedixelles.be

The commune of Ixelles possesses a remarkably rich art collection, presented in this small but highly rewarding gallery. It contains intriguing but little-known work by painters such as Rembrandt, Fragonard and Picasso and original posters by Toulouse-Lautrec. There is a good variety of work by the Belgian Symbolists Léon Frédéric and Léon Spilliaert. Other Belgian artists such as Magritte and Rik Wouters are represented with such pieces as a copy of the latter's exuberant bronze sculpture *La Vierge Folle* (The Mad Virgin). The museum is also noted for temporary exhibits.

❸ Musée Constantin Meunier

Rue de l'Abbaye 59, Ixelles, 1050 BRU. **Road Map** B4. **Tel** (02) 6484449. 🚋 38, 60. 🚌 7, 93, 94. **Open** 10am–noon & 12:45–5pm Tue–Fri. 📷 Ⓦ fine-arts-museum.be

Brussels-born Constantin Meunier (1831–1905) was an artist of great distinction, a realist who painted gritty industrial scenes in keeping with his socialist sympathies.

He is best known for bronze sculptures of factory workers, such as the *puddleurs* (forge-workers). These were largely inspired by his visits to industrial regions around Liège (*see pp220–23*) and Charleroi (*see p191*) in the 1870s and 1880s. The figures speak eloquently of that era – bent by their grim toil and hardships, they nonetheless retain an air of indomitable dignity.

This museum, a branch of the Musées Royaux des Beaux-Arts (*see pp72–7*), is located in Meunier's former home and studio, built in 1899, where Meunier lived and worked for the last five years of his life. In addition to the sculptures for which he is famous, the museum also has a good cross section of his paintings and documents, as well as informative exhibits that demonstrate some of his working techniques.

❹ Musée David et Alice van Buuren

Avenue Léo Errera 41, Uccle, 1180 BRU. **Road Map** B4. **Tel** (02) 3434851. 🚋 38, 60, 134. 🚌 3, 7. **Open** 2–5:30pm Wed–Mon. 🅿 📷 Ⓦ museumvanbuuren.com

Set in the prosperous, leafy suburb of Uccle, this museum delights on two levels. First, it is a comfortable, relaxed villa, originally built and furnished in the late 1920s in a user-friendly Art Deco style for the Dutch banker David van Buuren and his wife. Second, since the van

The iconic *Blacksmith* sculpture on view at Meunier's former home

Buurens used their fortune to invest in their passion for art, the house contains an outstanding private collection of artwork.

The art on display includes a priceless version of *The Fall of Icarus* by Pieter Brueghel the Elder, as well as paintings and sculptures by Vincent van Gogh, James Ensor and Rik Wouters. Artists from the St-Martens-Latem School of Art (*see p140*), such as Constant Permeke and Gustave van de Woestyne, are also well represented in the collection.

The van Buurens's quest for harmonious surroundings extended to the beautiful series of gardens outside, which were carefully designed according to Art Deco principles of stylistic geometry by the noted land-scape architects, René Pechère and Jules Buyssens.

Charmingly geometric Art Deco style at Musée David et Alice van Buuren

⑤ Art Nouveau Tour

The southern suburbs of Brussels grew rapidly in the late 19th century as wealthy industrialists commissioned grand new town mansions, or *hôtels*, from a new generation of architects. After 1895, Art Nouveau was the most fashionable style in Ixelles and St-Gilles, pioneered by Victor Horta (1861–1947) who built his house here. Much of Brussels's Art Nouveau heritage was lost over the next 60 years, until its revival in the 1960s, making these rare survivors more precious.

⑤ Rue Faider 83
A draughtsman from Horta's studio, Albert Roosenboom (1871–1943) designed this classic Art Nouveau façade in 1906, full of organic, counter-intuitive shapes.

③ Rue Defacqz 71
In 1894, architect Paul Hankar (1859–1901) designed his house in eclectic style, using a variety of models. There are indicators here of the evolving Art Nouveau style.

④ Hôtel Ciamberlani
Paul Hankar built this house at Rue Defacqz 48 for the Symbolist Albert Ciamberlani in 1897, with murals, ironwork and large round windows.

⑥ Hôtel Tassel
The first Art Nouveau building (1893–5) was designed by Victor Horta for a private client at Rue Paul-Émile Janson 6.

② Musée Horta
Horta's home and studio *(see p84)* is a masterpiece of Art Nouveau design.

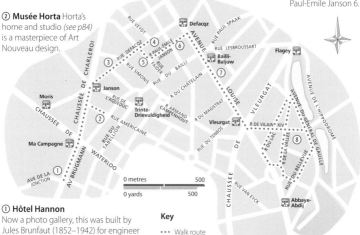

① Hôtel Hannon
Now a photo gallery, this was built by Jules Brunfaut (1852–1942) for engineer and photographer, Édouard Hannon.

Key

••• Walk route

Tips for Walkers

Starting point: Hôtel Hannon, on the corner of Avenue de la Jonction and Avenue Brugmann.
Distance: About 3 km (2 miles).
Getting there: Tram 3, 90, 91, 92; Bus 54. Return to the city from Avenue Louise: Tram 93, 94.
Walking time: 40 minutes, but allow 3 hours for sightseeing.
Cafés and restaurants: This is a residential area, but cafés and restaurants are present on the route.

⑦ Hôtel Solvay
A relatively restrained Horta building at Avenue Louise 224, this was built between 1894 and 1898 for the industrial magnate Ernest Solvay.

⑧ Quartier des Étangs
Around Rue de Vilain XIV, Rue de la Vallée and Rue de Bellevue, there are a number of notable Art Nouveau houses, many designed by Ernest Blérot (1870–1957).

❻ Musée Bruxellois de la Gueuze

Rue Gheude 56, Anderlecht, 1070 BRU. **Road Map** A4. **Tel** (02) 5214928. 27, 46, 49, 50, 78. Ⓜ Clemenceau, Gare du Midi. 3, 4, 31, 32, 81, 82, 83. **Open** 10am–5pm Mon, Tue & Thu–Sat. includes tasting. **w** cantillon.be

The valley of the River Senne possesses airborne yeasts called *Brettanomyces* that cause beer to ferment spontaneously. This rare phenomenon produces the famous local sour beer known as lambic, which is aged and blended to create gueuze *(see p278)*. The beer can only be brewed in winter. At Cantillon – the small family-run brewery museum – the copper cooling vat in the vented roof-top is on display along with the musty cellar full of barrels where beer froths and matures in time-honoured fashion.

❼ Erasmus House

Rue du Chapitre 31, Anderlecht, 1070 BRU. **Road Map** A4. **Tel** (02) 5211383. 46, 49. Ⓜ St-Guidon. 31, 81. **Open** 10am–6pm Tue–Sun. includes the Begijnhof van Anderlecht. **w** erasmushouse.museum

The great Dutch scholar and humanist Desiderius Erasmus (c.1469–1536) had a major role in the spread of Renaissance ideas in northern Europe. He travelled widely, was a friend to other humanists such as Thomas More in England, and became advisor to Emperor Charles V. He also unwittingly promoted the ferment of Protestant reforms through his challenging approach to knowledge, and so spent his final years as a refugee from the Catholic church in Germany and Switzerland. After helping found the College of Three Languages at Leuven *(see pp164–5)*, Erasmus lived in this pretty red-brick house for five months in 1521. Today, it is a museum with exhibits related to his life and times, including books censored in black ink by the infamous Spanish Inquisition.

The serene Erasmus House, briefly home to the famous philosopher

❽ Begijnhof van Anderlecht

Rue du Chapelain 8, Anderlecht, 1070 BRU. **Road Map** A4. **Tel** (02) 5211383. 46, 49. Ⓜ St-Guidon. 31, 81. **Open** 10am–noon & 2–5pm Tue–Sun. includes Erasmus House. **w** erasmushouse.museum

Close to the Erasmus House is the charming Begijhof van Anderlecht. Built in the 14th century, this was home to just eight béguines. The buildings are now a museum and one of the best ways to glimpse what these admirable institutions offered, both to the béguines and the public whom they served. The béguinage lies in the shadow of the 15th-century Gothic **Collegiale Kerk van St-Pieter-en-St-Guido**. The latter is a local saint, who was buried here in the 11th century.

🏠 Collegiale Kerk van St-Pieter-en-St-Guido

Place de la Vaillance, Anderlecht, 1070 BRU. **Tel** (02) 5230220. **Open** 2–5pm Mon–Fri, Sat on request. **Closed** during services. Procession of St Guidon (Sep).

❾ Basilique Nationale du Sacré-Coeur

Parvis de la Basilique 1, Koekelberg, 1083 BRU. **Road Map** A3. **Tel** (02) 4211667. 49, 87. Ⓜ Simonis. 19. **Open** 9am–6pm daily (Dome: Easter–Oct: 9am–4:30pm; Nov–Easter: 10am– 3:30pm). for dome. by request.

King Léopold II was keen to build a church which could hold the growing population of early 20th-century Brussels. He commissioned the striking Basilique Nationale du Sacré-Coeur, an Art Deco landmark, in 1904, although it would not be completed until 1970. Originally designed by Pierre Langerock (1859–1923), the final construc-tion of sandstone and terracotta is the less costly version by Flemish architect, Albert van Huffel. The predominant feature of the church, which rises 90 m (295 ft) above the ground, is a vast green copper dome that can be spotted from many places in the city. Very much a 20th-century church, it is dedicated to those who died for Belgium, particularly the thousands of soldiers killed on their own terrain during the two World Wars.

❿ René Magritte Museum

Rue Esseghem 135, Jette, 1090 BRU. **Road Map** A3. **Tel** (02) 4282626. 49, 53, 89. Ⓜ Belgica, Bockstael, Pannenhuis. 19, 51, 62, 93. **Open** 10am–6pm Wed–Sun. **w** magrittemuseum.be

The great Surrealist painter René Magritte *(see p27)* lived here with his wife from 1930 to 1954, during which time he became a widely recognized artist. Their apartment and his studio in the garden, where he produced almost half his total output, have been arranged in an understated and modest manner to look as they did in the artist's time. The museum includes original works, repro-ductions and material about Magritte and the Surrealists.

Basilique Nationale du Sacré-Coeur, a prominent Brussels landmark

For hotels and restaurants see p266 and pp282–3

The small-scale model of London's Houses of Parliament, Mini-Europe

⓫ Bruparck

Boulevard du Centenaire, 1020 BRU.
Road Map A3. **Tel** (02) 4748383.
🚌 84, 88. Ⓜ Heysel. 🚊 3, 7, 19,
51, 93. 🔲 bruparck.com
Mini-Europe: **Tel** (02) 4741313.
Open Apr–Jan; see website for
details. 🔲 minieurope.be
Océade: **Tel** (02) 4784320. **Open** year-
round. 🔲 🔲 oceade.be
Kinepolis: **Tel** (02) 4742600. 🔲 for
films. 🔲 🔲 kinepolis.be

Although nowhere near as large
or as grand as many of the world's
other theme parks, Bruparck is
nevertheless a popular family
destination. The first and favourite
port of call is **Mini-Europe**, where
more than 300 miniature reconstructions take visitors around
the buildings of the European
Union. Built on a scale of 1:25,
the collection displays buildings
of social or cultural importance,
including Athens's Acropolis,
Berlin's Brandenburg Gate and
London's Houses of Parliament.

For film fans, **Kinepolis** is
hard to beat. Popular films from
many different countries can be
viewed in large auditoriums and
on 25 screens. **The Village** is a
pedestrianized imitation Flemish
village, with plentiful food outlets and children's entertainment.

Another major attraction
is **Océade**, a tropically heated
water park complete with wave
machines, giant slides, bars, cafés
and even realistically re-created
sandy beaches.

⓬ The Atomium

Atomium Square, 1020 BRU.
Road Map A3. **Tel** (02) 4754775.
🚌 84, 88. Ⓜ Heysel. 🚊 3, 7, 19, 51, 93.
Open 10am–6pm daily. 🔲 🔲
🔲 atomium.be

Built for the 1958 World Fair, the
Atomium is arguably Brussels's
most famous landmark structure.
Representing an elementary
iron crystal magnified 165
billion times, it was designed
by the Belgian engineer André
Waterkeyn to reflect the new
age of science and space
travel, as well as to honour
the country's all-important
metal industry. Although the
Atomium was not originally
intended to be a permanent
structure, it proved to be a very
popular attraction. In recent
decades, it has undergone
several rounds of expensive
renovation, and has now
been restored to its original
gleaming vision.

Each of the nine spheres that
make up the crystal is 18 m (60 ft)
in diameter. They are linked
together by escalators and stairs
in the connecting tubes. Five
of the spheres, containing
exhibition rooms, are open to
the public. The uppermost,
rising 102 m (335 ft) above the
ground, provides a panoromic
view over the cityscape of
Brussels, and has a smart
restaurant at the top.

⓭ Domaine de Laeken

Laeken, 1020 BRU. **Road Map** A3.
🚌 47, 49, 53, 57, 84, 88, 89.
Ⓜ Heysel, Bockstael. 🚊 3, 7, 19, 62, 93.
Serres Royales: Avenue du Parc Royal,
1020 BRU. **Tel** (02) 5138940. **Open** late
Apr–early May. 🔲 🔲 reservations
required. 🔲 monarchie.be
Pavillon Chinois and Tour Japonais:
Avenue Van Praet 44, 1020 BRU.
Tel (02) 2681608. **Closed** for
renovations. 🔲 🔲
🔲 kmkg-mrah.be

The Belgian royal family's second,
and preferred, residence is a
large palace surrounded by
parkland in the northern suburb
of Laeken. The 19th-century
Château Royal de Laeken is not
open to the public. However, the
huge and beautiful greenhouses,
the **Serres Royales**, built in the
1870s, are open for guided tours
in spring. The park provides a
pleasant open space for walks

The gigantic Atomium towering above Bruparck

The Pavillon Chinois, housing a museum of Chinese ceramics, in the royal estate in Laeken

and picnics. To the northeast are two essentially authentic Oriental buildings, commissioned by King Léopold II at the start of the 20th century. These are the only completed pieces of a grandiose scheme to create an architectural world tour in his domain; they are now outposts of the Musées Royaux d'Art et d'Histoire (see p81). The **Pavillon Chinois** (Chinese Pavilion) contains a fine collection of Chinese ceramics, while the **Tour Japonais** (Japanese Tower) is a pagoda decorated in Japanese and Art Nouveau styles, and contains a collection of samurai armour and weapons. An additional museum space is devoted to exhibitions on Japanese art.

⓮ Musée du Transport Urbain Bruxellois

Avenue de Tervuren 364b, 1150 BRU. **Road Map** B4. **Tel** (02) 5153108.
🚌 36, 42. 🚋 39, 44, 94. **Open** Apr–Sep: 1–7pm Sat, Sun & public holidays.
🎫 includes ride in a vintage tram. ♿
🅿 📷 🌐 **trammuseumbrussels.be**

The main focus of the Musée du Transport Urbain Bruxellois is the tram, so it is often called the Musée du Tram. Here, lined up in a vast shed, are numerous beautifully restored historic vehicles, from the horse-drawn trams of the 1860s to the first electric trams and trolleybuses, through successive phases of modernization, each richly

redolent of its era. The fees include a 40-minute return journey in a vintage tram of the 1920s, to the Musée Royal de l'Afrique Centrale or to the Parc du Cinquantenaire (see pp80–81) and a ride to Place du Mont in Stockel.

⓯ Musée Royal de l'Afrique Centrale

Leuvensesteenweg 13, 3080 Tervuren. **Road Map** C4. **Tel** (02) 7695211.
🚋 44. **Closed** for renovations until autumn 2017; check website for latest information. 📷 🌐 **africamuseum.be**

One of the world's leading museums and research centres devoted to Africa, the Royal Museum of Central Africa first opened in 1899 and, after major renovations lasting several years, is reopening in autumn 2017. The dynamic museum features four main themed areas, with Central Africa forming the core: societies, showing daily life, rituals and ceremonies; history, featuring archaeological finds and displays on Colonial history; and landscape and biodiversity. Permanent and temporary exhibits include statues, religious idols, dugout canoes, weapons, masks, utilitarian objects, musical instruments, photographs and films, maps and a vast number of specimens of flora and fauna.

The Belgian Congo

During the "scramble for Africa" in the 19th century, Belgium was one of several nations that vied for a slice of that continent to colonize and call its own. In 1878, Belgium's King Léopold II commissioned the explorer Henry Morton Stanley (who famously sought and found Dr Livingstone) to map the uncharted Congo Basin. As a result, Belgium laid claim to a vast territory whose rich resources – gold, diamonds, timber, plantation crops – brought great wealth to the country. Known as the Congo Free State, this land remained the private fiefdom of Léopold II and eventually became notorious for brutality and exploitation. When this was made public knowledge, the Belgian government was forced to take over, in 1908. In 1960, amidst growing internal unrest, independence was hastily granted. The country's name was changed to Zaire in 1971, during the dictatorial rule of President Mobutu, and since his overthrow in 1997, it has been known as the Democratic Republic of Congo.

Léopold II (1835–1909), King of Belgium

SHOPPING IN BRUSSELS

Upmarket stores in Brussels have high-quality goods, elegant wrappings and professional service. International haute couture labels and top-brand chocolate shops radiate a sense of luxury, while the boutiques of up-and-coming designers have an off-hand nonchalance or an edgy intensity. However, all Belgians also have a well-tuned sense of value for money, and prices are keen at the high-street chain shops and supermarkets, for clothes, beers and biscuits. Bargain hunters in search of antiques and bric-a-brac stand a good chance of success, and will certainly enjoy Brussels's vibrant antiques and flea markets.

Window display at a designer fashion boutique on the Rue Neuve

Where to Shop

Brussels's Grand Place is surrounded by lace vendors, chocolate shops and souvenir outlets. The most impressive collection of shops nearby is Galéries St-Hubert (see p66), an opulent arcade housing upmarket outlets. Northwest of the Grand Place is Rue Antoine Dansaert, centre of the Bruxellois' contemporary fashion scene. For all major high-street chains, there is the pedestrianized Rue Neuve near the Grand Place. Between the Lower and Upper towns is the antiques district of Rue Haute and Rue Blaes. Close by is the Place du Grand Sablon where exquisite chocolate shops can be found alongside high-end florists and antique shops. South of the Palais de Justice lie Boulevard de Waterloo and Avenue Louise, with top boutiques such as Gucci.

Department Stores

City 2, at the northern end of Rue Neuve, is the largest urban shopping centre in Belgium and hosts the department store **Inno**. Further south on the same street lies **Hema**, a Dutch low-cost store, selling everything from clothes to kitchen utensils.

Markets and Antiques

During most weekends, visitors will find a *brocante* (a glorified car boot sale combined with street party) somewhere in the city. These are listed in most of the free events magazines, as are the various farmers' markets found across the city. The latter often have some remarkable local breads and cheeses. Cheapest and most extensive of the traditional markets is the **Marché du Midi** (6am–1pm Sundays) that reflects the tastes of the area's North African community. The eclectic **Marolles Marché aux Puces**, a flea market (7am–2pm daily, but best at weekends), dates from 1873 and is the starting point for any antiques hunter. It can take time to sort through the various boxes of items, but there are definitely bargains to be found. For pre-sorted antiques, it is best to head for the more expensive weekend market (9am–6pm Saturday, 9am–2pm Sunday) in front of the Notre-Dame du Sablon.

Fashion

Downtown's Rue Antoine Dansaert is at the heart of Brussels's thriving fashion industry. Its principal outlet **Stijl** has sold the work of fashion graduates from the Antwerp Art Academy since 1984, and still offers the best wares produced by domestic talent. Further down the street **Annemie Verbeke** offers beautiful knitwear. In the nearby Rue du Flandre is the shop of **Martin Margiela**, one of Belgium's most talked about designers. The radical Belgian hat designer, **Elvis Pompilio**, has a shop in Avenue Louise.

Chocolates

There are 81 chocolatiers listed in the Brussels phone book (not including franchise shops), almost all of high quality. The three biggest chains in Belgium are **Godiva**, **Neuhaus** and **Leonidas**. **Galler** and **Corné Port-Royal** are also excellent. All have numerous outlets throughout the city. The area around the Grand Place has many chocolate shops, but true

The Marolles flea market, perfect for bargain hunters

devotees will want to head for the Place du Grand Sablon, location of the **Wittamer** shop and café, which produces some of the finest chocolates and cakes in Brussels. Close by is **Pierre Marcolini**, a more recent star in the chocolate firmament.

Beer

Supermarkets such as Match, Carrefour (which have many outlets) and Delhaize *(see p297)* offer most of the country's finest beers. For rarer finds, as well as appropriate glasses for each beer, gift boxes and other beer paraphernalia, **Beer Mania, De Bier Tempel** and **Délices et Caprices** are recommended. Beer glasses can also be found at the Marolles flea market.

Comics

Brüsel has a vast collection of comics in French, Dutch and English. It also has a gallery of framed original art for sale on the second floor. **Utopia** leans towards American superhero strips and science fiction, but also has Japanese anime titles. A short walk from the Grand Place, **La Boutique Tintin** offers an interesting variety of Tintin-imprinted knick-knacks. The **Centre Belge de la Bande Desinée** *(see p66)* has one of the better stocked comic stores in the city.

Bookshops

Waterstone's and **Sterling** are the city's best English bookstores, while **Filigranes** also has an excellent English section.

Brüsel, one of Brussels's numerous well stocked comic-book stores

Nestled among the high-fashion boutiques of Rue Antoine Dansaert is **Passa Porta**, which calls itself a trilingual bookstore and an "international house of literature". Besides these, there is the exhaustive French book and CD emporium, **Fnac**.

DIRECTORY

Department Stores

City 2
Rue Neuve 123. **City Map** 2 D2. W city2.be

Hema
Rue Neuve 13.
City Map 2 D2. **Tel** (02) 2275210. W hema.be

Inno
Rue Neuve 111–123.
City Map 2 D2. **Tel** (02) 2112111. W inno.be

Markets and Antiques

Marché du Midi
Gare du Midi.
City Map 1 A5.

Marolles Marché aux Puces
Place du Jeu de Balle.
City Map 1 C5.

Fashion

Annemie Verbeke
Rue Antoine Dansaert 64.
City Map 1 C2.
Tel (02) 5112171.
W annemieverbeke.be

Elvis Pompilio
Avenue Louise 437.
City Map 2 D5.
Tel (02) 5128588.
W elvispompilio.com

Martin Margiela
Rue de Flandre 114.
City Map 1 B1. **Tel** (02) 2237520. W maison martinmargiela.com

Stijl
Rue Antoine Dansaert 74.
City Map 1 C2.
Tel (02) 5120313.

Chocolates

Corné Port-Royal
Rue de la Madeleine 9.
City Map 2 D3.
Tel (02) 5124314.
W corneportroyal.com

Galler
Rue au Beurre 44.
City Map 2 D3. **Tel** (02) 502 0266. W galler.com

Godiva
Place du Grand Sablon 47–48. **City Map** 2 D4.
Tel (02) 5029906.
W godivachocolates.eu

Leonidas
Rue au Beurre 34.
City Map 2 D3.
Tel (02) 5128737.
W leonidas.com

Neuhaus
Galerie de la Reine 25–27.
City Map 2 D3.
Tel (02) 5126359.
W neuhaus.be

Pierre Marcolini
Rue des Minimes 1. **City Map** 2 D4. **Tel** (02) 514 1206. W marcolini.be

Wittamer
Place du Grand Sablon 6.
City Map 2 D4.
Tel (02) 5123742.
W wittamer.com

Beer

Beer Mania
Chaussée de Wavre 174–6.
City Map 2 F5.
Tel (02) 5121788.
W beermania.be

De Bier Tempel
Rue Marché aux Herbes 56. **City Map** 2 D3.
Tel (02) 5021906.

Délices et Caprices
Rue des Bouchers 68.
City Map 2 D3.
Tel (02) 5121451.

Comics

La Boutique Tintin
Rue de la Colline 13.
City Map 2 D3.
Tel (02) 5145152.
W tintin.boutique.com

Brüsel
Boulevard Anspach 100.
City Map 1 C3.
W brusel.com

Centre Belge de la Bande Desinée
Rue des Sables 20.
City Map 2 E2.
Tel (02) 219 1980.
W comicscenter.net

Utopia
Rue de Midi 39. **City Map** 1 C3. **Tel** (02) 5140826.
W utopiacomics.be

Bookshops

Filigranes
Ave des Arts 39–40.
City Map 2 F3.
Tel (02) 511 9015.
W filigranes.be

Fnac
City 2, Rue Neuve 123.
City Map 2 D1. **Tel** (02) 2751111. W fnac.be

Passa Porta
Rue Antoine Dansaert 46.
City Map 1 C2.
Tel (02) 2260454.
W passaporta.be

Sterling
Fossé aux Loups 23–25.
City Map 2 D2.
Tel (02) 2236223.
W sterlingbooks.be

Waterstone's
Boulevard Adolphe Max 71–75. **City Map** 2 D1.
Tel (02) 2192708.
W waterstones.com

ENTERTAINMENT IN BRUSSELS

Lying at the crossroads of London, Paris, Amsterdam and Cologne, Brussels enjoys the presence of the best international touring groups. The calendar is full of first-rate opera, jazz, rock and classical and world music, glittering with performers of world renown. The city also generates its own productions of international acclaim, notably in opera and modern dance, while its cosmopolitan culture ensures that the latest films arrive quickly. There is a lively club scene, with venues attracting revellers from all over Europe. Many bars and cafés host live music, providing an easy continuum between traditional taverns and DJ-fuelled dance floors.

Listings and Tickets

Most expatriates in Brussels depend on the weekly English listings guide, **Brussels Unlimited**, and a monthly online magazine, **The Bulletin**, which also provides cultural information, weather reports, news, reviews and event listings. **Agenda** is a trilingual listings magazine that can be found in boxes outside supermarkets. Its website also has extensive, up-to-date listings in French and Dutch. The Brussels Tourist Office produces brochures, along with useful information on its website: www.visitbrussels.be. Tickets for many events are available from Fnac (see p91).

Classical Music

The **Théâtre Royal de la Monnaie** is one of Europe's best opera houses. Tickets can be cheap, but many productions sell out in advance. The Victor Horta-designed **Palais des Beaux-Arts** (BOZAR), the country's most notable cultural venue, is home to the Belgian National Orchestra.

Dance

Belgium is particularly strong in the field of modern dance. Its leading choreographers such as Michèle Anne de Mey and **Wim Vandekeybus** have enormous influence internationally. Another important figure, Anne Teresa De Keersmaeker, is the director of the world-renowned **Rosas Company**.

Jazz

Every May, jazz fans from around the world congregate for the **Brussels Jazz Marathon**, much of which is free.

The quintessential Brussels jazz venue is the venerable **L'Archiduc**, an Art Deco gem in the city centre which hosts regular concerts every weekend. **The Music Village** stretches across two 17th-century buildings near the Grand Place and features both local and international names. **Sounds**, in Ixelles, is another popular jazz club boasting a prolific agenda of concerts.

Rock, Reggae, Folk and World

Brussels is one of the best cities in Europe to catch up-and-coming acts, generally at reasonable ticket prices.

The **Forêt-National**, lying southeast of the city centre, is Belgium's top arena for big-name acts. Closer to the centre, Brussels's other venues tend to be more intimate, and each have their own favoured genres. **Café Central** leans towards R&B, blues, bossa nova and ambient, while **Cirque Royale** favours indie rock, and has a reputation for booking bands before they become household names. The downtown **Ancienne Belgique** has a similar line-up, but for more established acts.

The Flemish student venue **Kultuur Kaffee** at the Vrij Universiteit Brussel, the city's Dutch-language university, always has a strong line-up and serves the cheapest beer in the city. **Recyclart** plays avant-garde techno, hardcore, punk and some world music in a refitted train station. The impressive **Halles de Schaerbeek**, formerly a 19th-century market, hosts a range of different groups and other arts events. Reggae concerts are often held at the **VK Club** (Vaartkapoen), while Flemish acts are showcased at the **Beursschouwburg**, the Flemish cultural community centre.

Nightlife

Brussels's bright young things start the weekend in St Géry, a square in the fashion district of Rue Antoine Dansaert. This area is home to such bars as the

Dramatic performance at the prestigious Théâtre Royal de la Monnaie

latin-flavoured **Mappa Mundo**, popular **Le Roi des Belges** and elegant **Gecko**. The most renowned club in Brussels, **The Fuse**, has earned its reputation for having top-name techno and dance DJs. Once a month, it holds La Demence, a gay night that draws international crowds. **Le You** is another electro-psychedelic dance club with a gay night on Sundays. **Les Jeux d'Hiver** in the Bois de la Cambre woods attracts an affluent crowd. Cuban disco **Havana** is open till 7am on weekends. **Noctis** provides nightlife listings online.

Theatre

The most important Belgian theatre is the **Théâtre National**, which stages high-quality productions of mainly French classics. Young Belgian playwrights are showcased at the private **Théâtre Le Public**, while French 20th-century and burlesque pieces are staged in the beautifully restored **Théâtre Royal du Parc**. The main Dutch-language company is the **Koninklijke Vlaamse Schouwburg** (KVS) or the Royal Flemish Theatre, which uses several venues clustered in central Brussels.

Cinema

The massive **Kinepolis Bruxelles** at Laeken boasts 25 screens for the latest blockbusters, always in their original languages. Mainstream cinema can also be enjoyed at the two other central UGC cineplexes. A more intriguing ambience and eclectic line-up of films can be found at the **Arenberg-Galeries**. The **Nova** offers truly independent films, while the **Actors Studio** showcases foreign and art cinema. **Movy Club** screens mainstream films in opulent Art Deco movie-palace surroundings.

DIRECTORY

Listings and Tickets

Agenda
w agenda.be

The Bulletin
w xpats.com

Classical Music

Palais des Beaux-Arts
Rue Ravenstein 23.
City Map 2 E3.
Tel (02) 5078200.
w bozar.be

Théâtre Royal de la Monnaie
Place de la Monnaie.
City Map 2 D2.
w lamonnaie.be

Dance

Rosas Company
w rosas.be

Wim Vandekeybus
w ultimavez.com

Jazz

L'Archiduc
Rue Antoine Dansaert 6.
City Map 1 C2.
w archiduc.net

Brussels Jazz Marathon
w brusselsjazz
marathon.be

The Music Village
Rue des Pierres 50.
City Map 1 C3.
Tel (02) 5131345.
w themusicvillage.com

Sounds
Rue de la Tulipe 28.
w soundsjazzclub.be

Rock, Reggae, Folk and World

Ancienne Belgique
Boulevard Anspach 110.
City Map 1 C3.
Tel (02) 5482484.
w abconcerts.be

Beursschouwburg
Auguste Ortsstraat 20–28.
City Map 1 C2. Tel (02) 5500350. w beurss
chouwburg.be

Café Central
Rue de Borgval 14.
City Map 1 C2.
Tel (02) 5137308.
w lecafecentral.com

Cirque Royale
Rue de l'Enseignement 81.
City Map 2 F2.
Tel (02) 2182015.
w cirque-royal.org

Forêt-National
Avenue Victor Rousseau 208. Tel (09) 0069500.
w forestnational.be

Halles de Schaerbeek
Rue Royale Ste-Mairie 22b.
Tel (02) 2182107.
w halles.be

Kultuur Kaffee
Blvrd de la Plaine 2.
Tel (02) 6292325.
w kultuurkaffee.be

Recyclart
Rue des Ursulines 25.
City Map 1 C4.
w recyclart.be

VK Club
Schoolstraat 76.
Tel (02) 4142907.
w vkconcerts.be

Nightlife

The Fuse
Rue Blaes 208.
City Map 1 C5. Tel (02) 5119789. w fuse.be

Gecko
Place St-Géry 16.
City Map 1 C2.
w geckococktailbar.be

Havana
Rue de l'Epée 4.
City Map 1 C5.
w havana-brussels.com

Les Jeux d'Hiver
Chemin du Croquet 1.
Tel (02) 6497002.
w jeuxdhiver.be

Mappa Mundo
Rue du Pont de la Carpe 2. City Map 1 C2.
Tel (02) 5143555.

Noctis
w noctis.com

Le Roi des Belges
Rue Jules Van Praet 35.
City Map 1 C2.
Tel (02) 5034300.

Le You
Rue Duquesnoy 18.
City Map 2 D3. Tel (02) 6391400. w leyou.be

Theatre

Koninklijke Vlaamse Schouwburg
Arduinkaai 9. Tel (02) 2101112. w kvs.be

Théâtre National
Boulevard Emile Jacqmain 111–115. City Map 2 D1.
w theatrenational.be

Théâtre Le Public
Rue Braemt 64–70.
City Map 3 1A.
w theatrelepublic.be

Théâtre Royal du Parc
R de la Loi 3. City Map 2 F3. Tel (02) 5053040.
w theatreduparc.be

Cinema

Actors Studio
Petite Rue des Bouchers 16. City Map 2 D2.
Tel (02) 5121696.
w actorsstudio.
cinenews.be

Arenberg-Galeries
Galerie de la Reine 26.
City Map 2 D2.
w arenberg.be

Kinepolis Bruxelles
Bruparck, Boulevard du Centenaire 20.
w kinepolis.be

Movy Club
Rue des Moines 21.
Tel (02) 5376954.

Nova
Rue d'Arenberg 3.
City Map 2 D2.
Tel (02) 5112477.
w nova-cinema.org

Brussels's Cafés and Bars

A long history of conviviality lies behind Brussels's countless cafés and bars. Brewing has been a major industry here since medieval times, when the tavern was an important social hub. During the 19th century, the culture of the coffeehouse combined with the time-honoured traditions of the tavern to produce elegant and sophisticated cafés where men and women could meet with decorum and still enjoy a drink in the customary Belgian way. Many contemporary cafés and bars remain delightfully rooted in the past, while others bristle with ultra-modern style, but all are heirs to the same tradition of hospitality.

A waiter in a traditional tabard apron at Le Roy d'Espagne

Mappamundo, in the trendy St-Géry district, keeps long hours, like many bars. It often brims over with thirsty customers spilling out onto the outside tables. It serves a variety of Belgian beers and is a great place to unwind over a drink and snacks.

Places with Character

Le Roy d'Espagne is a two-tiered bar occupying the elegant guildhouse of the bakers in the Grand Place. The atmospheric interior famously has characterful decor. It is a fine place to sample the best Trappist beers and traditional tavern food.

Café Metropole is the café-cum-bar of one of Brussels's most prestigious hotels, with an interior lavishly decorated in 18th-century French style. The terrace is the place to see and be seen. Despite its grand air, everyone is made welcome.

Le Falstaff, facing the Bourse, is famous for its authentic Art Nouveau decor featuring stained glass, mirrors, lamps and woodwork. This popular bar, café and restaurant seems to have bottled the atmosphere of 1903, the year of its creation.

À La Mort Subite is a famous drinking place, given a Classical makeover in 1926. Its unnerving name, meaning Sudden Death, shared also with a brand of beer, in fact refers to a working men's dice game that used to be played here.

Le Cirio is a classic traditional café and bar with wall-mirrors, gilding, woodwork and an air of faded grandeur. Founded in 1886 and named after its owner, Le Cirio is famed for its speciality, *half en half* – half white wine, half sparkling wine.

On the Menu

There is no clear distinction drawn between a café and a bar. Most such establishments offer coffee, tea and hot chocolate, or beer, wine and stronger alcohols. Many of them also serve food of some kind. At its simplest, this will be a plate of rye-bread and cream cheese – traditionally served with beer – or a *croque-monsieur* (grilled cheese and ham on toast). However, many bars and cafés also offer a full menu of substantial bar meals such as steak and chips or mussels, as well as more elaborate dishes.

La Chaloupe d'Or, the Golden Boat, in the Grand Place, is a long-established café, bar and restaurant of timeless refinement and elegance. This is an excellent place for a light lunch, afternoon wheat beer with a slice of gâteau, or a pre-theatre drink. The staff glide swiftly among the tables, efficiently memorizing orders.

Steak and chips, a bar-food standard, with a garnish of salad and shallots

BRUSSELS STREET FINDER

The map given below shows the area of Brussels covered in the street finder maps. The Lower Town is the area around the Grand Place; the Upper Town includes the Musées Royaux des Beaux Arts, the Palais Royal and the Quartier Européen. Map references for all sights, hotels, restaurants, shopping and entertainment venues given in Brussels refer to the maps in this section. The key, set out below, indicates the scales of the maps and shows what other features are marked on them, including transport terminals, emergency services and information centres. Street names are in both French and Dutch. The first figure in the map reference indicates which street finder map to turn to. The letter and number that follow give the grid reference on that map.

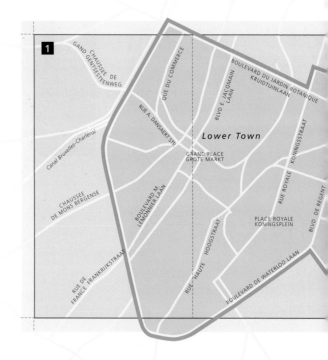

Key

- Major sight
- Other sight
- Other building
- M Metro station
- Train station
- Tram stop
- Bus station
- i Tourist information
- Hospital
- Police station
- Church
- Railway line
- Pedestrian street

Scale of Maps

| 0 metres | 250 |
| 0 yards | 250 |

Façade of La Maison des Ducs de Brabant, Grand Place (see pp60–61)

The triumphal arch in the Parc du Cinquantenaire, built in 1905 *(see pp80–81)*

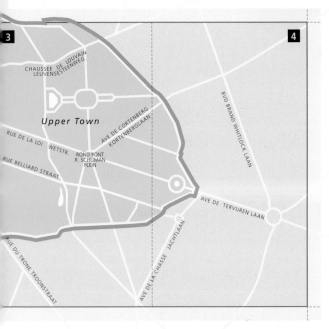

3

4

CHAUSSEE DE LOUVAIN
LEUVENSESTEENWEG

Upper Town

RUE DE LA LOI WETSTR.

RUE BELLIARD STRAAT

ROND PONT
R. SCHUMAN
PLEIN

AVE DE CORTENBERG
KORTENBERGLAAN

BVD BRAND WHITLOCK LAAN

AVE DE TERVUREN LAAN

AVE DE LA CHASSE JACHTLAAN

RUE DU TRONE TROONSTRAAT

| 0 metres | 500 |
| 0 yards | 500 |

Cathédrale Sts-Michel-et-
Gudule *(see p67)*

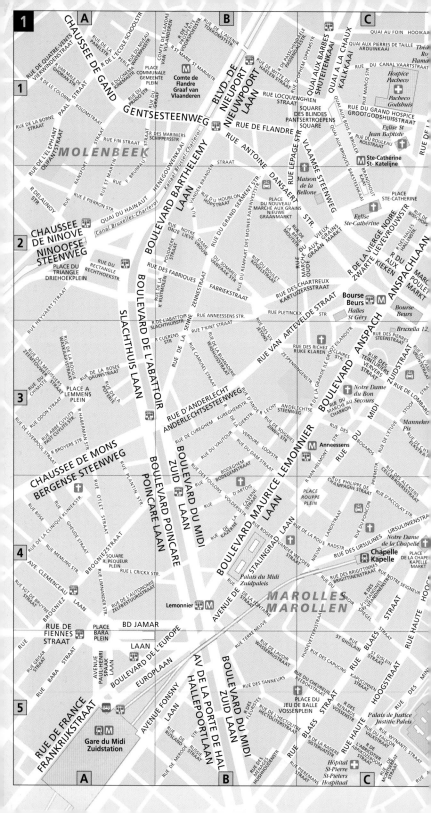

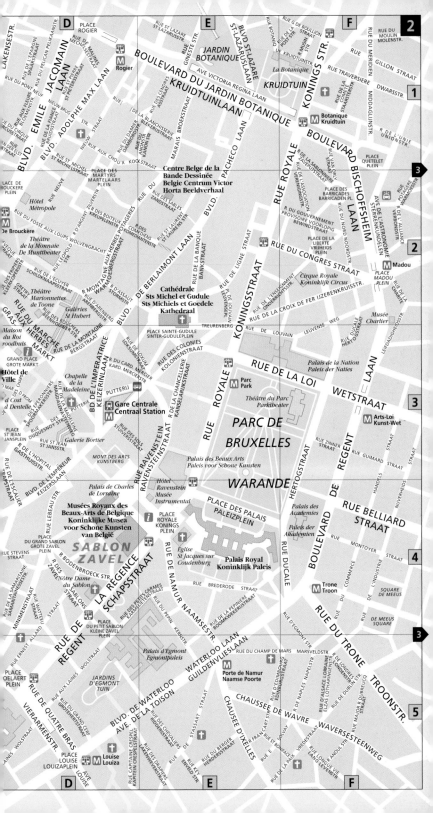

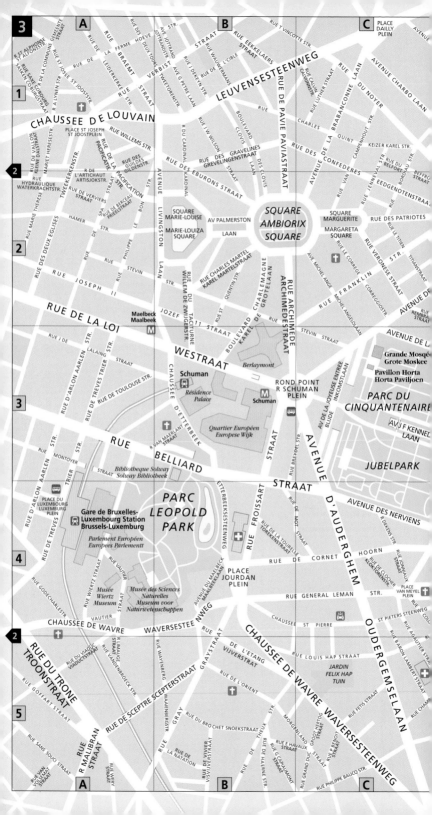

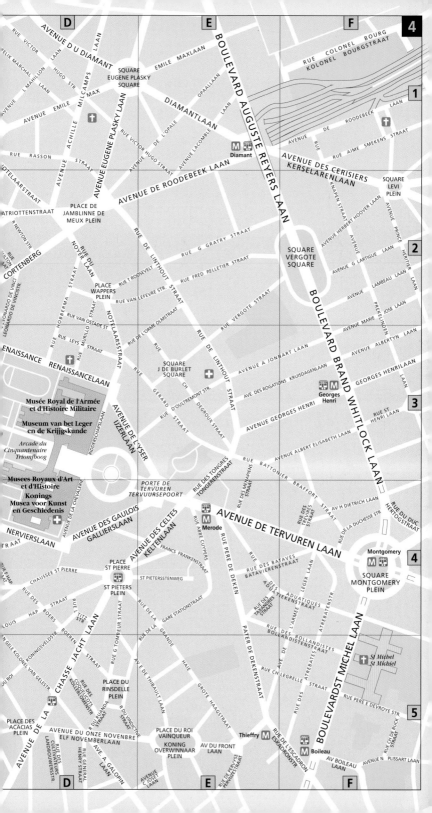

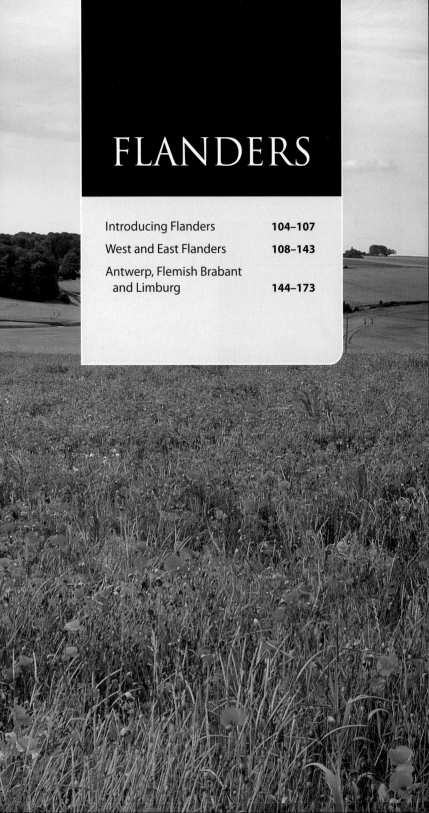

FLANDERS

Flanders at a Glance

Northern Belgium forms the Dutch-speaking region known as Flanders. The language here is spoken in Flemish dialects that vary hugely across the land. The western half of Flanders consists of two provinces – West Vlaanderen, which has a coast on the North Sea, and Oost Vlaanderen. The beautiful cities of Bruges and Ghent are the respective capitals. To the east lie three more provinces: Antwerpen, with its capital in the city of Antwerp; Limburg and Vlaams Brabant. Much of the north is flat, but towards the southern border with Wallonia, the land begins to rise into softly undulating hills.

Locator Map

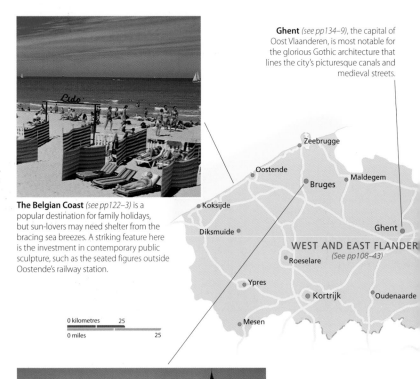

Ghent (see pp134–9), the capital of Oost Vlaanderen, is most notable for the glorious Gothic architecture that lines the city's picturesque canals and medieval streets.

The Belgian Coast (see pp122–3) is a popular destination for family holidays, but sun-lovers may need shelter from the bracing sea breezes. A striking feature here is the investment in contemporary public sculpture, such as the seated figures outside Oostende's railway station.

Zeebrugge

Oostende
Maldegem
Bruges

Koksijde

Diksmuide
Ghent

WEST AND EAST FLANDER
(See pp108–43)
Roeselare

Ypres

Kortrijk
Oudenaarde

Mesen

| 0 kilometres | 25 |
| 0 miles | 25 |

◀ Red poppies, a symbol of the war dead, carpeting the battlefields of Flanders

Bruges (see pp112–121) casts a romantic spell with its step-gabled façades and a skyline pricked by medieval towers. The canals that thread through this miniature city were used in the Middle Ages by barges laden with trade goods. The wealth and luxury this trade brought to Bruges is still very evident in the city's monuments and museums.

Grimbergen *(see p168)* – located just north of Brussels in the Province of Vlaams Brabant – has one of the finest Baroque churches in Belgium. Built between 1660 and 1725, it belongs to an abbey of the Premonstratensian Order, and has given its name to a respected abbey beer.

Hasselt *(see p170)*, thriving capital of the Province of Limburg, holds a number of surprises, such as an authentic Japanese Garden, complete with timber pavilions, a stimulating fashion museum and the National Museum of Jenever.

Turnhout

Antwerp

St-Niklaas   Lier   Geel

ANTWERP, FLEMISH BRABANT
AND LIMBURG
(See pp144–73)

Maaseik

Mechelen

Aarschot

Aalst   Grimbergen   Hasselt

Leuven *(see pp164–5)*, the capital of Vlaams Brabant, is the seat of Belgium's oldest university. Founded in 1475, it is wittily symbolized in the Font Sapienza fountain.

BRUSSELS
(See pp56–101)

Leuven

Gaasbeek   Tienen   St-Truiden

Tongeren

Kasteel van Gasbeek *(see p173)* sits in the beautiful rural region of Pajottenland, west of Brussels. This great medieval castle was renovated in sumptuous Flemish-Renaissance and Neo-Gothic styles in the late 19th century, creating a stylish aristocratic home, full of fascinating antique furniture, paintings and other *objets d'art*.

Flemish Masters

The early Flemish painters had a major impact on the history of European art. Pioneers of oil painting on wooden panels, they created masterpieces in the 15th century, which travelled along trade routes, notably to Italy where artists such as Leonardo da Vinci, stunned by their quality, in turn adopted oil painting. Many Flemish painters subsequently absorbed the advances of the Italian Renaissance, and the peculiarly Flemish qualities of their art softened. Most notably, Pieter Paul Rubens cut his teeth in Italy, then brought back an unprecedented swagger and dynamism, re-establishing Flanders as a European centre for artistic excellence.

Jan van Eyck's realistic portrait of his wife Margareta in 1439

Rogier van der Weyden is noted for his emotional intensity. A side panel from his triptych The Seven Sacraments (1445) depicts ordination, marriage and extreme unction.

Flemish Primitives

Early Flemish painters such as Jan van Eyck (c.1395–1441), Rogier van der Weyden (c.1400–64) and Hans Memling (c.1430–94) are often called the Flemish Primitives. The term comes from Latin primitivus, *or earliest of its kind, as their art was seen by later historians as a forerunner of the Renaissance. The Flemish Primitives' skills of fine detail and acute observation were based on monastic traditions of manuscript illustration, but used oils instead of water-based paints.*

Hans Memling created several paintings for St-Janshospitaal in Bruges. In The Mystic Marriage of St Catherine, from around 1479, the Christ Child places a ring on the saint's finger, attended by the hospital's patrons, St John the Baptist and St John the Evangelist.

Pieter Brueghel the Elder
(c.1525–69) was the greatest of a family of talented artists. He showed an earthy delight in Flemish rural life and used it as the context for scenes from the Bible or Greek mythology. In his *Fall of Icarus* (c.1558), the unfortunate pioneer aviator crashes into the sea beside a ship, unnoticed by the nearby ploughman who is concentrating on his work.

Jan van Eyck demonstrates his exceptional eye for detail, through contemporary touches such as the canon's spectacles, in *Madonna with Canon van der Paele* (1436).

Pieter Paul Rubens (1577–1640) was known as a master of composition. His *Adoration of the Magi* (1624) brings extraordinary energy to this well worn theme, making the viewer's eye dance around from face to face, although the prime focus always remains the baby Jesus.

Anthony van Dyck
(1599–1641) worked as Rubens's chief assistant in Antwerp. His gift for portraiture, seen in his self-portrait at the age of 30, later brought him great success at the court of Charles I in England.

Jacob Jordaens (1593–1678) worked with Rubens in Antwerp. He is famous for lively paintings such as *The Family Concert* (1638). The matronly central figure watches the others make raucous music, while, unobserved, the dog sniffs the food.

WEST AND EAST FLANDERS

Charming, fascinating and glorying in the treasures of its historic heritage, West and East Flanders is home to vibrant cities such as Bruges and Ghent, and smaller towns such as Oudenaarde, Kortrijk and Veurne. Around them lies a tranquil rural landscape of flat or gently hilly farmland, threaded with rivers and canals. To the north, sandy beaches face out on to the bracing North Sea.

Owing to its location at the crossroads of northern Europe, and to its boundary with the North Sea, this region has often been thrust into the forefront of historical events. Although a Flemish-speaking land, it was ruled during the Middle Ages by French kings *(see pp41–2)* – a cause of much frustration and strife. Despite this, many of the cities, notably Bruges, Ghent, Ypres, Kortrijk and Veurne, were rich from the cloth trade and industrious with crafts meticulously regulated by their proud guilds. The Golden Age followed in the 15th century, when the dukes of Burgundy took possession and made Bruges the glittering capital of their empire.

However, between 1500 and 1945, West and East Flanders was in the doldrums. The economy became largely rural, with small cottage industries such as lace-making. The land became a pawn in the big-game politics of Europe, battered by religious struggles in the 16th century as the Spanish Netherlands disintegrated, then fought over by the Austrians, the French and the English in succeeding centuries. The 20th century brought World War I, which scored a line through the region, creating a wasteland on either side and demolishing Ypres.

All this changed over the latter half of the 20th century with the rise of Flanders as one of Europe's most prosperous regions. The architectural treasures of the old medieval towns, sidelined and ignored for centuries, were restored, and the historic heritage of Flanders has become one of its greatest assets. Furthermore, West and East Flanders has done much to encourage visitors, be it in the great cities, the countryside, on the coast, or on the battlefields of the Western Front.

The traditional Flemish way of shrimp fishing from horse-drawn carts, at the Oostduinkerke beach

◀ Houses with Baroque-style gables along the banks of the Graslei, Ghent

Exploring West and East Flanders

The Belgian coast is a chain of beach resorts terminating in the north with the Zwin nature reserve. A little inland is Bruges, with the beautiful canal landscape around Damme to its northeast. The battlefields of World War I run in a strip from Diksmuide to Ypres (Ieper) and on to Mesen and the hills of Heuvelland. The delightful and historic city of Ghent is the biggest regional centre in East Flanders, ringed by interesting towns, from Kortrijk and Oudenaarde to Dendermonde and St-Niklaas. All these needed defences, and the green landscape is dotted with castles, such as Beauvoorde, Ooidonk and Laarne. Around Oudenaarde and Geraardsbergen, the landscape becomes quite hilly, inspiring the label the Flemish Ardennes.

Sand yachts with bright sails on the coast near De Panne

Sights at a Glance

Villages, Towns and Cities
❶ *Bruges pp112–121*
❷ Damme
❸ Knokke-Heist
❹ Zeebrugge
❻ Lissewege
❼ Oostende
❽ Veurne
❾ Koksijde
❸ Ypres
❹ Poperinge
❺ Kortrijk
❻ *Ghent pp134–9*
㉑ Oudenaarde
㉒ Geraardsbergen
㉓ Aalst
㉔ Dendermonde
㉕ St-Niklaas

Castles
❿ Kasteel Beauvoorde
⓲ Kasteel Ooidonk
⓳ Kasteel van Laarne

Museums
⓫ IJzertoren
⓴ Stoomcentrum Maldegem

Tours
⓬ *A Tour of World War I Battlefields pp130–31*
⓱ *A Tour Around St-Martens-Latem p140*

Areas of Natural Beauty
❺ Zwin Natuur Park

For hotels and restaurants see pp266–7 and pp283–6

Under the Blinde Ezelstraat bridge on a tour of Bruges

Flowering clumps of sea lavender on the flat expanse of marshland at the Zwin nature reserve

Getting Around

The motorways provide the fastest road links between main cities. Belgian National Railways has a network that reaches all major towns and many smaller communities, while De Lijn (Flanders' public transport service) runs a comprehensive bus service, including the Belbus and the Kusttram *(see p325)*. Scheduled boat trips on rivers and canals in and around Bruges and Ghent offer a different and more leisurely way of getting around.

Key

— Motorway

— Major road

— Secondary road

— Minor road

— Main railway

— Minor railway

— International border

— Provincial border

For keys to symbols *see back flap*

❶ Bruges

The city of Bruges originated as a 9th-century fortress built to defend the coast against the Vikings. Dominated by the French and then the dukes of Burgundy, Bruges became one of Europe's most sophisticated cities and an international trading hub, famed for its extravagance and luxury. Today, the city owes its pre-eminent position to the beauty of its historic centre, whose cobbled lanes and meandering canals are lined by medieval buildings. There is a lively cultural scene, embodied in the Concertgebouw, an innovative concert hall built to celebrate Bruges's status as a European City of Culture in 2002.

🏛 The Markt

Bruges's main square, an open space lined with 17th-century houses and overlooked by the Belfort on one side, has held a market since the 10th century. On the eastern side is the Neo-Gothic Provinciaal Hof, built between 1881 and 1921. This denotes Bruges's status as the capital of the Province of West Vlaanderen. In the middle of the square is a statue of Pieter de Coninck and Jan Breydel, two 14th-century guildsmen who led a bloody rebellion known as the Bruges Matins against French troops in 1302.

🏛 The Belfort

Markt 7. **Tel** (050) 448743.
Open 9:30am–6pm daily. 🖼

Built between the 13th and 15th centuries, the Belfort is an octagonal bell tower that rises to a height of 83 m (272 ft) and dominates the Markt. Inside the tower, 366 steps lead up, past

The medieval Belfort, towering over the roofs of the city centre

the treasury chamber where the town's rights and privileges were stored, to the roof, which offers delightful panoramic views of the city and its surroundings. The Belfort also contains a famous carillon, with 47 bells that can be played from a keyboard.

Bruges's medieval buildings flanking the canalized River Reie

🏛 Historium

Markt 1. **Tel** (050) 270311. **Open** 10am–6pm (last entry 5pm) daily. **Closed** 1 Jan. 🖼🖼🖼  historium.be

An interactive experience that takes visitors back in time, Historium shows what the city was like in the 15th century through displays, film, music and special effects. Using an audio guide in a choice of languages, visitors take a one-hour self-guided tour through the themed rooms and immerse themselves in historical scenes such as the bustling old port and painter Van Dyck's studio.

🏛 Choco-Story

Wijnzakstraat 2 (St-Jansplein), Bruges. **Tel** (050) 612237. **Open** 10am–5pm daily. **Closed** 2nd week of Jan. 🖼🖼 🟥 choco-story.be

Set in a 15th-century former wine tavern known as the Huis de Croon, this museum of chocolate shows, through exhibits and tastings, how cocoa is made into chocolate. Choco-Story's artifacts cover the history of chocolate from its origins in Central America to all aspects of its trade.
    The same building houses the **Lumina Domestica**, a museum of domestic lighting that displays the private collection of around 6,500 lamps, starting with pre-historic oil lamps.

🏛 Friet Museum

Vlamingstraat 33, Bruges. **Tel** (050) 340150. **Open** 10am–5pm daily. **Closed** second week of Jan. 🖼🖼 🟥 🟥 frietmuseum.be

Belgian chips or fries (*friet* in Dutch and *frites* in French) are widely acknowledged as the best in the world. The Friet Museum reveals the secrets of this national culinary triumph – the choice of potato, its cut and frying, its history (right back to the ancient Americas) plus everything associated with the Belgian passion for *friet*. Visitors can also taste the product of all this dedicated research. The museum is arranged in the modernized interior of the 14th-century Saaihalle (Serge-weavers' Hall), a building which, until 1516, had served as the Genoese Lodge, the headquarters of traders from the Italian port-city of Genoa.

The Burg

A cobbled square near the Markt, the Burg was once the political and religious focus of Bruges. It is also the site of the original fort around which the city grew. Some of the most imposing civic buildings are located here, including the **Stadhuis** and the **Oude Griffie** (Old Recorder's House) with its Renaissance façade. Next door is the **Renaissance Hall**, with a massive wood, marble and alabaster chimney designed by the Dutch architect Lanceloot Blondeel. On the nothern side of the Burg, the tree-shaded space was the site of the Cathedral of St Donation, destroyed by the French in 1799.

Stadhuis

Burg 12. **Tel** (050) 448711. **Open** 9:30am–5pm daily. **Closed** 1 Jan, 25 Dec. **bezoekers.brugge.be**

The intricately carved façade of the Stadhuis was completed in 1375, but the niche statues are modern effigies of the counts and countesses of Flanders. Much of this building is a triumph of restoration. Inside, a staircase

leads to the Gothic hall, a magnificent parliamentary chamber built around 1400. The ceiling has lavish woodcarvings including 16 corbels bearing representations of the seasons and the elements. A series of paintings, completed in 1895, portrays key events in the city's history.

Ornate statues decorating the façade of the Basilica of the Holy Blood

Heilig Bloed Basiliek

Burg 13 **Tel** (050) 336792. **Open** Apr–Sep: 9:30am–noon & 2–5pm daily; Oct–Mar: 10am–noon & 2–5pm daily.

One of Europe's most sacred reliquaries is held at the Basilica of the Holy Blood. The lower part is the 12th-century St Basil's chapel and has a plain stone-

pillared entrance and arches. The upper chapel was destroyed by the French in the 1790s and rebuilt in the 19th century. Here, colourful decorations surround a silver tabernacle from 1611 which houses a sacred phial, supposed to contain a few drops of blood and water washed from the body of Christ.

The Vismarkt

Braambergstraat. **Open** Tue–Sat am. From the Burg, an arched path called the Blinde Ezelstraat (Alley of the Blind Donkey) leads to this open-air fish market, where fish is still sold each morning.

Bruges

Key
Street-by-Street pp114–15

For keys to symbols see back flap

Street-by-Street: The City Centre

One of the most popular destinations in Belgium, Bruges is an unspoilt medieval town. The centre of the city is amazingly well preserved, with winding streets that pass by picturesque canals lined with fine buildings. When the River Zwin silted up at the end of the 15th century, the town's trade was badly affected. It was never heavily industrialized and has retained most of its medieval buildings. As a further bonus, Bruges also escaped major damage in both World Wars. Today, the streets are well maintained – there are no billboards or high-rises, and traffic is strictly regulated. All the major attractions are located within the circle of boulevards that marks the line of the old medieval walls.

The picturesque Rozenhoedkaai
A charming introduction to Bruges is provided by the boat trips along the city's canal network.

Onthaalkerk Onze-Lieve-Vrouw
The massive Welcome Church of Our Lady took 200 years to build and shows many architectural styles.

Sint-Janshospitaal
Six of the artist's works are shown in the chapel of the 12th-century St Janshospitaal that was functioning as late as 1976.

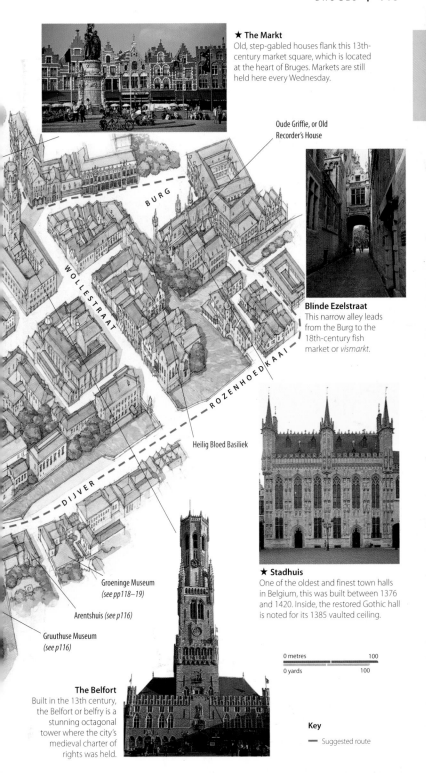

★ The Markt
Old, step-gabled houses flank this 13th-century market square, which is located at the heart of Bruges. Markets are still held here every Wednesday.

Oude Griffie, or Old Recorder's House

Blinde Ezelstraat
This narrow alley leads from the Burg to the 18th-century fish market or *vismarkt*.

BURG

WOLLESTRAAT

ROZENHOEDKAAI

Heilig Bloed Basiliek

DIJVER

★ Stadhuis
One of the oldest and finest town halls in Belgium, this was built between 1376 and 1420. Inside, the restored Gothic hall is noted for its 1385 vaulted ceiling.

Groeninge Museum
(see pp118–19)

Arentshuis (see p116)

Gruuthuse Museum
(see p116)

The Belfort
Built in the 13th century, the Belfort or belfry is a stunning octagonal tower where the city's medieval charter of rights was held.

0 metres   100
0 yards   100

Key

— Suggested route

The stately, pale brick tower of
St-Salvatorskathedraal, Bruges

St-Salvatorskathedraal

St-Salvatorskerkhof 1. **Tel** (050) 336188.
Open 10am–1pm & 2–5:30pm Mon–
Fri, 10am–1pm & 2–3:30pm Sat,
11:30am–noon & 2–5pm Sun.

Originally built as a parish church
between the 12th and 15th
centuries, this brick building
became Bruges's cathedral in
1834, following the destruction
of the Cathedral of St Donation
in the Burg (see p112), by the
French army in 1799. The
enormous but plain interior
of the building is offset by
the elaborate Baroque organ,
adorned with angels, which was
installed in 1682. The choir stalls
are decorated with the coats of
arms belonging to knights of the
Order of the Golden Fleece,
dating from a convention held
in 1478. The order, founded by
Philip the Good in Bruges in
1430, called together many of
Europe's rulers and powerbrokers
to settle disputes and uphold
the ideals of Christianity and
chivalry. Above the choir stalls
hang handsome Brussels
tapestries that date back to
the early 18th century and
depict scenes from the Bible.

Arentshuis

Dijver 16. **Tel** (050) 448763.
Open 9:30am–5pm Tue–Sun.
W museabrugge.be

An 18th-century mansion
overlooking the Dijver Canal,
the Arentshuis is now an annexe
of the Groeninge Museum (see
pp118–19), which stands nearby.
The ground floor is used to
house temporary exhibitions.
On the first floor are works by
Frank Brangwyn (1867–1956),

a painter and sculptor born in
Bruges of Welsh parents. His
father, William Curtis Brangwyn,
was an architect and painter,
and one of a number of British
residents closely involved in the
restoration of Bruges in the 19th
century. Most of Frank Brangwyn's
life was spent in Britain, but he
bequeathed this collection to
Bruges, along with his carpets,
drawings and furniture. His
dark and powerful canvases
depicting industrial scenes
are particularly striking, and
overall this is a surprising
and rewarding collection.

Gruuthuse Museum

Dijver 17. **Tel** (050) 448743.
Open 9:30am–5pm daily once
renovations completed late 2017.

Occupying a large medieval
mansion close to the Dijver
Canal, the Gruuthuse Museum
holds a priceless collection of
fine and applied arts. These
date from Bruges's heyday as
a wealthy trading city, and the
subsequent centuries.

In the 15th century, the
building was inhabited by the
merchant (or lord of the
Gruuthuse) who had the
exclusive right to levy a tax on
gruut – an imported mixture of
herbs added to barley during
the beer-brewing process. The
mansion's labyrinthine rooms,
with their ancient chimney
pieces and wooden beams,
have survived intact. Nowadays,
they house woodcarvings,
musical instruments, weapons,
furniture and tapestries. There is
even a medical section devoted
to cures of everyday ailments
such as haemorrhoids. One of
the museum's most treasured

possessions is the incredibly
lifelike wood and terracotta
bust of the Habsburg king
Charles V carved in 1520. This
is attributed to the German
sculptor Konrad Meit. There are
also a number of artifacts
recalling the exile of Charles II
of England in Bruges. On the
second floor is a wooden chapel
built in 1472 with a private
window into the Onthaalkerk
Onze-Lieve-Vrouw next door.

The soaring spire of the eclectic
Onthaalkerk Onze-Lieve-Vrouw

Onthaalkerk Onze-
Lieve-Vrouw

Mariastraat. **Tel** (050) 345314.
Open 9:30am–4:30pm Sat, noon–
4:30pm Sun. **Closed** for tours during
services. choir only.
W museabrugge.be

The construction of the
Onthaalkerk Onze-Lieve-Vrouw
(the Welcome Church of Our
Lady) began in 1220 and ended
200 years later. In consequence,
it incorporates a variety of
architectural styles. Its 122-m

An elaborate tapestry depicting the "free arts", Gruuthuse Museum

Warm brick tones in an inner courtyard of the Sint-Janshospitaal

(400-ft) tall spire is one of the tallest in Belgium. The interior, with its white walls, stark columns and black-and-white tiled floor has a medieval simplicity, while the side chapels and pulpit are lavishly decorated.

One of the church's artistic highlights is Michelangelo's 1505 sculpture, *Madonna and Child*, located at the end of the southern aisle. This marble statue was imported by a Flemish merchant, and was the only one of the artist's works to leave Italy during his lifetime. In the choir, there are fine paintings by Pieter Pourbus (1523–84), including his 1562 *Last Supper*, and the carved mausoleums of the Burgundian duke Charles the Bold and his daughter, Mary.

Sint-Janshospitaal
Mariastraat 38. **Tel** (050) 476100.
Open 10am–5pm daily.
museabrugge.be
This site has been occupied since the 12th century by the St-Janshospitaal, which closed as a working hospital only in 1976. During Bruges's Burgundian Golden Age in the 15th century, the great German-born painter Hans Memling (c.1430–94) created a number of exquisite paintings, commissioned specially for the hospital chapel in about 1479. The remarkable museum here today therefore has two aspects. First, there are the evocative medieval hospital wards with antique beds, medical instruments, paintings and documentation as well as an old *apotheek* (pharmacy). Then,

in the open-plan site of the old chapel, there is the small but supreme collection of Hans Memling's paintings. This includes the *St Ursula Shrine*, a reliquary painted with scenes from the legend of St Ursula, *The Adoration of the Magi* and the polyptych of *The Mystic Marriage of St Catherine (see p106)*. The martyrdoms of St John the Baptist and St John the Divine (to whom the hospital was dedicated) are illustrated in side-panels.

Brouwerij De Halve Maan
Walplein 26. **Tel** (050) 444222
Open 11am–4pm daily (to 5pm Sat).
halvemaan.be
The Halve Maan (Half Moon) is a historic brewery and museum in the centre of Bruges. The brewery is a family business with a tradition stretching back through six generations to 1856. This is where the Bruges city beer, Brugse Zot – a strong-tasting, high-fermentation beer based on malt, hops and special yeast – is brewed. Guided tours taking 45 minutes start on every hour and give an in-depth insight into the brewing process. They end with a beer tasting.

Begijnhof
Wijngaardplein 1. **Tel** (050) 330011.
Open daily.
The Bruges begijnhof was founded in 1245 by Margaret of Constantinople, Countess of Flanders. Entered via an 18th-century gatehouse at the end of a bridge that runs over a canal, this is an area of quiet tree-lined paths faced by white, gabled houses and a green at the centre. It is an enjoyable place for a stroll and visitors can also walk into the small church that was built here in 1602. The nuns who live in these houses today are no longer béguines *(see p65)* but Benedictine sisters who moved here in the 1930s. One of the houses is open to visitors and displays simple rustic furniture and artifacts that illustrate the béguines' contemplative lives.

Minnewater
Just south of the begijnhof, Minnewater is a peaceful park with a lake. The name probably means innerwater, but because *minne* is a Dutch word for love, Minnewater is often referred to as The Lake of Love. Swans have been here since 1488 when Maximilian of Austria ordered that they be kept in memory of his councillor, Pierre Lanchals, who was beheaded by the Bruges citizens. The Lanchals coat of arms features a swan.

Once a bustling harbour connected to canals and the sea, the Minnewater can today be reached by the barges that take visitors on a tour of Bruges. It is also a popular spot for walkers and picnickers, featuring a pretty 15th-century lock gate, sluicegate house and the 1398 gunpowder tower, Poedertoren.

The sluicegate house on the Southern Bridge at the Minnewater

Bruges: Groeninge Museum

The city's top fine-arts museum, the Groeninge holds a fabulous collection of early Flemish and Dutch masters, featuring artists such as Jan van Eyck (c.1400–41) and Hieronymous Bosch (1450–94), famous for the strange freakish creatures of his moral allegories. Hugo van der Goes (1440–82) is well represented too, as are Gerard David (c.1460–1523) and Hans Memling (c.1430–94). These early works are displayed on the ground floor of the museum along with a collection of later Belgian painters, most notably Paul Delvaux (1897–1994) and René Magritte (1898–1967). Originally built between 1929 and 1930, the museum is small and displays its collection in rotation along with various temporary exhibitions.

Museum Façade
This 1930 gallery was extended in 1994 by architect Joseph Viérin. The old entrance is based on that of a Romanesque convent.

★ *Death of the Virgin* (1470)
Hugo van der Goes's treatment of a popular and emotionally charged subject displays his imaginative use of composition. It is also remarkable for its range of carefully observed expressions.

★ *The Moreel Triptych* (1484)
Painted by German-born artist Hans Memling, this panel was designed to adorn the altar in a Bruges church. The triptych is said to be one of the earliest portaits of a family group.

★ *Madonna with Canon van der Paele* (1436)
Jan van Eyck's richly detailed work is noted for its precision. It shows St George presenting van Eyck's patron, the canon, to St Donatian.

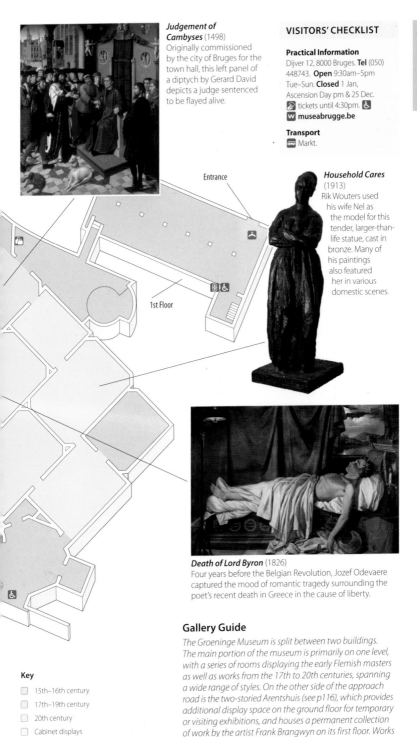

Judgement of Cambyses (1498)

Originally commissioned by the city of Bruges for the town hall, this left panel of a diptych by Gerard David depicts a judge sentenced to be flayed alive.

Entrance

1st Floor

Household Cares (1913)

Rik Wouters used his wife Nel as the model for this tender, larger-than-life statue, cast in bronze. Many of his paintings also featured her in various domestic scenes.

Death of Lord Byron (1826)

Four years before the Belgian Revolution, Jozef Odevaere captured the mood of romantic tragedy surrounding the poet's recent death in Greece in the cause of liberty.

Gallery Guide

The Groeninge Museum is split between two buildings. The main portion of the museum is primarily on one level, with a series of rooms displaying the early Flemish masters as well as works from the 17th to 20th centuries, spanning a wide range of styles. On the other side of the approach road is the two-storied Arentshuis (see p116), which provides additional display space on the ground floor for temporary or visiting exhibitions, and houses a permanent collection of work by the artist Frank Brangwyn on its first floor. Works are subject to relocation.

Key

- 15th–16th century
- 17th–19th century
- 20th century
- Cabinet displays
- Non-exhibition space

Exploring Eastern Bruges

Visitors pour into Bruges during the summer, crowding the city centre. Despite this, the narrow cobbled streets and picturesque canals to the east of the Markt remain free of throngs, and this fascinating area continues to be one of the most delightful parts of Bruges. Its avenues of picturesque terraced houses are dotted with grand and elegant 18th-century mansions. The best approach to this quarter is via Jan van Eyckplein, which in medieval times was the site of the busy canal-side tollhouse. A short stroll along the Spinolarei and Potterierei streets leads to the handful of intriguing churches and museums in this historic district.

The Museum voor Volkskunde, part of a row of 17th-century almshouses

Traditional bobbin-lace techniques demonstrated at the Kantcentrum

Kantcentrum

Balstraat 16. **Tel** (050) 330072.
Open Apr–Sep: 9:30am–5pm daily; Oct–Mar: 9:30am–5pm Mon–Sat.
W kantcentrum.eu

Lace-making skills are kept alive at the Kantcentrum, the Lace Centre. This neighbourhood is one of several where, in the past, the city's lace workers plied their craft. Most of the lace makers were women. They worked at home, receiving raw materials from a supplier who also bought the finished product.

The Kantcentrum also includes an exhibition of historic lace, and demonstrations on lace-making are held for visitors every summer afternoon. Finished pieces are sold in the Kantcentrum shop. The experts here can advise whether lace bought elsewhere is genuinely handmade or not.

Jeruzalemkerk

Peperstraat 1. **Open** 10am–5pm Mon–Sat.

One of Bruges's most unusual churches, the Jeruzalemkerk is based on the design of the Church of the Holy Sepulchre in Jerusalem. The structure possesses a striking tower with two tiers of wooden, polygon-shaped lanterns, topped by a tin orb. The present building dates from the 15th century, when it was commissioned by Anselmus Adornes and his spouse, members of a rich Italian merchant family, whose black marble tomb can be seen inside the church.

Inside the Jeruzalemkerk, the lower level contains a macabre altarpiece, carved with skulls in imitation of Golgotha, the site of Christ's crucifixion. Behind the altar is a smaller vaulted chapel leading to a narrow tunnel that is guarded by an iron grate. In the tunnel, a lifelike model of Christ in the Tomb can be seen at close quarters.

The distinctive tower of the Jeruzalemkerk

Volkskundemuseum

Balstraat 43. **Tel** (050) 448764.
Open 9:30am–5pm Tue–Sun, Easter & Whit Mon.
W museabrugge.be

One of the best folk museums in Flanders, the Volkskundemuseum occupies an attractive terrace of low brick almshouses located behind an old neighbourhood café called the Zwarte Kat, or Black Cat, which serves as the entrance. Each house is dedicated to a different aspect of traditional Flemish life, with workshops displaying old tools and other relevant artifacts. Several different crafts, such as cobbling and blacksmithing, are represented here, along with a series of typical historical domestic and shop interiors.

Guido Gezellemuseum

Rolweg 64. **Tel** (050) 448711.
Open 9:30am–12:30pm & 1:30–5pm Tue–Sun.
W museabrugge.be

The eldest of five children, the great Flemish poet Guido Gezelle was born and raised in a little red-brick house that is now a museum. With the help of a series of furnished rooms, it evokes the modest circumstances of his upbringing – his father was a gardener and his mother's family were farmers. Insights into Gezelle's work and life are offered through the museum's exhibits of books and documents. The charm of the building and of the garden outside reflect the character of the man, his piety and his love for nature, which evolved during the course of his childhood spent here.

🚇 Kruispoort

Open May–Aug (St-Janshuismolen) & Jul–Aug (Koelwereimolen): 9:30am–12:30pm & 1:30–5pm Tue–Sun. 🚻 🅦 **museabrugge.be**

Medieval Bruges was heavily fortified. It was encircled by a city wall that was itself protected by a moat and strengthened by a series of massive gates. Most of the wall was knocked down in the 19th century, but the moat and four of the city gates (poorten) have survived. One of these, the Kruispoort, is a monumental structure, dating from 1402, that guards the city's eastern approach. The earthen bank stretching north marks the old city

The massive Kruispoort, one of the original gates in Bruges's city walls

wall, and was once dotted with 20 windmills although only four stand here today. **Bonne Chieremolen**, the first one north of the Kruispoort, was brought here from a Flanders village in 1911. The second, **St-Janshuismolen**, is from the city. This restored structure was originally erected in 1770. **De Nieuwe Papegai**, an oil mill relocated here in 1970, is next, while the fourth, **De Koelweimolen**, is an old flour mill that arrived in the 1990s.

🚇 Schuttersgilde St-Sebastiaan

Carmersstraat 174. **Tel** (050) 331626. **Open** May–Sep: 10am–noon Tue–Thu, 2–5pm Sat; Oct–Apr: 2–5pm Tue–Thu & Sat. 🚻

The Longbow Archers' Guild (Schuttersgilde) was one of the most powerful militia guilds. Its 16th- and 17th-century red-brick guildhall now contains a small museum.

The commercial life of medieval Bruges was dominated by the guilds, each of which represented the interests of a group of tradesmen, craftsmen

The brick house and tower of the influential Longbow Archers' guild

or practitioners of a specific skill. This guild claimed the name of St Sebastian, an early Christian martyr who was sentenced by the Roman Emperor Diocletian to be executed by archers. The bowmen followed their orders, but the saint's wounds healed miraculously. He was ultimately executed by club-wielding assassins.

The guildhouse is notable for its collection of portaits of the guild's leading lights. This includes Charles II of England who caroused here during his exile. It also has a traditional shooting gallery for the still-active archery club.

🏛 Museum Onze-Lieve-Vrouw-ter-Potterie

Potterierei 79. **Tel** (050) 448711. **Open** 9:30am–12:30pm and 1:30–5pm Tue–Sun. 🚻 ♿ 🅦 **museabrugge.be**

Located by the canal in one of the quietest parts of Bruges, the Museum Onze-Lieve-Vrouw-ter-Potterie occupies part of an old hospital that was founded in 1276 to care for elderly women. There is a 14th- and 15th-century cloister, and some of the sick rooms house a selection of intriguing curios and a modest collection of paintings, the best of which are some 17th- and 18th-century portraits of leading aristocrats. The hospital church is a warm, intimate place, decorated with a set of impressive Baroque altarpieces and a number of fine stained-glass windows.

Guido Gezelle

One of Bruges's favourite sons, Guido Gezelle (1830–99) was a much-loved poet, priest and champion of the Flemish language. He is most famous for poetry about nature, which he acutely observed. On this basis, he produced poems that were filled with a sense of religious wonder and subtly drawn spiritual lessons. At the age of 16, Gezelle had finished his schooling in Bruges and began to study for the priesthood at Roeselare, 40 km (25 miles) to the south. Here, he soon began publishing his poetry. In 1853, Gezelle was ordained in Bruges, where he developed close friendships with members of the English community, many of whom were Roman Catholics involved in the restoration of the city. Gezelle went on to become the deputy rector of the Anglo-Belgian Seminary in Bruges, and later, the parish priest of St-Walburgakerk. In 1872, he moved to the Onze-Lieve-Vrouwekerk in Kortrijk, where he would spend the next 27 years. Through his enthusiastic and sometimes controversial promotion of the Dutch language and Flemish dialects, he became a leading figure in the Flemish Movement (see p129). In 1899, Gezelle became the Director of the English Convent in Bruges, but passed away shortly afterwards.

Statue of Guido Gezelle in Bruges's centre

The Belgian Coast

The Province of West Vlaanderen meets the North Sea in a 70-km (43-mile) long stretch of coast, whose beaches of soft white sand are rimmed by cheerful seaside resorts. With broad promenades, hotels and high-rise apartment blocks, campsites, seafood restaurants, ice-cream and waffle vendors, bucket-and-spade shops and electronic games arcades, these resorts can get very busy, especially in the high season of the summer months, but there is always an air of leisurely fun. Families return for their summer holidays year after year, generation after generation, relishing the comforts of familiar, time-tested pleasures.

Locator Map
Belgian Coast

De Panne is a comfortable, easy-going resort where old-fashioned bathing cabins on wheels line the broad beach, and sand yachts scud on windy days. De Panne is home to the popular Plopsaland theme park for children *(see pp308–309)*, while the nearby Westhoek dunes form a nature reserve with wilder landscapes.

Oostende *(see p126)* is the largest resort on the coast.

Nieuwpoort lies at the mouth of the IJzer and is a centre for water sports. A large circular monument overlooks the Ganzenpoot confluence of canals, commemorating the strategic flooding of the polders in World War I.

Bredene

Westende-Bad

Middelkerke

Nieuwpoort-aan-Zee

Lombardsijde-Bad

A18

Gist

Oostduinkerke

St-Idesbald

De Panne

Veurne

Koksijde has the Paul Delvaux Museum and the ruins of the Ten Duinen Abbey *(see p127)*.

Oostduinkerke has an interesting folklore museum and a Visserijmuseum (Museum of Fishing). However, the area is most famous for shrimp fishing, which is conducted here on horseback, with heavy draught horses pulling the nets through the shallows.

Middelkerke is a typical resort of the Belgian coast, dominated by apartment blocks and far removed from its origins as a 13th-century fishing village. It first developed as a resort in the late 19th century, when it became a link on the coastal tram route, the Kusttram – still the best way to travel from one end of the coast to the other.

De Haan is cherished as one of the most attractive and agreeable of the resorts, with a good beach, and controlled development that has preserved the handsome, early 20th-century villas. The name, meaning The Cock (Le Coq in French), was given to the town following a legend that fishermen were once led to safety here by a cock crowing on the beach.

Zwin Natuur Park *(see p125)* is a nature reserve containing dunes and tidal ponds, frequented by migratory birds.

0 km   5

0 miles   5

Blankenberge town has a pier, a 2-km (1-mile) long zeedijk (raised promenade), and plenty of holiday entertainment including the National Sealife Marine Park and the Serpentarium. The annual summer Sand Sculpture Festival is currently held here, inspiring breathtakingly ambitious work.

Zeebrugge *(see p124)* is the largest commercial port on this coast and also has a popular beach. A 1960s Soviet submarine and an old lightship are two of the exhibits at Seafront Zeebrugge, the town's main attraction.

Knokke-Heist *(see p124)* is considered the most chic of Belgium's coastal resorts. The tiny Neo-Gothic Fishermen's Chapel in Heist was built in 1892. Today, it is dwarfed by the modern architecture of this western urban end of Knokke-Heist.

❷ Damme

5 km (3 miles) NE of Bruges.
Road Map B1. 🏠 11,000. 🚌 🚲
ℹ️ Toerisme Damme, Huyse de Grote Sterre, Jacob van Maerlantstraat 3; (050) 288610. 🛒 2nd Sun of every month (books).
🌐 **damme-online.com**

This pretty village of historic red-brick buildings lies amidst a beautiful polder landscape of tree-lined canals and pasture. In the 14th and 15th centuries, it was a bustling port on the shores of the Zwin and at the head of the canal that led into Bruges. Standing witness to this golden era are the 15th-century **Stadhuis** and several other buildings. These include the **Huis St-Jan**, once a centre for the wine trade; the house where Charles the Bold, Duke of Burgundy, married Margaret of York in 1468; and the **St-Janshospitaal**, which houses a small museum of artifacts and church treasures. The **Huyse de Grote Sterre**, once the Spanish military governor's residence, now has the Visitor Centre and a museum devoted to Tijl Uilenspiegel. Also of interest are the half ruined **Onze-Lieve-Vrouwekerk** and the 19th-century windmill **Schellemolen**.

🏛 **St-Janshospitaal**
Kerkstraat 33. **Tel** (050) 461080.
Open Apr–Sep. ♿ &

🏛 **Huyse de Grote Sterre**
Jacob van Maerlantstraat 3. **Tel** (050) 288610. **Open** daily. **Closed** noon–2pm. ♿

🏚 **Schellemolen**
Damse Vaart-West. **Open** Easter and Apr–Sep: Sat, Sun & public holidays.

Tijl Uilenspiegel

A character that pops up regularly around Bruges and Damme is Tijl Uilenspiegel, a legendary roguish trickster. Originally a German creation known as Till Eulenspiegel, he came to Flanders with the advent of printing, and was adopted into the local mythology. The Flemish writer Charles de Coster (1827–79) revived the character in a book published in 1867, and placed him in 16th-century Damme, fighting for independence from Spain. Tijl, his fiancée Nele and his sidekick Lamme Goedzak are remembered in a number of statues, as well as in the names of several restaurants and other enterprises.

Bronze statue of Tijl Uilenspiegel

❸ Knokke-Heist

15 km (9 miles) NE of Bruges.
Road Map B1. 🏠 34,000. 🚌 🚆
ℹ️ Toerisme Knokke-Heist, Zeedijk-Knokke 660; (050) 630380.
🌐 **myknokke-heist.be**

Model of a boat at the Sincfala museum

Cited as the smartest seaside resort on the Belgian coast, Knokke-Heist is known for its casino, its streets of chic boutiques and art galleries, its elegant villas and select golf courses. It is in fact a conurbation stretching some 6 km (4 miles) from Heist in the west to Het Zoute in the east, where development is curtailed by the dunes of the Zwin nature reserve. The tale of the Zwin and the centuries-old fishing community of Heist – before tourism transformed the coast in the late 19th century – is eloquently told in **Sincfala**, the museum of the Zwin region.

As a result of the salt sea water, this natural reserve has some specific species of flora that are rarely found anywhere else, such as the exotic sea lavender. It also houses several species of migratory as well as native birds, including woodpeckers and the tiny egret.

🏛 **Sincfala**
Pannenstraat 140. **Tel** (050) 530730.
Open 10am–noon and 2–5:30pm daily. ♿ 🌐 **sincfala.be**

❹ Zeebrugge

Vismijnstraat 7; 15 km (9 miles) NE of Bruges. **Road Map** A1. 🏠 4,000.
Tel (050) 551415. 🚆 **Open** Jul–Aug: 10am–7pm daily; Sep–Jun: 10am–6pm daily. **Closed** 2nd two weeks of Jan. ♿ 🌐 **zeebrugge.net**

The deep-water seaport of Zeebrugge was built at the start of the 20th century. Under German occupation in World War I, it became a vital strategic port and U-Boat base, and the target of the daring Zeebrugge Raid by British forces in 1918. Today, Zeebrugge has a rugged industrial air, with its skyline dominated by cranes serving container ships. It is also Belgium's biggest fishing port. However, it has a softer side, with some good beaches and a sailing marina.

Close to the town's centre and occupying the quayside warehouses of the former fish-market is **Seafront Zeebrugge**. This mixed bag of a museum covers the history of the port and various maritime themes. Among the highlights are the gadget-encrusted chambers of a large 1960s Soviet submarine.

One of several canals that cut across the polders at Damme

For hotels and restaurants see pp266–7 and pp283–6

Path leading down from the dyke protecting the Visitor Centre into the wild coastal landscape of the Zwin nature park

❺ Zwin Natuur Park

24 km (15 miles) N of Bruges. **Road Map** B1. **Tel** (050) 607086. 🚌 13 (Jul and Aug). 🛈 Graaf Léon Lippensdreef 8, Knokke-Heist. **Open** 9am–4pm Tue–Sun. **Closed** 1 Jan, 25 Dec. 🚫 📷 on request. 📶 Ⓦ zwin.be

At the far eastern end of the Belgian coast, the border with the Netherlands is delineated by low-lying dunes, salt meadows and tidal inlets. Since 1952, this area has been a nature reserve, the Provinciaal Natuurpark Zwin, famed for its many nesting and migratory birds and its specialized wetland plantlife. There is little here now that speaks of the area's very different past, when the Zwin was a broad, deep channel, running some distance inland. During the medieval period, thousands of trading ships from all over Europe passed through here, bringing goods to Damme, where they were unloaded and transported to Bruges by canal. The navigable inlet was created by a massive storm in 1134 which inundated the coastline. However, it proved to be only temporary. During the 15th century, it began to silt up – partly because of the creation of polders around Damme. This gradually strangled trade, and by the 16th century Bruges's role as one of Europe's most prosperous cities was doomed.

Shelducks, the nature park's symbol

Today, the Zwin is a beautiful stretch of unspoilt tidal coastline, crossed by a number of footpaths. The main gateway is the Zwin Nature Centre, reached by an inland road, Graaf Léon Lippensdreef, from Het Zoute, the eastern portion of Knokke-Heist. The Nature Centre forms a triangular area within the reserve, set well back from the sea and protected from inundation by a long, high dyke. Within its large wooded compound are an interpretation centre and a bird park, which has a resident population of storks and various coastal and marshland birds such as owls and herons. The walkway along the dyke offers views over the Zwin, a broad expanse of dunes carpeted with salt-tolerant plants. The lake-like areas of water change with the tides. Simple hides along the dyke offer a good chance of seeing some of the birds that frequent the Zwin. These include geese, ducks, terns, harriers, avocets and egrets. Visitors can also follow paths that lead out from here into the wetland and dunes. Guided tours offer the opportunity to get off the beaten track and into some of the Zwin's more hidden corners.

There are two statues of note at the Zwin. One, near the information centre, is a bronze portrait of the founder of the park, the ornithologist Count Léon Lippens (1911–66). The other stands on the dunes that line the coast – a large, bronze sculpture of a running hare, by the British artist Barry Flanagan (b.1941).

The Zwin Natuur Park, which offers a nesting site to a large colony of storks

Brick clock tower of the Onze Lieve Vrouw Bezoekingskerk, Lissewege

❻ Lissewege

8 km (5 miles) N of Bruges.
Road Map B1. 🚏 2,500. 🚉 🚌
ⓘ VVV Lissewege-Bezoekerscentrum, Oude Pastoriestraat 5; (050) 552955.
🅦 lissewege.be

The white, flower-bedecked cottages nestling around its church and lining its canal have earned Lissewege a reputation as one of the prettiest villages in Flanders. The handsome church, the **Onze Lieve Vrouw Bezoekingskerk**, was built between 1225 and 1275 in Scheldt Gothic style, using local red brick and blue Tournai stone shipped in via the River Scheldt. Its tower rises to a height of 49 m (162 ft) and offers good views over the village and polders. The interior features a striking organ and a stunning rood loft and pulpit dating from 1652.

In the 12th century, land was donated in Lissewege to the Benedictines. Their Ter Doest abbey – a branch of the Ten Duinen abbey of Koksijde – flourished here until 1571, when it was destroyed by Protestant rebels. Virtually all that remains is the medieval **Abbey Barn**, located 1 km (half a mile) south of the village. This Gothic brick structure supported by oak beams is set in peaceful countryside.

🔲 **Onze Lieve Vrouw Bezoekingskerk and Abbey Barn**
Open 10am–5pm daily.

❼ Oostende

30 km (18 miles) W of Bruges.
Road Map A1. 🚏 69,000. ✈ 🚉 🚌
🚌 🚢 ⓘ Monacoplein 2; (059) 701199. 🎭 Bal du Rat Morte (Sat, early Mar). 🅦 visitoostende.be

Set in the middle of the Belgian coast, Oostende is an attractive, modern seaside resort as well as an active fishing and ferry port. It was favoured by royalty and the ruling classes in the late 19th century, and equipped itself with a *kursaal* (casino) and racecourse to complement their elegant villas. Summer holiday-makers arrive for the sand beaches and the seafront promenade, but visitors come all year round for the seafood.

Oostende also has a strong line in art. The **Mu.ZEE** contains a good collection of Belgian art including work by Symbolists such as Léon Spilliaert, Surrealists such as Magritte and Delvaux and by Expressionist artists such as Constant Termeke. The artist most associated with Oostende is James Ensor *(see p27)*. His home, the **Ensorhuis**, with its reconstruction of his aunt's novelty shop explains his influences and vision.

The town's connection with the sea is reflected in the **Mercator Marine Museum**, which is located on the three-masted training ship *Mercator* built in 1932; while what lies under the North Sea is shown at the **Noordzeeaquarium**. Oostende's location made it strategically important in war time. Vivid reminders of this are seen at **Fort Napoleon**, a muscular pentagonal fortress

built in 1811 among the dunes to the east of the town. To the west is the **Openluchtmuseum Atlantikwall**, with 2 km (1 mile) of tunnels, trenches and defences that show how the occupying German forces armed the coast against invasion during the World Wars.

Environs
At Jabekke, 16 km (10 miles) southeast of Oostende, the home and studio of Constant Permeke, one of St-Martens-Latem School of Art's leading figures, has been made the **Provinciaal Museum Constant Permeke**. This exhibits 150 of the artist's paintings, drawings and sculptures.

🔲 **Ensorhuis**
Vlaanderenstraat 27. **Tel** (059) 508 118. **Open** 10am–noon, 2–5pm Wed–Mon. 🗃

🏛 **Mercator Marine Museum**
Mercatordok. **Tel** (059) 517010. **Open** daily. 🗃 🅦 zeilschip-mercator.be

🏛 **Mu.ZEE**
Romestraat 11. **Tel** (059) 508118. 🅦 muzee.be

🏛 **Noordzeeaquarium**
Visserskaai. **Tel** (059) 500876. **Open** Apr–Sep: daily; Oct–Mar: Sat, Sun & public holidays. 🗃 ♿

🔲 **Fort Napoleon**
Vuurtorenweg. **Tel** (059) 320048. **Open** Apr–Oct: Tue–Sun; Nov–Mar: Wed–Sun. 🗃 ♿ 🗃 🗃 🗃
🅦 fortnapoleon.be

🏛 **Openluchtmuseum Atlantikwall**
Provinciaal Domein Raversijde, Nieuwpoortsesteenweg 636.
Tel (059) 702285. **Open** Apr–Nov. 🗃
🅦 raversyde.be

Displays of the North Sea's natural treasures at the Noordzeeaquarium

❽ Veurne

25 km (15 miles) SW of Oostende.
Road Map A2. 🏔 12,000. 🚊 🚌
ℹ️ Grote Markt 29; (058) 335531.
🌐 veurne.be

The pretty town of Veurne, sometimes called Little Bruges owing to its historic charm, clusters around an attractive Grote Markt rimmed with 15th- and 16th-century step-gabled façades. Its fine Flemish-Renaissance **Stadhuis**, built between 1596 and 1612, has interor walls lined with embossed Córdoba leather. This building served as headquarters for the Belgian army in 1914. Behind it is the 13th-century **St-Walpurgakerk**, with its soaring nave lit like a lantern by stained glass. St Walburga, an 8th-century missionary nun, is patron saint of the town. In the Appelmarkt close by is the 15th-century **St-Niklaaskerk**, with three coolly elegant aisles divided by sandstone arches. Its 13th-century brick tower is also a belfry, containing a carillon installed in 1961 and a small carillon museum.

On the southern outskirts is **Bakkerijmuseum**, a museum of bakery set in 17th-century almshouses and farm buildings. It takes visitors on a historic tour from grain to bread.

🏛 **Stadhuis**
Grote Markt 27. **Tel** (058) 335531.
Open Apr–mid-Nov. 🅿️

🏛 **St-Niklaaskerk**
Appelmarkt. **Tel** (058) 335531.
Open mid-Jun–mid-Sep. 🅿️
(tower and carillon museum).

🏛 **Bakkerijmuseum**
Albert I-laan 2. **Tel** (058) 313897.
Open Jul–Aug: daily; Sep–Jun: Sat–Thu. **Closed** Jan . 🅿️ 🖥 📷
🌐 bakkerijmuseum.be

❾ Koksijde

26 km (16 miles) W of Oostende.
Road Map A2. 🏔 21,000. 🚌 🚕
ℹ️ Zeelaan 303; (058) 512 910.
🌐 visitor.koksijde.be

A popular modern seaside resort, Koksijde has beachfronts at St-Idesbald and Koksijde-Bad. During the Middle Ages, the

Excavated ruins of the 12th-century Ten Duinen abbey at Koksijde

town was famed for its influential Abbey of Our Lady of the Dunes, called Ten Duinen (or Ter Duinen) for short. Founded by the Benedictines in 1107, it became Cistercian in 1138 and was destroyed by the Protestant rebels nicknamed *geuzen* (sea beggars) in 1566. The museum **Ten Duinen 1138** breathes life into the excavated remains that can be seen in the adjoining park. Just to the south is the **Zuid Abdijmolen**, a wooden windmill dating from the year 1773.

Located in St-Idesbald is the impressive **Museum Paul Delvaux**, containing the largest single collection of this great Surrealist's work. Set in a whitewashed villa built in traditional style, the museum was opened by the Paul Delvaux Foundation in 1982 with the artist's blessing. It includes a number of drawings, paintings and sculptures as well as personal possessions that have a bearing on the artist's work, as well as a reconstruction of his studio.

🏛 **Ten Duinen 1138**
Koninklijke Prinslaan 6, Koksijde.
Tel (058) 533950. **Open** Feb–Dec:
Tue–Sun. 🅿️ 🌐 tenduinen.be

🏛 **Museum Paul Delvaux**
Delvauxlaan 42, St-Idesbald.
Tel (058) 521229. **Open** Apr–Sep: Tue–Sun; Oct–Dec: Thu–Sun. 🅿️ 🖥 📷
🌐 delvauxmuseum.com

Procession of the Penitents at Veurne

Every year on the last Sunday of July – a day that coincides with the town's Kermis festival and its funfair in the Grote Markt – 1,000 citizens of Veurne dress in biblical costume for the Boetprocessie, the Procession of Penitence. Making a circuit of the centre of the town, successive groups recount the most famous stories of the Bible. Among them are 400 *boetelingen* (penitents) – anonymous men and women making a genuine act of religious devotion. Wearing monkish brown robes with masked hoods, and often barefoot, they carry large wooden crosses or pull heavy floats bearing religious statues. After the folkloric early scenes from Adam and Eve to the Nativity, the mood darkens as the Crucifixion of Christ approaches, surrounded by increasing numbers of penitents. The crowd looks on in near silence. The people of Veurne have been re-enacting this story since the 1640s. In charge is a venerable society called the Sodaliteit, whose members officiate wearing 17th-century outfits of black velvet robes and red hats.

Veurne's citizens dressed as figures from the Bible

The controversial IJzertoren with its striking cross-shaped profile

⑩ Kasteel Beauvoorde

Wulveringemstraat 10, Veurne.
Road Map A2. **Tel** (058) 299229. 🚍
Open Jul–Aug: daily; see website for
details. **Closed** Nov–Feb. 🦽 🎧 📷
W kasteelbeauvoorde.be

With its moat, brick turrets
and step gables as well as
its parkland setting, Kasteel
Beauvoorde is one of the
most attractive small castles
in Belgium. An earlier castle
on the site was destroyed
by Protestant rebels in
1584, and this classic
Flemish fortified
manor was built in
its place in the early
17th century.
Sympathetically
restored in the 19th
century, the interior
contains furniture, carved
wood panelling and ceramics.

Ceramic plate from
Kasteel Beauvoorde

⑪ IJzertoren

IJzerdijk 49, Diksmuide; 15 km (9 miles)
SE of Veurne. **Road Map** A2. **Tel** (051)
500286. 🚉 🚍 **Open** daily; see
website for details. **Closed** 3 weeks
in Jan. 🦽 💻 📷 **W** museum
aandeijzer.be

A vast cross, 84 m (275 ft) tall,
rises from the banks of the River
IJzer at Diksmuide and towers
over the surroundings. This is
the IJzertoren (IJzer Tower), a
monument to the Flemish dead
of World War I, and a physical
plea for peace. It contains an
impressive museum on 22 floors,
the **Museum aan de Ijzer**,
which tells the story of the
Belgian–German confrontation

during World War I and of
Flemish emancipation. With the
slogan „What remains of life?;
What remains of the country?",
the museum emphasises the
message of peace.

The tower is a controversial
monument; not only is it a
symbol of world peace but also
a mark of Flemish rights. In fact,
this is the second tower on the
site, completed in 1965. The
first, built between 1928 and
1930, was mysteriously blown
up in 1946, no doubt
because of its powerful
symbolic connotations.

Environs
Just 2 km (1 mile)
to the north of the
IJzertoren is the
Dodengang (Trench
of Death): preserved
trenches where, over 1915–18,
the Belgian army blocked
German troops from advancing
across the flooded IJzer. The
German military cemetery at
Vladso, 6 km (4 miles) northeast,
contains the heartrending
sculptures *Grieving Parents* by
celebrated Expressionist artist
Käthe Kollwitz (1867–1945). Her
17-year-old son, killed in 1914,
is buried here.

🏛 Dodengang
IJzerdijk 65, Diksmuide. **Tel** (051)
505344. **Open** Apr–Sep: 10am–5pm
daily (Oct–mid-Nov: Mon–Fri, mid-
Nov–Apr: Tue–Fri).

⑫ A Tour of World War I Battlefields
See pp130–31.

⑬ Ypres

32 km (20 miles) S of Veurne.
Road Map A2. 🚹 35,000. 🚉 🚍
ℹ Lakenhalle, Grote Markt 34; (057)
239220. **W** ieper.be

Ieper in Flemish and "Wipers" to
the thousands of British troops
who passed this way during
World War I, Ypres was once a
prosperous medieval cloth town.
In 1914, it found itself just to the
west of the front line, the Ypres
Salient, and was demolished by
shelling over the next four years.
When peace returned, the
citizens reconstructed their town.
Today, the town acts as a centre
for visitors to the battlefields
and military cemeteries. Its
superb World War I museum,
In Flanders Fields provides a
moving background, focussing
on the experiences of individuals,
with touch screens, video
projections and soundscapes.The
Last Post is played every evening at the Menin Gate, a huge
stone arch with the names of
55,000 missing soldiers.

Environs
Located 5 km (3 miles) east of
Ypres, **Bellewaerde Park** is a large
theme park with an open-air zoo.

🏛 In Flanders Fields
Grote Markt 34, Ypres. **Tel** (057) 239
220. **Open** Apr–mid-Nov: 10am–6pm
daily; mid-Nov–end Mar: 10am–5pm
Tue–Sun. 🦽 🧑‍🦽 📷
W inflandersfields.be

🎠 Bellewaerde Park
E17/A19 Ypres, exit 3 Beselare,
Meenseweg 497, Ypres. **Tel** (057)
468686. **Open** late Mar–Jan. 🦽 🧑‍🦽
🍴 💻 📷 **W** bellewaerde.be

Moving displays at In Flanders Fields,
Ypres's Word War I museum

Talbot House chapel, where British soldiers gathered in Poperinge

⓮ Poperinge

12 km (8 miles) W of Ieper. **Road Map** A2. 🏛 20,000. 🚌 💬 ℹ️ Stadhuis, Grote Markt 1; (057) 34 66 76. 🗓 Fri. 🌐 toerismepoperinge.be

A cloth town in medieval times, Poperinge became a centre for production of hops (used in beer-making) in the 15th century. Today, this is celebrated in the **Hopmuseum**, an old hop processing plant. The town centres on a Grote Markt with a Neo-Gothic **Stadhuis** built in 1911. Close by is the 15th-century, late-Gothic church, the **Hoofdkerk St-Bertinus**, which contains fine woodcarving in its organ loft and Baroque pulpit. Its tower has an unusual lantern.

Lying some 15 km (8 miles) behind the World War I front line, Poperinge served as a transit point and a recuperation centre for Allied troops. Testimony of this is the **Talbot House**, an 18th-century townhouse that was operated by army chaplain Philip Clayton (1885–1972) as an informal club for British soldiers. The Edwardian-style rooms and the makeshift chapel in the roof are redolent of the era. The grim death cells where deserters awaited the firing squad have been preserved behind the Stadhuis.

🏛 **Hopmuseum**
Gasthuisstraat 71, Poperinge.
Tel (057) 337922. **Open** Mar–Nov: Tue–Sun & public holidays. 🖼
🏠 💻 🌐 hopmuseum.be

🕌 **Talbot House**
Gasthuisstraat 43, Poperinge.
Tel (057) 333228. **Open** Tue–Sun.
🖼 🏠 🌐 talbothouse.be

⓯ Kortrijk

37 km (23 miles) E of Ypres.
Road Map B2. 🏛 80,000. 🚌 💬
ℹ️ Begijnhofpark; (056) 277840.
🌐 toerismekortrijk.be

A vibrant city with a historic centre, Kortrijk (Courtrai in French) owed its prominence in medieval times to the cloth trade, and textiles still play a key role in its economy. The Battle of the Golden Spurs *(see p42)* was fought near this city, and the museum **Kortrijk 1302** explains the battle and why it is an important Flemish landmark. The captured spurs were triumphantly exhibited in the **Onze-Lieve-Vrouwekerk** until the French recovered them in 1382. Today, this atmospheric church contains two notable treasures – *The Raising of the Cross* (1631), a painting by Anthony van Dyck, and an alabaster statue of St Catherine (1380). The statue stands in the spacious 14th-century

The sturdy Broeltoren guarding a bridge over the River Leie

Chapel of the Counts, which is decorated with portraits of the counts of Flanders. Located a short walk from here is the **Begijnhof St Elisabeth**, one of Flanders's most enchant-ing béguinages.

The town's **Grote Markt** has a fine late-Gothic Stadhuis and a 14th-century brick belfry whose bell is rung by gilded mechanical statues. Close to the medieval Broeltoren – twin towers protecting a bridge over the River Leie – is the **Broelmuseum**, an 18th-century mansion with a collection of paintings that includes work by Kortrijk-born Roelandt Savery (1576–1639).

In a former linen warehouse on the banks of the Leie is the **Museum Texture**, which tells how flax and linen played a key role in Kortrijk. River Leie was once called the "golden river" because of all the flax processed in it.

🏛 **Kortrijk 1302**
Begijnhofpark. **Tel** (056) 277850.
Open Tue–Sun. 🖼 🏠
🌐 kortrijk1302.be

🕌 **Onze-Lieve-Vrouwekerk**
Open daily.

🕌 **Begijnhof St Elisabeth**
Open sunrise–sunset daily.

🏛 **Broelmuseum**
Broelkaai 6. **Tel** (056) 277780.
Open 2–6pm Tue–Fri, 11am–6pm Sat, Sun & public holidays. 🏠

🏛 **Museum Texture**
Noordstraat 28. **Tel** (056) 277470.
Call for opening timings. 🖼

Flemish Nationalism in Belgium

The sense of grievance felt by the people of Flanders towards the French-speaking community has a long history, dating back to the 9th century when Flanders was under French rule. The latter's high-handed treatment of successful Flemish cities resulted in an uprising, and a short-lived triumph in 1302 *(see p42)*. French, then Burgundian rule favoured French-speakers, a situation that became etched in society and intensified as Wallonia became the economic force of 19th-century industrialization. At the start of World War I, army officers were all French-speaking. King Albert I rallied Flemish troops by promising equality after the war, but this was not fulfilled. The resentment over historic injustice is still palpable at some Flemish museums.

The 1302 Battle of the Golden Spurs

⓬ A Tour of World War I Battlefields

In 1914, the invading German army forced the Belgians to retreat to the far northeast, behind the River IJzer. To impede further German advance, the Belgians opened the sluicegates of the river and flooded the landscape, which formed an effective obstacle as far south as Diksmuide. South of here, the Germans confronted the Allies along a ridge to the east of Ypres (Ieper) called the Ypres Salient. Between 1915 and 1917, this was the front line, where the gruelling stalemate of trench warfare cost more than 500,000 lives. Today, the area around the Salient is a beguilingly pretty landscape dotted with monuments, museums and numerous cemeteries.

① Diksmuide and Dodengang
The Belgians dug in along the canal of Diksmuide. Some of their trenches have been preserved at Dodengang (see p128).

② John McCrae Site
Bunkers, dressing stations and the Essex Farm Cemetery recall where Canadian medic John McCrae served, and wrote his poem "In Flanders Fields". The poem established the poppy as the symbol of the war dead.

③ Langemark This haunting German military cemetery has the flat tombstones of some 44,000 soldiers laid out beneath a cloak of trees.

④ Guynemer Monument A sculpture of a stork at Poelkapelle celebrates the pioneer of military aviation Georges Guynemer, who was lost, presumed dead, near here in 1917.

⑤ Canadian Forces Memorial At St-Juliaan, the large bust of *The Brooding Soldier* commemorates the 2,000 soldiers who died after the first ever gas attack in 1915.

⑥ Tyne Cot Cemetery The largest Commonwealth cemetery in the world contains nearly 12,000 graves. The walls bear the names of 35,000 missing soldiers.

⑦ Memorial Museum Passchendale
This 19th-century mansion, located in Zonnebeke, contains numerous World War I artifacts, and includes impressively reconstructed dugouts and trenches.

Tips for Drivers

Starting point: Diksmuide.
Length: 60 km (37 miles).
Duration of drive: A thorough tour will require two days. It can be done in one day, but visitors may need to be selective.
Driving conditions: The roads are good and usually fairly quiet. Signposting can be random.
Where to stay and eat: The main centre is Ypres, but there are restaurants and accommodation all along the route, especially in the smaller centres such as Diksmuide, Zonnebeke, Zillebeke, Kemmel and Mesen.

⑧ Menin Gate
Each evening in Ypres, the Last Post, played by buglers at the Menin Gate, echoes beneath the huge arch which lists the names of 55,000 missing Commonwealth soldiers.

```
0 kilometres      2
0 miles              2
```

⑨ Hill 62, Sanctuary Wood Museum
A private collection of military jumble leads to a wood where original trenches have been preserved.

Langemark ③

Poelkapelle ④

⑤

JEZNGR STR

ZONNEBEKSTRAAT

N313

N332

A19

⑥

⑦ Zonnebeke

N37

N8

Zillebeekse rijver

⑨

Zillebeke

⑩

ARTSTRAAT

N336

⑩ Hill 60, Zillebeke
A battered, scarred hilltop, the much disputed Hill 60 faced devastating attacks from underground mines.

⑪ Pool of Peace
Underground mining and a huge explosion beneath German lines in 1917 resulted in the water-filled Lone Tree Crater, which has now been designated the Pool of Peace.

⑬ Irish Peace Tower
This Irish monastic round tower in early medieval style was built in 1998 at Mesen to commemorate the Irish dead, and as a symbol of reconciliation.

⑫ French Memorial and Ossuary
The land rises dramatically in Heuvelland (Hill Country) and around Kemmel. The French fatalities in a battle of 1918 are remembered in a monument on Kemmel Hill, and 5,000 lie nearby in the French Ossuary.

Key
 Tour route
━━━ Motorway
═══ Other road
••• Battlefront 1915–17

⑯ Street-by-Street: Ghent

As a tourist destination, the Flemish city of Ghent (Gent in Dutch) has long been overshadowed by its neighbour, Bruges. In part, this reflects their divergent histories. The success of the cloth trade during the Middle Ages was followed by a period of stagnation for Bruges, while Ghent became a major industrial centre in the 19th century. The resulting pollution coated the city's antique buildings in layers of grime from its factories. In the 1980s, Ghent initiated a restoration programme. The city's medieval buildings were cleaned, industrial sites were tidied up and the canals were cleared. Today, the intricately carved stonework of its churches and old buildings, as well as the city's excellent museums and stern, forbidding castle give the centre its character.

Het Gravensteen
Ghent's centre is dominated by the thick stone walls and imposing gatehouse of its ancient Castle of the Counts.

★ The Design Museum Gent
This elegant 19th-century dining room is just one of many charming period rooms in the decorative arts museum. The collection is housed in an 18th-century mansion and covers art and design from the 1600s to the present.

To Ghent St-Pieters and Stadsmuseum (STAM)

★ Graslei
One of Ghent's most picturesque streets, the Graslei overlooks the River Leie on the site of the city's medieval harbour. It is lined with perfectly preserved guildhouses; some date from the 12th century.

Korenmarkt
This busy street was once the corn market, the commercial centre of the city since the Middle Ages. Today, it is lined with popular cafés.

For hotels and restaurants see p267 and pp284–5

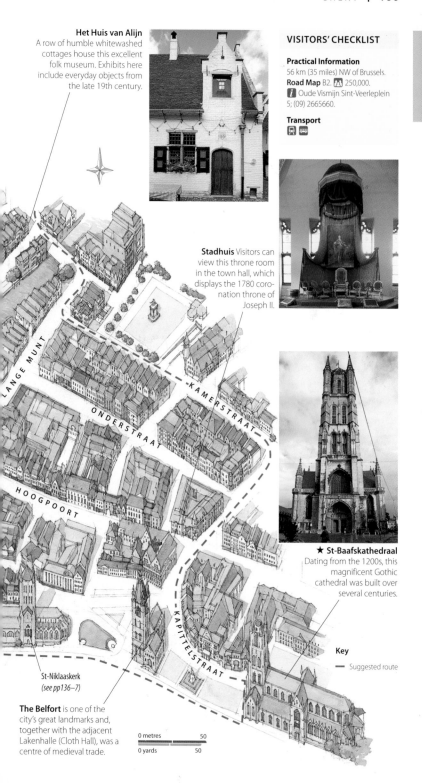

Het Huis van Alijn
A row of humble whitewashed cottages house this excellent folk museum. Exhibits here include everyday objects from the late 19th century.

VISITORS' CHECKLIST

Practical Information
56 km (35 miles) NW of Brussels.
Road Map B2. 250,000.
Oude Vismijn Sint-Veerleplein 5; (09) 2665660.

Transport

Stadhuis Visitors can view this throne room in the town hall, which displays the 1780 coronation throne of Joseph II.

★ **St-Baafskathedraal**
Dating from the 1200s, this magnificent Gothic cathedral was built over several centuries.

LANGE MUNT

ONDERSTRAAT

KAMERSTRAAT

HOOGPOORT

KAPITTELSTRAAT

St-Niklaaskerk
(see pp136–7)

The Belfort is one of the city's great landmarks and, together with the adjacent Lakenhalle (Cloth Hall), was a centre of medieval trade.

Key

— Suggested route

0 metres   50
0 yards   50

Exploring Ghent

In the 9th century, Baldwin Iron-Arm, the first Count of Flanders, laid the foundations of Ghent when he built a castle to protect two abbeys from Viking raids. Ghent's historic centre was originally built during the 13th and 14th centuries, when the city prospered as a result of the cloth trade. Despite the many religious and dynastic conflicts, Ghent flourished throughout the 16th and early 17th centuries. After 1648, the Dutch sealed the Scheldt estuary near Antwerp, closing vital canal links, which led to a decline in the fortunes of both cities. The 19th-century boom in cotton spinning reinvigorated Ghent and led to the building of wide boulevards in the city's south. Today, textiles still feature in Ghent's industry, while its university lends a youthful vibrancy to city life.

Tiled flooring forming a maze in the Pacification Hall in Ghent's Stadhuis

🏛 St-Baafskathedraal

St-Baafsplein. **Tel** (09) 2692045. **Open** daily. Adoration of the Mystic Lamb: **Open** Apr–Oct: 8:30am–6pm Mon–Sat, 10am–6pm Sun; Nov–Mar: 8:30am–5pm Mon–Sat, 10am–5pm Sun. 🅿 ♿
W sintbaafskathedraal.be

St Bavo, who was Ghent's own 7th-century saint, left the life of a wealthy degenerate to become first a missionary in Flanders and France and then a hermit. Built in several stages, St-Baafskathedraal represents every phase of Gothic style, from the 13th- and 14th-century chancel to the later cavernous nave that is supported by slender columns. The main attraction here is van Eyck's polyptych *Adoration of the Mystic Lamb*, housed in a side chapel.

🏛 Stadhuis

Botermarkt 1. **Tel** (09) 2665111. 🅿 ♿
May–Oct: 3pm Mon–Thu; tours depart 2pm from the tourist office.

The façade of Ghent's town hall displays two distinctly different architectural styles. Overlooking Hoogstraat, the older half dates from the early 16th century and its tracery is in the elaborate Flamboyant Gothic style. The plainer, newer part, which flanks the Botermarkt, is characteristic of post-Reformation architecture. The statues seen in the niches on the exterior were added in the 1890s. Among this group of figures, it is possible to spot the original architect, Rombout Keldermans, who is shown studying his plans.

The building is still the city's administrative centre. Guided tours pass through a series of rooms, the most fascinating of which is the Pacification Hall. This was once the Court of Justice and the site of the signing of the Pacification of Ghent (a treaty between Catholics and Protestants under Habsburg rule) in 1576.

🏛 Belfort

St-Baafsplein. **Tel** (09) 3753161. **Open** daily. **Closed** 1 Jan, 25 Dec. 🅿 ♿ May–Oct.

Ghent's Belfort (Belfry), a famed landmark rising 91 m (299 ft) high to the gilded-copper dragon on the tip of its spire, is situated between the cathedral and the town hall. Originally built in 1313, the Belfort was restored in the 19th and 20th centuries. Its bells today include a 54-bell carillon, which is used to play tunes to accompany the clock chimes every 15 minutes, and for concerts on the first Friday of the month, as well as every Sunday. A lift to its parapet at a height of 65 m (213 ft) offers magnificent views over the city.

Below the Belfort is the **Lakenhalle** (Cloth Hall), a fine Flemish-Gothic building from 1425 where the city's cloth-trade was carried out. The building incorporates a small town prison; guided tours are provided on request.

🏛 St-Niklaaskerk

Cataloniëstraat. **Open** 10am–5pm Tue–Sun, 2–5pm Mon.

Built by merchants between the 13th and 15th centuries, this church was dedicated to their patron saint, St Nicholas, Bishop of Myra (and model for

Gothic towers of St-Niklaaskerk and the Belfort from St-Michielsbrug

The Graslei and 16th-century guildhouses along the River Leie

fruit and cartouches. The earliest building in this embankment is the 12th-century **Spijker** (Staple House). This simple Romanesque structure stored the city's grain supply for hundreds of years until a fire destroyed its interior.

Facing the Graslei across the water, the gabled buildings of the Korenlei date from later centuries, but gracefully complement the architecture of the Graslei. The views of the city's iconic buildings from **St-Michielsbrug**, the bridge at the southern end, crossing the River Leie, are among the most beautiful in Ghent.

Design Museum Gent
Jan Breydelstraat 5. **Tel** (09) 2679999. **Open** 10am–6pm Tue–Sun.
w designmuseumgent.be

This excellent decorative arts museum occupies an elegant 18th-century townhouse. The displays are arranged in two sections, beginning at the front with a series of lavishly furnished period rooms that feature textiles, furniture and artifacts from the 17th to the 19th centuries. At the back, an airy, modern extension completed in 1992 focusses on 20th-century design ranging from Art Nouveau to contemporary works, and includes furniture by the architects Victor Horta (see p84), Marcel Breuer and Ludwig Mies van der Rohe.

Santa Claus). The church is a fine example of the distinctive and austere style called Scheldt Gothic. The interior was once filled with guild shrines and chapels, until Protestant church-wreckers destroyed them in 1566. Today, it is remarkable for its pure architectural forms, with soaring columns brightly lit by high windows. The space is punctuated by a massive and extravagantly Baroque altar screen, a clarion call to the Counter-Reformation period; unusually for such latter-day alterations, it harmonizes with the rest of the church's interior to exhilarating effect.

Graslei and Korenlei
These are two embankments that face each other across the Tusschen Brugghen, once Ghent's main medieval harbour. The Graslei, on the eastern side, possesses a fine set of guildhouses. Among them is the sandstone façade of the guildhouse of the free boatmen, which is decorated with finely detailed nautical scenes. The corn measurers' guildhouse next door is adorned by bunches of

---

The Adoration of the Mystic Lamb

One of the greatest cultural treasures of northern Europe, *The Adoration of the Mystic Lamb* is a monumental, multi-panelled work by the first of the great, early Flemish artists, Jan van Eyck, and his lesser-known brother, Hubrecht. Completed in 1432, it is exquisitely painted with rich glowing colours and meticulously depicted details. It is also an expression of the deepest beliefs of Christianity – that human salvation lies in the sacrifice of Christ, the Lamb of God. What can be seen today in St-Baafskathedraal is almost entirely original; only one panel on the lower left is a modern copy, following the theft of the original in 1934. This is a remarkable achievement, given the painting's tumultuous history. It survived Protestant church-wreckers in 1566; sections of it were taken apart and removed by French soldiers in 1794; and several of the panels were sold in 1816. It even had to be rescued from fire in 1822. Audio-guides to the painting (included in the price of the entry ticket) explain the significance of each of the 12 panels, the largest of which depicts the Mystic Lamb.

Central panels of the painting, with the Mystic Lamb as the focal point

🏛 Groot Vleeshuis

Groentenmarkt 7. **Tel** (09) 2232324.
Open 10am–6pm Tue–Sun. 🖉 📷
W grootvleeshuis.be

Literally the Great Meat Hall, the Groot Vleeshuis was built between 1407 and 1419. Its long, low interior space still reflects the area's original purpose as a covered butchers' market, complete with ancient beams and uneven flooring. A large modern glass box has been ingeniously inserted into this to house a centre that promotes local Flemish food. One side is a restaurant that serves good Flemish dishes; the other is a delicatessen.

The original covered butchers' market of the Groot Vleeshuis

🏛 Dulle Griet

Groot Kanonplein.

This 5-m (16-ft) long giant cannon, sitting on the embankment of the River Leie, is famous in Ghent folklore. Cast in about 1450 and weighing 16,000 kg (35,300 lb), it could fire stone cannonballs the size of beach-balls. It was brought to Ghent in 1578, during an era of the Calvinist government. The name Dulle Griet means Mad Meg, a legendary medieval character who embodied mad, violent frenzy and disorder. The cannon has been repainted in its original red which reflects its other nickname, the Groten Rooden Duyvele (Great Red Devil).

🏰 Het Gravensteen

St-Veerleplein. **Tel** (09) 2259306.
Open Apr–Sep: 9am–6pm daily;
Oct–Mar: 9am–5pm daily. 🖉
W gent.be/gravensteen

Once the seat of the counts of Flanders, the imposing bulk of Het Gravensteen, or the Castle of the Counts, eloquently recalls the unsettled and violent context of Ghent's early medieval past. Parts of the castle date back to the late 1100s, but most of it comprises later additions. Until the 14th century, the castle, with its massive stone walls, was Ghent's main military stronghold. It was then used as the city's jail until the late 1700s. Later, it became a cotton mill.

From the gatehouse, a long and heavily fortified tunnel leads up to the courtyard, which is overlooked by two large buildings, the count's medieval residence and the earlier keep. Arrows guide visitors around the interiors of both buildings, and in the upper rooms there is a spine-chilling collection of medieval torture instruments.

Het Gravensteen, a classic medieval castle

🏛 Het Huis van Alijn

Kraanlei 65. **Tel** (09) 2353800.
Open 11am–5:30pm Tue–Sat,
10am–5:30pm Sun. 🖉 📷
W huisvanalijn.be

This is one of Belgium's best folk museums, graphically evoking daily life of the past through a huge collection of fascinating artifacts. This includes dolls and other toys, clothes, games, furniture, kitchenware and funerary mementos as well as complete shops and craftsmen's workshops. The complex also has a puppet theatre that presents plays throughout the year in Dutch. The museum is set out in a sequence of rooms located in a pretty group of whitewashed almshouses (the House of Alijn) surrounding a grassy courtyard. Although mainly 16th-century, the almshouses were originally founded in 1363 as a children's hospital – not out of philanthropy, but as an act of penance by the Rijm family for the murder of two members of the rival Alijn family.

The surrounding area, known as the **Patershol**, is a grid of quaint little lanes and low brick houses that developed in the 17th century to house the city's weavers. This once down-at-heel area underwent extensive refurbishment in the 1980s and is now one of the trendiest parts of town, but retains a bohemian flair.

Het Huis van Alijn, housed in atmospheric 16th-century almshouses

Opera Ballet Vlaanderen

Schouwburgstraat 3.
Tel (09) 2681011. **Open** for performances. 3rd Sat of each month. **W** operaballet.be

This classic opera house, built between 1837 and 1840, has been restored to reclaim its reputation as one of the most spectacular theatres in Europe, with an auditorium and adjoining salons encrusted with gilding, chandeliers, mural paintings and sculptural decorations. The resident companies are Opera Vlaanderen, which was formed when the opera companies of Ghent and Antwerp merged, and the Royal Ballet Flanders.

The opulent, renovated interior of the Opera Ballet Vlaanderen

Stadsmuseum Gent (STAM)

Godshuizenlaan 2. **Tel** (09) 2671400.
Open 10am–6pm Tue–Sun. on request. **W** stamgent.be

This city museum offers a historic view of Ghent through multi-media presentations and a wide variety of artifacts, treasures and documentation. STAM is located in the old **Abdij van de Bijloke**, a rambling set of historic red-brick buildings. This abbey, originally founded in 1204, has over time been a nunnery, a hospital and a museum. The old cloisters, dormitories and refectory (with its 14th-century wall paintings) provide a restful backdrop to the exhibits, which take visitors through all the phases of Ghent's history. This includes its medieval heyday, the rebellion against Charles V in 1539 *(see p44)* and the industrial revolution.

A small courtyard surrounded by step-gabled houses in the Klein Begijnhof

Klein Begijnhof

Lange Violettestraat 205.
Open 6:30am–9:30pm daily.

The prettiest of Ghent's three béguinages, the Klein Begijnhof (Small Béguinage) was founded as a community of single women in 1235 and has been continuously occupied ever since, although the residents are no longer béguines *(see p65)*. The rows of step-gabled whitewashed houses here, most dating from the 17th century, enclose a small park and a Baroque church. Although just the grounds are open to the public, the structure is a beautiful site to behold.

Stedelijk Museum voor Actuele Kunst (SMAK)

Citadelpark. **Tel** (09) 2407601.
Open 10am–6pm Tue–Sun. **W** smak.be.

One of Europe's most dynamic modern art galleries, SMAK is a force in the art world that, over the past two decades, has helped bring the spotlight to the Belgian art scene. Its permanent collection includes

works by artists such as Bacon, Beuys, Broodthaers, Long, Muñoz, Nauman, Tuymans, Panamarenko and Warhol. Temporary exhibitions feature international artists at the cutting edge of contemporary art. The airy and attractive building dates from 1949 but was remodelled in the 1990s.

Museum voor Schone Kunsten

Ferdinand Scribedreef 1, Citadelpark. **Tel** (09) 2400700.
Open 10am–6pm Tue–Sun. **W** mskgent.be

Ghent's impressive collection of pre-modern fine art is displayed in this Neo-Classical building. Medieval paintings include the *Bearing of the Cross* by Hieronymus Bosch as well as work by such artists as Rogier van der Weyden and Hugo van der Goes. Jordaens, Rubens, and van Dyck are also represented here, along with James Ensor, Belgian Symbolists and artists belonging to the St-Martens-Latem School of Art *(see p140)*.

Grand Neo-Classical façade of the Museum voor Schone Kunsten

⑰ A Tour Around St-Martens-Latem

The pretty stretch of countryside along the River Leie just before it reaches Ghent, was famously adopted at the start of the 20th century by a number of Belgian artists who were collectively known as the St-Martens-Latem school. Mostly Symbolists, they included Gustave van de Woestyne, Valerius de Saedeleer, Frits van den Berghe, Albert Servaes, Gustave de Smet and the sculptor Georges Minne. Constant Permeke arrived in 1909, bringing a more radical Expressionistic tone. Many galleries in this part of the Leiestreek (Leie region), display their work.

① St-Jan-Baptistkerk
The distinctive octagonal tower and spire of the 13th-century Church of St John the Baptist in Afsnee is seen in many paintings.

② Gemeentelijk Museum Gevaert-Minne
This museum has a major collection of work by the artists of the St-Martens-Latem school.

③ St-Martens-Latem
A short detour along Meerstraat at St-Martens-Latem leads to a curving stretch of the river that makes clear why artists were attracted to this area.

④ Museum Gustave de Smet
Surrounded by trees in a quiet quarter of Deurle, the house where artist Gustave de Smet (1877–1943) lived and worked has been preserved as an art gallery and museum.

| 0 km | 2 |
| 0 miles | 2 |

Key

━━ Tour route
━━ Motorway
═══ Other road

⑦ Museum van Deinze en de Leiestreek (MuDeL)
On the eastern outskirts of Deinze, this museum has a fine collection of art, antique furniture and crafts.

⑥ Kasteel Ooidonk
A short detour to this elegant château and its gardens provides an opportunity to see the tranquil farm and woodland areas around the river.

Tips for Drivers

Starting point: Afsnee, just north of the A10 motorway outside Ghent.
Length: About 15 km (10 miles).
Duration: Allow half a day.
Driving conditions: The roads are narrow but good.
Where to eat: Restaurants are at Deinze and St-Martens-Latem.
Visitors' Information: Deinze: Emile Clausplein 4, (09) 3804601; St-Martens-Latem: Dorp 1, (09) 2821700.
Ⓦ toerisme-leiestreek.be

⑤ Museum Dhondt-Dhaenens
Named after its art-collector founders, this dynamic museum specializes in exhibitions of contemporary art, but also displays selections of its impressive permanent collection.

Corner tower with bulbous spire overlooking the moat at Kasteel Ooidonk

was remodelled and enlarged in the 17th century to make it a more habitable château. Since 1953, it has been in the hands of the Royal Association of Historic Residences and Gardens. The interior, which can be visited only by a guided tour, holds 17th-century furniture, an exceptional collection of 15th- to 18th-century silver and 16th-century Brussels tapestries depicting domestic and hunting scenes. There is also a well-respected restaurant that occupies the outbuildings.

⑱ Kasteel Ooidonk

Ooidonkdreef 9, Deinze; 24 km (15 miles) SW of Ghent. **Road Map** B2. **Tel** (09) 2822638. **Open** Apr–mid-Sep: 2–5:30pm Sun & public holidays; Jul–Aug: 2–5pm Sat, Sun & public holidays. 🅿 🚗 🆆 **ooidonk.be**. Gardens: **Open** 9am–4pm Tue–Sun.

The impressive castle of Ooidonk sits on a meandering loop of the River Leie, surrounded by **Gardens**, woodland and a moat. It occupies the site of a 13th-century fortress that was wrecked in 1491 by the citizens of Ghent in a revolt against Habsburg ruler Maximilian I. It was then the home of Philip de Montmorency, Count of Hornes, until 1568, when he was executed for opposing the introduction of the Spanish Inquisition. His castle was destroyed by Protestants in 1579. The corner towers are all that remain of this earlier fortress. The rest was rebuilt after 1595 in a mixture of Renaissance and Hispano-Flemish styles, with step-gabled façades and bulb-shaped crests on the towers. The interior was refurbished sensitively in the 19th century to sumptuous standards, and has a fitting collection of antique furniture, tapestries, paintings, *objets d'art* and the kind of detail which is seen in a castle that is still lived in by its owners.

⑲ Kasteel van Laarne

Eethoekstraat 5, Laarne; 19 km (12 miles) SE of Ghent. **Road Map** B2. **Tel** (09) 2309155. 🚗 🅿 mandatory; Easter–Sep: 3pm Sun; Jul–Aug: 3pm Thu & Sun. 🚗 🆆 **slotvanlaarne.be**

A remarkable castle, Laarne is surrounded by a broad moat and accessed by a long bridge. The castle is artistically set at an angle both to the moat and to the large square forecourt, with corner buildings, that leads up to it. Originally a pentagonal fortress dating from the 12th to 14th centuries, with unusual spires on the towers, it was used by the counts of Flanders, and was the target of repeated sieges. Laarne

⑳ Stoomcentrum Maldegem

Stationsplein 8, Maldegem; 32 km (20 miles) from Ghent. **Road Map** B1. **Tel** (050) 716852. 🚌 **Open** early May–Sep: 10am–5:30pm Sun; Jul–Aug: noon–5pm Wed & Fri, 10am–5:30pm Sun. 🅿 🚗 Steam Festival (1st weekend of May). 🆆 **stoomcentrum.be**

The Stoomcentrum (Steam Centre) in Maldegem is the largest collection of steam engines in Flanders. It has agricultural and industrial machines, fire-engines, steamrollers and steam locomotives. The museum is operated by enthusiasts, and visitors can see them working on machines currently under restoration. Steam and diesel trains take visitors for rides on a track to Eeklo 10 km (6 miles) away, and a diesel train runs on a narrow-gauge line to Donk, about 1.5 km (1 mile) away.

Old-fashioned diesel train at Stoomcentrum Maldegem

For hotels and restaurants see pp266–7 and pp283–6

The Flamboyant Gothic façade of Oudenaarde's elegant Stadhuis

㉑ Oudenaarde

30 km (19 miles) S of Ghent.
Road Map B2. 🏔 28,000. 🚌 🚍
🛈 Stadhuis, Markt 1; (055) 317251.
🌐 oudenaarde.be

Founded as a fortress on the River Scheldt in the 11th century, Oudenaarde (Old Landing Place) has had a long and troubled history, scrapping with the rival city of Ghent in the Middle Ages, and often besieged. Developing as a cloth town, it became celebrated for its tapestries in the 15th century, but fell into decline thereafter.

Oudenaarde has preserved many of its great monuments, chief among which is the outstanding 16th-century Stadhuis built in Flamboyant Gothic style. It houses the **Museum of Oudenaarde and the Flemish Ardennes**. Of particular note here are the carved wood furnishings, the fine silverware collection, and the works of art by Adriaen Brouwer (1605-1638), famed for his rumbustious paintings of peasants. There are informative displays that feature the life and culture of the Flemish Ardennes region. The museum also incorporates the nearby Lakenhalle (Cloth Hall), which contains an exceptional collection of tapestries. Overlooking the River Scheldt is the grand 16th- to 18th-century mansion **Huis de Lalaing**, now a municipal tapestry workshop. A little way up-river, the 13th-century **Onze-Lieve-Vrouwekerk van Pamele** is a classic example of Scheldt Gothic *(see p32)*; Pamele was the name of the twin town that developed on the south bank of the Scheldt.

The undulating countryside around Oudenaarde is known as the Vlaamse Ardennen, or the Flemish Ardennes.

🏛 Museum of Oudenaarde and the Flemish Ardennes

Stadhuis, Grote Markt. **Tel** (055) 317251. **Open** summer: 10am–5:30pm Tue–Sun; winter: 10am–5pm Tue–Fri, 2–5pm Sat & Sun. 🚻 🗾

🏛 Huis de Lalaing

Bourgondiestraat 9.
Closed to the public. 🚻

㉒ Geraardsbergen

41 km (25 miles) S of Ghent.
Road Map B2. 🏔 31,000. 🚌 🚍
🛈 Stadhuis, Grote Markt; (054) 437289. 🌐 Krakelingenfeest (Feb).
🌐 geraardsbergen.be

The agreeable town of Geraardsbergen (Grammont in French) is situated in the Vlaamse Ardennen, on the River Dender. The nearby hill of **Oudenberg** rises above the town to a height of 110 m (360 ft), and the steep, cobbled road up it is known to all cycle-race enthusiasts as the Mur de Grammont, a gruelling feature of the Tour of Flanders *(see p36)*. The summit, with its Baroque chapel dating from 1648, is where 8,000 ring-shaped pastries are thrown into the crowd after a costumed parade known as the Krakenlingenstoet *(see p39)*. However, bakers from Geraardsbergen pride themselves more on a sweet cheese tartlet called *mattentaart*.

The Grote Markt, at the centre of the town, has an impressive Stadhuis. The version of the **Manneken-Pis** found outside

the Stadhuis was originally installed in 1459, so it predates the one in Brussels by nearly 200 years. The statue's 235 costumes can be admired in a small museum by the tourist office. The 15th-century stone fountain and cross in the square is a town emblem known as the **Marbol**.

㉓ Aalst

33 km (21 miles) SE of Ghent.
Road Map B2. 🏔 82,000. 🚌 🚍
🛈 Hopmarkt 51; (053) 723880. 🌐 Carnival (Feb). 🌐 aalst.be/toerisme

Aalst is the second largest city in East Flanders. It has a splendid town square (Grote Markt) featuring the Alderman's House, which was originally the town hall and dates to the 13th century, making it one of the oldest town halls in the Low Countries. The beautiful adjacent belfry has a carillon of 52 bells. The old town hall now serves as the deputy mayor's office, while a 19th-century building with a rococo façade in its inner court houses the present-day town hall. Other notable buildings include the Old Hospital (15th century) and the Gothic-style St Martin's Collegiate Church (built in 1480), which contains the painting *Saint Rochus Beseeching Christ to Terminate the Plague at Aalst* (1623–6) by Rubens. The Municipal Museum has displays about local history and folklore, including carnival masks.

Aalst's Shrove Tuesday Carnival *(see p39)* is a popular three-day festival.

The 15th-century belfry tower on the Grote Markt, Aalst

㉔ Dendermonde

30 km (19 miles) E of Ghent.
Road Map C2. 🚇 43,000. 🚉 🚌
ℹ️ Stadhuis, Grote Markt; (052)
213956. 🎪 Mon.
🌐 toerismedendermonde.be

Its position at the confluence
of the Scheldt and Dender has
made Dendermonde (literally,
Mouth of the River Dender)
a strategically important
location throughout history,
even in 1914, when the town
was sacked by the Germans.
Today, it is a quiet commuter
town, famed above all for its
celebrated pageant of the steed
Bayard, which dates back to the
15th century and is performed
every ten years, with the next
such triumphal procession of a
horse and its four riders due to
take place in 2020.

Dendermonde's attractive
Grote Markt is flanked by the
steepled turret and step-gables
of its 15th-century **Vleeshuis**
(Meat Hall), which now contains
a town museum. The Stadhuis
was originally built as a cloth
hall in the 14th century. It was
wrecked in 1914 and restored to
its original medieval architectural
splendour in the 1920s. Its belfry
has a carillon of 49 bells. The
town's **Onze-Lieve-Vrouwekerk**,
built between the 13th and
15th centuries, has a remarkable
12th-century carved stone font,
and two paintings by Anthony
van Dyck – the *Adoration of the
Shepherds* (c.1616) and the
Crucifixion (c.1628).

To the south of the River
Dender, in the beguiling
St-Alexiusbegijnhof, are rows
of attractive 17th-century
houses lining a triangular green.
Located here is a small museum
about the béguinage as well as
a folk museum.

Environs
Situated 15 km (9 miles) to the
west, **Donkmeer** is a lakeland
area famed as the place to eat
eel dishes such as *anguilles au
vert – paling in't groen* in Dutch –
(*see p274*). There is also an
agreeable nature reserve known
as **De Eendenkooi** (The Duck
Pen), where visitors can spot
herons, storks and other birds.

A statue of the benevolent saint outside the
Stadhuis at St-Niklaas

㉕ St-Niklaas

39 km (24 miles) NE of Ghent.
Road Map C1. 🚇 70,000. 🚉 🚌
ℹ️ Grote Markt 45; (03) 7783500.
🎪 Thu. 🌐 sint-niklaas.be

The sprawling town of
St-Niklaas is the commercial
centre of Waasland, an area of
drained marshes that have
become productive farmland.
St-Niklaas's Grote Markt is the
largest market square in the
country. Surrounded by a
number of attractive 17th-
century buildings and an
elegant 19th-century **Stadhuis**,
the square really comes alive
on market days as well as in
early September when scores
of hot-air balloons gather for
the Vredesfeesten (literally,
Peace Festivities).

The intriguing **Ste.M** (Stedelijk
Museum) includes a collection
of music recording machines –
from musical boxes to early
gramophones – historical hair-
dressing salons (the Barbierama),
18th-century apothecary jars
and reconstructions of life in
medieval times based around
archaeological finds at the
Boudelo Abbey close by.
Interactive touchscreens give
more background information.

Set in a Neo-Classical town
mansion built during 1928 and
1929, the **Salons voor Schone
Kunsten** has elegantly furnished
rooms and a collection of
paintings by noted 19th-century
Belgian artists such as Henri de
Braekeleer, Henri Evenepoel,
James Ensor, Jan Stobbaerts
and Hippolyte Boulenger.

The great Renaissance
geographer and cartographer
Gerardus Mercator (1512– 94),
creator of the familiar Mercator
Projection, was born nearby at
Rupelmonde. Dedicated to him,
the **Mercatormuseum** explores
his contributions to the history
of cartography.

🏛️ **Ste.M**
Zwijgershoek 14. **Tel** (03) 7783450.
Open 2–5pm Tue–Sat and
11am–5pm Sun. 🚫

🏛️ **Salons voor Schone Kunsten**
Stationsstraat 85. **Tel** (03) 7781745.
Open 2–5pm Thu–Sat & 11am–5pm
Sun. **Closed** mid-Dec–mid-Jan. 🚫

🏛️ **Mercatormuseum**
Zamanstraat 49. **Tel** (03) 7603783.
Open 2–5pm Tue–Sat, 11am–5pm
Sun. 🚫

The Legend of the Steed Bayard

Set in the times of Charlemagne, the legend of the steed Bayard
recounts the derring-do of four knights and a powerful horse.
The knights were the four sons of Aymon, Lord of
Dendermonde, and Aya, Charlemagne's sister. One of
them, Reinout, subdued the ferocious steed Bayard.
In a quarrel over the horse, Reinout killed
Charlemagne's jealous son Lodewijk, after
which the brothers, riding the mighty steed,
defended themselves from the emperor's
wrath. Finally, as a condition of peace,
Reinout agreed to kill the steed Bayard.
Seeing how Reinout had rejected him, the
valiant horse sacrificed himself in the river.
Dendermonde's famous pageant today, the
Ros Beiaardommegang, centres upon a
giant model of the horse ridden by the
Aymon brothers in full armour, a role
always taken by four real brothers
from Dendermonde.

Statue of the steed Bayard with
three of the Aymon brothers visible

ANTWERP, FLEMISH BRABANT AND LIMBURG

Magnificent castles and Gothic churches speak eloquently of this region's rich historic heritage. The busy axis between Brussels and Antwerp is a hothouse of contemporary culture and fashion. Further east, the beauty and tranquillity of the countryside become the keynotes, in the heaths and woodlands of the Kempen and the sweetly rolling farmlands of the south.

From the River Scheldt in the west to the Province of Limburg is an area of age-old natural and historical beauty, with the straight roads built by the Romans around Tongeren, in eastern Limburg, still in use today.

In AD 843, the lands to the south and east of the River Scheldt were an area called Lotharingia. These followed a trajectory within the Holy Roman Empire, separate from that of the rest of Flanders. Over the next few centuries, the land was further divided between the duchies of Brabant and Limburg, with the prince-bishopric of Liège gaining control of southern Limburg. During this period, the remote forests and woodlands of Eastern Flanders attracted religious communities, most notably the Premonstratensians at Tongerlo and Averbode. In the 15th century, the dukes of Burgundy slowly pulled the region under their control – by marriage, diplomacy or ruthless force. Towns such as Mechelen and Leuven began to flourish, and by the 17th century, the port-city of Antwerp had entered a Golden Age, echoed in the flamboyant paintings of Rubens.

Today, visitors come to admire the many vestiges of this history that are etched into the countryside and the fabric of the towns. They also come to immerse themselves in the natural charm of the landscape, to walk and cycle, and to enjoy the great range of *streekproducten*, the food specialities of the region, particularly from the farmlands and orchards of the Hageland and the Haspengouw.

A flat and tranquil landscape, characteristic of the agricultural regions of Antwerp, Flemish Brabant and Limburg

◄ Ornate doorway of the Cathedral of Our Lady, built between the 14th and 16th century, Antwerp

Exploring Antwerp, Flemish Brabant and Limburg

The main attractions of Antwerp, Flemish Brabant and Limburg lie in the west of the region. Antwerp has a clutch of top-quality museums and historic buildings, as well as a celebrated club scene. Leuven and Mechelen are beautiful medieval towns, with outstanding architectural treasures. There are castles at Beersel and Gaasbeek, gardens at Nationale Plantentuin and a World War II concentration camp memorial at Breendonk. More to the east, the beguiling little town of Diest is close to sites such as the pilgrimage shrine at Scherpenheuvel and the Abdij van Averbode. The abbey of Tongerlo is famous for its copy of Leonardo's *Last Supper*, while Hasselt is the place for those who wish to sample *jenever* gin. Roman history is very much in the air in Tongeren. The highlight of the region is Bokrijk's open-air museum, a collection of historic rustic buildings set out in a large park, bringing to life Flanders's rural past.

Sights at a Glance

Villages, Towns and Cities
- ❶ Antwerp *pp148–59*
- ❷ Sint-Amands
- ❹ Turnhout
- ❻ Lier
- ❼ Mechelen
- ❽ Leuven *pp164–5*
- ❾ Aarschot
- ⓬ Diest
- ⓭ Zoutleeuw
- ⓮ Tienen
- ⓱ Halle
- ㉑ St-Truiden
- ㉒ Hasselt
- ㉔ Maaseik
- ㉗ Tongeren

Castles
- ⓲ Kasteel van Beersel
- ⓳ Kasteel van Gaasbeek
- ㉖ Landcommanderij Alden Biesen

Churches and Abbeys
- ❺ Abdij Tongerlo
- ❿ Onze-Lieve-Vrouw van Scherpenheuvel
- ⓫ Abdij van Averbode
- ⓰ Sint-Servaasbasiliek Grimbergen

Museums
- ❸ Memorial Breendonk
- ㉓ Bokrijk Openluchtmuseum *p171*

Parks and Gardens
- ⓯ Nationale Plantentuin
- ㉕ Nationaal Park Hoge Kempen

Areas of Natural Beauty
- ⓴ Forêt de Soignes

The stately 16th-century castle and grounds at Landcommanderij Alden Biesen

For hotels and restaurants see p268 and pp286–8

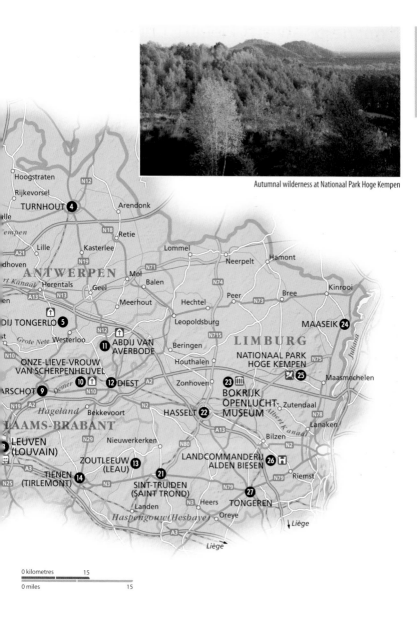

Autumnal wilderness at Nationaal Park Hoge Kempen

Hoogstraten

Rijkevorsel

N12

TURNHOUT **4**

Arendonk

N18

Retie

Lille

A21

Kasterlee

Lommel

Neerpelt

Hamont

ANTWERPEN

N71

Mol

Balen

N74

Bree

Kinrooi

Herentals

Geel

A13 N13

Meerhout

Hechtel

Peer

N73

MAASEIK **24**

ABDIJ TONGERLO **5**

Leopoldsburg

Grote Nete Westerloo

N12

ABDIJ VAN AVERBODE **11**

N715

Beringen

LIMBURG

N10

ONZE-LIEVE-VROUW VAN SCHERPENHEUVEL

Houthalen

NATIONAAL PARK HOGE KEMPEN

N75

Maasmechelen

ARSCHOT **9**

10 N10

12 DIEST A2

Demer

Zonhoven

23 BOKRIJK OPENLUCHT MUSEUM

Zutendaal

N78

Lanaken

N19 A2

Hageland

Bekkevoort

N2

HASSELT **22**

VLAAMS-BRABANT

LEUVEN (LOUVAIN)

N29

Nieuwerkerken

N80

Bilzen

N2

ZOUTLEEUW (LEAU) **13**

LANDCOMMANDERIJ ALDEN BIESEN **26**

Riemst

A3

TIENEN (TIRLEMONT) **14**

21

SINT-TRUIDEN (SAINT TROND)

N79

N25

N3

Landen

N3

Heers

Oreye

TONGEREN **27**

Haspengouw (Hesbaye)

↓ Liège

A3

Liège

↓ Liège

0 kilometres 15

0 miles 15

Key

Motorway

Major road

Secondary road

Minor road

Main railway

Minor railway

International border

Provincial border

Getting Around

None of the distances are very great. Maaseik, which lies close to the border with the Netherlands, is only 100 km (62 miles) east of Brussels. Motorways straddle the region, linking Antwerp and Brussels in the west to Tongeren in the southeast (and Liège further south), and provide important transport links to Germany and the Netherlands. Travelling to the many towns and villages is made possible by buses operated by De Lijn, which also runs the tram service in Antwerp. Most towns are also on the national rail network.

For keys to symbols *see back flap*

❶ Antwerp

The largest city in Flanders and one of Europe's busiest ports, Antwerp is also known as Belgium's second city. Beginning as a settlement on the banks of the Scheldt in the 2nd century AD, Antwerp went on to become part of the Duchy of Brabant, and its main port, in 1106. Over the next 200 years, it was a thriving hub of the European cloth industry. However, its golden age came during the era of Spanish rule (*see p45*), when it was illuminated by the artistic genius of its most famous son, Pieter Paul Rubens (1577–1640). Today, mirroring this vigorous mercantile and cultural past, Antwerp is undergoing a spirited regeneration, seen in its widespread programme of rebuilding and renovation, and in its reputation as a key European centre of cutting-edge fashion design.

Carvings around the door at the Onze-Lieve-Vrouwekathedraal

Brabo Fountain portraying the story of the legendary Roman hero Brabo

Brabo Fountain is an Antwerp landmark, commemorating the legend of a Roman soldier, Silvius Brabo, who killed an evil giant terrorizing shipping. A Christmas market is held here annually.

Key

☐ Street-by-Street
pp150–151

🏛 Grote Markt

Tel (03) 2320103. ♿

Antwerp's central square, or Grote Markt, is flanked by the ornately gabled **Stadhuis**, which was completed in 1564 by the architect and sculptor Cornelis Floris. The square's north side has a series of guildhouses, all decorated with gilded figures. The tallest building is the **House of the Crossbowmen**, on top of which is a statue of St George and the dragon. The central

Murals depicting the dukes of Brabant in Antwerp's Stadhuis

🏛 Onze-Lieve-Vrouwekathedraal

Handschoenmarkt 1. **Tel** (03) 2139951.
Open 10am–5pm Mon–Fri, 10am–3pm Sat, 1–4pm Sun. 🔊 🏛 ♿

The building of Antwerp's Onze-Lieve-Vrouwekathedraal (Cathedral of Our Lady) took almost two centuries, from 1352 to 1521. It has a graceful tiered spire that rises to a height of 123 m (404 ft) above the winding streets of the medieval city centre. Inside, the impression of light and space owes much to the seven-aisled nave and vaulted ceiling. The cathedral's large collection of paintings and sculptures, some on loan from the Koninklijk Museum voor Schone Kunsten (see p156) until 2017, includes three works by Rubens, of which two – *Raising of the Cross* (1610) and *Descent from the Cross* (1612) – are triptychs.

🏛 Vleeshuis

Vleeshouwersstraat 38. **Tel** (03) 2926100. **Open** 10am–5pm Thu–Sun & Easter Mon.

There has been a Vleeshuis (Meat Hall) on this site since 1250, but the present hall was designed by the architect Herman de Waghemakere and completed in 1504. It features slender

towers with five hexagonal turrets and rising gables, all built in alternate strips of stone and brick. The Gothic interior holds a museum, Sounds of the City, which presents artifacts from over 600 years of music in Antwerp.

🏛 Het Steen

Steenplein 1.
Antwerp's castle, Het Steen, was built on the banks of the Scheldt to protect the town and control shipping. Although a castle stood on this site in the 10th century, during the Viking raids, the lower section, which is the oldest part of the present building, dates only from the 13th century. Above that section are vestiges of the rebuilding ordered in 1520 by Charles V. For many centuries, until 1823, Het Steen served as the town's prison. Eventually, the whole edifice underwent a romanticized restoration in the year 1890. According to legend, the castle was once home to the evil giant Druon Antigoon, who exacted a heavy toll on shipping and cut off the hands of captains who failed to pay him. He was eventually slain by the brave Roman soldier Silvius Brabo, who chopped off the giant's hand in turn and threw it into the River Scheldt. This *handwerpen*, or hand-throwing, is said by one legend to be the gesture that gave Antwerp its name. The bronze statue dating from 1963

Het Steen, Antwerp's castle on the banks of the Scheldt

at the base of the entrance ramp depicts another legendary local giant, the jovial rogue Lange Wapper, who could grow taller at will and played alarming tricks on drinkers. Over the main gate is an old sculpture of Semini, Scandinavian god of fertility – the statue was once held to be a talisman for Antwerp's people.

Lange Wapper guarding Het Steen

🏛 St-Pauluskerk

St-Paulusstraat 22. **Tel** (03) 2323267. **Open** Apr–Oct: 2–5pm daily. 3pm Sun & public holidays.

Completed in the early 17th century, this splendid church displays a mix of Gothic and Baroque features. The exterior dates from about 1571, and has an elaborate Baroque gateway, while the interior has intricately carved wooden choir stalls. St-Pauluskerk possesses a series of paintings illustrating the Fifteen Mysteries of the Rosary, one of which, *The Scourging of the Pillar*, is an exquisite canvas by Rubens. There are also paintings by van Dyck and Jordaens.

🏛 Museum aan de Stroom (MAS)

Hanzestedenplaats 1. **Tel**(03) 338 4400. **Open** 10am–5pm Tue–Fri, 10am–6pm Sat & Sun (until 5pm in winter). mas.be

Set in a spiralling building in the old docks area just north of the historic centre is the Museum aan de Stroom, (Museum on the River). It combines artifacts formerly held in the Maritime, Folklore and Ethnographic museums and the Vleeshuis to present a portrait of Antwerp's historic relationship with the River Scheldt and the world beyond.

Antwerp

Street-by-Street: Around the Grote Markt

Fanning out from the east bank of the River Scheldt, Antwerp has been one of the leading trading cities of northern Europe for centuries. Today, the city's industries lie away from its medieval core whose narrow streets and fine buildings cluster around the cathedral and the Grote Markt. Packed with evidence of Antwerp's rich history, this is a delightful area to wander in. Most sites of interest are within walking distance of the Grote Markt whose surrounding streets house museums, shops and exuberant cafés and bars.

Het Steen *(see p149)*

STEENPLEIN

JORDAENSKAAI

KUIPERSSTRAA

SUIKERRUI

OUDE KOORNMARKT

Vleeshuis
Occupied by the butcher's guild for three centuries, this beautiful 1504 building has striking layers of brick and stone that look like alternating strips of fat and lean meat.

Stadhuis
Flanking Antwerp's spectacular central square is the elegant 16th-century Stadhuis, designed by Flemish architect Cornelis Floris.

Key

— Suggested route

| 0 metres | 50 |
| 0 yards | 50 |

Brabo Fountain
Set in the centre of the Grote Markt, this statue (1887) by Antwerp-born sculptor Jef Lambeaux depicts the Roman soldier Silvius Brabo throwing the hand of the mythical giant Druon Antigoon into the River Scheldt.

For hotels and restaurants see p268 and pp286–7

St-Pauluskerk
This imposing church was built in 1571, but has a magnificent Baroque gate and spire dating from the late 17th century. Inside, there is a noted collection of paintings, including a particularly fine work by Rubens.

★ Grote Markt
Antwerp's golden age of trade in the 16th century is reflected in the square's impressive line-up of elaborate 16th- and 17th-century guildhouses.

★ Onze-Lieve-Vrouwekathedraal
The largest Gothic cathedral in Belgium, this building occupies a 1-ha (2.5-acre) site in Antwerp's centre. Work began on the church in 1352, and after two centuries, the second spire was left incomplete.

ZIRKSTRAAT

VERSMIDSTRAAT

To Rubenshuis and Centraal Station

To Koninklijk Museum voor Schone Kunsten

Groenplaats
The Groenplaats or Green Square is a pleasant open space with trees and a statue of Rubens. Lined with cafés and bars, the square is a popular spot with both locals and visitors for a relaxed stroll or drink.

Exploring Central and Southern Antwerp

Antwerp stretches from its centre out into sprawling suburbs for a distance of 7 km (4 miles). Since it was badly damaged in both World Wars, the city has a broad mix of architecture, ranging from the medieval to the ultramodern. The old city centre is concentrated around the Onze-Lieve-Vrouwekathedraal and the Grote Markt. To the east of the cathedral – beyond Antwerp's pioneering 1930s skyscraper, the Boerentoren – lies the Meir, a premier shopping street. The Zuid (South) district is an area of drained docks. Now rejuvenated, this is a vibrant part of the town, and the old dockland architecture of the streets Waalse Kaai and Vlaamse Kaai now houses a variety of clubs, bars and museums.

Late 16th-century printing press in the Museum Plantin-Moretus

Modernist interior of the reputed Modemuseum

🏛 Modemuseum (MoMu)

Nationalestraat 28. **Tel** (03) 4702770. **Open** 10am–6pm Tue–Sun (until 9pm on the first Sun of the month). 🖼 **W** momu.be

Following the rise to celebrity in the 1980s of the influential fashion designers called the Antwerp Six, the city has entered the stratosphere of international haute couture, and maintains a glowing reputation for nurturing new talent. Stars such as Dries van Noten, Ann Demeulemeester, Walter van Bierendonck and Martin Margiela all have a presence in the city.

This museum provides the historical context to Antwerp's rise to glory in the fashion world. Stylish items and accessories are innovatively displayed in changing exhibitions, allowing the museum to serve as a resource for both instruction and inspiration.

🏛 Museum Plantin-Moretus

Vrijdagmarkt 22. **Tel** (03) 221450. **Open** 10am–5pm Tue–Sun, Easter Mon & Whit Mon. 🖼 free on last Wed of month. **W** museumplantin moretus.be

This fascinating museum and World Heritage Site occupies a large 16th-century house that belonged to the printer Christopher Plantin, who moved here in 1576. The house is built around a courtyard with ancient rooms and narrow corridors that resemble the types of interiors painted by Flemish and Dutch masters. The museum is devoted to the early years of printing, when Plantin and others began to produce books that bore no resemblance to earlier illuminated medieval manuscripts.

Antwerp was a centre for printing in the 15th and 16th centuries, and Plantin was its most successful printer. His legacy was carried on by his son-in-law Jan I Moretus. Today, his workshop displays several historic printing presses, as well as woodcuts and copper plates. Plantin's library is also on show. One of its gems is an edition of the Gutenberg Bible – the first book to be printed using moveable type, a technique that was invented by Johannes Gutenberg in 1455.

🏛 Maagdenhuis

Lange Gasthuisstraat 33. **Tel** (03) 3382620. **Open** 10am–5pm Mon & Wed–Fri, 1–5pm Sat & Sun. 🖼

Literally the Maidens' House, this orphanage and foundling hospital for girls was built in two phases during the 16th and 17th centuries, and remained in operation until 1882. It is a delightful historic building with a footnote of tragedy – baby girls were abandoned here by their mothers, often anonymously in a "foundling drawer" set into an outer wall. One half of a playing card was attached to the child, and the mother kept the other half, in the hope that one day they might be reunited. Such cards are among the quirky but intriguing collection of items now on view in a series of rooms that includes furniture, paintings

The charming inner courtyard of the Maagdenhuis

by artists such as van Dyck and Rubens, sculpture, silverware, pottery, needlework and porridge bowls, all belonging to the orphanage, or bequeathed to it. There is also a reproduction of the original foundling drawer that used to be in Rochusstraat.

🏛 Rockoxhuis
Keizerstraat 12. **Tel** (03) 2019250. **Open** 10am–5pm Tue–Sun. 🖼
W rockoxhuis.be

Nicolaas Rockox (1560–1640) was the mayor of Antwerp as well as a humanist, philanthropist and a friend and patron of Rubens. These attributes are reflected in his beautifully renovated home – a series of rooms set around a formal courtyard garden. They hold a fine collection of contemporary furniture and miscellaneous artifacts, all interesting and well chosen. The paintings include work by Pieter Brueghel the Younger, Rubens, Jordaens and van Dyck, as well as by his neighbour, Frans Snyders (1579–1657), who was much admired by Rubens, and painted the fruit and flowers in Rubens's work.

🏛 St-Jacobskerk
Lange Nieuwstraat 73–75. **Open** Apr–Oct: 2–5pm daily. **Closed** Nov–Mar. 🖼 **W** sintjacobantwerpen.be

Noted as Pieter Paul Rubens's burial place, this sandstone church was built between 1491 and 1656. Rubens's tomb, in his family's chapel behind the high altar, displays his painting of *Our*

Stained-glass window in the sandstone church of St-Jacobskerk

Lady and the Christ Child Surrounded by Saints, into which the artist inserted the faces of himself and his family. The rich interior of St-Jacobskerk contains the tombs of several notable Antwerp families, and a fine collection of 17th-century art that includes sculptures by Verbruggen as well as paintings by van Dyck, Otto Venius – who was Rubens's first master – and Jacob Jordaens *(see p107)*.

Fishmarket Antwerp at the Rockoxhuis

🏛 Rubenshuis
See pp154–5.

🏛 Museum Mayer van den Bergh
Lange Gasthuisstraat 19. **Tel** (03) 3388188. **Open** 10am–5pm Tue–Sun & Easter Mon. 🖼 **W** museum.antwerpen.be/mayervandenbergh

Fritz Mayer van den Bergh (1858–1901) was the scion of a

wealthy trading family, but instead of following in his father's footsteps, he devoted himself to collecting works of art. After his death at the age of 43, his mother created this museum to display his collections. Among the many treasures on display here are tapestries, furniture, ivory carvings, medieval and Renaissance sculpture, stained glass, and a number of excellent paintings. In particular, *Dulle Griet* (Mad Meg) is a powerful image of a chaotic world, painted in 1562 by Pieter Brueghel the Elder *(see p107)*.

🏛 Koninklijk Museum voor Schone Kunsten
See pp156–7.

🏛 Museum van Hedendaagse Kunst Antwerpen (M HKA)
Leuvenstraat 32. **Tel** (03) 2609999. **Open** 11am–6pm Tue–Sun (until 9pm Thu). 🖼 🖼 🖼 **W** muhka.be

This museum fits perfectly into a city famed for its sense of style and design. Once a 1920s dockside grain silo and warehouse, the huge, sculptural building has been transformed into a series of unusual spaces to display works from the front line of international contemporary art. It includes work by many of the artists who helped place Belgium at the forefront of the art scene in recent years, including Luc Tuymans, Panamarenko, Jan Fabre and Wim Delvoye.

🏛 FotoMuseum
Waalse Kaai 47. **Tel** (03) 2429300 **Open** 10am–6pm Tue–Sun. 🖼
W fotomuseum.be

The city's excellent museum of photography displays a broad variety of historical artifacts and images. The museum has now undergone a complete makeover and has embraced the moving image by incorporating the Antwerp Film Museum. The latter offers regularly scheduled film viewings. In addition to its extensive permanent collection, the museum mounts a series of photography exhibitions that feature both local and international artists.

Choice antique furniture and art in the Museum Mayer van den Bergh

Antwerp: Rubenshuis

Located on Wapper Square, Rubenshuis was Pieter Paul Rubens's home and studio for the last 29 years of his life, from 1611 to 1640. The city bought the premises just before World War II, but by then the house was little more than a ruin, and what can be seen today is the result of careful restoration. It is divided into two sections. To the left of the entrance are the narrow rooms of the artist's living quarters, equipped with period furniture. Behind this is the Kunstkamer, or art gallery, where Rubens exhibited both his own and other artists' work, and entertained his friends and patrons such as the Archduke Albert and Infanta Isabella. To the right of the entrance lies the main studio, a spacious salon where Rubens created – and showed – his works. A signposted route guides visitors through the house.

Façade of Rubenshuis
The older Flemish part of the house sits to the left of the later section, whose elegant early-Baroque exterior was designed by Rubens himself.

Pavilion and Garden
Rubens was greatly influenced by Italian Renaissance architects such as Alberti. In the 1620s, he added an Italian Baroque pavilion to his house, charmingly set in a small, formally laid-out garden.

★ Rubens's Studio
It is estimated that Rubens produced some 2,500 paintings in this large, high-ceilinged room. In the Renaissance manner, Rubens designed the work, which was usually completed by a team of other artists employed in his studio.

KEY

① **Entrance passage**

② **The Living Room** is a cosy sitting room with a pretty tiled floor and view of Wapper Square.

③ **Chequered mosaic tiled floor**

Bedroom
The Rubens family lived in the Flemish section of the house with its small rooms and narrow passages. The furniture in the room, including the bed, is all from Rubens's time.

VISITORS' CHECKLIST

Practical Information
Wapper 9–11. **Tel** (03) 2011555.
Open 10am–5pm Tue–Sun,
Easter Mon, Whit Mon.
W rubenshouse.be

Transport
22, 25, 26. 3, 4, 5, 9, 15.

Dining Room
Intricately fashioned leather panels line the walls of this room, which displays a noted self-portrait.

★ Kunstkamer
This art gallery contains a series of painted sketches by Rubens. At the far end is a semicircular dome, modelled on Rome's Pantheon, displaying a number of marble busts.

Baroque Portico
One of the few remaining original features, this portico was designed by Rubens and links the older house with the Baroque section. It is adorned with a frieze showing scenes from Greek mythology.

Antwerp: Koninklijk Museum voor Schone Kunsten

Antwerp's largest art collection is exhibited in the Museum voor Schone Kunsten, housed in a massive late 19th-century Neo-Classical building. The permanent collection contains both ancient and modern works. The earlier collection contains medieval Flemish painting and continues through the 19th century, with the "Antwerp Trio" of Rubens, van Dyck and Jordaens. Modern exhibits include the work of Belgian artists Magritte, Ensor, Delvaux and Rik Wouters. Foreign artists on display are Tissot and van Gogh. The museum is currently closed for renovations. Collection highlights can be seen at the Cathedral of our Lady and the Museum aan de Stroom, MAS *(see p149).*

First floor

Madame Récamier
(1967), Magritte's macabre version of David's painting, is a classic Surrealist work.

Main entrance

Façade of Main Entrance
Building began on the imposing museum in 1884. The Neo-Classical façade, with its vast pillars, features winged women charioteers on each side. It was opened in 1890.

★ Woman Ironing (1912)
A domestic scene painted by Rik Wouters is animated by bright Fauvist colours. This was a productive period for Wouters who painted 60 canvases in that year.

In the Pink Bows
(1936), Paul Delvaux's dream-like style shows the influence of Freud's psychoanalytic theories on Surrealist painting.

Ground floor

Gallery Guide

The gallery is divided into two floors. Flemish Old Masters and 19th-century painters are housed on the first floor, which also has an area devoted to sculpture. The ground floor focuses on James Ensor and the 20th century, with a large portion set aside for temporary exhibitions. The museum is currently closed for renovations.

★ *Saint Barbara* (1437)
Jan van Eyck's painting of St Barbara, in tones of grey, shows her sitting in front of a huge Gothic cathedral tower still under construction. A prayer book lies open on her lap.

★ *The Lance* (1620)
One of Pieter Paul Rubens's best-known religious masterpieces, this painting displays a remarkable freedom of composition.

Woman Ironing by
Rik Wouters

Key to Floorplan

- 15th-century paintings
- 16th-century paintings
- 16th–18th-century sketches
- 17th-century paintings
- 19th-century sculpture
- 19th-century paintings
- 19th-century salon
- 20th-century paintings
- Temporary exhibitions
- Museum history
- Non-exhibition space

The Lamentation over the Dead Christ (1629)
Anthony van Dyck painted several versions of this subject, with different notes of emotional intensity in each.

Antwerp: Beyond the Centre

There are a number of interesting suburbs that lie outside the historic hub of Antwerp. To the east is the magnificent Centraal Station, surrounded by the surprisingly unglamorous Diamond District – centre of Europe's biggest international diamond trade – whose streets are lined with diamond outlets. Further south, the suburb of Zurenborg, in Berchem, has some of Europe's most exuberant mansions, created in a wide variety of styles for Antwerp's wealthy merchant classes. The eastern suburb of Deurne has a silver museum, set in a charming castle, while to the south, Middelheim contains an outdoor sculpture museum of exceptional quality.

Antwerp's steel-and-glass Centraal Station, a monument to the railroad era

🚇 Centraal Station

Koningin Astridplein. **Open** daily.

Antwerp's main railway station is a grand building designed in extravagant Neo-Classical style by the well known Bruges architect Louis Delacenserie, and built over seven years, between 1898 and 1905. With its grand staircases, columns, marble and gold decorative flourishes, Antwerp's palatial station speaks of a bygone age, when rail was considered the king of luxury travel. A family theme park, **Comics Station Antwerp**, featuring all the most popular Belgian comic strip characters, is scheduled to open in a corner of the Centraal Station by the end of 2017.

🐾 Antwerp Zoo

Koningin Astridplein 20–26. **Tel** (03) 2024540. **Open** 10am–6pm Mon–Sat (until 7pm on Sun). ♿
W zooantwerpen.be

Founded in 1843, the Antwerp Zoo is one of the oldest zoos in the world. It emphasizes wildlife conservation with a resolutely modern approach. It has a superb tropical

reptile house and a giant reef aquarium with more than 4,000 fish and a wealth of tropical corals, along with all the other usual favourites - penguins, elephants and hippos. The zoo offers plenty for children of all ages to enjoy.

🏛 Middelheimmuseum

Middelheimlaan 61. **Tel** (03) 2883360. **Open** Tue–Sun. 📷 ♿
W middelheimmuseum.be

The large, wooded park of the open-air Middelheimmuseum (or the Openluchtmuseum voor Beelhouwkunst) provides a sympathetic setting for 215 sculptures from the 19th century to the present day. Works by artists such as Auguste Rodin, Henry Moore, Barbara Hepworth, Georges Minne, Rik Wouters, Juan Muñoz, Panamarenko, Chris Burden, Dan Graham, Ai Weiwei and Roman Signer give a unique overview of more than a century of visual arts. The open spaces form the perfect backdrop for the sculptures to come into their own. The museum represents the pinnacle of a policy to decorate public spaces with contemporary sculpture, a trend that can be seen all over Belgium.

Every year renowned and promising artists are invited to create new work. Freed from the constraints of the typical "white cube" of a museum hall, the artists interact with the endless opportunities offered by the park and the existing collection, which inspires them to create original pieces, custom-made for the museum. Artists with whom the museum has collaborated include Berlinde De Bruyckere, Wim Delvoye, Yoshitomo Nara, Paul McCarthy, Chris Burden, John Körmeling and Erwin Wurm.

With an average of 300,000 visitors per year and free entry, the Middelheimmuseum is a gateway to modern and contemporary art for young and old, from nature lovers to art experts. It provides an environment where culture and recreation come together in perfect harmony.

A Dog of Flanders

The suburb of Hoboken is the setting for the children's book *A Dog of Flanders*, which is most popular in Japan. It was written by the British author Marie Louise de la Ramée (1839–1908), an animal rights activist and literary figure, under the pen-name Ouida. Inspired by a visit to Antwerp in 1871, the story is of an orphaned boy, Nello, and his dog Patrasche, who take a milk cart into Antwerp each day. A series of tragic events leads to their deaths in front of Rubens's *Descent from the Cross* in Onze-Lieve-Vrouwekathedraal. Fans travel from Japan to visit the bronze statue of these two figures at Kapelstraat 3, Hoboken, and the commemorative bench by the cathedral.

Statue of Nello and Patrasche

A 60-Minute Walk Around Cogels-Osylei

The most famous street in the district of Zurenborg in southern Antwerp, Cogels-Osylei developed as a home of the wealthy between 1894 and 1906. Local architects designed mansions using a vast range of styles: Gothic, Byzantine, Baroque, Neo-Classical, a fusion of historic influences (Eclectic style), and even the newly minted Art Nouveau. With mosaics, statues, turrets and ironwork, the houses can be palatial, artistic or splendidly flamboyant. The most striking characteristic is the extraordinary individuality expressed in such a concentrated area.

⑤ Pure lines and white shades at the mansion at Cogels-Osylei 32–36

② Decorative summer mosaic on one of the four De Vier Seizoenen

Waterloostraat

Beginning at Guldenvliesstraat, walk straight up Waterloostraat till De Slag van Waterloo (The Battle of Waterloo) house ①, which has Art Nouveau ironwork and a mosaic commemorating the battle as well as profiles of Wellington and Napoleon. At the crossroads is a quartet of houses by Joseph Bascourt (1863–1927). Known as De Vier Seizoenen (The Four Seasons) ②, each has an Art Nouveau mosaic depicting a season. Take a right turn at the end of the street.

Transvaalstraat

Another Bascourt house stands on the left at No. 56. Built in

1898, it is named Boreas ③, after the Greek god of the north wind, and has an unusual projecting oriel window. Continue till the Tramplein and take the first right turn.

Cogels-Osylei

A set of contrasting houses line up at the turn into Cogles-Osylei. De Zevensterre (The Seven Stars) ④, at No. 17, has turrets and gables. Further down, at a roundabout, is the white palace

at 32–36 ⑤, dominated by French Neo-Classical taste and built between 1897 and 1899. Next is De Huize Zonnebloem (The Sunflower House) ⑥. Art Nouveau-style organic shapes cover this pretty mansion designed in 1900. Many other styles are seen down the road, ending at Uitbreidingsstraat.

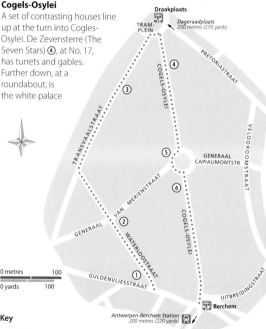

Key

••• Walk route

Tips for Walkers

Starting point: Guldenvliesstraat and Waterloostraat junction.
Length: 2 km (1.5 miles).
Getting there: Bus 9, 20 or Tram 6, 11 to Cogels-Osylei, a short walk from Guldenvliesstraat.
Cafés and restaurants: Try Dageraadplaats, which is 200 m (660 ft) to the north of Tramplein.

① Horseshoe arches and Art Nouveau ironwork at De Slag van Waterloo

For keys to symbols see back flap

❷ Sint-Amands

25 km (15 miles) SW of Antwerp.
Road Map C2. 🚉 8,000. 🚍 🚊
🛈 Livien van der Looystraat 10; (052) 399862. 🅦 sint-amands.be

Lying along a broad stretch of the River Scheldt, the small town of Sint-Amands is a popular destination for cyclists. It is celebrated as the birthplace of the Symbolist poet Emile Verhaeren (1855–1916), who lies buried, along with his wife, under a black marble tomb near the river. The town has a collection of his manuscripts, early editions, paintings and mementos, which is presented beautifully at the **Provinciaal Museum Emile Verhaeren**. Verhaeren wrote affectionately of a ferryman who took people across the river. The ferryman's house, **Het Veerhuis** has been restored and is used for exhibitions.

Environs
Just to the north is a defunct branch of the River Scheldt, called the **Oude Schelde**, an area of pretty countryside and cycling routes. The **Kasteel van Bornem** (Château Marnix de Ste Aldegonde) is a late 19th-century Neo-Gothic château located by the river.

🏛 **Provinciaal Museum Emile Verhaeren**
E Verhaerenstraat 71. **Tel** (052) 330 805.
Open Mar–Jun and Sep–Nov: 11am–6pm Sat, Sun and public holidays; Jul–Aug: 11am–6pm Tue–Sun. 🚻

🏰 **Kasteel van Bornem**
Kasteelstraat 34, Bornem. **Tel** (03) 8899009. **Open** Aug: 1:30–4pm 15 and last two Sun; Sep: 1:30–4pm first two Sun. 🚻 🅦 chateaumarnixde saintealdegonde.be

❸ Memorial Breendonk

Brandstraat 57, Willebroek; 5 km (3 miles) S of Antwerp. **Road Map** C2. **Tel** (03) 8607525. **Open** daily. 🚻 🔊 ♿ 🎧 🅦 breendonk.be

Prior to World War I, three squat, moated fortresses were built to the south of Antwerp to protect the city. They were militarily ineffective, but the Nazis turned one of them, Fort Breendonk,

into a concentration camp for 3,500 Belgian political prisoners and Jews during World War II. Today, the grim, labyrinthine interior has been converted into a museum that reveals the shocking events that took place here. It pulls no punches and even includes the role of Flemish Nazis in this horror.

Environs
Another fort in this group, **Fort Liezele** is a museum covering its military history from construction to World War II.

🏛 **Fort Liezele**
Hoogstraat 29, Puurs. **Tel** (03) 8907620. **Open** 1:30–5:30pm Sat, Sun & public holidays. 🚻 🖥 🅦 fortliezele.be

❹ Turnhout

42 km (26 miles) NE of Antwerp.
Road Map D1. 🚉 40,000. 🚍 🚊
🛈 Grote Markt 44; (014) 443355.
🅦 turnhout.be

Capital of the flat, marshy heathland area known as the Kempen, Turnhout thrives on a range of light industries such as

Photographs from the World War II era on view at Memorial Breendonk

The stately Kasteel Hertogen van Brabant, close to Turnhout's Grote Markt

printing. A rich collection of historical artifacts on the Kempen region is exhibited in the town's **Taxandria Museum**. Just to its north is the tranquil **Begijnhof**, lined with houses dating from the 16th and 17th centuries. It also has a small museum about béguinage life.

Turnhout was once a part of Brabant and close to its Grote Markt is the old centre of power, the robust **Kasteel Hertogen van Brabant** (Castle of the Dukes of Brabant), surrounded by a moat. Since 1826, the town has also been famous as a manufacturer of playing cards. A former card factory here is now home to the **Nationaal Museum van de Speelkaart** (National Playing Card Museum), which exhibits printing machines and historical cards dating from 1500.

Environs
A popular theme park located 12 km (7 miles) to the south of Turnhout, **Bobbejaanland** has more than 50 thrilling rides and live shows.

🏛 **Taxandria Museum**
Begijnenstraat 28. **Tel** (014) 436335.
Open 2–5pm Tue–Sat, 11am–5pm Sun. 🚻

🏛 **Begijnhof**
Begijnhof 56 (museum). **Tel** (014) 421248. **Open** 2–5pm Tue–Sat, 11am–5pm Sun. 🚻 ♿

🏛 **Nationaal Museum van de Speelkaart**
Druivenstraat 18. **Tel** (014) 415621.
Open 10am–5pm Tue–Fri, 11am–5pm Sat & Sun. 🚻

🎡 **Bobbejaanland**
Olensteenweg 45, Kasterlee. **Tel** (014) 557811. **Open** end Mar–Oct; see website for details. 🚻 ♿ 🚻 🖥 📷
🅦 bobbejaanland.be

⑤ Abdij Tongerlo

Abdijstraat 40; 40 km (25 miles) SE of Antwerp. Road: **Map** D1. **Tel** (014) 539900. 🚌 **Open** Mar–Oct; see website for details. 🐾 🎦 Apr–Sep: 2:30pm Sun. 🌐 tongerlo.org

Founded in about 1130, Abdij Tongerlo is Belgium's largest Premonstratensian abbey. It is home to an almost full-size oil-on-canvas copy of Leonardo da Vinci's *Last Supper*, which was painted by an unknown artist over 1506–7. This contains many details now lost in his 1498 original in Milan. The copy came to Tongerlo in 1545, and is the centrepiece of the **Da Vinci Museum**.

Jubilee Clock with its 13 faces, on the façade of Lier's Zimmertoren

⑥ Lier

17 km (11 miles) SE of Antwerp. **Road Map** C1. 🚹 34,000. 🚃 🚌 ℹ️ Grote Markt 57; (03) 8000555. 🗓️ Sat. 🌐 visitlier.be

Built where the rivers Grote Nete and Kleine Nete meet, Lier was once a wealthy medieval town. Its **Grote Markt** is a spacious cobbled square lined with old guildhouses, an elegant Stadhuis and a fairytale belfry. Nearby is the **Stedelijk Museum Wuyts-Van Campen en Baron Caroly**, with a fine collection of paintings by Flemish masters and early 20th-century Belgians. In 1496, the marriage of Philip the Fair and Joanna of Castile took place in **Sint-Gummaruskerk**, a Brabant Gothic church, whose stained-glass windows were given by Emperor Maximilian I in 1516. Lier is above all famous for its **Zimmertoren**, a 14th-century

watchtower that now houses the clocks and workshop of clockmaker Lodewijk Zimmer (1888–1970).

🏛️ **Stedelijk Museum Wuyts-Van Campen en Baron Caroly**
Florent van Cauwenberghstraat 14. **Tel** (03) 8000396. **Open** Tue–Sun. 🐾

⛪ **Sint-Gummaruskerk**
Kardinaal Mercierplein 8. **Open** Easter–Oct. 🐾 🌐 sintgummaruskerktelier.be

🕰️ **Zimmertoren**
Zimmerplein 18. **Tel** (03) 8000395. **Open** Tue–Sun. 🐾 🌐 zimmertoren.be

⑦ Mechelen

25 km (15 miles) S of Antwerp. **Road Map** C2. 🚹 80,000. 🚃 🚌 ℹ️ Hallestraat 2-6; (070) 222800. 🎭 Hanswijk Processie (Sun before Ascension Day). 🌐 toerisme. mechelen.be

The historic city of Mechelen, on the River Dijle, has exceptional charm. Its large Grote Markt has a curious **Stadhuis** that combines a 14th-century Lakenhalle and a Flamboyant Gothic galleried wing, begun in 1530 but completed only in 1911. The city's magnificent **Sint-Rombout-skathedraal** is the seat of the Catholic archbishop of Belgium. The cathedral took some 300 years to build and its colossal 97-m (318-ft) high tower is one of the tallest in Belgium. Its interior is part Gothic, part Baroque, and has many prized paintings, including a *Crucifixion* (1627) by van Dyck. Mechelen's **Hof van Busleyden** museum occupies a 16th-century mansion, and

Mechelen's magnificent Stadhuis decked in flowers and flags

The large Grote Markt at Mechelen busy with stalls and shoppers

owns a collection that includes the city's mascot, a wooden doll called Op Signoorke. The nearby **Sint-Janskerk** has a rich Baroque interior and a version of *The Adoration of the Magi* (1619) by Rubens.

Mechelen owes its riches to the cloth trade and tapestry weaving. This heritage can be seen at the royal tapestry workshops of **Koninklijke Manufactuur de Wit**. The city also has **Speelgoedmuseum**, an excellent toy museum. In the north of Mechelen are 18th-century barracks from where, in 1942–4, 25,484 Jews and 352 Roma were deported to Auschwitz, Poland. This chilling story is told at **Kazerne Dossin**.

Just southeast of Mechelen is a branch of Antwerp Zoo, **Planckendael Animal Park**, with several trails, exotic animals and treetop walkways.

⛪ **Sint-Romboutskathedraal**
Sint-Romboutshof. **Tel** (015) 297655. **Open** 1:30–5:30pm daily (Tower: 1–6pm Thu–Tue). 🎦 for tower.

🏛️ **Hof van Busleyden**
Frederik de Merodestraat 65-7. **Tel** (015) 294030. **Open** Thu–Sun.

🏛️ **Koninklijke Manufactuur de Wit**
Refugie van de Abdij van Tongerlo, Schoutetstraat 7. **Tel** (015) 202905. **Open** by reservation only at visitdewit@telenet.be. 🐾 🎦 🌐 dewit.be

🏛️ **Kazerne Dossin**
Goswin de Stassartstraat 153. **Tel** (015) 290660. **Open** Thu–Tue. **Closed** Jewish holidays. 🌐 kazernedossin.eu

🐾 **Planckendael Animal Park**
Leuvensteenweg 582. **Tel** (015) 414921. **Open** daily. 🐾 🚲 🍴 🛒 📷 🌐 planckendael.be

A row of high-gabled, brick houses in the Oud Markt, Leuven ▶

❽ Leuven

Located within easy striking distance of Brussels, the historic Flemish town of Leuven traces its origins to a fortified camp constructed here by Julius Caesar. In medieval times, the town became an important centre of the cloth trade, but it was as a seat of learning that it achieved international prominence. In 1425, Pope Martin V and Count John of Brabant founded Leuven's university, and by the mid-1500s it was one of Europe's most prestigious academic institutions, the home of such famous scholars as Erasmus and Mercator. Today, the university exercises a strong influence over the town, and its students give Leuven a vibrant atmosphere. The bars and cafés flanking the Oude Markt, a large square in the centre of town, are especially popular. Adjoining the square is the medieval Grote Markt and just out of town is the Stella Artois Brewery.

Huge buttresses supporting the Gothic structure of St-Pieterskerk

Lively café society at the Oude Markt

▣ Oude Markt

This handsome, cobblestoned square is flanked by a tasteful ensemble of high-gabled brick buildings. Some of these date from the 18th century, while others are comparatively new. At ground level, these buildings house the largest concentration of bars and cafés in town, and as such, attract the town's university students in droves.

▣ Stadhuis

Grote Markt. **Tel** (016) 203020. **Open** daily. 🕌 🎫 obligatory; 3pm daily.

Built between 1439 and 1463 from the profits of the cloth trade, Leuven's Stadhuis was designed to demonstrate the wealth of the city's merchants. This tall and distinctive building is renowned for its lavishly carved and decorated façade. A line of narrow windows rises up over three floors beneath a steeply pitched roof adorned with dormer windows and pencil-thin turrets. However, it is in the exquisite quality of

its stonework that the building excels, with delicately carved tracery and detailed medieval figures beneath 300 niche bases. There are grotesques of every description as well as representations of folktales and biblical stories, all of which are carved in an exuberant late-Gothic style. Within the niche alcoves are 19th-century statues depicting local dignitaries and politicians. Guided tours (in Dutch and several other languages) of the interior include three lavish reception rooms. When visitors

The elaborate stonework and spires of Leuven's Gothic town hall

buy a ticket, they receive an informative booklet in a choice of several languages.

🏛 St-Pieterskerk and Museum Schatkamer van St Pieter

Grote Markt. **Tel** (016) 295133. **Open** 10am–4:30pm Mon–Sat, 11am–4:30pm Sun & public holidays. **Closed** Wed. 🕌 to museum.

Across the square from the Stadhuis rises St-Pieterskerk, a massive church built over a period of 200 years from the 1420s. The nave and aisles were completed first, but when the twin towers of the western façade were finally added in 1507, the foundations proved inadequate and it soon began to sink. With money in short supply, it was decided to remove the top sections of the towers – hence the truncated versions of today.

Inside the church, the sweeping lines of the nave are intercepted by an impressive 1499 rood screen and a Baroque wooden pulpit depicting the conversion of St Norbert (see p167). Norbert was a wealthy but irreligious German noble, who was hit by lightning while riding. His horse died, but he was unhurt and this led him to devote himself to the Church.

The church also houses the treasury of St Peter which has three exquisite paintings by Dirk Bouts (1415–75), including his *Last Supper* triptych, painted in 1468, and the gory yet sedate *Martyrdom of Saint Erasmus*. Both provide vivid glimpses of

15th-century life in Flanders. Although he was born in the Netherlands, Dirk Bouts spent most of his working life in Leuven, where he won himself a position as the town's official artist.

M-Museum Leuven
Leopold Vanderkelenstraat 28.
Tel (016) 272929. **Open** 11am–6pm Tue–Sun, 11am–10pm Thu.
mleuven.be

The former Museum Vander Kelen-Mertens was revamped as M in 2009 to provide a dynamic space for high-profile temporary art exhibitions and underline Leuven's claim to be a major city of the arts. The original collection still remains in the 17th–18th century mansion, owned by the Vander Kelen-Mertens family until it was donated to the city in 1918. The rooms were refurbished in a variety of historical styles, ranging from a Renaissance salon to a Rococo dining room, each with the appropriate antique furniture, silverware and ceramics.

Much of the art on permanent display is by the early Flemish Masters, including Quentin Metsys (1466–1530), who was born in Leuven and is noted for introducing Italian style to northern European art. It also houses a lovely version of the *Holy Trinity* by the famed artist, Rogier van der Weyden (*see p106*).

University Library
Monseigneur Ladeuzeplein 21.
Tel (016) 203020 **Open** 10am–5pm Mon, Wed, Fri, Sat & Sun; 1pm–5pm Tue & Thu. **bib.kuleuven.be**

Risen from the ashes of World War I and World War II, this imposing Renaissance-style palace was rebuilt twice as "a cathedral of knowledge", with more than 1.5 million books stored over five floors. A photographic exhibition details the history of the library, and the Great Reading Room is worth a visit. Visitors can also climb the 300 steps of the library tower to the balcony from which there is a panoramic view of the city.

The ILuvLeuven combi ticket allows entry to the University Library and Tower, as well as to the Stadhuis, M-Museum Leuven and the Treasury of St-Pieterskerk.

Groot Begijnhof
Schapenstraat.
Founded around 1230, the Groot Begijnhof was once one of the largest béguinages in Belgium and home to several hundred béguines (*see p65*). The

VISITORS' CHECKLIST

Practical Information
64 km (40 miles) SE of Antwerp.
Road Map D2. 97,300.
Naamsestraat 3; (016) 203020.
Christmas Markt (10 days in Dec). **leuven.be**

Transport
Bondgenotenlaan. 20, 50.

complex of 72 charming red-brick cottages, dating mostly from the 17th century, is set around grassy squares and cobbled streets near the River Dijle. The university in Leuven bought it in 1962 and converted the cottages into student accommodation which can be viewed from outside.

The 17th-century red-brick houses of Leuven's Groot Begijnhof

Leuven

① Oude Markt
② Stadhuis
③ St-Pieterskerk and Museum Schatkamer van St Pieter
④ M-Museum Leuven
⑤ University Library

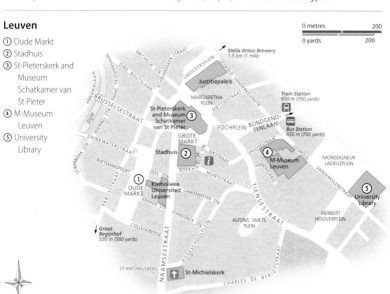

The distinctive bulbous spire of Aarschot's Onze-Lieve-Vrouwekerk

❾ Aarschot

16 km (10 miles) NE of Leuven.
Road Map D2. 🚉 28,000. 🚗 🚌
ⓘ Elisabethlaan 103; (016) 569705.
ⓦ hetgasthuis.be/toerisme

The pleasant, busy town of Aarschot on the River Demer lies in the undulating, agricultural region of eastern Vlaams-Brabant known as Hageland (Hedge Country). The town's most striking building is the 14th-century **Onze-Lieve-Vrouwekerk** built in the Gothic style, with iron-rich, rust-red sandstone, and an immediately recognizable black onion-shaped spire. The striped interior contains an ornate stone rood screen and an elaborately carved wooden pulpit and choir stalls. Among the church's notable collection of paintings is *The Mystic Winepress*, a work by an unknown artist, dating from 1525. In it, a series of scenes show how Christ's blood is treated just like wine by his apostles, the Church and the Holy Roman Emperor.

West of the church along the river is the **Begijnhof**, with fetching rows of 17th-century houses forming a U-shape around a large garden. The tourist office, to the north of the river, is attached to a small local history museum.

🏛 **Onze-Lieve-Vrouwekerk**
Jan van Ophemstraat 23. **Tel** (016) 560930. **Open** 9am–noon daily.

❿ Onze-Lieve-Vrouw van Scherpenheuvel

Isabellaplein, Scherpenheuvel; 10 km (6 miles) E of Aarschot. **Road Map** D2. **Tel** (013) 355641. 🚌 ⓘ Basilieklaan 16; (013) 772081. **Open** 7:30am–6:30pm daily. ♿ 📷 ✝
🎭 Kaarskensprocessie (Nov).

Once the site of a sacred oak tree, Scherpenheuvel (Sharp Hill) remains a revered pilgrimage site. In the 14th century, a statue of Mary and the child Jesus was placed here and became known for the miraculous healing powers it was reputed to have. However, it was destroyed by Protestant iconoclasts in 1580.

In 1605, the Infanta Isabella and Archduke Albert, joint governors of the Spanish Netherlands, ordered the construction of the present elegant Baroque Basilica of Our Lady. Mass is held four times a day in its richly ornate interior before an elaborately dressed copy of the original statue.

⓫ Abdij van Averbode

Abdijstraat 1B, Averbode, 11 km (7 miles) NE of Scherpenheuvel. **Road Map** D2. **Tel** (013) 780440. 🚌 **Open** 10am–12pm and 1–5:30pm daily. 📷 ⓦ abdijaverbode.be

A large and active abbey of the Premonstratensian Order, Abdij van Averbode was founded in 1134–35. Its entrance gate dates from the 14th century, while

Baroque ornament on the façade of Averbode's abbey church

many buildings of the inner court are from the 17th century. This was built over 1664–72 with an icing-sugar-white interior offset by Baroque ornamentation in black and grey marble, all lit by clear-glass windows. South of the abbey, marked walking trails lead into the **Averbode Bos en Heide**, a large area of woodland and heath. Although the abbey is closed to visitors, the church and its grounds are open.

⓬ Diest

10 km (6 miles) S of Averbode.
Road Map D2. 🚉 23,000. 🚗 🚌
ⓘ Grote Markt 1; (013) 353274.
ⓦ toerismediest.be

As it belonged to the House of Orange from 1499 to 1794, and has connections with the present royal family of the Netherlands, Diest calls itself the "Oranje stad". A network of shopping streets leads up to the handsome, L-shaped Grote Markt, overlooked by the 18th-century Neo-Classical **Stadhuis**. The medieval crypt of the Stadhuis contains the **Stadsmuseum de Hofstadt**, which has an admirable collection of paintings, sculpture, armour, furniture and silverware. Next to it stands the Gothic **St-Sulpitiuskerk**, the church of St Sulpice who was a 7th-century saint. Much of the exterior of the splendid church is built of red, iron-rich sandstone. Its dainty little spire over the crossing, where the transept meets the nave, is known affectionately as the "mustardpot" and has a carillon of 32 bells. The soaring and richly decorated interior includes a treasury museum, with precious reliquaries and chalices, as well as an exceptional collection of religious sculptures. Some of these masterpieces of artistry in painted wood date from the 15th century.

Prefaced by an elaborate Baroque entrance, Diest's vast **Begijnhof** is one of the most beautiful in Belgium. Its grid of cobbled streets is lined with whitewashed or brick houses, mainly from the 16th century. Its Church of St Catherine, or **St-Catharinakerk**, was built

The striking red-and-white St-Sulpitiuskerk, in the heart of Diest

during the 14th century and has a charming interior of white and red sandstone, with a fine Baroque wooden screen and pulpit.

🏛 Stadsmuseum de Hofstadt
Stadhuis, Grote Markt. **Tel** (013) 353274. **Open** Apr–Oct: 10am–noon and 1–5pm Tue, Thu–Sat (1–5pm Wed and Sun); Nov–Mar: 1–5pm Tue–Sun. **Closed** Oct–Apr: Mon. 🚫

⛪ St-Sulpitiuskerk
Grote Markt. **Tel** (013) 353271. **Open** mid-May–mid-Sep: 2–5pm Tue–Sun. 🚫 treasury. 📷

⑫ Zoutleeuw

29 km (18 miles) E of Leuven. **Road Map** D2. 🚶 8,000. 🚌 ℹ Grote Markt; (011) 781288. 🌐 zoutleeuw.be

Before falling on leaner times, Zoutleeuw was a prosperous cloth town in the Middle Ages. This explains its 16th-century **Stadhuis**, the 14th-century cloth hall in the Grote Markt and above all, the scale and splendour of the medieval **St-Leonarduskerk**, the Church of St Leonard. The exterior of the structure has an unusual lopsided pair of towers and a bulbous spire, but the interior of the church is magnificent, since it escaped vandalization both by Protestants in the 16th century and by French Revolutionaries in the 1790s. Today, it is richly decorated with paintings and sculpture. Suspended in the nave is an unusual **Marianum**, a painted wrought-iron image of the Virgin Mary surrounded by angels, dating to 1533. In the

north transept, the **Sacramentstoren** (Tower of the Sacraments) is decorated with dozens of statues by Cornelis Floris, the designer of Antwerp's town hall

⛪ St-Leonarduskerk
Grote Markt. **Open** Apr–Sep: 2–5pm Tue–Sun; Oct: 2–5pm Sat and Sun. 🚫

⑭ Tienen

20 km (12 miles) SE of Leuven. **Road Map** D2. 🚶 32,000. 🚆 🚌 ℹ Grote Markt 6; (016) 805738. 🌐 tienen.be

Sugar beet is a key crop for Tienen (Tirlemont in French), the largest town in the largely agricultural Hageland region. It has been refining sugar since the 19th century, an occupation that has given it the nickname

Sugar Town. In celebration of this industry, the town has an interactive **Suikermuseum**, or Sugar Museum, which occupies a former courthouse in the vast **Grote Markt**, the second-largest market square in Belgium. A stone star in the square marks the place of execution and pillory which was in use until the 1840s. To the rear of the Sugar Museum is the **Stedelijk Museum Het Toreke**, housed in a 19th-century building that once served as the town's prison. Its archaeological collection explores Tienen's Gallo-Roman past and more recent history, focussing on special themes such as death rituals.

Tienen's Brabant Gothic **Onze-Lieve-Vrouw-ten-Poelkerk** was built beside a *poel* (pool) and sacred spring between the 13th and 15th centuries. It has a strangely truncated look as there is no nave. The west door, built in 1360, has an unusually deep, arched portal that leads straight into the transept.

🏛 Suikermuseum
Grote Markt. **Tel** (016) 805686. **Open** 10am–5pm Tue–Sun. 🚫 📷 🌐 erfgoedsitetienen.be

⛪ Onze-Lieve-Vrouw- ten-Poelkerk
Grote Markt. **Open** 9am–7pm Mon and Thu, 9am–6pm Tue, Wed and Fri, 3–6pm Sat, 9am–12:30pm Sun.

The Premonstratensians

St Norbert (1080–1134) was a German noble who underwent a sudden conversion at the age of 35 and abandoned his wealth to devote his life to religion. In 1120, he established a community at Prémontré, in northeastern France. Although members of the order wore white habits, they were not monks cloistered in monasteries. Instead, they were canons – priests who live in a community but actively engage with the world outside. St Norbert's approach to religious devotion proved influential in the Low Countries and Germany. The order was suppressed by the French occupation of the 1790s, but dramatically revived in 19th-century Belgium. Today, the abbeys of Averbode, Tongerlo, Parc, Grimbergen and Postel are active houses of the order.

St Norbert, founder of the Premonstratensian Order

The medieval castle of Bouchout at the Nationale Plantentuin

⓯ Nationale Plantentuin

Nieuwlaan 38, Meise; 12 km (7 miles) N of Brussels. **Road Map** C2. **Tel** (02) 2600970. 🚌 **Open** Apr–Sep: 9:30am–6:30pm daily, Oct–Nov: 9:30am–5pm daily. 🚻 ♿ 🚻 🍴
W br.fgov.be

The Domein van Bouchout is the old estate of the 14th-century castle of **Bouchout**. In 1938, the Belgian state bought the domain and made it the Nationale Plantentuin (National Botanic Garden), essentially a research institution that is also open to the public.

Marked paths take visitors around the arboretum and lake, and to the greenhouses which contain some 18,000 plant species from all of the world's climates. The **Balat Greenhouse** was designed by Alphonse Balat in 1854, in advance of his spectacular greenhouses at Laeken (see p88). The **Plantenpaleis** (Plant Palace), a cluster of 35 hothouses, includes **Victoria House** with its giant lillies.

⓰ St-Servaasbasiliek Grimbergen

Kerkplein 1, Grimbergen; 2 km (1 mile) E of Meise. **Road Map** C2. **Tel** (02) 2724060. 🛈 Prinsenstraat 22; (02) 2601296. **Open** 7am–6pm daily. ♿
W abdijgrimbergen.be

The town of Grimbergen is well known for its abbey of the Premonstratensian Order (see p167) and its abbey beer. Founded by St Norbert in 1128, the abbey was destroyed by

Protestants in 1579. When it was re-established, the St-Servaasbasiliek was built in glorious Baroque style with a soaring interior that rises to a large lantern over the crossing. The black-and-white marble altarpiece clamours with apostles, prophets, trumpeting cherubs and garlands, reaching a crescendo at the shining cross. The oak pulpit and the elaborate confessionals were the work of noted Antwerp-born sculptor and architect Hendrik Verbruggen (c.1655–1724). The tower contains a carillon of 48 bells.

⓱ Halle

19 km (10 miles) SW of Brussels. **Road Map** C2. 🚆 36,830. 🚉 🚌 🛈 Grote Markt 1; (02) 3564259.
W toerisme-halle.be

Since its early history, Halle has played an important role as a strategic border town between Brabant and Hainaut. In 1267, a

The sacred Black Virgin at the St-Martinusbasiliek in Halle

miraculous wooden statue of the Virgin Mary named the **Black Virgin** was brought here, making Halle a major pilgrimage centre, visited by nobility and royalty, including Edward I of England, Louis XI of France and Philip, Duke of Burgundy (who died here in 1404). The statue is the most precious treasure of the **St-Martinusbasiliek**. This 14th-century basilica is a fascinating confection. Its tower, with a 54-bell carillon, has a 17th-century lantern. Next to it stands the octagonal baptistery with a curious ball-shaped top. The sublime interior contains many treasures, including a second Black Virgin. Cannon balls in the porch are relics of sieges that occurred in 1489 and 1580. Close to the choir is the tomb and effigy of Joachim, infant son of the Louis XI who died in 1460 while Louis was hiding from his father under the protection of Philip the Good.

🏛 St-Martinusbasiliek

Grote Markt. **Open** 8am–6pm daily. 🚪 tower and crypt (treasury).

⓲ Kasteel van Beersel

Lotsestraat, Beersel; 9 km (6 miles) NE of Halle. **Road Map** C2. **Tel** (02) 3591646. **Open** Mar–Nov: 10am–6pm daily. 🚪

Rising out of its broad moat, the 14th-century castle of Beersel cuts a distinctive profile. Its three semicircular red-brick towers have robust exterior walls, while their flat, step-gabled sides face inwards onto a galleried courtyard. The castle was badly damaged during the 1489 rebellion against Maximilian I (see p44), but was rebuilt. It became a cotton factory in the 19th century, but fell into disrepair and was restored to its present condition only in the 20th century.

Environs
Located 4 km (2 miles) to the southwest, **Provinciedomein Huizingen** is the old estate of a

château and is now an extensive recreational park with playgrounds, sports facilities, a swimming pool, mini-golf, rowing on the lake and imaginative gardens that include a garden for the blind.

🏠 **Provinciedomein Huizingen**
Torleylaan 100, Huizingen. **Tel** (02) 3830020. **Open** Apr–Sep: 9am–8pm daily; Oct–Mar: 9am–sunset daily. 🅿️
W **vlaamsbrabant.be**

⑲ Kasteel van Gaasbeek

Kasteelstraat Gaasbeek; 8 km (5 miles) NW of Beersel. **Road Map** C2. **Tel** (02) 5310130. 🚌 **Open** Apr–Nov: 10am–6pm Tue–Sun. 🅿️ 🖼️ 📷 📷
W **kasteelvangaas beek.be**

Essentially a Neo-Renaissance and Neo-Gothic reconstruction, the castle of Gaasbeek was built on a grand scale and in great detail by Marie, Marquise Arconati Visconti (1840–1923). She donated it to the Belgian state in 1921. Tours led by well-informed guides pass through a series of luxurious rooms, decorated in a way that medieval nobles might have enjoyed. To achieve this effect, the Marquise amassed a wealth of exquisite artifacts, including medieval sculpture, valuable paintings, antique furniture and Brussels tapestries. The castle also runs temporary exhibitions. Gaasbeek is located on the site of an ancient and important 13th-century fortress that was

Wood-panelled walls and paintings in the hall at Kasteel van Gaasbeek

the home of Count Egmont (*see p45*). Some of the original castle is still visible within the current one. It stands in a commanding position, surrounded by beautiful wooded parkland, which includes a "museum garden" in the 19th-century style.

Beyond the castle lies the **Pajottenland**, an area of rolling hills and farms, often painted by Pieter Brueghel the Elder in the 16th century.

⑳ Forêt de Soignes

15 km (9 miles) E of Gaasbeek. **Road Map** C2. 🚌 41, 71, 72. M Hermann Debroux. 🚋 23, 44, 90.
W **sonianforest.be**

An old ducal hunting forest, the Sonian Forest (Forêt de Soignes in French and Zoniënwoud in Dutch) once covered much of

southern Brabant. Today, it stretches for 44 sq km (17 sq miles) and is a popular place for walking, cycling and horse riding. Splendid beech trees arch over a network of pathways like cathedrals, turning golden in autumn. In fact, this was formerly an oak forest, but was ransacked by Napoleon to build a fleet. Several monasteries were founded here in medieval times, but most have vanished. Among those that have survived are buildings of the **Abbaye de Rouge-Cloître** at Auderghem, which now house an arts centre and restaurant. The beautiful grounds of a 14th–18th-century priory at Hoeilaart form the **Groenendaal Arboretum**, with more than 400 tree species. The **Geografisch Arboretum** at Tervuren, with 460 species, also adjoins the forest.

The Forêt de Soignes, once a royal hunting ground and now a park

Gin and distilling apparatus at the Nationaal Jenevermuseum, Hasselt

㉑ St-Truiden

20 km (12 miles) E of Tienen.
Road Map D2. 🚗 39,800. 🚉 🚌
ℹ️ Grote Markt 44; (011) 701818. 🛒
🌐 toerisme-sint-truiden.be

The attractive market town of
St-Truiden lies in the western
sector of the Haspengouw, a
region noted for its spring
blossom and for orchards of
apples, pears and cherries.
The town is named after its
Benedictine abbey, founded
around AD 660 by St Trudo, a
nobleman-turned-evangelist.
The abbey was closed during the
French Revolutionary occupation
in the 1790s. Its 11th-century
Abdijtoren is one of three towers
that line up on the northern
side of the large Grote Markt.
The second is the **Belfort**, built in
1606 and attached incongruously
to the red 18th-century Stadhuis.
In front of the Belfort is a perron,
a place marked by a column,
where laws were promulgated
and justice meted out. The
perron was a symbol of liberty
under the rule of the prince-
bishops of Liège (13th–15th
centuries). The third tower is
the 19th-century spire of the
Onze-Lieve-Vrouwkerk.

In the northeast of the town,
a set of pretty 16th- to 18th-
century houses cluster around
a square in the begijnhof.
The charming barrel-vaulted
church, the **Begijnhofkerk**,
has a remarkable set of murals
dating from the 13th to the
17th centuries.

The **Festraetsstudio** contains
a famous astronomical clock,
6-m (20-ft) tall, created by
master clockmaker Kamiel
Festraets between 1937 and

1942. It has 20,000 parts and is
animated by moving figures
when the clock strikes.

🕐 Abdijtoren
Abdijstraat. **Open** 9am–5pm daily.
Closed 1 Jan, 25, 26 & 31 Dec. 🎫

🕐 Begijnhofkerk
Begijnhof. **Open** Apr–Sep:
10am–12:30pm & 1:30–5pm
Mon–Fri, 2–5pm Sat & Sun.

🏛️ Festraetsstudio
Begijnhof. **Open** 10:30am–12:30pm
& 1:30–4:30pm Mon–Fri, 1:30–4:30pm
Sat & Sun.

St-Truiden's 18th-century Stadhuis with the
Belfort rising behind it

㉒ Hasselt

20 km (12 miles) NE of St-Truiden.
Road Map E2. 🚗 80,000. 🚉 🚌
ℹ️ Maastrichterstraat 59; (011)
239540. 🌐 visithasselt.be

Capital of the Province of Limburg,
Hasselt is a busy modern town,
famous as a historic centre of
jenever (gin) production. The
history of *jenever* is stylishly
explained in a former distillery at
the **Nationaal Jenevermuseum**.
The fashion museum, the
Modemuseum Hasselt, mounts
thematic exhibitions drawing
on its extensive collection of
historical costumes.

Hasselt also has the **Japanse
Tuin**, a remarkable garden
created with its Japanese twin
town, Itami. With rocks, winding
paths, waterfalls, blossom trees
and ceremonial buildings by a
large carp pond, the garden has a
refreshing air of authenticity. On
the other side of the ring road is
Plopsa Indoor Hasselt, an all-
weather theme park for children.

🏛️ Nationaal Jenevermuseum
Wittenonnenstraat 19. **Tel** (011)
239860. **Open** Tue–Sun. **Closed**
3 weeks in Jan, 24, 25 & 31 Dec. 🎫
📷 🌐 jenevermuseum.be

🌷 Japanse Tuin
Gouverneur Verwilghensingel.
Open Apr–Oct: 10am–5pm
Tue–Fri, 2–6pm Sat, Sun &
public holidays. 🎫

🎡 Plopsa Indoor Hasselt
Gouverneur Verwilghensingel 70.
Tel (011) 293040. **Open** school holidays:
daily; school term: 10am–6pm Wed–
Sun (until 5:30 pm Sat & Sun).
📱 📷 ♿ 🌐 plopsa.be

Jenever

The original gin, *jenever* is a strong alcoholic drink distilled
from grain, usually malted barley. Invented in the 16th century,
jenever was originally a medicine named
after its key ingredient, juniper berries.
Today, it is produced in Belgium and
the Netherlands in countless different
styles, and with flavourings such as
orange, lemon, apple, hazelnut, vanilla
and chocolate. *Oude* (old) and *jonge*
(young) describe variant distilling
techniques (rather than ageing) – *jonge*
styles, introduced in around 1900, have a
lighter, less malty flavour. *Jenever*,
in all its various forms, is always
consumed neat.

Ceramic bottles of
flavoured *jenever*

For hotels and restaurants see p268 and pp286–8

㉓ Bokrijk Openluchtmuseum

Rescued, transported to and preserved in a large park of woodland and pasture, the Bokrijk Openluchtmuseum, or Open-air Museum, is a fascinating collection of over a 100 historic rural buildings from across Flanders. Grouped by their regional origins into three village areas, the buildings are open, revealing dimly lit interiors full of authentic furniture, furnishings and tools. Staff in traditional costume demonstrate crafts such as spinning and baking, and help create a convincing image of what daily life was like in rural Flanders before 1914.

VISITORS' CHECKLIST

Practical Information
Domein Bokrijk, Bokrijklaan 1, Genk; 8 km (5 miles) E of Hasselt. **Road Map** E2. **Tel** (011) 265300. **Open** end-Mar–end Sep: 9am– 6pm Tue–Sun (Mon in Jul & Aug).

W bokrijk.be

Transport

Interior Features
Most buildings here have original interior features, such as 18th-century fireplaces with Delft tiles that depict scenes from the Bible.

Agricultural Architecture
This 16th-century farmhouse is built in the style familiar from Brueghel's paintings. The windmill dates from 1788 and still contains the original millstones.

The fertile lowlands: East and West Flanders

The old town

The poor heathlands or the Kempen

The fertile uplands: Limburg, Haspengouw and the Maasland

0 metres 200
0 yards 200

Village Priest
Many of Bokrijk's costumed workers are on hand to explain what life was like in the pre-industrial rural areas.

Grain Store
This timber-framed *spijker* (grain store) dates from the 16th century. The building is from Limburg province, where it probably formed part of a brewery.

Display in the courtyard of the Museactron in Maaseik

㉔ Maaseik

28 km (17 miles) NE of Genk.
Road Map E1. 🚄 26,000. 🚌 🚃
ℹ️ Markt 1; (089) 819290. 🚲
Halfvastenstoet (Mar). 🅆 **maaseik.be**

Lying close to the River Meuse (Maas in Dutch), which now forms the border between Belgium and the Netherlands, Maaseik developed as a cloth town during the Middle Ages. It is thought to have been the birthplace, in about 1395, of the great pioneer oil painters Jan van Eyck and his brother Hubrecht. A statue of the siblings stands in the tree-lined **Markt**, surrounded by 17th- and 18th-century mansions.

The 19th-century Neo-Classical **St-Catharinakerk**, or St Catherine's Church, has a treasury, containing items from a local abbey, including the 8th-century *Codex Eyckensis*, which is believed to be the oldest book in Belgium. The **Regionaal Archeologisch Museum**, a revamped, inter-active archaeological museum, covers the history of the region starting from the Stone Age. It also provides access to a 17th-century apothecary shop, the Apothekersmuseum, the earliest of its kind in Belgium. Finally, Maaseik's **John Selbach Museum** is housed within a former Ursuline convent. One collection displays more than 400 antique dolls and their accessories, the earliest dating from 1780. The second collection consists of paintings in the Romantic mode from the 16th to the 20th centuries and includes works by notable

Belgian artists such as Ferdinand Braekeleer the Elder (1792–1883).

↑ St-Catharinakerk
Kerkplein. **Open** Jan–Jun: Tue–Sun; Jul–Dec: daily. 🚲

🏛 Regionaal Archeologisch Museum
Lekkerstraat 5. **Tel** (089) 566890. **Open** Apr–Oct: 10am–5pm Tue–Sun; Nov–Mar: 10am–4pm Tue–Sun. 🚲 📷

🏛 John Selbach Museum
Boomgaardstraat 20. **Tel** (089) 622000. **Open** May–Oct: 11am–5pm Wed–Sat; Nov–Apr: 11am–4pm Wed–Sat. 🚲

㉕ Nationaal Park Hoge Kempen

Winterslagstraat 87, Genk.
Road Map E2. **Tel** (089) 655665. 🚃
ℹ️ Kattevennen (Genk), Pietersheim (Lanaken), Lieteberg (Zutendaal), Mechelse Heide (Maasmechelen) and Station As (As). 🚲 🅆 **rlkm.be**

The Kempen region of Belgium stretches from the eastern part of the Province of Antwerpen through Limburg and across the border into the Netherlands. It

Visitors enjoying a nature trail in the Nationaal Park Hoge Kempen

has a varied landscape of heath, marsh, woodland and farms. The area is sparsely populated and consequently, cherished by those seeking natural beauty and tranquillity.

A portion of this region between Maaseik and Genk was set aside in 2006 as Belgium's first national park, the Hoge Kempen (High Kempen). It covers 50 sq km (20 sq miles), containing pinewoods and quarry lakes, and features marked walking paths and cycling routes of varying lengths. The land rises to an altitude of 100 m (330 ft) in places, affording fine views.

Environs
South of the Nationaal Park Hoge Kempen, the town of **Maasmechelen** has a large "fashion village", built in an engaging traditional style. With nearly 100 outlets selling both Belgian and international labels at discount prices, plus restaurants and cafés, it attracts shoppers from neighbouring countries such as Germany and the Netherlands.

Maasmechelen
15 km (9 miles) E of Genk.
Tel (089) 774000. **Open** 10am–6pm Mon–Fri, 10am–7pm Sat & Sun. 🅆 **maasmechelenvillage.com**

㉖ Landcommanderij Alden Biesen

Kasteelstraat 6 Bilzen; 20 km (12 miles) S of Nationaal Park Hoge Kempen.
Road Map E2. **Tel** (089) 519393.
🚃 **Open** summer: 9am–5pm daily; winter: 10am–5pm daily.
Closed mid-Dec–Jan. 🚲 for permanent display and garden. 🚲
📷 🅆 **alden-biesen.be**

A magnificent red-brick castle, Alden Biesen was built between the 16th and 18th centuries with courtyards, turrets, a moat and a large Baroque chapel. It was originally founded in 1220 on land that was given to the German Order of the Teutonic Knights, whose mission was to defend Christendom. By the 16th century, the power of the order rested mainly in land-

The stately Alden Biesen castle, former headquarters of the German Order of the Teutonic Knights

holdings. Alden Biesen, as the regional headquarters, or *landcommanderij*, was an expression of this wealth, until the order was evicted in 1795 by the armies of the French Revolution. It then became a private residence.

In 1971, the main part, called the Water Castle, was gutted by fire. Although it has been restored, little of the original interior has survived. Today, the castle is used primarily as a cultural centre by the Flemish community, hosting concerts and exhibitions. The castle complex also offers a permanent display about its history, a formal French garden and beautiful parkland.

27 Tongeren

10 km (6 miles) SW of Alden Biesen.
Road Map E2. 32,000.
Via Julianus 2; (012) 800070.
Sun. tongeren.be

Tournai *(see pp184–8)* and Tongeren both claim to be Belgium's oldest town due to their Roman origins. This heritage is seen in Tongeren's **Gallo-Romeins Museum**, built on the site of a Roman villa. It contains an extensive collection of artifacts and sculptures, extending up to the Middle Ages, from the prehistoric era to the Middle Ages.

Tongeren evolved into a prosperous medieval trading centre, as can be seen in the existing traces of its city walls,

such as the **Moerenpoort**, a 14th-century city gate. Today, the **Begijnhof** nearby is a pretty area to wander in. The town is also famous for its huge antiques market.

Another landmark, the **Onze-Lieve-Vrouwebasiliek**, stands on the site of a 4th-century church. The current basilica was built between the 11th and 16th centuries. Its high and elegant Gothic interior is rich in statues and paintings, while the organ loft is a superb example of Baroque extravagance. It is famous for a miraculous statue, in painted wood, of Our Lady of Tongeren. This statue, dating from 1476, is the focal point of the Seven-yearly Kroningsfeesten, or Coronation Festival *(see p37)*, attended by what is said to be the biggest procession in the country. The church treasury

contains more early wooden sculpture, including a vividly expressive head of Christ, as well as impressively bejewelled chalices and reliquaries. The 12th-century cloister is a rare example of Romanesque architecture in Belgium

The **Haspengouw** region surrounding Tongeren is celebrated for its bountiful farms and orchards and the appealing *hoevetoerisme*, or farmhouse accommodation *(see p262)* that showcases the area's charming rural assets.

🏛 **Gallo-Romeins Museum**
Kielenstraat 15. **Tel** (012) 670330.
Open 9am–5pm Tue–Fri, 10am–6pm Sat & Sun.
W **galloromeinsmuseum.be**

🏠 **Onze-Lieve-Vrouwebasiliek**
Stadhuisplein. **Open** 9am–5pm daily.

Ambiorix and "The Bravest of the Gauls"

The leader of a Belgic tribe called the Eburones, Ambiorix is famous for mounting a fierce campaign against the Romans, who had conquered the area in 57 BC. Three years later, they wanted provisions from the Eburones to feed their troops. Ambiorix, who had gained the confidence of the Roman leaders, warned them that a massive army of Germanic tribes was on its way and persuaded them to retreat. As the Romans did so, the Eburones swooped down and massacred them. Julius Caesar decided to reap his revenge personally, and in the resulting campaign he crushed the Belgae completely. For his part, Ambiorix vanished along with his troops. These events inspired Caesar to record that "of all the Gauls, the Belgae are the bravest". Today, a 19th-century statue of Ambiorix stands in the Grote Markt of Tongeren.

Ambiorix of the Eburones

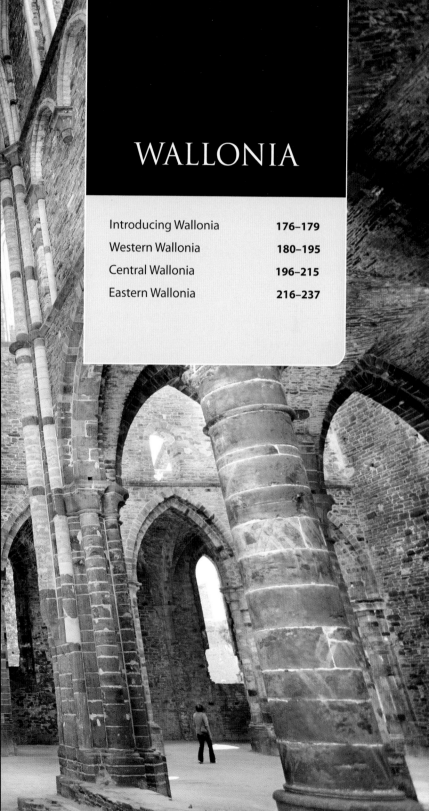

WALLONIA

Wallonia at a Glance

The southern, French-speaking part of Belgium, Wallonia gets its name from a Romanized Celtic tribe known as the Wala, whose people spoke a French-related language, Walloon. There are five provinces in this region: Hainaut forms Western Wallonia; the provinces of Namur and Brabant Wallon lie in Central Wallonia; and the provinces of Liège and Luxembourg (not to be confused with the independent Grand Duchy of Luxembourg) make up Eastern Wallonia. The largest cities lie in the old industrial heartland that stretches across the north from Charleroi to Liège. Further south, the landscape rises into the Ardennes, with its forested hills and riverside towns and hamlets.

Locator Map

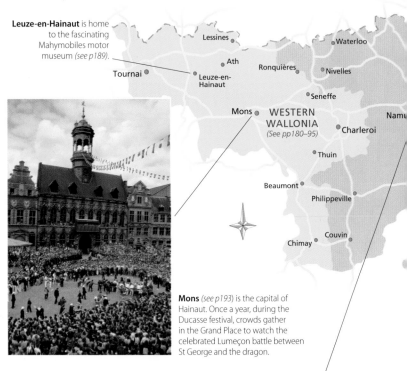

Leuze-en-Hainaut is home to the fascinating Mahymobiles motor museum (see p189).

Mons (see p193) is the capital of Hainaut. Once a year, during the Ducasse festival, crowds gather in the Grand Place to watch the celebrated Lumeçon battle between St George and the dragon.

Namur (see pp206–7), capital of the Province of Namur, lies on the confluence of the rivers Sambre and Meuse. Dominating this busy city is the massive Citadelle, a stronghold reinforced over 2,000 years of military use, which finally ended in 1977.

◄ Ruins of the Cistercian Abbeye de Villers in Villers-la-Ville, Central Wallonia

Rochefort *(see p215)*, in the Province of Namur, is one of many places in the Ardennes to have an extensive cave system *(see pp212–13)*. The Grotte de Lorette-Rochefort has a visitor centre, from where paths lead sharply down for 80 m (262 ft), past encrustations of stalactites and stalagmites, to halls of vast, rugged rock.

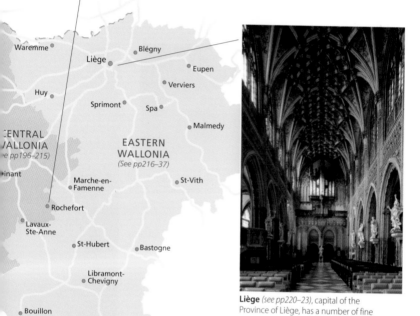

Liège *(see pp220–23)*, capital of the Province of Liège, has a number of fine churches. This includes the superb Église St-Jacques, which fuses the Romanesque with Flamboyant Gothic.

| 0 kilometres | 25 |
| 0 miles | 25 |

Bouillon *(see pp234–7)*, located in the south of the Ardennes, is famous for its picturesque medieval castle set on a rocky spur near the Semois. Once the home of the 11th-century crusader knight Godefroi de Bouillon, the castle now forms a romantic backdrop to this quiet and elegant little town.

The Ardennes

The region known as the Ardennes stretches across southern Belgium and into Luxembourg, France and Germany. Located south of the River Meuse, it comprises forested hills and valleys cut by a network of winding, picturesque rivers, notably the Lesse, Semois, Ourthe and Amblève. Namur, Liège and Dinant are the main urban centres, but the Ardennes is predominantly rural and sparsely populated, with river-basin farms and small villages, and areas of upland pasture. The Romans named this forested land after the local Celtic goddess Arduinna. For centuries, it was a backwater, but today its large expanses of unspoilt nature attract numerous visitors who come to walk, cycle, canoe or simply to motor and enjoy the views.

Locator Map
◼ Ardennes

The River Meuse *(see p210)* forms the natural northern boundary to the Ardennes region. This navigable waterway links the cities of Dinant and Namur to Liège. Beyond that, it leads eventually to the North Sea. When Wallonia was the centre of Belgium's old heavy industries, the river was a vital transport artery.

An Astonishing Landcape

Beauty and variety of landscape: these are the principal attractions of the Ardennes. In places, the rivers and hills conspire to produce dramatic effects, as seen at the famous Tombeau du Géant (The Giant's Tomb), a strangely regular wooded hill almost encircled by a typically extravagant loop of the River Semois.

Han-sur-Lesse *(see p215)* has the best of the many caves that are open to public. Over thousands of years, water has drilled away the limestone rock, creating spectacular tunnels and galleries dripping with stalactites.

Kayaking *(see p305)* is a major holiday pursuit on rivers such as the Semois, Amblève and Ourthe. Often too rocky for larger boats, they provide excellent kayaking conditions as they wind their way through steep, picturesque valleys.

The Hautes Fagnes *(see p227)* is an extensive raised plateau of boggy moorland in the east of the Province of Liège. In winter, and on days of mist and low cloud, these moors can be powerfully gloomy and desolate, but they also have an austere beauty and an abundance of unusual flora and fauna. Here and there, raised walkways have been built to provide access to the marshy interior.

Walkers are rewarded by a landscape that is both gently challenging and remarkably varied. The tourist offices have maps of recommended walks, which include a part of the network of Grande Randonnée (GR) long-distance paths.

Mountain bikers will find ideal terrain here. There are well-organized, signposted routes for *vététistes* (from VTT for Vélo Tout Terrain, or All Terrain Bicycle). This includes Grand Raid Godefroy, a 160-km (100-mile) circuit around Bouillon.

Rock formations, created where blocks of harder rock have resisted erosion, form major landmarks and are often named after or associated with legends. There are noted rock climbing sites on the River Meuse and in the valley of the River Ourthe.

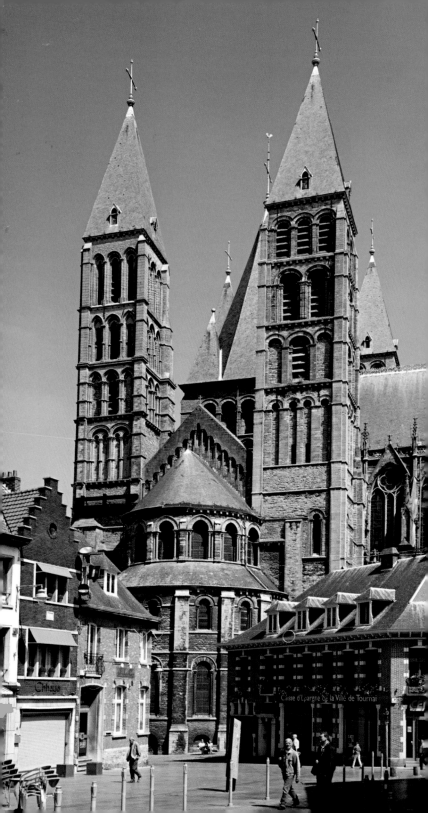

WESTERN WALLONIA

Stretching across the Province of Hainaut, Western Wallonia is redolent with the romance of history in such impressive châteaux as Beloeil, Seneffe and Attre, and the intimate medieval centre of Tournai. Hainaut also played a key role in Belgium's industrial development, a past that is now celebrated in several fascinating showpieces of industrial heritage across the region.

Historically a border county, Hainaut has been contested over the centuries between France and the rulers of the rest of central Belgium. The region around Tournai, a city with Roman origins, was the centre of the Frankish empire in the 5th century and remained French until 1513. After a brief English occupation under Henry VIII, it was French again during the time of Louis XIV and through the turmoil that followed the French Revolution (1789–99). This influence is reflected in the local language, Picard, which is distinct from Wallon and shared with Nord-Pas-de-Calais in neighbouring France.

In the 19th century, the green hills of central Hainaut, around the historic cities of Charleroi and Mons were found to contain rich seams of coal. This led to the development of the Région du Centre, around La Louvière, as a powerhouse of industrial development within Belgium. Canals and waterways were built to link the area to Germany, France and the North Sea. The region's affluence grew owing to the mines and factories, but districts around the major cities struggled with growing industrialization and the resultant poverty.

Today, Western Wallonia remains the epitome of Belgium's varied history. The industrial areas across the centre of the region have redefined their collieries and mines as dynamic museums and centres for the arts that draw hundreds of enthusiasts. In addition, the stately châteaux dotting the region bring the splendour of the late medieval period to life for Belgians and visitors alike. The most popular times to visit are when towns across Western Wallonia hold lively carnivals, steeped in pageantry, that attract people from across the world.

Immaculately costumed participants at the bold and sparkling carnival of Binche

◄ Pedestrians walking past the historical Cathédrále Notre-Dame, Tournai

Exploring Western Wallonia

The Province of Hainaut can be divided into three areas. The north is attractive farmland, with châteaux at Beloeil, Attre, Seneffe and Ecaussinnes-Lalaing as well as the impressive cathedral city of Tournai. The central band is the old industrial area running from Mons to Charleroi via La Louvière. This not only has exhilarating industrial constructions, such as the colossal canal lift at Ronquières, but also some exquisite cultural treasures, as at the Musée Royal de Mariemont. In the southern sector, the rural landscape becomes wooded as it rises into the Ardennes hills. The lakes of L'Eau d'Heure are a huge water sports centre.

One of many statues located on the grounds of the Domaine de Mariemont

Sights at a Glance

Villages, Towns and Cities

- ❶ Tournai pp184–8
- ❸ Ath
- ❼ Soignies
- ⓫ Charleroi
- ⓭ La Louvière
- ⓰ Mons
- ⓱ Grand Hornu
- ⓲ Binche
- ⓳ Thuin
- ㉒ Chimay

Castles

- ❺ Château d'Attre
- ❻ Château de Beloeil
- ❾ Château-Fort d'Ecaussinnes-Lalaing
- ❿ Château de Seneffe

Churches and Abbeys

- ⓴ Abbaye d'Aulne

Museums

- ❷ Mahymobiles
- ❹ Hôpital Notre-Dame à la Rose
- ⓬ Musée Royal de Mariemont
- ⓮ Ecomusée Regional du Centre

Areas of Natural Beauty

- ㉓ Vallée de la Sambre

Sites of Interest

- ❽ Plan Incliné de Ronquières
- ⓯ Canal du Centre
- ㉑ Lacs de l'Eau d'Heure

Dottigniés (Dottenijs)
Espierres (Spiere)
Pecq
Celles
Nechin
Escaut
Rhosnes
Frasnes-les-Anvaing
A17
N60
TOURNAI ❶
N508
N7
MAHYMOBILE
Antoing
A16
Blato

Terrace cafés lining the Grand Place of Mons, capital of Hainaut

Key

- ━ Motorway
- ━ Major road
- ━ Secondary road
- ━ Minor road
- ━ Main railway
- ━ Minor railway
- ━ International border
- ━ Provincial border

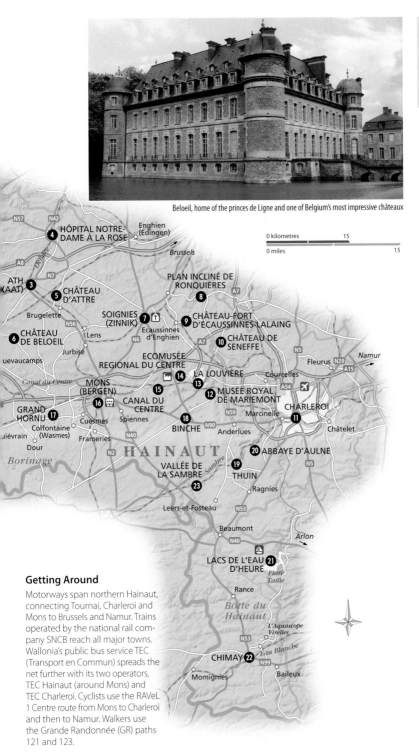

Beloeil, home of the princes de Ligne and one of Belgium's most impressive châteaux

0 kilometres 15

0 miles 15

Getting Around

Motorways span northern Hainaut, connecting Tournai, Charleroi and Mons to Brussels and Namur. Trains operated by the national rail company SNCB reach all major towns. Wallonia's public bus service TEC (Transport en Commun) spreads the net further with its two operators, TEC Hainaut (around Mons) and TEC Charleroi. Cyclists use the RAVeL 1 Centre route from Mons to Charleroi and then to Namur. Walkers use the Grande Randonnée (GR) paths 121 and 123.

For keys to symbols *see back flap*

❶ Street-by-Street: Tournai

One of Belgium's oldest urban centres, Tournai has origins dating back to AD 60. A Roman city, it became the focus of early Christian activity, beginning with St Piat's efforts in the 3rd century AD. Clovis I (AD 465–511), King of the Franks and the first major ruler of the Merovingian dynasty and the French royal line, was perhaps born here. The much-venerated St Eleutherius was his first bishop. Although badly damaged by German bombing in World War II, Tournai's long history is written into the city centre. The awe-inspiring Cathédrale Notre-Dame, the soaring belfry and the impressive Grand Place are surrounded by old cobbled streets which provide a constantly changing view of the city skyline.

Église St-Jacques
This 13th-century church was built for pilgrims en route to Santiago di Compostela in Spain.

★ Grand Place
The town square is bounded by numerous 17th-century façades and the cathedral's towers loom in the east. On the western side, the Halle des Draps (Clothmakers' Hall), built in 1610, has a gilded façade. A statue of Christine de Lalaing, local 16th-century heroine, stands in the centre of the square.

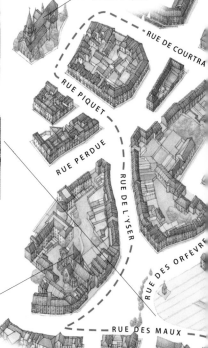

RUE DE COURTRA
RUE PIQUET
RUE PERDUE
RUE DE L'YSER
RUE DES ORFÈVRE
RUE DES MAUX

Key

— Suggested route

Église St-Quentin
The grey-stone columns and vaulting give this 12th-century church a tranquil austerity. It was restored in the 1960s, following wartime damage. Its greatest treasure is the silver statue of Notre Dame de la Treille (1724).

★ Cathédrale Notre-Dame

The colossal and magnificent cathedral is enriched with a wealth of detail, including tiers of ornate sculpture at the entrance and an elaborately carved 16th-century rood screen inside.

Cathédrale Notre-Dame's treasury is one of the most precious collections of church treasures in Belgium. It includes the reliquary shrine of St Eleutherius, completed in 1247, which is paraded in the Grande Procession festival.

The River Scheldt
Known here as the Escaut, the river gave Tournai vital, navigable access to the sea, making it a trading hub in the Middle Ages.

RUE DU CURÉ NOTRE-DAME

RUE DE L'HÔPITAL NOTRE-DAME

QUAI DU MARCHÉ AU POISSON

RUE DE LA LANTERNE

RUE DES CHAPELIERS

RUE DE LA WALLONIE

0 metres 50
0 yards 50

★ The Belfry

Begun in the 12th century, but dating mainly from the 14th century, the belfry in Tournai is the oldest in Belgium, a UNESCO World Heritage Site, and unusual in that it is free-standing. Its carillon of 55 bells sings melodies out over the city centre. The belfry's 257 steps take visitors to the top, where a parapet offers excellent views.

The Musée de la Tapisserie celebrates Tournai's tradition of tapestry weaving.

Tournai: Cathédrale Notre-Dame

One of the great landmarks of Belgium, Cathédrale Notre-Dame has a long history. Tournai's first bishop, St Eleutherius, built a cathedral on this site in the 5th century. The existing church, however, was begun in the 12th century. Construction started at the western end in Romanesque style, and progressed eastwards, becoming Gothic in the 13th-century chancel. The impressive interior was once more elaborate, but much of the decoration was destroyed by Protestant iconoclasts in 1566. Considerable damage was also inflicted by German bombing in 1940. A tornado struck in 1999, highlighting the fragility of the building. In 2000, the cathedral became a UNESCO World Heritage Site. Some areas of the cathedral will be closed to the public until 2025 while resoration work is ongoing.

★ **The Five Towers**
The cluster of pyramid-tipped towers soaring from the transept and crossing, impart a distinctive individuality to the cathedral. Completed in the early 13th century, they reach a height of 83 m (272 ft).

KEY

① **The Chapelle St Louis** contains paintings by Jordaens and Rubens.

② **The Romanesque nave** has three external tiers of rounded arches. Two flanking aisles help support its high vaulted ceiling.

③ **The central tower**, the oldest, is a "lantern tower", allowing light into the crossing between the nave and the transept.

④ **The chancel**, built between 1243 and 1255, was the first example of the new French Gothic style in Belgium.

⑤ **The transept** separates the Romanesque nave from the Gothic choir, both of which, unusually, are almost of equal length.

West Porch The west façade has an arched 14th-century porch decorated with a line of statues dating from between the 14th and 17th centuries.

Rose Window Set in the west façade, the rose window was installed in the 19th century, replacing a Gothic window from 1526. The stained glass depicts Virgin Mary in the centre and the 16 compartments portray the Prophets.

For hotels and restaurants see p269 and p289

★ Rood Screen
The line between the nave and the choir is marked by an elegant rood screen in polychrome marble. It was designed in Italian-Renaissance style and completed in 1572.

VISITORS' CHECKLIST

Practical Information
Place de l'Evêché 1, Tournai.
Tel (069) 452650. **Open** Apr–Oct: 9:15am–noon and 2–6pm daily; Nov–Mar: 9:15am–noon & 2–5pm daily. Treasury: **Open** Apr–Oct: 9:30am–noon & 2–6pm Sun–Fri; Nov–Mar: 9:30am–noon & 2–5pm Mon–Fri, 2–5pm Sat, Sun & public holidays.
W **cathedrale-tournai.be**

Transport

High Altar
With the structural weight on external buttresses, the walls of the chancel could be filled with glass. The Gothic pillars and arches are made of the city's famous blue stone. This area is not accessible to the public during the restoration work.

★ Treasury
Rooms in the cathedral contain a wealth of church treasure. Most precious are the large reliquary chests gilded and encrusted with gems. There is also a long tapestry from 1402 depicting St Eleutherius and St Piat, who brought Christianity to Tournai.

Exploring Tournai

A ring of boulevards encircles the centre of Tournai, with the River Escaut slicing through the middle, passing beneath the triple arches of the 13th-century bridge, Pont de Trous. The boulevards follow the path of the 14th-century city walls. The street plan of the centre has remained almost unchanged since the walls were built. From 1187 onwards, Tournai was often under French control; in 1513, it fell to the English, whose five-year rule is commemorated in the Henry VIII Tower. This is a pleasant place to wander, with the museums clustered to the west of the cathedral.

Belfry
Vieux Marché aux Poteries.
Tel (069) 222045. **Open** Tue–Sun.
W visittournai.be

The city's famous belfry, a UNESCO World Heritage site, rises to a height of 72 m (236 ft). In 1187, the Tournaisiens wrangled freedom from the count of Flanders and placed themselves under the protection of the king of France. However, they retained a good degree of autonomy – the belfry was a symbol of this, serving as a watchtower, clock tower, place of public announcements, prison and stronghold for town charters. The belfry was revamped after a fire in 1391, and the spires date from between the 16th and 19th centuries.

Musée de Folklore
Réduit des Sions. **Tel** (069) 224069.
Open Wed–Mon. **Closed** Nov–Mar:
Sun mornings.

Set out in two 17th-century step-gabled houses called La Maison Tournaisienne, this extensive folklore collection is spread over a series of 23 rooms and reconstructions depicting daily life in the past – school and home, the pub, workshops of printers, clog-makers, weavers and coopers, as well as the worlds of the priests, doctors, soldiers, women and children.

Musée des Beaux-Arts
Enclos St-Martin. **Tel** (069) 332431.
Open Wed–Mon. **Closed** Nov–Mar:
Sun mornings.

Often referred to as Musée Horta, this art museum was designed by the great Art Nouveau architect Victor Horta *(see p84)* in his later, more sober, Classical style. It opened in 1928. In galleries fanning out from a central polygonal sculpture hall, its impressive collection covers work from the 15th century onwards and includes art by many of the greatest Belgian painters and sculptors. Among them are Rogier van der Weyden, Rubens, Constantin Meunier and James Ensor. International artists such as Watteau, Manet, Monet, Toulouse-Lautrec and van Gogh are also represented.

Musée de la Tapisserie
Place Reine Astrid. **Tel** (069) 234285.
Open Wed–Mon. **Closed** Nov–Mar:
Sun mornings.

Occupying a grand Neo-Classical mansion, this museum focusses on the celebrated quality of Tournai's tapestry, notably of the 15th and 16th centuries. It has a small but fine collection of historic tapestries, some contemporary tapestries and an active workshop where tapestries are restored.

Detail from a tapestry at the Musée de la Tapisserie

Musée des Arts de la Marionnette
Rue St-Martin 47. **Tel** (069) 889140.
Open 9am–12:30pm & 2–5pm Tue–Fri, 2–6pm Sat, Sun & public holidays.
W maisondelamarionnette.be

Housed in a 19th-century mansion, this puppetry arts museum within the Centre de la Marionnette brings together a large collection of almost 2,500 puppets from all over the world, many of which are on show to the public in the form of a permanent exhibition. A multi-media documentation centre offers further opportunity to find out more about puppetry.

Musée d'Archéologie
Rue des Carmes 8. **Tel** (069) 221672.
Open Wed–Mon. **Closed** Nov–Mar:
Sun mornings.

Archaeological remains from Tournai's prehistoric, Gallo-Roman and Frankish past are exhibited here. Many of the finds come from recent excavations of graveyards in the city centre, and include sarcophagi, glassware, pottery, weapons and jewellery.

Display of costumes at the Musée de Folklore

❷ Mahymobiles

Rue Erna 3, Leuze-en-Hainaut; 16 km (10 miles) E of Tournai. **Road Map** B3. **Tel** (069) 354545. ▣ **Open** mid-Mar–Oct: 1–5pm Thu & Sat, 10am–5pm Sun & public holidays. 🅿 ♿ 💻
W **mahymobiles.be**

Some 300 veteran and vintage vehicles, mainly cars, are on display at this museum, set in an old factory. They are chosen from over 1,000 vehicles assembled since 1944 by the collector Ghislain Mahy. The earliest dates from 1890. Also on show are historic motorbikes and bicycles, toy cars and the paraphernalia of past decades of motoring.

❸ Ath

42 km (26 miles) E of Tournai. **Road Map** B3. 🏔 28,500. 🚋 🚌 🛈 Rue de Pintamont 18; (068) 265170. 🎭 Ducasse (4th weekend in Aug). W **ath.be**

A busy industrial town, Ath comes alive during its famous festival Ducasse, when giant figures are carried through the streets *(see p37)*. This Parade of the Giants is celebrated all year round at the **Maison des Géants**. Set in the Château de Cambier, an 18th-century mansion, it explores the folkloric background of the giants, Ducasse itself and parallel traditions elsewhere using film and pictures.

🏛 Maison des Géants

Rue de Pintamont 18. **Tel** (068) 265170. **Open** 10am–5pm Tue–Fri (until 6pm Jun–Sep), 2–6pm Sat, Sun & public holidays. 💻 🎭
W **maisondesgeants.be**

Ornately decorated interior of the Hôpital Notre-Dame à la Rose

❹ Hôpital Notre-Dame à la Rose

Place Alix de Rosoit, Lessines; 10 km (6 miles) N of Ath. **Road Map** B2. **Tel** (068) 332403. **Open** 2–6pm Tue–Sun & public holidays. 🅿 🎭 3pm Sat, Sun & public holidays. 🏠 ♿
W **notredamealarose.com**

Founded in 1242 by a French princess called Alix de Rosoit as a refuge for the poor, sick and needy, this establishment ran as a hospital, and more recently as an old people's home, for nearly 750 years, until 1980. Today, its tranquil convent buildings, dating to the 16th to 18th centuries, serve as a museum, presenting the work of the institution. There are wards, beds, medical instruments and information about the medicines that were dispensed, the pewter dishes used by patients, Tournai porcelain used by the sisters, a library of 2,000 antique books, paintings and sculpture and precious gold- and silverware. A cloister, chapel, herb garden

and ice house all add to the picture of this community.

The town of Lessines was famous for its quarries producing porphyry, a flecked, deep-red stone used for architectural sculpture. The open pits can still be visited.

❺ Château d'Attre

Avenue du Château 8, Attre; 5 km (3 miles) SE of Ath. **Road Map** B3. **Tel** (068) 454460. **Open** Jul–Aug: 1–6pm Sat, Sun & public holidays; Apr–Jun & Sep–Oct: 2–6pm Sun & public holidays. 🅿 🎭 🏠
W **jardins.tourismewallonie.be**

This elegant château, built in 1752 in French Neo-Classical style, still contains its original decoration, furniture and furnishings. The suite of sumptuous rooms evokes the Rococo tastes of the era. It also has a large park, crossed by the River Dender, that includes a ruined belvedere, dovecote, Swiss chalet, bathhouse and the remains of a celebrated marvel of the 1780s known as the Rocher (Rock). This is an artificial mound, with a castle-like hunting platform on top.

Environs

Pairi Daiza, 5 km (3 miles) to the southeast, is a large, child-friendly zoo set in the former domain of the Château de Cambron-Casteau.

🦜 Pairi Daiza

Domaine de Cambron, Brugelette. **Tel** (068) 250850. **Open** late Mar–early Nov. 🅿 ♿ 🚻 💻 🏠
W **pairidaiza.eu**

Formal gardens adding to the grandeur of the well-maintained Château d'Attre

Stately avenues leading up to the grand Château de Beloeil, set in green parkland

❻ Château de Beloeil

Rue du Château 11; 10 km (6 miles) SW of Attre. **Road Map** B3. **Tel** (069) 689426. 🚌 **Open** Easter–Apr: 1–6pm Sat and Sun; Apr–Jun & Sept: 1–6pm Sat, Sun & public holidays; July & Aug: daily. 🅿️
W chateaudebeloeil.com

Standing on a site that has been home to the eminent princes de Ligne since the 14th century, Beloeil is a moated château built originally in the 16th century. Until the French Revolutionary Army took over in 1792, it was the domain of Charles-Joseph Lamoral, 7th Prince de Ligne (1735–1814). Field marshal, diplomat and a close confidant of Joseph II of Austria, he was at the courts of France and Russia and interacted with many of the leading political figures of his day.

Château de Beloeil was remodelled in the French style during the 17th and 18th centuries with Versailles-like grandeur, but a disastrous fire in 1900 badly damaged the central block. The reconstructed château displays furniture, tapestries, paintings and a 20,000-volume library. An enormous artificial water basin, parklands and formal gardens lie outside.

❼ Soignies

30 km (19 miles) E of Beloeil. **Road Map** C3. 🚊 27,000. 🚍 🚌
ℹ️ Rue du Lombard 2; (067) 347376.

The agreeable little town of Soignies was once surrounded by woods linked to the Forêt de Soignes *(see p169)* near Brussels. It later became well known for its blue limestone quarries. Today, its great treasure is the robust **Collégiale St-Vincent**, named after St Vincent Madelgaire, Governor of Hainaut, husband of St Waudru of Mons and founder of an abbey built here in AD 650. The church was built between the 10th and 13th centuries, largely in Romanesque style. The pastel interior is impressive for its scale and understated style. It has a polychrome 14th-century statue of the Virgin and Child, in a niche beneath the marble rood loft, as well as carved Renaissance choir stalls dating from 1576.

Coat of arms at Soignies's church

🏛 Collégiale St-Vincent
Grand Place. **Tel** (067) 331210. **Open** Apr–Sep: 8am–6pm daily; Oct–Mar: 8am–5pm daily. ♿ access via Porte du Chevet. **W** collegiale-soignies.be

The control tower rising above the *plan incliné* at Ronquières

❽ Plan Incliné de Ronquières

Route Baccara 1; 14 km (9 miles) NE of Soignes. **Road Map** C3. **Tel** (078) 059059. **Open** Apr–Oct: 10am–7pm (last entry 5pm). **Closed** Thu–Sun of 1st weekend in Aug. 🅿️ 🚻 May–Aug: Sun (boat trips). 🚻 ♿ except boat trips. **W** voiesdeau.hainaut.be

Modern canal engineering has achieved some impressive feats in the region. One of the most interesting structures is on the Brussels–Charleroi canal at Ronquières. Boats weighing up to 1,350 tonnes (1,500 tons) can negotiate a difference in the canal levels of 68 m (221 ft) in a single operation, by using a transporter lock. Called the *plan incliné* (literally, inclined plane), this is a sloping boat lift almost 1.5 km (1 mile) long. Boats enter one of the two vast water-filled containers at either end of the *plan incliné*. The containers then ride on rollers through the length of the canal lift.

When it was completed in 1968, the lift reduced the time taken by barges to travel between Charleroi and Brussels by some seven hours. To the north, the canal follows a 300-m (984-ft) long aqueduct. A visitors' centre in the soaring control tower explains the system through an audiovisual presentation. Glass footbridges allow a bird's-eye view of the operations of this colossal machine and the landscape. Visitors can also take boat trips through the *plan incliné*.

❾ Château-Fort d'Écaussinnes-Lalaing

Rue de Seneffe 1, Écaussinnes-Lalaing; 6 km (4 miles) SW of Ronquières. **Road Map** C3. **Tel** (067) 442490. 🚌 **Open** Apr–Sep: 2–6pm Sun; group visits can be booked in advance for a minimum of 10 people daily Apr–Oct. 🖼 🔲 chateaufort-ecaussinnes.be

The small, historic village of Écaussinnes-Lalaing is dominated by a gaunt and mighty fortress. Built during the 12th century on a rocky spur, it played a vital strategic role in the Centre Region, a much-disputed border area between France and the Low Countries. During World War I, it served as a German barracks, prison, munitions store and infirmary. Now restored, the echoing interior contains period furniture and armour, as well as a dungeon, a Gothic chapel and a 15th-century kitchen.

❿ Château de Seneffe

Rue Lucien Plasman 7–9, Seneffe; 10 km (6 miles) SE of Écaussinnes-Lalaing. **Road Map** C3. **Tel** (064) 556913. **Open** 10am–6pm Tue–Sun. 🖼 🔲 🔳 🔲 🔲 chateaudeseneffe.be

An elegant château, Seneffe was built in the Neo-Classical style during the 1760s as a grand residence for wealthy entrepreneur Julien Depestre. Its interior matches the refined exterior with parquet floors, panelling, stucco work and ornate marble fireplaces. It is now the setting for an important collection of gold and silverware, within a permanent exhibition called The Art of Living in the 18th Century. Outside, there is an extensive garden and park, with an open-air theatre and an orangery. During World War II, the château was the local headquarters of General von Falkenhausen, the Nazi military governor of occupied Belgium.

⓫ Charleroi

25 km (16 miles) SE of Seneffe. **Road Map** C3. 🏙 210,000. 🚉 🚍 🚌 ℹ Place Charles II; (071) 861414. 🔲 charleroi.be

As capital of the Pays Noir (Black Country), surrounded by coal pits and monuments to Belgium's age of booming industrial growth, Charleroi is an important city. Set on the Sambre, it was first called Charnoy, but when it became a military base to fend off the threat of Louis XIV of France in 1666, it was renamed after Charles II, King of Spain and the Spanish Low Countries. Glass has been a key industry here since 1577, but it was the combination of iron and the local abundance of coal that turned Charleroi into an industrial powerhouse in the 19th century. The Brussels–Charleroi canal linked the city ultimately to the North Sea, as did the Sambre, contributing to its reputation as a major centre for industrial transport.

Charleroi's impressive Hôtel de Ville, dominated by its belfry

The main sight in the city is the massive **Hôtel de Ville** and its belfry, built in a blend of Neo-Classical and Art Deco styles in 1936. The stylish interior includes the **Musée des Beaux-Arts**, on the second floor, which has a good collection of paintings, featuring François-Joseph Navez (1787–1869), pupil of Jacques Louis David and a leader of the Belgian Neo-Classical movement. It also includes works by the sculptor Constantin Meunier as well as Surrealist artists such as René Magritte and Paul Delvaux.

Housed in a Neo-Gothic former monastery, the **Musée de la Photographie** has a significant collection of photography from the 19th century to the present day.

Environs

The former colliery of **Le Bois du Cazier** at Marcinelle, 3 km (2 miles) to the south, has become an industrial heritage centre with a Musée de Verre (Glass Museum) and a Musée l'Industrie.

🏛 **Musée des Beaux-Arts**
Hôtel de Ville, Place Charles II. **Tel** (071) 861134. **Open** 9am–5pm Tue–Fri, 10am–6pm Sat. 🖼 🔳 🔲 charleroi-museum.be

🏛 **Musée de la Photographie**
Avenue Paul Pastur 11. **Tel** (071) 435810. **Open** 10am–6pm daily. 🖼 🔲 museephoto.be

🏛 **Le Bois du Cazier**
Rue du Cazier 80, Marcinelle. **Tel** (071) 880856. **Open** 9am–5pm Tue–Fri, 10am–6pm Sat, noon–6pm Sun. 🖼 🔳 🔲 🔲 🔲 🔲 🔲 leboisducazier.be

Formal lines of the elegant Neo-Classical Château de Seneffe

Pillars and sphinx – ruins of the old castle at Domaine de Mariemont

⑫ Musée Royal de Mariemont

Chaussée de Mariemont 100, Morlanwelz; 24 km (15 miles) W of Charleroi. **Road Map** C3. **Tel** (064) 212 193. **Open** 10am–6pm Tue–Sun (to 5pm Oct–Mar). **W** musee-mariemont.be

Built in 1975 in the **Domaine de Mariemont**, a large park with an arboretum, this modern museum is home to a major collection of decorative arts. The estate once belonged to a castle built in 1546 by Mary of Hungary. This was destroyed by the French Revolutionary Army in 1794, and its ruins can be seen today. Another mansion, constructed by the Warocqué family of industrialists in the 20th century, was also destroyed, but many of its contents were saved. Today, the museum also has sculpture and artifacts from ancient Egypt, Greece, the Far East and Gallo-Roman times; illuminated manuscripts; lace; and the world's largest collection of Tournai porcelain.

⑬ La Louvière

20 km (12 miles) NW of Charleroi. **Road Map** C3. 80,000. *i* Place Mansart 21-22; (064) 261500. **W** lalouviere.be

The town of La Louvière was once the hub of the coal and steel enterprise. Industrial heritage is a big theme here, but the town also has art centres. The **Centre de la Gravure et de l'Image Imprimée** mounts

exhibitions of prints and engravings. The **Musée Ianchelevici** celebrates the life and work of Romanian-born sculptor Idel Ianchelevici, who came to Belgium in his youth. The **Centre Keramis** has a large collection of ceramics.

Centre de la Gravure et de l'Image Imprimée
Rue des Amours 10. **Tel** (064) 278727. **Open** during exhibitions only: 10am–6pm Tue–Sun. **W** centredelagravure.be

Musée Ianchelevici
Place Communale 21. **Tel** (064) 282530. **Open** 11am–5pm Tue–Fri, 2–6pm Sat & Sun. **W** ianchelevici.be

Centre Keramis
1 Place des Fours Bouteilles. **Tel** (064) 236070. **Open** 10am–6pm Wed–Sun. **W** keramis.be

⑭ Écomusée Regional du Centre

R St-Patrice 2B, Houdeng-Aimeries; 4 km (3 miles) NW of La Louvière. **Road Map** C3. **Tel** (064) 282000. **Open** May–Oct: 9am–5pm Mon–Fri, 2–6pm Sat & Sun; Nov–Apr: 9am–5pm Mon–Fri. **W** ecomuseeboisduluc.be

This UNESCO World Heritage Site has been in existence since 1983, recalling the long history of coal mining in Belgium (1685–1973)

and at the St Emmanuel mine in particular. It features a paternalistic industrial village with its orderly grid of more than 166 miners' dwellings, plus shops, a church, schools and an infirmary. Offices, workshops and equipment stores cluster around the mine shaft that descends 558 m (1,830 ft) below the surface.

⑮ Canal du Centre

Rue Tout-y-Faut 90, Houdeng-Goegnies; 3 km (2 miles) N of La Louvière. **Road Map** C3. **Tel** (064) 847831. *i* Place Mansart 21; (064) 261500. Apr–Oct: Tue–Sun (boat trips). **W** canalducentre.be

Forged between 1882 and 1917, Canal du Centre was used to transport raw materials and goods to the North Sea, France and Germany. The original canal tackled the 68-m (223-ft) rise in the land with locks and four hydraulic boat lifts between Thieu and Houdeng-Goegnies. Boats – one going up and the other down – enter a pair of metal counterbalanced containers. As water is pumped, one rises and the other goes down.

After nearly a century, a more efficient system was devised for a new cut of the canal designed to take the canal boats of the modern era. Here, the rise of 73 m (240 ft) is dealt with by a single

The gigantic Ascenseur Funiculaire de Strépy-Thieu at Canal du Centre

huge lift about 2 km (1 mile) to the northeast of the old lift at Thieu. Built from 1982 to 2002, the **Ascenseur Funiculaire de Strépy-Thieu** is a marvel of modern engineering. Raising and lowering boats in two water-filled tanks, it has fine views from its visitor centre.

The four old boat lifts on the original branch are now UNESCO World Heritage Sites. They still function, but are used only for pleasure crafts. There are 2-hour boat trips between La Cantine des Italiens and Bracquegnies.

Ascenseur Funiculaire de Strépy-Thieu
Tel (064) 671200. **Open** Apr–Oct: daily.
W voiesdeau.hainaut.be

⑯ Mons

18 km (11 miles) W of La Louvière.
Road Map C3. 92,669.
Grand Place 27; (065) 335580.
W mons.be

Despite its location in the heart of the Borinage mining district, Mons, the vibrant capital of the Province of Hainaut, has considerable charm. On the contours of the hill for which it is named are cobbled streets with 17th- and 18th-century merchant's houses. The city's patron saint, Ste Waudru, built a convent here in AD 650; and the main church, the Brabant Gothic **Collégiale Ste-Waudru** that was built between 1449 and 1686, is dedicated to her. It houses the splendid Car d'Or (Chariot of Gold), built in 1781, which is used to carry the saint's relics in the parade during the annual Ducasse, or Doudou, festivities *(see p37)*.

Mons is particularly proud of its unusual, free-standing, Baroque belfry. Built over 1661–9 and rising to a height of 87 m (285 ft), it contains a carillon of 49 bells. The Gothic **Hôtel de Ville** in the Grand Place dates from 1458, but its distinctive copper-clad, pepperpot tower was added in 1718. Stroking the head of the little cast-iron monkey by the front entrance, the Singe du Grand-Garde, is said to bring good luck. There

Brabant Gothic exterior of Collégiale Ste-Waudru, Mons

are two museums close to the Grand Place. The **Musée des Arts Décoratifs François Duesberg** contains an extraordinary collection of elaborate clocks made in Paris in Louis XIV and Empire styles between 1795 and 1815. There are also exquisite decorative arts from the same era. The art museum **Beaux-Arts Mons** focusses on hosting temporary exhibitions. South of here is the **Mons Memorial Museum** charting the history of the city and of World Wars I and II.

South of the city centre is the **Maison de van Gogh**, a tiny brick house that was once owned by a miner's family. The artist Vincent van Gogh stayed here while training to be a missionary among the Borinage miners.

Around Mons are a number of cemeteries and monuments that serve as reminders that this region was the scene of fierce battles during both World War I and World War II.

Environs
About 7 km (4 miles) to the southwest is **Parc d'Attractions Scientifiques (PASS)**, a family-oriented, interactive museum demonstrating the concepts of science and technology. At **Spiennes**, 3 km (2 miles) to the southeast, an extensive Neolithic flint mine is a UNESCO World Heritage Site.

Mons Memorial Museum
Boulevard Dolez 51. **Tel** (065) 405320.
Open 10am–6pm Tue–Sun.
W polemuseal.mons.be

Maison de Van Gogh
Rue du Pavillon 3, Cuesmes. **Tel** (065) 355611. **Open** Tue–Sun.

Parc d'Attractions Scientifiques (PASS)
Tel (070) 222252. **Open** Thu–Tue.
Closed part of Sep, Dec.
W pass.be

⑰ Grand Hornu

R Ste-Louise 82, Hornu; 10 km (6 miles) SW of Mons. **Road Map** B3.
Tel (065) 652121. **Open** Tue–Sun.
W grand-hornu.eu

The remains of the large Neo-Classical buildings of Grand Hornu are the vestiges of a great industrial enterprise. This idealistic colliery complex, built around an oval courtyard with engineering workshops, forges and 440 workers' houses, was created between 1810 and 1830 by French industrialist Henri de Gorge. In 1971, it was made a centre for industrial arts and design. In 2002, new buildings meshing with the old became the home of the **Musée des Arts Contemporains de la Fédération Wallonie-Bruxelles**, housing exhibitions of contemporary art.

Arches in a curved wing around Grand Hornu's large oval courtyard

Posters outside Musée International du Carnaval et du Masque in Binche

⑱ Binche

16 km (10 miles) SE of Mons.
Road Map C3. 🚹 33,000. 🚋 🚌
i Grande Place Binche; (064) 336727. 🎭 Carnival (Feb or Mar).
W binche.be

Set amid the old industrial heartlands between Mons and Charleroi, Binche is celebrated for its extraordinary, colourful and elaborate pre-Lenten Carnival, the most famous of Belgium's carnivals. This event takes place mainly in the Grand Place, which is overlooked by a 16th-century Gothic town hall. Those who are unable to visit Binche during the carnival can experience it to an extent at the town's prestigious **Musée International du Carnaval et du Masque**. Occupying an 18th-century building that was formerly an Augustinian college, the museum takes a global look at festivities, masks and carnivals, with special focus on the carnivals of Wallonia and Binche.

The town's long history is underscored by the restored remains of its extensive walls. Built between the 12th and 14th centuries, they stretch continuously across a distance of 2 km (1.5 miles) and include 25 towers.

🏛 **Musée International du Carnaval et du Masque**
Rue St-Moustier 10, Binche. **Tel** (064) 335741. **Open** 9:30am–5pm Tue–Fri, 10:30am–5pm Sat–Sun. **Closed** Ash Wednesday, 1 Nov, 24 Dec–2 Jan. 🈺
W museedumasque.be

⑲ Thuin

14 km (9 miles) SE of Binche.
Road Map C3. 🚹 15,000. 🚋 🚌
i Maison du Tourisme Val de Sambre, Place Albert 1; (071) 595454.
🎭 Marche Militaire St Roch (May)
W thuin.be

Located close to the French border, Thuin was at the western end of the Principality of Liège, whose ribbon of territory stretched right across the central band of Belgium during the Middle Ages. The upper town was reinforced by Prince-Bishop Notger in the 10th century, but of this work, only the tower, Tour Notger, can be seen today. There are also remnants of 15th-century ramparts – Remparts du Midi.

The military significance of Thuin is further remembered in traditional *spantôle* biscuits, shaped and named after a French cannon captured in 1654. The Place du Chapitre at the town centre has the free-standing 17th-century belfry, **Beffroi de Thuin**. This has an interactive exhibition and also offers enchanting views over the River Sambre, lined with barges.

Environs

At Ragnies, 3 km (2 miles) to the south, is the **Distillerie de Biercée**, famed for flavoured spirits such as Eau de Villée and Poire Williams. At Leers-et-Fosteau, 5 km (3 miles) southwest of Thuin, is the **Château du Fosteau**, which exhibits antique furniture.

🏛 **Beffroi de Thuin**
Place du Chapitre. **Tel** (071) 595454.
Open Tue–Sun (Easter holidays, Jul, Aug: daily). 🈺 🈺

🏛 **Distillerie de Biercée**
Ferme de la Cour, Rue de la Roquette 36. **Tel** (071) 591106. **Open** Mar–mid-Nov. 🈺 🈺 🈺 🈺
W distilleriedebiercee.com

🏛 **Château du Fosteau**
Rue du Marquis 1. **Tel** (071) 592344.
Open Apr–mid-Dec: 2–6pm Mon, Thu–Fri; mid-Dec–Mar: 2–6pm Sat & Sun. 🈺 🈺 **W** chateaufosteau.be

⑳ Abbaye d'Aulne

Rue Vandervelde 275, Thuin. **Road Map** C3. **Tel** (071) 595454. 🚌 **Open** Apr–Oct: Wed–Sun; Jul–Aug: daily. 🈺 🈺 🈺 🈺 **W** abbayedaulne.be.

The extensive ruins of the Abbey d'Aulne create a picturesque ensemble along the banks of the

---

The Carnival at Binche

Rooted in a long and obscure history, the Carnival at Binche begins as a gradual build-up of festivities over a series of Sundays preceding Lent. This explodes into a frenzy of fancy-dress processions, folk music and street dancing over three days, with the climax on Shrove Tuesday. This is the day of the *gilles* (clowns) – all native men of Binche dressed in the dun-coloured motley of court jesters, heavily padded and rotund, and decorated with heraldic symbols, ribbons and bells. They wear clogs on their feet, and bandaged to their heads are sinister pink masks with moustaches and wire-rimmed green glasses. In the afternoon they put on colossal ostrich-feather headdresses – a reference to Inca costumes at the time of the Spanish conquests during the reign of Emperor Charles V – and parade about tossing oranges at the onlookers. The day ends in dancing and fireworks. For more information about the event, visit www.carnavaldebinche.be.

Binche's quirkily costumed *gilles* at the annual Carnival

Sambre. It is said to have been founded in AD 657 by St Landelin in an act of contrition for his former life as a notorious brigand. It rose in wealth and prominence as a Cistercian monastery until it was set ablaze by the French Revolutionary Army in 1794. Dominating the ruins is the 13th-century Gothic abbey church and its contrasting 18th-century Neo-Classical west front. The complex now also includes a brewery, the Brasserie du Val de Sambre.

The opulently furnished theatre at the Château des Princes de Chimay

㉑ Lacs de l'Eau d'Heure

22 km (14 miles) S of Thuin. **Road Map** C3. 🚌 ℹ️ Centre d'Acceuil de la Plate Taille; (071) 509292. **Open** daily (Barrage de la Plate Taille); Mar–Sep: daily (Relais de Falemprise). 🏊 W **lacsdeleaudheure.be**

In the 1970s, the River l'Eau d'Heure was dammed twice to regulate the flow of water in Charleroi canal. The main dams, **Barrage de la Plate Taille** and **Barrage de l'Eau d'Heure**, and a series of subsidiary dams form a set of five lakes – the Lacs de l'Eau d'Heure. These are now a major resort area focussing on water sports. There are also signposted paths for walkers and barbecue sites for picnickers.

Barrage de la Plate Taille, the largest dam in Belgium, has a visitors' centre and a viewing tower 107 m (351 ft) high. Tours in the Crocodile Rouge, an extraordinary bus that also goes on water, begin here. Just 2 km (1 mile) to the east is the **Relais de Falemprise**, a recreational centre that offers a sand beach, pedalos, restaurants, mini-golf, tennis courts, and facilities for beach volleyball and pétanque.

㉒ Chimay

38 km (24 miles) S of Thuin. **Road Map** C4. 🚉 10,000. 🚌 ℹ️ (060) 211846. W **ville-de-chimay.be**

The pretty town of Chimay is the main centre of the Botte du Hainaut, the boot-shaped southern part of the province. The town's

main attraction is the **Château des Princes de Chimay**, a medieval castle that has been the home of the de Croy family and the princes de Chimay since the 15th century. It contains memorabilia of the family, including those of the lively and beautiful Spanish-born Madame Tallien (1773–1835), Princess of Chimay, who escaped the guillotine during the French Revolution and helped engineer the downfall of Robespierre. The castle also has an elaborate 19th-century Rococo theatre.

Chimay's 13th–16th-century **Collégiale des Sts-Pierre-et-Paul** contains tombs of the castle's lords and ladies and a memorial to the medieval chronicler Froissart, who was a canon here. Chimay is also the name of a Trappist beer, brewed under the auspices of monks of the Abbaye Notre-Dame-de-Scourmont, 10 km (6 miles) to the south.

Environs
L'Aquascope Virelles, 3 km (2 miles) to the northeast, is a nature reserve focussing on Belgium's largest natural lake. A popular park and adventure playground, it is linked to Chimay by a train in summer.

🏰 **Château des Princes de Chimay**
Tel (060) 214531. **Open** late-Mar–mid-Nov: Tue–Sun. 🏊 🎫 tours depart 2:30pm & 3:45pm daily (11am Thu–Sat as well). W **chateaudechimay.be**

🦆 **L'Aquascope Virelles**
Rue du Lac 42. **Tel** (060) 211363. **Open** varies, check website. 🏊 ♿ 🚻 W **aquascope.be**

㉓ Vallée de la Sambre

Road Map C3. 🚌 ℹ️ Maison du Tourisme Val de Sambre, Place Albert 1; (071) 595454. W **valdesambre-thudinie.be**

The River Sambre is a major thoroughfare in Hainaut's old industrial centre, but it has a very pretty, countrified stretch to the west of Charleroi. This makes an attractive excursion. The river passes the Abbaye d'Aulne and Thuin as well as **Lobbes**, which is noted for its fine Romanesque collegiale church, dating in part to about AD 825 and dedicated to St Ursmer (c.644–713). St Ursmer was the influential abbot of the monastery of Lobbes, said to have been founded by his predecessor St Landelin. It was destroyed by the French Revolutionary Army in 1794.

The River Sambre winding through the pretty countryside

CENTRAL WALLONIA

Comprising the provinces of Namur and Brabant Wallon, Central Wallonia is characterized primarily by rural landscapes. However, scattered across this expanse are numerous fine castles and abbeys, and some of the most impressive caves of the Ardennes. The city of Namur, capital of Wallonia, sits at its heart, on the broad and busy convergence of the rivers Meuse and Sambre.

The many fortresses of Central Wallonia's provinces bear witness to the military significance of these lands, which have been fending off invaders from the south, east and west for centuries. For instance, the rock on which the formidable Citadelle of Namur was built was once the site of a Roman fortress, and was refortified incessantly over nearly 2,000 years. The dark castles and fortified manor houses are strongly evocative of the region's medieval history. In the southwest are garrison towns dating from the 16th century. One of Europe's most famous battlefields is in the Province of Brabant Wallon – Waterloo, scene of the final defeat of Napoleon in 1815. Central Wallonia also saw much fighting during the World Wars, and Dinant marks the furthest point west reached by the German army during the 1944 Ardennes Offensive.

In parallel with these political and military events, religion left its mark on the land via a number of superb abbeys and cathedrals, such as the Romanesque church in Nivelles. Some buildings, such as the 12th-century Abbaye de Villers, are now no more than spectacular ruins, while others, such as the 19th-century Neo-Gothic Abbaye de Maredsous, are still active monasteries.

While Charleroi to its west and Liège to its east became centres of heavy industry in the 19th century, Central Wallonia remained largely agricultural. Today, its châteaux and abbeys, the picturesque River Meuse and the cities located on its banks are the main draw for visitors. Towards the south, where the Belgian landscape rises to form the Ardennes, limestone caves bristling with stalactites and stalagmites offer an equally appealing attraction.

Fortress city of Dinant, with the onion-domed Collégiale Notre-Dame dominating the banks of River Meuse

◀ The commemorative Butte de Lion providing a lofty vantage point at Waterloo

Exploring Central Wallonia

The fertile, undulating lowlands of Brabant Wallon are the farmland setting for the battle site of Waterloo and for the university at Louvain-la-Neuve. The River Meuse forms a centrepiece, linking Dinant and Namur. It is flanked by the Citadelle of Namur and the châteaux of Annevoie and Freÿr, as well as the abbeys of Floreffe and Maredsous. Couvin nestles in the forested Fagne region, close to the famous Grottes de Neptune at Petigny. Steam engines puff their way through the Viroin valley between Mariembourg and Treignes. The hills of the Ardennes begin to rise further to the south and east, where the River Lesse carves a path out of the limestone hills. The spectacular caves of Han-sur-Lesse lie in the far southeast of the region.

Sights at a Glance

Villages, Towns and Cities

- ❶ Waterloo pp200–201
- ❼ Nivelles
- ❽ Namur pp206–207
- ⓭ Dinant
- ⓳ Mariembourg
- ⓴ Couvin
- ㉔ Rochefort

Castles

- ❾ Corroy-le-Château
- ⓰ Château de Freÿr
- ⓱ Château de Vêves
- ㉒ Château de Lavaux Ste-Anne

Museums

- ❷ Fondation Folon
- ㉑ Treignes

Churches and Abbeys

- ❻ Abbaye de Villers
- ⓾ Abbaye de Floreffe
- ⓮ Abbaye de Maredsous
- ⓲ Basilique St-Materne

Parks

- ⓫ Jardins d'Annevoie

Areas of Natural Beauty

- ❺ Folx-les-Caves
- ⓯ River Meuse
- ㉓ Domaine des Grottes de Han

Sites of Interest

- ❸ Walibi
- ❹ Louvain-la-Neuve
- ⓬ Brasserie du Bocq

The resplendent interior of De Groesbeeck de Croix museum at Namur

For hotels and restaurants see pp269–70 and pp289–90

Visitors descending the cavernous depths of the grotto at Rochefort

Key

--- Motorway

--- Major road

--- Secondary road

--- Minor road

--- Main railway

--- Minor railway

--- International border

--- Provincial border

Getting Around

The main motorway, the E411 (A4), slices southwards across the region, connecting Brussels with Luxembourg. It intersects the main east–west link, E42 (A15), just north of Namur. The SNCB railway network covers all major towns, but fewer areas in the more remote regions, for instance, in the area between Couvin and Dinant. A more comprehensive coverage is offered by the bus network of TEC Namur-Luxembourg and TEC Brabant Wallon. Cruises on the River Meuse link Namur and Dinant. For walkers and cyclists, there is the RAVeL 2 all the way from Mariembourg in the south to Hoegaarden, near Leuven in Flanders. It follows disused railways and the River Meuse, via Dinant and Namur. The GR paths for walkers are concentrated in the south.

For keys to symbols *see back flap*

❶ Waterloo

The Battle of Waterloo, which took place on 18 June 1815, marked the final defeat of the French emperor Napoleon Bonaparte. This was immediately recognized as a pivotal event in European history and the battlefield became an attraction almost before the bodies of the dead had been removed. Memorials and exhibits were set up in the town of Waterloo as well as at the main scene of the battle, which lies 3 km (2 miles) to the south. As a result, some of the exhibits are themselves historic relics.

Wax models of French army generals debating the battle plans, Musée de Cire

Église St-Joseph

This church was built as a royal chapel in the 17th century. On the walls and floors of the interior are dozens of memorial plaques dedicated to British soldiers who died at Waterloo, some of whom had fought loyally with Wellington through the Peninsular War (1808–14) in Portugal and Spain.

The Battle of Waterloo

The legendary Battle of Waterloo was the culmination of the Hundred Days – Napoleon's brief but explosive return to power. He had previously been defeated, after his ill-fated invasion of Russia, and exiled to the Italian island of Elba. In February 1815, he escaped from Elba and rallied his many supporters in a final bid for European domination. Heading to retake Brussels, Napoleon reached Waterloo, where his army faced the British, under the Duke of Wellington, and their allies, the Prussians and other German states, the Dutch and Belgians. The ensuing battle lasted nine hours; the noise of gunnery could be heard across the Channel in Britain. The allied victory was, as Wellington put it, "a damned near thing", and was only assured by the last-minute arrival of the Prussian cavalry under Marshal Blücher. It had cost the lives of 13,000 men; 35,000 were wounded. Napoleon and his defeated army fled back to France in disarray, and Napoleon eventually surrendered a month later near Rochefort on the west coast. He was exiled, this time to the remote island of St Helena, where he died six years later.

Charge of the Scots Greys and Gordon Highlanders at the Battle of Waterloo, by English artist Richard Caton Woodville in c.1890

For hotels and restaurants see p269 and pp289–90

★ Musée Wellington
A former inn where the Duke of Wellington spent the night before the battle, the museum has narrow rooms packed with weapons and uniforms. There are many other curios, including plans and models of the battle.

VISITORS' CHECKLIST

Practical Information
16 km (10 miles) S of Brussels.
Road Map C2. ℹ Chaussée de Bruxelles 218; (02) 3520910.
🔲 visitwaterloo.be
Waterloo Battlefield Visitors' Centre: 1815 Rte du Lion, Braire-Lalleud. **Tel** (02) 3851912. **Open** Apr–Oct: 9:30am–5pm daily; Nov–Mar: 10am–5pm daily. 🚻 ♿ 🚻
🔲 🏠 🔲 waterloo1815.be
Musée Wellington: Chaussée de Bruxelles 166. **Tel** (02) 3572860.
Open daily. 🔲 museewellington.be 🚻 🏠 Napoleon's Last Headquarters: Vieux-Genappe.
Tel (02) 3842424. **Open** daily. 🚻

★ Panorama de la Bataille Created by artist Louis Dumoulin and erected in 1912, this vast circular painting of the battle, 110 m (360 ft) long, stretches around the inside of a circular gallery.

KEY

① **Musée Wellington.**

② **Musée de Cire** or the Waxwork Museum provides an insight into the elaborate uniforms of the time.

Key

━━ Motorway
━━ Major road
━━ Minor road
── Railway

② **Waterloo Battlefield Visitor Centre**

Battlefield of Waterloo *Vieux Genappe ↓*

★ Butte du Lion
The bronze figure of a lion sits on top of a large artificial mound, raised in 1826 as a battle memorial. A climb up 226 steps rewards visitors with views over the battlefield.

0 kilometres   1
0 miles   1

For keys to symbols *see back flap*

Statue by Jean-Michel Folon at the Fondation Folon, Domaine Solvay

❷ Fondation Folon

Ferme du Château de la Hulpe, Drève de la Ramée, La Hulpe; 10 km (6 miles) SE of Brussels. **Road Map** C2. **Tel** (02) 6533456. 🚌 **Open** 9am–5pm Tue–Fri, 10am–6pm Sat & Sun. 🚗 🚻 ⏁ 🍴 **W** fondationfolon.be

The **Domaine Solvay** is a large and beautiful park with woodland and lakes, and an elegant château dating from 1842. This estate was once owned by the philanthropic mega-industrialists, the Solvay family. In 1972, the family gave the estate to the nation and the château is now used for receptions and seminars.

The old farm complex located on the domain is now the Fondation Folon – a large exhibition centre that celebrates the life and work of Belgian painter, illustrator and sculptor Jean-Michel Folon (1934–2005). Folon's deceptively simple style, using bright watercolour washes and stylized figures, is instantly recognizable. Over his career, Folon was much in demand as the creator of prints, posters, magazine covers and stamps. His art is hugely popular and is noted for its wry, poetic comments about the human condition. With numerous examples of his work, audiovisual presentations, installations and beguiling sculpture, Fondation Folon is a museum that delights visitors of all ages.

❸ Walibi

Blvd de L'Europe, Wavre; 15 km (9 miles) E of Waterloo. **Road Map** D2. **Tel** (010) 421500. 🚌 **Open** Easter–Oct; see website for details. 🚗 🚻 ⏁ 🖥 🍴 **W** walibi.be

Named after the three surrounding communities, Wavre, Limal and Bierges, as well as the Australian marsupial that is its mascot, Walibi is one of Belgium's most popular theme parks. It has a host of heart-stopping rides plus many gentler attractions, traditional fairground rides and live shows. The park also includes a large swimming complex called **Aqualibi**, with various pools, hot baths, Jacuzzis and themed rapids.

❹ Louvain-la-Neuve

16 km (10 miles) SE of Waterloo. **Road Map** D2. 🚶 32,000. 🚌 🚍 ℹ️ Galerie des Halles; (010) 474747. 🛒 Tue & Sat. **W** uclouvain.be

The origin of the university town of Louvain-la-Neuve is linked to Belgium's oldest university, in Leuven *(see pp164–5)*, in Dutch-speaking Flanders. Until the 1920s, courses at the University of Leuven were held in French, causing resentment in the Flemish community. Following riots, teaching in Dutch was introduced, but in the 1960s protesters demanded that French be abandoned altogether. The authorities then decided to build a completely new university at Ottignies, in French-speaking Wallonia, called Louvain-la-Neuve (New Leuven). The

institution opened in 1980. Its campus is an ingenious complex raised above road level. There are two museums to attract visitors. The **Musée L à Louvain-la-Neuve** presents selections from its rich collection of donations to the university. These include prints and paintings (from Dürer to Magritte and Delvaux), sculpture of all eras and various fascinating historical, anthropological and scientific artifacts. The **Musée Hergé** occupies a striking, prism-shaped building. It celebrates the life and work of the creator of Tintin through a collection of artworks and exhibitions.

🏛 **Musée L à Louvain-la-Neuve** Place des Sciences. **Tel** (010) 474841. **Open** Tue–Sun. 🚗 **W** museelin.be

🏛 **Musée Hergé** Rue du Labrador 26. **Tel** (010) 488421. **Open** 10:30am–6pm Tue–Sun. 🚗 🍴 🖥 **W** museeherge.com

❺ Folx-les-Caves

Rue Auguste Baccus 35; 32 km (20 miles) E of Louvain-la-Neuve. **Road Map** D2. **Tel** (081) 813620. **Open** by appointment only; phone ahead. 🚗 **W** folx-les-caves.com

In the soft tufa rock beneath Orp-Jauche, in the fertile Hesbaye (Haspengouw) region, an extraordinary labyrinth of underground caves has been excavated by human hands since Neolithic times. They now cover an area of 6 ha (15 acres). Over the centuries, the caves have been used as dwellings, a quarry for phosphates

Walibi's wallaby mascot welcoming visitors to the theme park

For hotels and restaurants see pp269–70 and pp289–90

Atmospheric ruins of the Cistercian Abbaye de Villers, the backdrop for summer concerts

and lime, and a refuge in times of war. Between 1793 and 1797, they were a haven for those enduring the suppression of religion by the French Revolutionary armies. Later, the caves were used as a dance hall and, after 1886, for the cultivation of mushrooms.

❻ Abbaye de Villers

Rue de l'Abbaye 55, Villers-la-Ville; 15 km (9 miles) S of Louvain-la-Neuve. **Road Map** C3. **Tel** (071) 880980. 🚃 **Open** Apr–Oct: 10am–5pm Wed–Mon. 🏠 📷 W villers.be

The great Cistercian Abbaye de Villers was founded in 1146 and its large church was built over the following half-century. However, the abbey suffered the familiar fate of so many ecclesiastical buildings in Belgium – it was wrecked by Protestant rebels in the 16th century and finally destroyed by the French Revolutionary Army in 1794. The result is the largest set of church ruins in Belgium – a haunting ensemble surrounded by a park. Much of the essential architecture of the monastery is visible, including the cloisters, refectory, dormitory and brewery. There is a re-created medieval medicinal garden. The site makes a spectacular venue for open-air concerts and theatre productions during the summer.

❼ Nivelles

21 km (13 miles) SW of Louvain-la-Neuve. **Road Map** C3. 🏔 26,700. 🚃 🚌 **i** Rue de Saintes 48; (067) 840864. 🎭 Carnival (weekend after Mardi Gras). W **tourisme-nivelles.be**

The capital of the Roman Païs (Roman Land), a region so named for the Latin-based dialect formerly spoken here, Nivelles is a pretty town with a long history dating back to an abbey founded in around AD 650 by the ancestors of Charlemagne. The first abbess was a famously gentle-natured daughter of the family, to whom the abbey church, the **Collégiale Ste-Gertrude**, is dedicated. The abbesses thereafter were all of noble birth, and the abbey became a rich and powerful institution right up to the time that it was closed by the French Revolutionary Army in 1798. The abbey's massive church survived

The awe-inspiring west façade of Collégiale Ste-Gertrude in Nivelles

this turbulent period. Completed in 1046, it was built in a Byzantine-influenced style called Ottonian (after the three 10th-century Holy Roman Emperors called Otto). The dominant feature, the towering west façade, the Westbau, effectively forms a second transept. It has a semicircular apse and rises five storeys high, flanked by towers and topped by an octagonal bell tower containing a carillon of 49 bells. The sheer scale, simplicity and dignity of the interior are impressive, underlined by the contrasting exuberance of the 18th-century Baroque oak-and-marble pulpit. Also on display is the 15th-century wooden cart, which, drawn by horses, carries the reliquary of Ste Gertrude in a costumed procession through the town and surrounding countryside each autumn. Inside the Westbau are two gallery chapels and a large Salle Impériale (Imperial Hall). The cloisters outside once connected the church to the abbey.

The town itself suffered widespread damage in 1940, when much of the historic centre was set alight, but all has been meticulously restored.

🏛 Collégiale Ste-Gertrude

Grand Place. **Tel** (067) 840864. **Open** 9am–5pm Mon–Sat, 2–5pm Sun. 🏠 for guided tours only. 🕑 2pm daily, 3:30pm Sat, Sun & public holidays; compulsory for Westbau and crypt.

The Collegiate Church of Our Lady by the river Meuse ▶

❽ Namur

A stately university town, a centre of trade and the capital of Wallonia, Namur straddles the confluence of the rivers Sambre and Meuse. The town's dominant feature is the massive, gaunt Citadelle, mounted on a spur of rock that sits on the Grognon, a dagger-shaped spit of land between the two rivers. The Romans built defences here, and the Citadelle has since seen action in just about every war that has swept across Belgium; the last, World War II, brought widespread damage to the city from air raids. Little remains of the medieval town, the seat of the counts of Namur, but its old residential areas are dotted with elegant 17th- and 18th-century civic buildings and mansions. The suburb to the south of the Meuse, called Jambes, was, until the 15th century, ruled separately by the prince-bishops of Liège.

Namur's mighty Citadelle rising above the banks of the River Meuse

🏰 The Citadelle

Route Merveilleuse 64. **Tel** (081) 654500. **Open** 10am–5pm daily. 🖼
📷 Ⓦ citadelle.namur.be

The strategic value of the Champeau hill that rises up from the Grognon has been recognized since prehistoric times. Julius Caesar is said to have laid siege to this rock to oust the Aduatuci Gauls. It has since been fortified and embattled on numerous occasions, most significantly in 1692, when it was seized by the army of French monarch Louis XIV. Louis's great military engineer, Marquis de Vauban, then set his stamp on the fortress with his signature triangular bastions, but it was retaken by William III of Orange three years later. The Citadelle saw action right up to the end of World War II, and was only fully demilitarized in 1977.

The winding road leading up to the top of the Citadelle is called Route Merveilleuse. On the south side, it offers panoramic views over the Sambre and Meuse.

The fortress itself is a sprawling complex of robust defensive ramparts, built between the 16th and 20th centuries. Its network of underground passages inspired Napoleon to call it "the termite hill of Europe". There are various exhibits, activities and audiovisual presentations, plus a little train that ferries visitors about. Also on the hill, close to the 17th-century Fort d'Orange, is a small amusement park for children called the Parc d'Attractions Reine-Fabiola.

🏛 Musée Archéologique de Namur

Rue du Pont 21. **Tel** (081) 231631. **Open** 10am–5pm Tue–Fri, 10:30am–5pm Sat & Sun. 🖼 📷

The impressive 16th-century Halle al'Chair (Meat Hall) is home to a remarkable collection of prehistoric, Gallo-Roman and Merovingian artifacts such as statues, pottery, mosaics, jewellery, glassware and weapons. The most celebrated exhibits are the late-Roman treasures of the 4th–5th centuries, excavated from tombs in various local sites. The museum also has a beautiful 17th-century scale model of Namur, made for Louis XIV. In 2018, the collection will move to become part of the Musée des Arts Décoratifs.

🏛 Musée Provincial des Arts Anciens

Rue de Fer 24. **Tel** (081) 776754. **Open** 10am–6pm Tue–Sun. **Closed** 14–25 Dec. 🖼
Ⓦ museedesartsanciens.be

Home to medieval and Renaissance pieces from Namur, the Musée Provincial des Arts Anciens has a remarkable collection of sculptures, paintings, altarpieces, metalwork, armour, stained glass and embroidery. These are elegantly displayed in a fine 18th-century mansion, the Hôtel de Gaiffier d'Hestroy.

Housed in Musée Provincial des Arts Anciens, Le Trésor d'Oignies has exquisite examples of medieval Mosan (of the Meuse) silver and gold work, ivory carvings, enamelware, glass and mitres. The treasury once belonged to the Priory of Oignies in Hainaut, but was whisked away and hidden from the armies of the French Revolution who destroyed the priory in 1794. The most celebrated pieces are by the 13th-century monk, Hugo d'Oignies, and include bejewelled reliquaries, crosses and ecclesiastical book covers.

Modern galleries at the Musée Provincial des Arts Anciens

The lofty nave and unusual sandstone ceiling at the Église St-Loup

🏛 Église St-Loup
Rue du Collège.
🌐 eglisesaintloup.be

One of the great Baroque churches of Belgium, the Église St-Loup was built for the Jesuits between 1621 and 1645. Its striking façade, adorned by muscular banded pillars, gives way to an equally robust interior with banded pillars of coloured marble and a contrasting ceiling of carved sandstone. The French poet Charles Baudelaire, a friend of the Namur artist Félicien Rops (1833–98), suffered a stroke here in 1866, the year before his death; he was fascinated by the church, which he found to be

deliciously funereal. It is now used for concerts.

🏛 Musée Provincial Félicien Rops
Rue Fumal 12. **Tel** (081) 776755.
Open Jul–Aug: 10am–6pm daily;
Sep–Jun: 10am–6pm Tue–Sun.
Closed 24, 25 & 31 Dec, 1 Jan. 🅿 🔇
🌐 museerops.be

A gifted Symbolist artist, Félicien Rops was born in Namur. He is known for his vividly imagined compositions, often macabre and sacrilegious. Rops moved to Paris in 1874, where he led a colourful life among the avant-garde literary set and became a successful illustrator of their

work. Set in an 18th-century townhouse, Musée Provincial Félicien Rops has a collection of about 3,000 paintings, prints and drawings by Rops. It showcases a large selection of the best, assisted by audio guides and multimedia presentations.

🏛 Musée des Arts Décoratifs
Rue Saintraint 3. **Tel** (081) 248723.
Open Call or see website for opening hours. 🅿 ✏ 📷 🌐 ville.namur.be

The magnificent 18th-century Groesbeeck de Croix mansion has been preserved and restored in Enlightenment and Louis XV styles to provide a sympathetic backdrop for an impressive collection of paintings, sculpture, antique furniture, tapestries, gold and silverwork, clocks and *objets d'art*. Outside the mansion is a pleasant formal garden.

Namur

① The Citadelle
② Musée Archéologique de Namur
③ Musée Provincial des Arts Anciens
④ Église St-Loup
⑤ Musée Provincial Félicien Rops
⑥ Musée des Arts Décoratifs

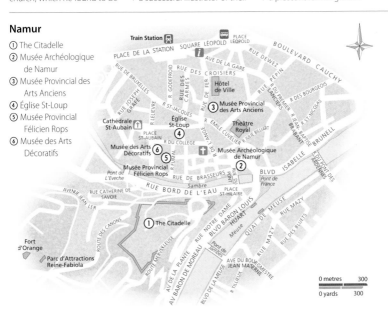

For keys to symbols *see back flap*

❾ Corroy-le-Château

Rue de Corroy-le-Château 4, Gembloux; 20 km (12 miles) NW of Namur. **Road Map** D3. **Tel** (081) 633232. ℹ Office du Tourisme de Gembloux, Rue Sigebert 1; (081) 626960. **W** **corroy-le-chateau.com**

Its woodland setting gives this splendid medieval fortress a romantic appeal. The robust 13th-century towers and gateway over the moat lead to an intimate U-shaped courtyard inside. The interiors, however, have been much altered over the centuries and are mainly in the 18th- and 19th-century styles. The castle had been in the same family since 1270, but a protracted succession dispute led to its sale in 2008. Many concerts and special events are held throughout the year, including a medieval fête in late April, with jousting knights on horseback.

❿ Abbaye de Floreffe

Rue du Séminaire 7, Floreffe; 11 km (7 miles) SW of Namur. **Road Map** D3. **Tel** (081) 445303. **Open** Jul–Aug: 10:30am & 11:30am; Apr–Jun & Sep: every hour 10:30am–5:30pm. 🖉 📷 📷 **W** **abbaye-de-floreffe.be** Moulin-Brasserie: **Open** 11am–6pm Mon–Fri, 11am–8pm Sat & Sun.

Occupying a commanding position on a hilltop above River Sambre, the Abbaye de Floreffe exudes a reassuring authority. St Norbert (*see p167*) founded a

The moat and towers at the entrance to Corroy-le-Château

monastery on this site in 1121 and it became one of the region's leading Premonstratensian abbeys. Wrecked many times by military action, it was largely remodelled in the 18th century in an imposing late-Renaissance style. It was then closed during the French Revolution, but reopened as a seminary in 1830. The church, dating from the 13th century, is an atmospheric potpourri of styles ranging from Neo-Classical to Romanesque. The highlights are the exceptional Baroque choir stalls, masterpieces of the German-born sculptor Pieter Enderlin, who devoted 16 years (1632–48) to the intricate carvings.

The abbey is also famous as a producer of beer, cheese and bread, and its products can be sampled at the now restored 13th-century brewery, the **Moulin-Brasserie**.

⓫ Jardins d'Annevoie

Rue des Jardins d'Annevoie 37, Annevoie; 12 km (7 miles) SE of Floreffe. **Road Map** D3. **Tel** (082) 679797. 🚃 🚃 **Open** Apr–Nov: 9am–5pm Mon–Fri. 🖉 ♿ 📷 📷 **W** **annevoie.be**

The elegant 18th-century **Château d'Annevoie** is famous for its beautiful park packed with water features. Supplied by four springs filling a long basin called the Grand Canal, they include a number of fountains, pools and waterfalls including the strangely hushed corrugated waterfall. Statues, formal gardens, woodland glades and a grotto help create an enchanting environment, all of which was designed in the 18th-century to reflect French and Italian tastes of the period. The château itself has been in the Montpellier family since 1675, and is unfortunately not open to visitors.

⓬ Brasserie du Bocq

Rue de la Brasserie 4, Purnode; 8 km (5 miles) SE of Annevoie-Rouillon. **Road Map** D3. **Tel** (082) 610780; (082) 610790 for reservations. 🚃 **Open** Jul–Aug: daily; late Mar–Jun and Sep–Oct: Sat & Sun. 📷 📷 2pm & 5pm. 📷 **W** **bocq.be**

The picturesque, whitewashed Brasserie du Bocq at Purnode was founded by Martin Belot in 1858 and is still run by the family. It makes a wide range of beers, including St Benoît, Triple Moine,

Fountains at the extensive and beautiful gardens of the Château d'Annevoie

For hotels and restaurants see pp269–70 and pp289–90

Saison Régal and Blanche de Namur. Guided tours take in the old copper brewing vessels and the various stages of production, and end with a tasting. Nearby, **Spontin**, also in the Bocq valley, is famous for its mineral water as well as a fairytale medieval château, but this is no longer open to the public.

A river cruise boat passing beneath a bridge on the River Meuse at Dinant

❸ Dinant

23 km (14 miles) S of Namur.
Road Map D3. 🚉 13,900. 🚗 🚌 🚆
ℹ️ Avenue Cadoux, 8; (082) 222870.
🖥️ dinant-tourisme.com

The small town of Dinant has one of the most beguiling and distinctive settings in Belgium. Standing on the east bank of the River Meuse, it clusters around the black onion dome of a Gothic church and under the shadow of a fortress on an escarpment above. Dinant was occupied by the Romans and valued for its commanding position on the navigable River Meuse. It became prosperous in the Middle Ages as a centre for metal-working, earning an international reputation for ornately decorated copperware and brassware known as *dinanderie*.

Dominating the town is the church **Collégiale Notre-Dame** whose interior contains two paintings by the Dinant-born, macabre-Romantic painter Antoine Wiertz (1806–65). The Place Reine Astrid, just to the south of the church, is the departure station for the *téléphérique* (cable car) to the **Citadelle**, which is also accessible to walkers via 408 steps. In 1466, Charles the Bold, Duke of Burgundy, sacked the town, after which the Citadelle was rebuilt and reinforced in an effort to prevent such invasions. More changes were made over the centuries and the Citadelle is now primarily 19th-century, and offers glorious views over the Meuse. Its military museum recalls the conflicts that took a heavy toll on Dinant, notably in the two World Wars. About 1 km (half a mile) to the south of the town is the **Rocher Bayard**, a pinnacle of rock, which marks

the most westerly point reached by German troops in the Ardennes Offensive *(see p235)*. The name, however, comes from the legend of the rock's creation, supposedly by the hoof of the mighty steed Bayard *(see p143)*.

Dinant is famous for its hard, sculptured honey-based biscuits called *couques de Dinant*, which are used as much for decoration as eating. The town is also the home of the famous abbey beer Leffe. Opposite the old Abbaye de Leffe, located inside Hotel La Merveilleuse, is its brewery museum called the **Musée de la Leffe**.

Quays beside the Avenue Winston Churchill are the departure point for cruises on the River Meuse. On its west bank, 500 m (547 yards) west of the bridge, is the **Grotte la Merveilleuse**, one of Belgium's best caves for stalactites.

🚡 Citadelle
Place Reine Astrid 3–5 (cable car and ticket office). **Tel** (082) 223670. **Open** Apr–mid-Nov: daily; mid-Nov–Mar: Sat–Thu (Jan: open only Sat, Sun & school hols). 🅿️ 📷 summer only. 💻
🖥️ citadellededinant.be

🏛️ Musée de la Leffe
Charreau des Capucins 23. **Tel** (082) 229191. **Open** Easter–mid-Nov: 11am–6pm Tue–Sun; winter: 11am–6pm Fri–Sun. 🅿️ 📷 🖥️ breweryvisits.com

🏰 Grotte la Merveilleuse
Route de Philippeville 142. **Tel** (082) 222210. **Open** Apr–Oct daily; Nov–Mar: school holidays. 🅿️ 📷

Adolphe Sax

Dinant was the birthplace of one of the most successful and innovative inventors of musical instruments of all time, Adolphe Sax (1814–94). He followed his father's profession as an instrument maker and musician, moving permanently to Paris in 1841. He is said to have been working on a kind of keyed bugle called the ophicleide when he hit upon the idea of combining this with the single-reed mouthpiece

Adolphe Sax, famed Belgian innovator

of a clarinet. The saxophone was born, and in 1846, it was patented in seven registers, from contrabass to sopranino. With its conical metal bore and set of keys to operate the valves, it could produce just the kind of volume and expression demanded by opera orchestras, military bands and music halls. It later turned out to be a perfect instrument for jazz. Adolphe Sax did not stop there – he also invented the saxhorn (a family of valved bugles) and a number of other, less successful, instruments, including the saxtuba and saxotromba, and a trombone with seven tubes and bells.

The saxophone, Sax's best-known creation

Cruise boats line up along the tree-lined banks of the River Meuse

⓮ Abbaye de Maredsous

Rue de Maredsous 11, Denée; 12 km (7 miles) NW of Dinant. **Road Map** D3. **Tel** (082) 698211. **Open** daily. 🔁 📧 🏠 **W** maredsous.com

A vast Neo-Gothic monastery founded by the Benedictines in 1872, Abbaye de Maredsous is set in the tranquil Molignée valley and built in austere grey stone. The abbey offers insight into the lives of the monks and a chance to sample two of the institution's famous products – a soft, orange-rind cheese and the respected abbey beer. The grounds have gardens, a playground and walks into the surrounding countryside. There is also a shop selling regional produce at the Centre d'Acceuil St-Joseph.

The soaring and polished chancel of the Abbaye de Maredsous

Environs

With **Railbikes of the Molignée**, visitors can pedal along the Molignée valley on a four-person *draisine* (railbike), on disused railway lines linking Falaën, Maredsous and Warnant. Falaën, set 4 km (3 miles) southeast of Maredsous, has the ruins of a mighty 14th-century castle, **Château-Fort de Montaigle**, which was destroyed by the French in 1554.

Railbikes of the Molignée

Rue de la Molignée 116, Anhée. **Tel** (082) 699079. **Open** daily (Falaën); Apr–Oct: Tue–Sun (Warnant). 🚲 🔁 **W** draisine.be

🏰 Château-Fort de Montaigle

Rue du Marteau 10, Falaën. **Tel** (082) 699585. **Open** Jul–Aug: daily; Apr–Jun & Sep–Oct: Sat & Sun. 🚲 **W** montaigle.be

⓯ River Meuse

Road Map D3. ℹ️ La Compagnie des Bateaux Touristes de la Meuse, Rue Daoust 64, Dinant; (082) 223670. **W** croisieres-mosanes.be

Flowing north out of France, River Meuse enters Belgium via the Province of Namur, coursing past Hastière and the Château de Freÿr to Dinant (*see p209*), and then on to Namur (*see pp206–207*). Here, it is joined by River Sambre and heads east to Liège. The prettiest part runs between Dinant and Namur and many long-established boat cruises offer trips along

this stretch. Fully-equipped sightseeing boats make scheduled excursions up and down the river. The main departure points are at Dinant and Namur. The round-trip between the two takes about 9 hours, but there are numerous shorter trips to points in between. It is necessary, however, to check about landing possibilities as most boat trips do not stop at their destination, but simply turn round. Landscape, and the pleasure of being on water, are the main attractions. The river banks are dotted with rocky outcrops and ruined castles. Points in between include the pretty towns of **Profondeville** and **Wépion**, the most famous source of strawberries in Belgium.

South of Dinant, the stretch up to Hastière and Waulsort is also rewarding and includes the splendid castle at Freÿr. The main season for river trips runs from May to September, with mid-July to late August being busiest.

⓰ Château de Freÿr

Domaine de Freÿr, Hastière; 5 km (3 miles) S of Dinant. **Road Map** D3. **Tel** (082) 222200. 🚌 **Open** Apr–Jun & Sep–mid-Nov: Sat, Sun & public hols; Jul–Aug: 11am–5pm Tue–Fri. 🚲 🔁 **W** freyr.be

One of the most impressive châteaux in Belgium stands right beside the broad River

Meuse. Originally a medieval fortress commanding the river, it was destroyed by the French in 1554, then rebuilt as a palatial residence in fetching Mosan Renaissance style, with touches of French château grandeur, between the 16th and 18th centuries. This was the home of the influential dukes of Beaufort-Spontin. Louis XIV of France stayed here during his siege of Dinant in 1675 and, later that year, signed the Treaty of Freÿr with Charles II of Spain. In the 1770s, the Austrian governor of the Netherlands, Charles of Lorraine, was a visitor.

The château is still owned by the 20th generation of the Beaufort family. Its Italianesque interior is decorated with wood panelling, tapestry, paintings and murals. Outside is a large formal garden in 18th-century French style, with parterres, fountains, pools, an orangery (with 300-year-old orange trees), follies, hedged mazes and an ornate Rococo pavilion overlooking the River Meuse.

The name Freÿr relates to the legend that Freya, the Scandinavian goddess of fertility, stopped to rest here in a cave on the rocky banks of the Meuse, and had to be rescued from a band of naughty Nutons – the elves that play a major role in local mythology.

The medieval frame and conical towers of the Château de Vêves

⑰ Château de Vêves

Noisy 5, Celles-Houyet; 8 km (5 miles) SE of Dinant. **Road Map** D3. **Tel** (082) 666395. **Open** Easter, Jul–Aug & 1 Nov: 10am–5pm daily; Apr–early Nov: 10am–5pm Sat, Sun & public hols. 🅿 🆆 chateau-de-veves.be

Perched on a grassy hillock with massive walls, five tall, cone-topped towers and high windows, the 15th-century Château de Vêves resembles a child's drawing of a fantasy castle. Its half-timbered galleries overlook a fully enclosed courtyard. Parts of the interior, such as the huge medieval kitchens, are pleasingly robust, but the private family rooms have been softened by 18th-century refinements. The Seigneurs de Celles, who took possession of

a fortress on this site in the 12th century, came from the Beaufort family, and their descendants still use the castle as a residence, giving it the rare feeling of live-in continuity. The nearby village of **Celles** is considered to be one of the prettiest in Wallonia.

⑱ Basilique St-Materne

Rue de la Basilique 12, Walcourt; 18 km (11 miles) S of Charleroi. **Road Map** C3. **Tel** (071) 611366. 🚆 🚌 🅸 Grand Place 25. **Open** daily. 🅿 treasury. 🆆 walcourt.be

A large 13th- to 15th-century church, Basilique St-Materne is distinguished by its turrets and peculiar onion-shaped tips on its spire. Said to be founded by the 4th-century St Maternus of Tongeren, the church became a pilgrimage site focussing on devotion to Notre Dame de Walcourt, a wooden statue dating from the 10th century (with 17th-century silver plating) that now stands in the north transept. This history explains the basilica's size, as well as the richness of its interior, which includes a flamboyant Gothic *jubé* (rood screen), believed to have been presented by Charles V in 1531. The church's **Treasury** also has many exquisite devotional objects, some of which may be the work of the great 13th-century goldsmith Hugo d'Oignies (*see p206*).

Environs

Philippeville, 9 km (6 miles) to the southeast, was a fortress town built by Emperor Charles V in 1555 and modernized by the French military architect Vauban in the 17th century. The fortress was demolished in 1860, leaving 10 km (6 miles) of underground passages, called **Les Souterrains**, part of which can be visited by a guided tour.

Les Souterrains

Philippeville. 🅸 Rue des Religieuses 2; (071) 662300. **Open** call or check website for times. 🆆 philippeville.be
🆆 valleesdeseauxvives.be

Stately grandeur of the Mosan Renaissance Château de Freÿr

Caves of the Ardennes

Large areas of the Ardennes consist of karst – areas of soft, porous limestone that, over the centuries, have been gouged out, tunnelled and dissolved by rivers, streams and rain. In numerous places, this has created honeycombs of underground passageways and galleries, some still filled with lakes and rivers and containing fantastical arrays of stalactites and stalagmites. The best of these caves, or *grottes*, have now become major attractions. Visitors are led deep into the landscape, sometimes in boats, to see these extraordinary sculptural formations under dramatic illumination. There is evidence too, that some of these caves were shelters for prehistoric people.

Grottes de Goyet at Gesves, occupied by Neanderthals 40,000 years ago

Grotte la Merveilleuse in Dinant is celebrated for its "frozen waterfalls": stalactites and stalagmites with the glistening limestone seemingly captured in mid-flow. Guided tours, lasting about 50 minutes, lead visitors through successive chambers via a series of pathways and steps.

Sink holes allow water into the bed of limestone.

Cave Systems

The limestone caves of the Ardennes are celebrated for their astonishing range of concretions of fused stalactite and stalagmite. Streams that are formed by surface water enter cave systems through a sink hole, replenishing the underground rivers. Water dripping through the cave ceiling deposits particles of limestone that slowly build up stalactites, and corresponding stalagmites on the cave floor. The underground river, on a bed of harder rock, continues to carve a path through the softer limestone.

The Grottes de Hotton *(see p230)* form a network of deep, underground passages. Narrow paths lead down to a succession of dripping galleries draped with sculptural limestone, noted for its extraordinary range of delicate shapes and colours. The base is flooded by a siphon that marks the modern water table.

The Grottes de Lorette at Rochefort *(see p215)* has been revamped and now has a visitors' centre that delves into the broader realms of geology, including plate tectonics. A man-made corridor cuts through impervious marble to reach the largest of its underground chambers called the Sabbath, the setting for a son-et-lumière presentation.

Former sink holes provide water-free entrances to the cave system.

The Grottes de Remouchamps *(see p229)* have an 8,000-year-old history of human encounter. They opened to visitors in 1912 and were illuminated in 1924. A walkway leads down to a giant chamber called the Cathedral, from where boats follow the underground river, Rubicon, which carved out these caves on its way to the Amblève.

Stalactites and stalagmites line the limestone caves, and over the years, fuse to form a single structure.

The Grottes de Han at Han-sur-Lesse *(see p215)* is the most famous cave system of the Ardennes. In boats and on foot, visitors can see about 3 km (2 miles) of a huge cave system carved out by the River Lesse. Mirror-still pools reflect the bejewelled ceilings.

The Grottes de Neptune near Couvin *(see p214)* take visitors through three levels of caves and underground rivers, with a boat trip leading to a spectacular son-et-lumière presentation.

⓳ Mariembourg

34 km (21 miles) SW of Dinant.
Road Map C4. 🚉 3,000. 🚌 🚐
ℹ️ (060) 340140 (Couvin).

The old frontier fortress-town of Mariembourg was built in 1542 by Holy Roman Emperor Charles V and his sister, Mary of Hungary, after whom it was named. Although supposedly impregnable, it was captured by the French in 1554, but retaken by the Spanish in 1559. Exactly a century later, it was handed over to Louis XIV of France by treaty, and remained French until taken by the Prussians in 1815. The fortifications were demolished in 1855, leaving only the star-shaped grid of the street plan.

Mariembourg became an important railway junction. It is now the starting point for historic steam trains that journey through the beautiful Les Trois Vallées. The **Chemin de Fer des Trois Vallées** (Railway of the Three Valleys) takes a 14-km (8-mile) long route by the Viroin valley. Mariembourg's **Karting des Fagnes** has one of Europe's longest go-kart tracks.

🚂 Chemin de Fer des Trois Vallées

Chaussée de Givet 49–51 **Tel** (060) 312440. **Open** Jul–Aug: daily; Mar–Jun & Sep–Oct: Sat & Sun. 🚫 ♿
W cfv3v.in-site-out.com

🏁 Karting des Fagnes

Parc Industriel, 13. **Tel** (060) 312670. **Open** Jul–Aug: daily. **Closed** Thu during the off season. 🚫 📷
W kartingdesfagnes.com

A historic steam engine running on the tracks at Mariembourg

Slate-roofed houses of Couvin, a pretty setting for industrial history

⓴ Couvin

5 km (3 miles) S of Mariembourg.
Road Map C4. 🚉 14,000. 🚐
ℹ️ Office du Tourisme de Couvin, Rue de la Falaise 3; (060) 340140.
W couvin.be

A fetching little slate-roofed town set on the River Eau Noire, Couvin is a popular centre for exploring the Fagnes – an unspoilt region of forests and meadows on a bed of clay, slate and limestone. Couvin was once an important iron- and steel-working centre and vestiges of its industrial past are still evident. The town's prettiest quarter is set on a rocky crag, formerly the site of a castle destroyed by the French in 1672. This area was inhabited by Neanderthals in prehistoric times, as witnessed in the caves and museum of the **Cavernes de l'Abîme**. A combination ticket includes the **Grottes de Neptune**, 3 km (2 miles) to the northeast. These are classic limestone caves of stalactites and stalagmites through which flows the River Eau Noire.

Environs

Near the historic village of Nismes, 5 km (3 miles) to the northeast, is a curious canyon-like weathered limestone formation called the **Fondry des Chiens**. Also of interest are the wooded hills near Brûly-de-Pesche, 8 km (5 miles) southwest of Couvin, which form the setting of the **Grand Quartier Général Allemand 1940** (German Headquarters 1940). Called Wolfsschlucht (Wolf's Ravine), they include

bunkers from which Hitler directed his assault on France in July 1940, plus a small museum.

🏛️ Cavernes de l'Abîme

Rue de la Falaise. **Tel** (060) 311954. **Open** Jul–Aug: daily; Feb–Dec: Thu–Tue. 🚫

🏛️ Grottes de Neptune

Route du l'Adugeoir. **Tel** (060) 311954. **Open** Feb–mid-Nov: see website as some days require reservations. 🚫
📷 W grottesdeneptune.be

㉑ Treignes

15 km (9 miles) E of Couvin.
Road Map D4. 🚉 700. 🚌 ℹ️ Office du Tourisme de Viroinval, Rue Vieille Église 2; (060) 311635. 🚪 Tue–Sun.
W treignes.info

Styling itself as the *village des musées*, Treignes is home to four museums. Formerly a key railway hub for trains crossing into France, the town now serves as the terminus of the Chemin de Fer des Trois Vallées. Treignes's **Musée du Chemin de Fer à Vapeur** (Museum of Steam Railways), is located on the grounds of the old international railway station and contains a major collection of historic trains and associated memorabilia. The station itself was bought by the Université Libre de Bruxelles in 1972 as a centre for environmental studies. The university now also runs the **Ecomusée du Viroin**, lodged in an old *château-ferme* (fortified farm), presenting the traditional crafts and agricultural heritage of the Viroin valley, as well as its flora and fauna. The **Musée Malgré du Tout et Parc de la Préhistoire** explores the lives of prehistoric hunters and farmers through archaeological finds and reconstructions. Lastly, the **Espace Arthur Masson**, in an old boys' school, celebrates the life and work of local novelist Arthur Masson (1896–1970).

🏛 Musée du Chemin de Fer à Vapeur
Plateau de la Gare 1. **Tel** (060) 300948. **Open** Jul–Aug: daily; Mar–Jun & Sep–Nov: Tue–Sun. 🅿 💻 📷
🚂 Steam Festival (2nd weekend of Sep). **W** insiteout.brinkster.net

🏛 Ecomusée du Viroin
Rue Eugène Defraire 63. **Tel** (060) 399624. **Open** daily. 🅿 💻 📷
W ecomuseeduviroin.be

🏛 Musée du Malgré Tout
Rue de la Gare 28. **Tel** (060) 390243. **Open** Thu–Tue. 🅿 📷
W museedumalgretout.be

🏛 Espace Arthur Masson
Rue Eugène Defraire 29. **Tel** (060) 391500. **Open** Mar–Oct: Tue–Sun; Nov, Dec & Feb: Tue–Thu, Sat, Sun. 🅿 🔇 💻 📷 **W** espacemasson.be

㉒ Château de Lavaux-Ste-Anne
Rue du Château 8, Lavaux-Ste-Anne; 44 km (27 miles) E of Couvin. **Road Map** D4. **Tel** (084) 388362. **Open** 10am–6pm Wed–Sun & public hols (daily in school hols). **Closed** 1 Jan, 24, 25 & 31 Dec. 🅿 💻 📷
W chateau-lavaux.com

Located on the plains of the Famenne region, part fortress, part château, Lavaux-Ste-Anne is a fusion of power and elegance. Dating to 1193, it has round 15th-century corner towers, topped by onion domes, rising from a moat. In contrast, the courtyard inside is flanked by arcaded Renaissance façades. The interior has a series of furnished rooms with museums on local wildlife and traditions of Famenne rural life. Visitors can also join tours of the surrounding wetlands.

Environs
Beauraing, 11 km (7 miles) to the west, has numerous sanctuaries that serve pilgrims

Striking corner towers of the sturdy Château de Lavaux-St-Anne

visiting the site where the Virgin Mary appeared to five children in 1932 and 1933.

㉓ Domaine des Grottes de Han
Rue J Lamotte 2, Han-sur-Lesse; 7 km (4 miles) E of Lavaux-Ste-Anne. **Road Map** D4. **Tel** (084) 377213. 🚌 **Open** Apr–Aug: daily; Sep–Mar: more restricted timetable, see website for details. **Closed** Jan. 🅿 🔇 💻 📷
W grotte-de-han.be

The most celebrated limestone cave system of the Ardennes, the Grottes de Han is situated in the pretty valley of River Lesse. The river also flows through the cave and has created its impressive water features. Access to the cave entrance is by means of a historic tram from the centre of the village of Han-sur-Lesse. There are impressive galleries of stalactites and stalagmites, but boat rides through the caverns are perhaps the most memorable highlight. Part of

the same complex is **Réserve d'Animaux Sauvages**, a safari-style park featuring animals once native to the Ardennes. These include bears, lynx, bison, wild boar and wolves. Tours of the reserve are conducted in open-sided coaches.

㉔ Rochefort
5 km (3 miles) NE of Han-sur-Lesse. **Road Map** D4. 🏔 12,500. 🚉 🚌
ℹ Maison du Tourisme du Val de Lesse, Rue de Behogne 5; (084) 345172. **W** valdelesse.be

A pleasant town, Rochefort serves as a good base from which to fan out into the wooded hills and valleys of the Ardennes. Rochefort's big attraction is the **Grottes de Lorette**, a limestone cave that is unusual for its towering verticality. There are good views over the town from the **Château Comtal**, set upon a rocky outcrop. The château consists of a Neo-Gothic castle dating from 1906, built next to the ruins of a castle dating from 1155 and demolished in the 1740s. The celebrated Trappist beer called Rochefort is made at the monastery at St Rémy 2 km (1 mile) to the north, but the brewery is not open to the public.

🕳 Grottes de Lorette
Drève de Lorette. **Tel** (084) 212080. **Open** Jul & Aug: 10:30am–4:15pm (visits every 45 mins); Apr–early-Nov: daily. **Closed** Wed.

🏰 Château Comtal
Rue Jacquet. **Tel** (084) 214409. **Open** call or check website for times. 🅿 **W** chateaurochefort.be

Visitors near a bear enclosure in the Réserve d'Animaux Sauvages

EASTERN WALLONIA

Known above all for its slice of the Ardennes, Eastern Wallonia is a dramatically hilly area of farmland and forests, threaded by fast-flowing rivers and dotted with tranquil towns and villages. Comprising the provinces of Liège and Luxembourg, this once remote region now attracts many visitors, who come to walk or cycle through the beautiful landscape or go kayaking on its swift rivers.

Throughout much of its history, Liège traced a path different from that of the rest of Belgium. Ruled by prince-bishops since the 10th century, it was a principality of the Holy Roman Empire, but was fiercely proud of its autonomous status. Its territory stretched at times right across the central band of Belgium to the French border. Liège retained its prince-bishops until they were overthrown by rebels during the French Revolution in 1789–94. In 1830, it joined Belgium in the struggle for independence. The Belgian industrial revolution also began near Liège, kick-started by the English entrepreneurs William and John Cockerill, who brought the age of steam to Wallonia's textile industry in the 1800s and set up iron mills just outside the city.

Maps have been repeatedly redrawn in the border areas between Belgium and its neighbours. The Province of Luxembourg formerly belonged to the Duchy of Luxembourg, but under the Treaty of London of 1839, the Duchy was split in two. The eastern part became an independent country, the Grand Duchy of Luxembourg, while the western part was incorporated into Belgium. Similarly, having been intermittently in Belgian possession, Eupen and the German-speaking community in the Cantons de l'Est have been reclaimed into the Province of Liège since the end of World War II.

Over the years, the once sparsely populated region of Eastern Wallonia has become popular with holiday-makers and outdoor enthusiasts. In winter, skiers flock to the highest areas of the Ardennes, around Spa and the Haute Fagnes. Several medieval castles, modern battlefields and museums attract summer visitors.

The immaculately maintained and serene Abbaye d'Orval, a functioning Cistercian monastery

◀ The river Semois running through a valley in Bouillion, Eastern Wallonia

Exploring Eastern Wallonia

The city of Liège, on the broad River Meuse, remains the main urban centre, surrounded by modern enterprises. Vestiges of the more distant industrial past can be seen at the coal mine at Blégny. Durbuy ranks as one of the prettiest towns in Belgium, while the rural traditions of the Ardennes are presented at Fourneau St-Michel's museums. To the east, the Hautes Fagnes, a wild area of moorland, are the highest part of the Ardennes. Many of the towns in the Province of Luxembourg, notably Bastogne, have monuments and museums that recall the devastation at the end of World War II. Further south, the River Semois runs through wooded hills, passing beneath the dramatic medieval castle of Bouillon, and forming some of the most beautiful landscapes in all Belgium.

The eye-catching Renaissance façade of the Château de Jehay

Sights at a Glance

Getting Around

Liège airport focusses on cargo transport, but is also used for passenger (mainly charter) flights. Motorways link the city to Brussels, Luxembourg, Charleroi, Antwerp and major cities across the border in the Netherlands and Germany. SNCB rail routes connect many of the main towns, but, owing to the rugged landscape, are relatively sparse. TEC Namur-Luxembourg provides a bus network to complement the trains, and includes a phone-a-ride Telbus service reaching 270 villages in Luxembourg. The greatest concentration of GR paths in Belgium are in the north of this region, around the Hautes Fagnes and the valleys of the rivers Ourthe and Amblève.

Key

	Motorway
	Major road
	Secondary road
	Minor road
	Main railway
	Minor railway
	International border
	Provincial border

0 kilometres 15

0 miles 15

Majestic and elegant, the Gothic interior of the basilica at St-Hubert

For keys to symbols *see back flap*

❶ Liège

A busy port-city straddling the River Meuse, Liège has a 20th-century industrial air peppered with medieval and Baroque exuberance. It is known as La Cité Ardent (The Hot-Blooded City), a reference to its fractious history as part of the fiercely independent Principality of Liège. The Coeur Historique (Historic Heart) of the city lies to the north of the River Meuse, around the parallel roads Féronstrée and Rue Hors-Château. Tiny dead-end alleys called Impasses thread north from here, and steps climb up to the old Citadelle, with its panoramic views and interesting hill walks. The Place St-Lambert is the city's main square, overlooked by the Palais des Princes-Évêques. A modern commercial area lies to its southwest, which is served by the Gare du Palais train station.

Display at the Musée des Beaux-Arts de Liège (BAL)

🏛 Place St-Lambert

Junction of Rue Joffre and Rue Léopold. Palais des Princes-Évêques: **Open** 10am–6pm Mon–Sun. Archéoforum: **Tel** (04) 2509370. **Open** 9am–5pm Tue–Fri, 10am–5pm Sat & Sun. **Closed** Mon & Sun. 🕐 🅿 📷 🖼 🚻 archeoforum deliege.be

The vast central square of Liège, Place St-Lambert, is dominated by **Palais des Princes-Évêques** (Palace of the Prince-Bishops), a mainly 18th-century building in Neo-Classical style. It now houses the Palace of Justice and other government offices, but visitors can explore its 16th-century Renaissance courtyard, which has notable relief sculptures on the columns. The square was the site of the huge Cathédrale St-Lambert, a major pilgrimage centre built in honour of St Lambert of Maastricht, who was murdered here in AD 705. Liégoise revolutionaries destroyed the cathedral between 1794 and 1803, but its foundations, some Roman remains and a history of the city can be seen at **Archéoforum**, a subterranean museum under the square.

🏛 Le Perron

Hôtel de Ville, Place du Marché 2.

A symbol of civic liberty in the principality, Le Perron is a large stone pillared monument with fountains and balustrades, topped by a single column. The first perrons date from the 11th century, when town guilds bought liberties from their rulers, and laws and judgements were announced in front of them. The association of Le Perron with Liège's independence was so strong that when Charles the Bold suppressed the city's rebellion in 1468, he took the column back to Bruges. It was not restored till his death. The current monument is from the late 17th century, and is crowned by the Three Graces and the symbol of the authority of the

Carving atop Le Perron

prince-bishops, a pine cone and cross. Nearby, the elegant red **Hôtel de Ville** dates from 1718. Its beautiful Italianate entrance hall has a balcony supported by expressive wood sculptures of classical gods.

🏛 Musée de la Vie Wallonne

Cour des Mineurs 1. **Tel** (04) 2379060. **Open** 9:30am–6pm Tue–Sun. **Closed** 1 Jan, 2nd week in Jan, 1 May, 1 Nov & 25 Dec. 🕐 🅿 📷 🚻 province deliege.be/viewwallonne

One of the best folklore and local history museums in the country, the Musée de la Vie Wallonne (Museum of Walloon Life) is housed in a former convent, which was recently modernized. The courtyard is in the austere style of late 17th-century Mosan (that is, of the Meuse) architecture, while the interior provides a fascinating tour of daily life in this region until the recent past. The large collection features historic crafts and industries, furniture and domestic wares, religious fetishes and medical equipment, as well as antique posters, old photographs that can be seen through antique stereoscopes, and some splendid oddities such as a real guillotine, which was last used in 1824.

🏛 Musée des Beaux-Arts de Liège (BAL)

Ilôt St-Georges Féronstrée 86. **Tel** (04) 2219231. **Open** 10am–6pm Tue–Sun. **Closed** 1 Jan, 1 May, 1, 2 & 11 Nov, 25 Dec. 🕐 📷 🚻 beauxartsliege.be

Spiralling floors in a 1970s building display the permanent collection of the Musée des Beaux-Arts de Liège, containing

The elegant façade behind Hôtel de Ville in Liège's Coeur Historique

For hotels and restaurants see pp270–71 and pp290–91

more than 3,000 works of art. It features work by Liège's Renaissance genius Lambert Lombard (1505–66) and by the outstanding 18th-century sculptor Jean Del Cour (1627–1707). There are also paintings by the leading Belgian Neo-Classical artist François-Joseph Navez and a single work by Antoine Wiertz (see p27). Other famed Belgian artists such as Félicien Rops, René Magritte, Alfred Stevens, Henri Evenepoel, Paul Delvaux and Constantin Meunier are also represented.

Also housed within the Musée des Beaux-Arts de Liège is the exquisite collection originally part of the Musée d'Art Moderne et d'Art Contemporain (MAMAC). This collection dates back to the late 19th century and is presented on a rotating basis.

Period furniture at the Musée d'Ansembourg

It includes work by Belgian artists such as Theo van Rysselberghe, Fernand Khnopff, Emile Claus, James Ensor, Constant Permeke and Rik Wouters (see p77), as well as such international luminaries as Pissarro, Signac, Gauguin, Kokoschka, Monet, Picasso and Chagall.

🏛 Musée d'Ansembourg

Féronstrée 114. **Tel** (04) 2219402. **Open** 10am–6pm Thu–Sun. 🅿 🖼 🖥 liege.be

Set in the Coeur Historique, this 18th-century banker's mansion contains authentic rooms filled with high-quality 18th-century furniture and furnishings. Many of them were produced locally by the skilled craftsmen of Liège.

🏛 Musée Grand Curtius

Féronstrée 136. **Tel** (04) 2216840. **Open** 10am–6pm Wed–Mon. 🅿 📷 🔖 🖥 grandcurtiusliege.be

Reopened with great fanfare in 2009, the Musée Grand Curtius brings together the contents of several Liège museums to create one of Europe's best centres for the decorative arts.

VISITORS' CHECKLIST

Practical Information
87 km (54 miles) SE of Brussels.
Road Map E2. 🅰 195,000.
ℹ Féronstrée 92; (04) 2219221.
🛒 La Batte (Sun). 🎭 Festival of the Republique Libre d'Outremeuse (15 Aug). 🖥 **liege.be**

Transport
🚊 🚌 🚆 🚇

The main building is the striped red-brick Maison Curtius, which was the home and headquarters of the wealthy entrepreneur and arms dealer, Jean de Curtius (1551–1628). The current collection of the museum features several archaeological treasures from Ancient Egypt and the Roman and Frankish eras, masterpieces of magnificent medieval Mosan craftsmanship, tapestries, ceramics and many impressive paintings. It also contains world-class collections of fine antique glassware; French clocks dating from 1775 to 1825, in lavish Louis XVI and Empire styles; as well as historic weapons and firearms. It also regularly mounts temporary exhibitions of high international calibre.

Liège

① Place St-Lambert
② Le Perron
③ Musée de la Vie Wallonne
④ Musée des Beaux-Arts de Liège (BAL)
⑤ Musée d'Ansembourg
⑥ Musée Grand Curtius
⑦ Cathédrale St-Paul
⑧ Église St-Jacques
⑨ Aquarium-Muséum
⑩ Musée Tchantchès

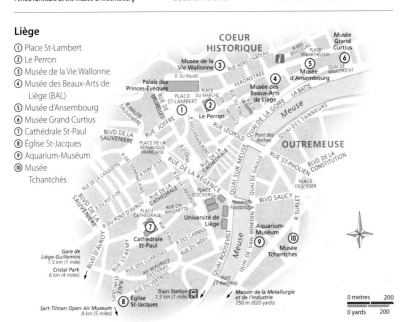

For keys to symbols see back flap

Exploring Liège

South of the Coeur Historique, the commercial heart of Liège is clustered around two fine churches, the Cathédrale St-Paul and Église St-Jacques. Further south is the city's prestigious architectural project, the Gare de Liège-Guillemins. Bridges across the River Meuse lead eastwards to the Outremeuse district, which is actually an island formed by a split in the river at its confluence with the River Ourthe. This is an area with its own accent and traditions and was once the haunt of the author Georges Simenon. The annual Festival of the République Libre d'Outremeuse held in August, is an expression of its independent spirit. There are a number of interesting museums on the island and to its east.

Graceful Gothic vaulting spanning the nave of the Cathédrale St-Paul

🔒 Cathédrale St-Paul

Place Cathédrale. **Tel** (04) 2326131.
Open 8am–5pm daily. 🚫 🎧 ♿
🎧 W tresordeliege.be
Treasury: **Open** 2–5pm Tue–Sun.

This grand though austere church was built over six centuries, beginning in the 13th century. It was promoted to its high status following the destruction of the Cathedral of St Lambert in 1794. Its real attraction is the treasury in the cloister. This contains elaborate pieces of the Mosan school in gold, silver, ivory and enamel. Its supreme treasure is the huge Reliquary of St Lambert – created in about 1512, it is a silver-and-gold bust of the saint and contains his skull. Equally spectacular is the Reliquary of Charles the Bold, which was donated to the city by the duke in 1471. Two statues in gold, silver and enamel depict Charles holding a relic of

St Lambert, with St George standing behind him.

🔒 Église St-Jacques

Place St-Jacques. Tel (04) 2221441.
Open 10am–noon Mon–Fri, 9am–noon Sat & Sun. ✝ 4:30pm Sat, 11am Sun.
🎧 10am–noon, 2–6pm Mon–Fri (5pm Mar & Oct), 10am–noon, 2–4:30pm Sat, 2–6pm Sun (5pm Mar & Oct).

The best church in Liège, the Église St-Jacques still has its original Romanesque narthex, or portico, at its western end. The rest of the church is a triumph of Flamboyant Gothic, built between 1514 and 1538, with a wonderful ceiling of interlaced vaulting high above the nave. The 17th-century statues of the saints lining the nave are painted limewood, carved by Liège's most celebrated sculptor Jean Del Cour. The intense clusters of architectural detail, combined with 19th-century Neo-Gothic decoration, create a rich and uplifting impact.

🐟 Aquarium-Muséum

Quai Van-Beneden 22. **Tel** (04) 3665021. **Open** 9am–5pm Mon–Fri, 10am–6pm Sat, Sun & public holidays; Jul & Aug: 10am–6pm daily. 🚫 🎧 W aquarium-museum.ulg.ac.be

This excellent aquarium has marine and freshwater creatures from all over the world, with 2,500 specimens in 46 tanks. The museum holds a collection of 20,000 stuffed animals and skeletons. Both sets of exhibits belong to the Université de Liège and were founded in the 19th century; hence their location in a 19th-century Neo-Classical building.

🎭 Musée Tchantchès

Rue Surlet 56. Tel (04) 3427575.
Open Sep–Jun: 2–6pm Tue & Thu; Oct–Apr: 10:30am Sun, 2:30pm Wed (performances). 🚫 W tchantches.eu

The vibrant mascot of Liège, Tchantchès is an irreverent, freedom-loving and courageous lover of pékèt (jenever gin) who is said to embody the typical characteristics of the Liégeois. He is usually depicted as a puppet dressed in traditional costume. The original legend places him in Charlemagne's era. Born between the paving stones of the Outremeuse in AD 760, he served the emperor valiantly and chaotically, with his large nose as his sole weapon. His love of boasting is habitually crushed by his equally colourful wife, Nanèsse. The small museum devoted to Tchantchès has costumes, puppets and memorabilia, with a theatre for puppet shows.

The puppet theatre and costume display at Musée Tchantchès

🏛 Sart-Tilman Open-air Museum

Université de Liège-Domaine du Sart-Tilman. **Tel** (04) 3662220. **Open** daily.
🖼 📷 ♿ W **museepla.ulg.ac.be**

Located on the outskirts of Liège, this museum opened in 1977 as a result of a collaboration between the University of Liège and the Ministry of Culture. A perfect blend of nature and architecture, the museum's permanent collection includes more than 110 pieces. They represent the history of modern open-air sculpture in French-speaking Belgium over the past 40 years. Notable works include *The Mad Virgin* by Rik Wouters, *The Eagle* and *Memory* by André Willequet and *Spring* and *The Prostrate* by George Grard. Charles Leplae's *Young Woman Kneeling* is scheduled to be added to the collection.

The Mad Virgin (1912) by artist Rik Wouters

🚉 Gare de Liège-Guillemins

Place des Guillemins 2. **Tel** (04) 2292610.

In 1843, a link was forged between Liège and Aachen, in Germany, making the Gare de Liège-Guillemins the world's first international railway station. Opened in 2009, it forms a major hub on the international TGV high-speed rail network. To mark the station's significance, Liège commissioned award-winning Spanish-Catalan architect Santiago Calatrava to redesign it as an eye-catching landmark. It is a huge, stunning confection of curving steel and glass, a breathtaking introduction to the city, where visitors immediately get a sense of Liège's newly reinvigorated dynamism.

Historic industrial tools at the Maison de la Métallurgie et de l'Industrie

🏛 Maison de la Métallurgie et de l'Industrie

Boulevard Raymond-Poincaré 17. **Tel** (04) 3426563. **Open** Apr–Oct: 9am–5pm Mon–Fri, 2–6pm Sat & Sun; Nov–Mar: 9am–5pm Mon–Fri. 🖼 💻 W **mmil.be**

Located on the site of an old metalwork factory dating from 1845, this museum is the best place to gauge Liège's history as an industrial centre. Steam power was first used by textile mills in nearby Verviers *(see p226)*, and the iron-and-steel-industry developed at Seraing, outside Liège, where Belgium's first railway engines were built in the 1830s. It displays equipment and machinery spanning four centuries, such as forges, iron-furnaces, steam engines and hydraulic hammers.

🏛 Cristal Park

6 km (4 miles) SW of Liège, Esplanade du Val, Seraing. **Tel** (04) 3303620. **Open** Easter–1 Nov: daily; 2 Nov–Easter: Wed, Sat & Sun. 🖼 ♿ 📷 🏛 W **cristalpark.com**

The Cristallerie du Val St Lambert, a famous glass-manufacturer established in 1826, has its headquarters at Cristal Park and the Château du Val St-Lambert. There is a glass workshop where visitors can observe glass being blown, cut and engraved, a museum and a showroom displaying glass for sale.

Georges Simenon

Georges Simenon, alias The Man with the Pipe

Belgium's bestselling author of all time, Georges Simenon (1903–89) was born in Liège, at Rue Léopold 24. When he was two, his family moved across the river to Outremeuse, to a street now renamed Rue Simenon. He trained as a journalist and wrote his first novel in 1919, before heading off to Paris, in 1922, at the age of 19. He went on to write some 350 novels and novellas, translated into many languages; 75 of them feature his most famous creation, the French detective Inspector Maigret, who first appeared in 1931. Maigret reached an even wider audience through the many French feature films based on the novels. After World War II, Simenon lived in the USA and in Switzerland, but Liège continued to occupy his imagination and he set a number of his novels here. The total number of Simenon books printed is thought to be about 550 million. The city's tourist office has a leaflet on the Simenon Trail, which links sites in the Coeur Historique and the Outremeuse districts that are connected to his life.

The fawn-and-white patterned Château de Jehay, rising from its moat

❷ Château de Jehay

Rue du Parc 1, Amay; 20 km (12 miles) SW of Liège. **Road Map** E3. **Tel** (085) 824400. **Open** Apr–Nov: 2–6pm Tue–Fri, 11am–6pm Sat, Sun & Easter weekend. 🅿 🐾
W provincedeliege.be/chateaujehay

With its chequerboard walls of limestone and brown sandstone and its pepperpot towers, this is one of the most delightful castles in Belgium. Although founded in the 11th century, the building dates largely from the 16th century and has a Renaissance feel. In 1698, it was taken over by the van den Steen family. Count Guy van den Steen (1905–99), its most recent owner, was an artist and sculptor who left many works, notably bronze female nudes, *in situ* when he bequeathed the castle to the Province of Liège. The interior contains tapestries, antique furniture, pottery, silverware, maps and manuscripts, as well as archaeological finds.

❸ Huy

28 km (17 miles) SW of Liège. **Road Map** D3. ⬚ 21,350. 🚉 🚌
i Quai de Namur 1; (085) 212915.
W pays-de-huy.be

Founded as a Roman military base, Huy was an important town in the Principality of Liège between AD 985 and 1789. It was renowned in the Middle Ages as a centre for textiles, metal and gold work. Its castle, perched above the town, repeatedly attracted the attention of passing armies,

notably that of Louis XIV of France in the late 17th century; for that reason, the Hutois destroyed it in 1717. Notwithstanding, the Dutch built the massive **Fort de Huy** on the same site in 1818–23. It was used by the Nazis between 1940 and 1944 as a concentration camp – author PG Wodehouse was interned here for a month in 1940. The darker truths of this period are the subject of the **Musée de la Résistance et des Camps de Concentration**. In summer, the fort is accessible by a cable car departing from the left bank of the Meuse.

Huy's main church is the Gothic **Collégiale Notre Dame**, built between 1311 and 1536. Its treasury has fine examples of 12th- to 13th-century Mosan silver and gold work, but the

church is best known for its 15th-century rose window, Li Rondia. This is cited as one of the four wonders of Hutois heritage, the others being Li Tchestia (The Fort), Li Bassinia (the 15th-century fountain in the Grand Place) and Li Pontia (a bridge over the Meuse).

🏰 Fort de Huy
Chaussée Napoléon. **Tel** (085) 215334. **Open** Easter–Sep. 🐾

❹ Château de Modave

11 km (7 miles) SE of Huy.
Road Map E3. **Tel** (085) 411369. **Open** Apr–mid-Nov: 10am–6pm Tue–Sun (Jul–Aug: daily). 🐾 🅿 🚫
W modave-castle.be

Built on a steep rocky spur with views over River Hoyaux, Château de Modave owes its appearance mainly to its overhaul in Flemish Renaissance style by the count of Marchin in 1652–73. The well-furnished rooms are decorated with tapestries, panelling and impressive polychrome stuccowork, and 17th–18th century furniture.

The gardens and fountains of Versailles were fed by a massive hydraulic waterwheel designed by Renkin Sualem (1645–1708), royal engineer to Louis XIV: the 1667 prototype for it was built at Modave, as an exhibition here explains.

Magnificently furnished interior of the Château de Modave

River Vesdre passing under a flag-decked bridge at Chaudfontaine

❺ Chaudfontaine

8 km (5 miles) SE of Liège.
Road Map E3. 🏯 21,000. 🚌
𝑖 Ave des Thermes 78 bis; (04)
3615592. 🆆 chaudfontaine.be

Sitting prettily on a curve of
River Vesdre, Chaudfontaine
is the site of the only natural
hot springs in Belgium. It first
developed its therapeutic
activities in 1676, when a
local landowner installed
rudimentary baths and
proclaimed the water's
medical benefits. Today,
the main treatment
centre is the luxurious
**Château des
Thermes**, a restored
18th-century
residence set in a
wooded park. At the interactive
Source O Rama museum,
multimedia techniques provide
an educational exploration of
cold-water and thermal spas.

🛢 **Château des Thermes**
Rue Hauster 9. **Tel** (04) 3678067.
Open daily. 🛇 🅰 ⚕ 🏠
🆆 chateaudesthermes.be

🏛 **Source O Rama**
Avenue des Thermes 78(b). **Tel** (04)
3642020. **Open** Sun–Fri; school hols.
🛇 🅰 🏠 🆆 sourceorama.com

❻ Blegny-Mine

Rue Lambert Marlet 23, Blegny; 11 km
(7 miles) NE of Liège. **Road Map** E2.
Tel (04) 3874333. 🚌 **Open** mid-Feb–
Easter & mid-Dec: weekends &
public hols; Easter–early Sep: daily.
🛇 🛇 🛇 ⚕ 🏠
🆆 blegnymine.be

The last coal mine in the
Province of Liège was forced
to close in 1980, but parts of it

have been meticulously kept
in working order and opened to
the public. After an introductory
film, visitors don helmets and
jackets to go down a shaft in a
lift cage. This reaches a depth
of 60 m (197 ft) – a mere one-
tenth of the full depth of this
mine. Guided by a former miner,
the tour offers a taste of the
noise, danger and harsh working conditions that the so-called
gueules noires
(black faces)
had to endure
at the coal-
face. The
Musée de
la Mine provides
more of this history.
For a rural contrast,
a little tourist
road train takes visitors on a
50-minute jaunt through the
local orchards and meadows.

The tourist train at Blegny's
Musée de la Mine

❼ Eupen

21 km (13 miles) E of Blegny.
Road Map F2. **Tel** (03) 84635082.
🏯 19,250. 🚉 🚌 𝑖 Marktplatz 7;
(087) 553450. 🆆 eupen.be

The capital of Belgium's German-
speaking community, Eupen is
part of the border-land Cantons
de l'Est given to Belgium by the
Treaty of Versailles after World
War I. From the town's pleasant
streets, a massive carnival erupts
to mark the start of Lent each
year *(see p39)*. The **Stadtmuseum**
(Town Museum), set in a late
17th-century cloth-merchant's
house, tells Eupen's story,
alongside local historic craft
products such as cloth, pottery,
goldwork and furniture. On
the northern edge of town,
the chocolate manufacturers
Jacques & Callebaut have a
Musée du Chocolat, presenting
the history of chocolate and
how it is made.

🏛 **Stadtmuseum**
Gospert 52. **Tel** (087) 740005.
Closed for renovation; call for latest
information. 🛇 🆆 eupener-
stadtmuseum.org

🏛 **Musée du Chocolat**
Rue de l'Industrie 16. **Tel** (087) 592967.
Open 11am–4:30pm Tue–Thu,
11am–3:30pm Fri. **Closed** public
holidays and during Carnival. 🛇 🏠
🆆 chocojacques.be

Belgian Spas

Chaudfontaine is one of two main spa towns of Belgium –
the other one being Spa itself *(see p226)*. At Chaudfontaine,
the water is naturally hot, while at Spa it is cold. It was Spa,
however, that first attracted visitors convinced of the medical

Façade of the Pouhon Pierre-le-Grand
spring building at Spa

benefits of mineral-rich waters.
They began arriving in 1550 and
soon established the town as
a destination for nobility and
royalty. Waters of both towns
are still believed to help sufferers
of various maladies, including
rheumatism, gout and heart and
circulatory disorders. Until the
1860s, visitors tended to drink
the waters. Today, the centres
offer a full range of treatments,
from bathing in pools, saunas
and Jacuzzis, to steam rooms,
mud baths and beauty therapies.
Both towns also produce bottled
mineral water bearing their name.

❽ Limbourg

27 km (17 miles) E of Liège.
Road Map E2. 🗺 6,000. 🚊 🚌

Set on a rocky spur above a hairpin bend in the River Vesdre, Limbourg developed after 1033 as the fortified capital of the Duchy of Limburg, a historic region between the Meuse and the city of Aachen. As the vestiges of the city walls testify, Limbourg was a military stronghold, besieged on many occasions – notably in 1578 by the Spanish, in 1675 by French king Louis XIV and in 1715 by the Austrians. Today, the upper town, where little has changed since the 18th century, is picturesque, with tree-lined cobbled streets and window boxes full of flowers.

❾ Verviers

20 km (12 miles) E of Liège.
Road Map E3. 🗺 55,750. 🚊 🚌
ℹ️ Maison du Tourisme du Pays de Vesdre, Rue Jules Cerexhe 86; (087) 307926. 🌐 paysdevesdre.be

Straddling the River Vesdre, which was vital to the textile industry, Verviers is adorned with numerous fountains and water features, and calls itself the Walloon Capital of Water. Belgium's industrial revolution began here in 1799, when the English entrepreneur William Cockerill (1759–1832) established steam-powered woollen textile mills. This history is remembered in the exhibits of **Centre Touristique de la Laine et de la Mode**, set out in a restored Neo-Classical wool factory. The **Musée des Beaux-Arts et de la Céramique** has a major collection of porcelain and art. There is also the **Musée**

d'Archéologie et du Folklore, housed in an 18th-century townhouse, with antique furnishings and a lace collection.

🏛 **Centre Touristique de la Laine et de la Mode**
Rue de la Chapelle 24-30. **Tel** (087) 307920. **Open** 10am–5pm Tue–Sun. 🚻 ♿ & 🌐 aqualaine.be

🏛 **Musée des Beaux-Arts et de la Céramique**
Rue Renier 17. **Tel** (087) 331695. **Open** 2–5pm Mon, Wed & Sat, 3–6pm Sun. 🚻 🌐 paysdevesdre.be

❿ Theux

20 km (12 miles) SE of Liège.
Road Map E3. 🗺 12,000. 🚊 🚌
🌐 theux.be

The attractive town of Theux developed in the shadow of the medieval **Château de Franchimont**. The town was sacked by Charles the Bold, Duke of Burgundy, in 1468, during his conquest of Liège. The castle was reinforced in the 16th century by Erard de la Marck, Prince-Bishop of Liège, but fell into ruin after the 1780s. Theux is also noted for its remarkable **Église Sts-Hermès-et-Alexandre**. A hall-church built from the 9th-century onwards in Gothic and Romanesque styles, its naves have rare, painted, flat ceilings.

Environs
Banneux, 6 km (4 miles) to the west, is a major pilgrimage site, where in 1933 apparitions of the Virgin of the Poor revealed a healing spring to 11-year-old Mariette Beco.

🏛 **Château de Franchimont**
Allée du Château. **Tel** (087) 530489. **Open** Easter, Apr–Oct & 1 Nov. 🚻 ♿ 🚻 🌐 chateau-franchimont.be

One of many picturesque fountains in the original spa town

⓫ Spa

28 km (17 miles) SE of Liège.
Road Map E3. 🗺 10,600. 🚊 🚌
ℹ️ Place Royale 41; (087) 795353.
🌐 villedespa.be

The heyday of Spa was in the 18th and 19th centuries, when the well-to-do came here to take the waters, turning the town's name into a generic term for water therapy. Spa retains a leisurely grandeur, with its Neo-Classical **Hôtel de Ville**, the original, now disused baths and the casino. Six springs can still be visited, including the **Pouhon Pierre-le-Grand**, housed in an elegant stone pavilion built in 1880. The modern **Thermes de Spa** (Baths) are at the top of a hill, accessed by cable railway. Spa also has three intriguing museums. Sharing the same location at the **Villa Royale** are Musée de la Ville d'Eaux and Musée Spadois du Cheval: the former has a collection of antique, intricately painted wooden souvenirs (jolités), while the latter is devoted to horse-racing and carriages. The enterprising **Musée de la Lessive** takes a historical look at laundry.

♨️ **Thermes de Spa**
Colline d'Annette et Lubin.
Tel (087) 772560. **Open** Mar–Oct: 2–6pm daily. 🚻 ♿
🌐 thermesdespa.be

🏛 **Villa Royale**
Avenue Reine Astrid 77b.
Tel (087) 774486. **Open** daily.
🚻 ♿ 🌐 spavillaroyale.be

🏛 **Musée de la Lessive**
Rue Hanster 10. **Tel** (087) 771418.
Open Easter & Jul–Aug: 2–6pm daily; Mar–Oct: 2–6pm Sat. 🚻

Moated entrance to the atmospheric ruins of Château de Franchimont

⑫ The Hautes Fagnes

A large area of raised, boggy moorland, the Hautes Fagnes (High Fens) extends over much of the eastern part of the Province of Liège. The region straddles the border to form part of a German-Belgian Nature Reserve, and includes some of the German-speaking Belgian areas of the Cantons de l'Est. The centre, around the Signal de Botrange, is a remote and wild bog, admired for its untamed beauty on fine days, but also famous for its desolate, foggy gloom when the weather closes in. At an altitude of 694 m (2,277 ft), this is also the highest point of Belgium.

VISITORS' CHECKLIST

Practical Information
35 km (22 miles) SE of Liège.
Road Map F3. 𝒊 Centre Nature de Botrange, Route de Botrange 131, Robertville; (080) 440300.
Open 10am–6pm daily; in Zone B areas, access is limited to paths; Zone C areas can be accessed only with a registered guide. 🎫 📷 ♿ 🏪 W botrange.be

Transport
🚌

Bogs of the High Fens
The deep peat bogs, created over 7,500 years, sustain a rich diversity of plant life, including heather and purple moor grass. It is also a haven for rare wild cats and birds.

Trails and Boardwalks
The treacherous bogs have claimed many lives in the past. Today, visitors can admire this unique natural habitat from the safety of walkways.

0 kilometres 5
0 miles 5

Barrage de la Gileppe, a dam built between 1867 and 1875, has created a lake surrounded by woodland.

★ **Signal de Botrange**
A tower, attached to a restaurant, takes visitors 28 m (92 ft) above the highest point in Belgium, and offers views out over the plateau.

Centre Nature de Botrange is an information and exhibition centre. It is also the starting point for guided walks and cross-country skiing.

Key
▬▬ Motorway
▬▬ Major road
▬▬ Minor road
── Railway
– – Trail
▬ · International border

For keys to symbols *see back flap*

Racing exhibits at the Musée du Circuit de Spa-Francorchamps, Stavelot

⓭ Château de Reinhardstein

Chemin du Cheneux 50, Ovitat; 17 km (15 miles) SE of Spa. **Road Map** F3. **Tel** (080) 446868. **Closed** Mon, Wed, Fri. 🚗 📷 11:30am, 12:30pm, 1:30pm, 2:30pm & 3:30pm Sat & Sun, also 11:30am & 2:30pm public hols. 🕸 reinhardstein.net

The 14th-century fortress of Reinhardstein was built by the lords of Waimes and owned by their descendants, the German Metternich family. The château was attacked by the French Revolutionary Army in 1795, after which it fell into ruin. In 1969, historian and collector Jean Overloop rebuilt it. Today, tours take visitors through stone-walled rooms containing furniture, tapestries, sculpture and armour.

⓮ Malmedy

13 km (8 miles) SE of Spa. **Road Map** F3. 🚶 12,350. 🚗 🚌 🛈 Place Albert 1er, 29a; (080) 330250. 🕸 malmedy.be

The mainly French-speaking town of Malmedy is one of the main towns of the Cantons de l'Est (Oostkantons in Dutch) – a borderland district that has been swapped back and forth with Germany. Until its conquest in 1795 by the French Revolutionary Army, Malmedy was ruled by prince-abbots as part of the twin Principality of Stavelot-Malmedy, which was based on two 7th-century abbeys. The town became rich through production of cloth, gunpowder, leather-tanning and paper. Today, it is a base for

walkers heading to Hautes Fagnes. Its main attraction is the 18th-century **Cathédrale Sts-Pierre-Paul-et-Quirinn**, set in the main square, Place Albert 1er. Malmedy is most famous for its four-day pre-Lenten carnival, Cwarmê *(see p39)*.

⓯ Castle of Burg-Reuland

38 km (24 miles) SE of Malmedy. **Road Map** F3. **Tel** (080) 329131. 🚌 **Open** 9am–5pm daily. 🚗 🕸 burg-reuland.be

Located in the south of the Cantons de l'Est, the pretty slate-roofed village of Burg-Reuland is home to one of the most impressive sets of castle ruins in Belgium. The Romans built a fort on this site and the Franks made it a royal castle: Charlemagne is said to have stayed in it. However, the ruins seen today date from the 10th to 16th centuries. The round corner tower and high curtain walls were built by the counts of Reuland, vassals of the Holy Roman Empire. Decline set

in after the castle was sacked by Louis XIV of France in 1689; it was dismantled after 1804.

⓰ Stavelot

10 km (6 miles) SW of Malmedy. **Road Map** E3. 🚶 6,920. 🚗 🚌 🛈 Abbaye de Stavelot, Place St Remacle 32; (080) 862706. 🕸 stavelot.be

Founded in the 7th century as an abbey, Stavelot is an attractive town whose old centre is a cluster of little streets and squares lined with 17th-century half-timbered houses. Here, the **Église St-Sébastien** houses a masterpiece of Mosan art – the 13th-century reliquary of St Remaclus, founder of the abbey at Stavelot. The striking deep-red **Abbaye de Stavelot** dates from the 18th century. It now contains three museums. The **Musée du Circuit de Spa-Francorchamps**, with its collection of cars, motorcycles and memorabilia, documents the history (from 1896) of the Grand Prix motor-racing track at Francorchamps, which lies about 10 km (6 miles) to the north. There is also the Musée de la Principauté de Stavelot-Malmèdy and the Musée Guillaume Apollinaire, dedicated to this French poet (1880–1918) who wrote eloquently about the Ardennes. Stavelot is also known for its carnival, the Laetare *(see p36)*.

🏛 **Abbaye de Stavelot**
Tel (080) 880878. **Open** 10am–6pm daily. **Closed** Sun & Mon of carnival weekend. 🚗 🖥 📷
🕸 abbayedestavelot.be

The village of Burg-Reuland, dominated by the ruins of its lofty castle

⓱ A Tour of the Amblève

One of the key rivers of the Ardennes, the Amblève carves a picturesque path through hills and forests. Walks here lead off along the river's edge or to the woodland waterfalls of the tributaries. Quarries and a railway line are seen early on, but after Aywaille, a busy centre for summer visitors, the landscape becomes wilder and the road hugs the river, giving access to picnic sites on the banks. It then rises to villages such as Stoumont, which offer fine views over the valley. The famous waterfalls at Coo are an impressive note on which to end the drive.

Tips for Drivers

Starting point: Comblain-au-Pont – exit to Sprimont from A26.
Tour length: 55 km (35 miles).
Duration: Allow half a day.
Driving conditions: The roads are narrow and busy, but good.
Where to eat: Restaurants can be found at Comblain-au-Pont, Aywaille and Stoumont.
Visitors' information:
Remouchamps: (04) 3843544,
Ⓦ ourthe-ambleve.be

① Comblain-au-Pont
South of the Amblève's scenic confluence with the River Ourthe are strange sculptures formed by hard dolomitic rock that has resisted erosion. Equally sculptural stalactites can be seen in Comblain's Découvertes Mystères limestone caves.

② Château d'Amblève
A walk across the river from Aywaille ends in a ruined castle linked to the steed Bayard legend *(see p143)*.

③ Sougné-Remouchamps
Visits to the Grottes de Remouchamps include a subterranean boat trip.

④ Ninglinspo
A signposted walk through woodland leads along a stream called Ninglinspo to La Chaudière (The Cauldron), where the stream falls into a basin.

⑤ Fonds de Quarreux
Large quartzite rocks, formed 400 million years ago, lie scattered across the river, which ripples, gurgles and sparkles in the current. Signposts lead to a number of riverside paths.

⑥ Coo
Belgium's most impressive cascade is a pair of falls roaring down a rocky drop of 15 m (50 ft). Coo is also a resort with the children's theme park, Plopsa Coo *(see p309)*.

Key

▬ Tour route
▬ Motorway
═ Other road
— Railway

0 kilometres 3
0 miles 3

Durbuy, sheltered by the forested Ardennes, often cited as one of the prettiest towns in Belgium

⑱ Durbuy

17 km (11 miles) S of Modave.
Road Map E3. 🚍 11,300. 💬
ℹ️ Place aux Foires 25; (086) 212428.
🅦 durbuyinfo.be

Established by charter in 1331, Durbuy calls itself the world's smallest town. Its cobbled streets of stone houses wind down to a bridge over the River Ourthe under the gaze of an 18th-century château. The main attraction, the **Parc des Topiaires**, takes topiary to surreal extremes: the box-tree hedges have been sculpted into 250 subjects including crocodiles, birds, a mermaid, and even the Manneken- Pis.

Environs
Near **Wéris**, 7 km (4 miles) to the southeast, there are two dolmens and many menhirs and megaliths dating back to the Neolithic era. There is also a Musée des Mégalithes.

🎋 Parc des Topiaires
Rue Haie Himbe 1. **Tel** (086) 219075.
Open Feb–Oct: 10am–6pm daily; Nov: 10am–5pm daily; Dec: 10am–4pm Sat, Sun & public holidays. **Closed** Jan. ♿
♿ 🖥️ 🅦 topiaires.durbuy.be

⑲ Grottes de Hotton

11 km (7 miles) S of Durbuy.
Road Map E3. **Tel** (084) 466046. 💬
Open Apr–Oct: 10am–5pm daily (till 6pm Jul & Aug); Nov–Mar: tours on Sat & Sun at 12:30pm, 2pm & 3:30pm. ♿
📷 🖥️ ♿ 🅦 grottesdehotton.be

Located on the River Ourthe, Hotton has some of the area's most impressive limestone caves. Over the millennia, the river has carved out chasms, which are draped with stalactites, stalagmites and sculptural concretions and mineral formations of the utmost delicacy. Staircases and walkways lead down through a series of illuminated chambers to Belgium's largest cave gallery – 200 m (656 ft) long and 35 m (115 ft) high. The gardens at the head of the cave have a path leading to fine views of the area.

⑳ La Roche-en-Ardenne

16 km (10 miles) SE of Hotton.
Road Map E3. 🚍 4,300. 💬
ℹ️ Place du Marché 15; (084) 367736.
🅦 la-roche-tourisme.com

Set in a deep valley on a loop of the River Ourthe, La Roche provides an attractive base for exploring the Ardennes. The grim ruins of the imposing 11th–12th-century **Château Féodal** (Feudal Castle) overlook the town from a rocky spur known as the Deister.

Arrays of stalactites on the ceiling of Grottes de Hotton

Destroyed by the Austrians in the late 18th century, the château provides a dramatic backdrop when illuminated at night during the summer months. The pottery museum, **Les Grès de la Roche**, explains the history and practicalities of making traditional blue stoneware, called *grès*. It also covers local culinary traditions, most notably the manner of curing hams to make *jambon d'Ardennes*.

La Roche was damaged by bombing during the Battle of the Bulge (*see p235*). This action is remembered in a collection of uniforms, weapons, vehicles, photographs and maps in the **Musée de la Bataille des Ardennes**.

Environs
River Ourthe winds through one of the most beautiful valleys in the Ardennes. The most scenic stretch runs from **Houffalize**, 25 km (16 miles) east of La Roche, to Liège, 95 km (59 miles) north of La Roche. Kayaking is popular and equipment can be rented at La Roche and other locations.

🏰 Château Féodal
Rue du Vieux Château 4. **Tel** (084) 411342. **Open** Apr–Oct: daily; Nov–Mar: Mon–Thu. ♿ 📷
🅦 chateaudelaroche.be

🏛️ Les Grès de la Roche
Rue Rompré 28. **Tel** (084) 411239.
Open check website for latest information. 📷 📷 📷
🅦 gresdelaroche.be

🏛️ Musée de la Bataille des Ardennes
Rue Châmont 5. **Tel** (084) 411725.
Open late Mar–Dec: Tue–Sun; Jan–Mar, Jul & Aug: Sat, Sun & public hols.
♿ 🅦 batarden.be

㉑ St-Hubert

25 km (16 miles) SW of La Roche.
Road Map E4. 5,700.
Rue Saint-Gilles 12; (061) 613010.
Journées Internationales de la Chasse et de la Nature (1st weekend of Sep). **saint-hubert-tourisme.be**

Greatly venerated during the Middle Ages, St Hubert was an 8th-century bishop of Tongeren-Maastricht and successor to St Lambert *(see p220)*. According to legend, he was converted to Christianity as a young man after encountering a stag with the image of a crucifix between its antlers. Upon his death, St Hubert became the patron saint of hunting and the stag became his emblem. In the 9th century, the saint's relics were brought to a Benedictine abbey in the present-day Belgian town of St-Hubert, which became a pilgrimage site for hunters. The monks here are said to have developed the blood-hound breed called the St Hubert Hound.

The abbey was rebuilt in 1729, but suppressed in the 1790s. However, its large church, the **Basilique St-Hubert**, remains the centrepiece of the town. Its Baroque façade (1700–1702), crested by twin domes, fronts an impressive late-Gothic interior (1526–64). This is a focal point of Journées Internationales de la Chasse et de la Nature, the festival of hunting, which also holds a costumed procession.

The **Centre Pierre-Joseph Redouté** presents a collection of exquisite watercolours by the celebrated flower artist Pierre-Joseph Redouté (1759–1840). The artist was born in St-Hubert but moved to Paris, where he was appointed to the court of Marie-Antoinette.

Basilique St-Hubert
Place de l'Abbaye. **Tel** (061) 612388.
Open daily.

Centre Pierre-Joseph Redouté
Rue Redouté 11. **Tel** (061) 611467.
Open Jul–Aug: 1–5pm daily; Sep–Jun: by reservation. **musee-pierre-joseph-redoute.be**

The mighty organ of the 16th-century Basilique St-Hubert

㉒ Fourneau St-Michel

8 km (5 miles) N of St-Hubert.
Road Map E4. **Tel** (084) 210890.
Open Mar–Jun & Sep–Nov: 9:30am–5pm Tue–Sun; Jul & Aug: 9:30am–5:30pm daily; Dec–Feb : access to the grounds only.
fourneausaint michel.be

The word *fourneau* literally means furnace, and the aptly named community of Fourneau St-Michel was involved in a flourishing iron-smelting business in the 17th and 18th centuries. Scattered in a beautiful forest clearing here are two rewarding museums revealing local life in the past. A rare surviving high furnace from the 18th century and forge workshops, set up by the last abbot of St-Hubert, form the crux of the **Musée du Fer** (Museum of Iron). Close by

Industrial relic at Fourneau St-Michel

is the **Musée de la Vie Rurale en Wallonie** (Museum of Rural Life in Wallonia), also called the Musée Plein Air (Open Air Museum). This has some 50 rural buildings from the 19th century, rescued from all over Wallonia. Many have been fully restored, with interiors containing authentic furniture and domestic items. A team of animators on site demonstrate rural activities and crafts.

㉓ Redu

17 km (11 miles) W of St-Hubert.
Road Map D4. **Tel** (061) 656699.
500. Maison du Tourisme du Pays de la Haute-Lesse, Place de l'Esro 63, Redu-Libin. **haute-lesse-tourisme.be**

Often nicknamed Belgium's Hay-on-Wye, in reference to the town of books that developed in Wales in the 1960s, Redu is above all a book village. It has some 20 bookshops selling new and used books, as well as workshops for papermaking, printing, engraving and other crafts. This tradition was founded in 1984 by Liège-born writer Noël Anselot (b.1924), who was directly inspired by the example of Hay-on-Wye.

Environs
The **Euro Space Center** at Transinne, 6 km (4 miles) to the east, is a family-oriented museum on space exploration.

Euro Space Center
Rue Devant les Hêtres 1, Transinne.
Tel (061) 656465. **Open** late Mar–Jun: 10am–4pm Tue–Sun (& weekends in Mar); Jul & Aug: 10am–5pm daily.
eurospacecenter.be

Full-size replica of a shuttle at the Euro Space Center, Transinne

㉔ A Drive Along the Semois

The River Semois flows westwards across the southern parts of the Belgian provinces of Luxembourg and Namur into France, where it joins the River Meuse. Along much of its course, the river cuts an exaggeratedly serpentine path through a dramatic landscape of steep and forested hills. The roads that wind through these valleys have plenty of stop-off points from which to admire the breathtaking scenery and panoramic views.

① Jambon de la Semois
Signposted from the road, a high viewpoint offers the first glimpse of the river below.

② Membre
This small resort village is also a gateway to the Parc Naturel de Bohan-Membre.

③ Vresse-sur-Semois
Located close by the river, this attractive village is the main visitors' centre for the Namur sector of the Semois valley.

④ Rochehaut
As its name suggests, Rochehaut (High Rock) provides a fine vantage point. Nestling below, in a curve of the river, is the pretty hamlet of Frahan.

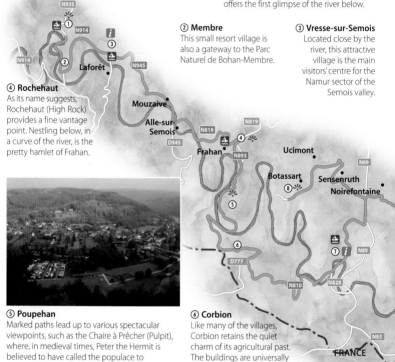

⑤ Poupehan
Marked paths lead up to various spectacular viewpoints, such as the Chaire à Prêcher (Pulpit), where, in medieval times, Peter the Hermit is believed to have called the populace to participate in the First Crusade.

⑥ Corbion
Like many of the villages, Corbion retains the quiet charm of its agricultural past. The buildings are universally roofed in locally-mined slate.

⑦ Bouillon
The largest town at the heart of the valley is dominated by a medieval fortress (see pp236–7).

⑧ Tombeau du Géant
A detour through upland pasture and woodlands leads to a famous viewpoint, just past Botassart. Below, the river sweeps around a forested hillock known as the Giant's Tomb (see pp178–9).

⑨ Dohan
The road crosses the river at Dohan, then provides a series of notable viewpoints. The first of these is near the riverside rocks of the Rocher de Dampiry. Beyond it, the next point lies where the river performs a series of hairpin bends.

⑩ Herbeumont
A 13th-century castle here commanded a vital strategic position, with extensive views along the river, until it was wrecked by the French in 1657. The castle is under restoration.

Tips for Drivers

Starting point: Jambon de la Semois on the N935 is accessed from the A4-E411 Namur–Arlon motorway; from Exit 23, take the N835, then the N952.

Length: About 80 km (50 miles).

Duration of drive: Allow at least a whole day; better to break the journey into two days.

Driving conditions: Roads are small and winding, but wide enough for comfortable driving.

Where to stay and eat: There are restaurants, cafés and accommodation in villages and towns all along the way. Bouillon is the main centre. Many of the viewpoints have picnic tables.

Visitors' Information: Vresse-sur-Semois: Rue Albert Raty 83, (061) 292827; Bouillon: Quai des Saulx 12 and at the château-fort, (061) 464202 **W** **bouillon-initiative. be**; Florenville: Place Albert 1er, (061) 311229 **W** **semois-tourisme.be**

0 kilometres   3

0 miles   3

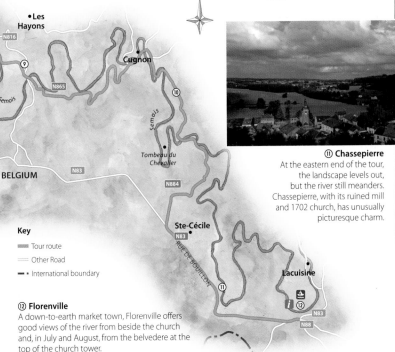

⑪ Chassepierre
At the eastern end of the tour, the landscape levels out, but the river still meanders. Chassepierre, with its ruined mill and 1702 church, has unusually picturesque charm.

Key
▬ Tour route
═ Other Road
▬ • International boundary

⑫ Florenville
A down-to-earth market town, Florenville offers good views of the river from beside the church and, in July and August, from the belvedere at the top of the church tower.

Courtyard of the renowned Cistercian Abbaye d'Orval

㉕ Bouillon

34 km (21 miles) SW of St-Hubert.
Road Map D4. 🚉 5,500. 🚌
ℹ️ Quai des Saulx 12; (061) 465211.
🌐 **bouillon-tourisme.be**

The elegant town of Bouillon straddles the River Semois beside the rock on which its famous fortress stands. The town offers activities such as walking, horse riding and kayaking as well as mountain bike circuits. On the castle hill, the **Musée Ducal** has various mementos relating to the history of the castle and town. Housed in a 17th-century convent on the banks of the river, the **Archéoscope Godefroid de Bouillon** presents an innovative multimedia show on this leading knight of the First Crusade.

Environs
At Bertrix, 25 km (15 miles) to the northeast, there is a remarkable underground slate mine and museum called **Au Coeur de l'Ardoise**.

🏛 **Musée Ducal**
Rue du Petit 1–3. **Tel** (061) 464189.
Open Easter–Nov. 🚫
🌐 **museeducalbouillon.be**

🏛 **Archéoscope Godefroid de Bouillon**
Quai des Saulx 14. **Tel** (061) 468303.
Open Feb–Dec. 🚫 💻 📷
🌐 **archeoscopebouillon.be**

🏛 **Au Coeur de l'Ardoise**
Domaine de la Morépire, 1 Rue du Babinay, Bertrix. **Tel** (061) 414521.
Open see website for times. 🚫 📷
🌐 **aucoeurdelardoise.be**

㉖ Château-Fort de Bouillon

See pp236–7.

㉗ Abbaye d'Orval

Villers-devant-Orval; 25 km (15 miles) SE of Bouillon. **Road Map** E5. **Tel** (061) 311060. **Open** Mar–Oct: 9:30am–6:30pm daily; Nov–Feb: 10:30am–5:30pm. 🚫 🚫 📷 🌐 **orval.be**

Set in a forested area of the Gaume region, the Cistercian abbey of Notre-Dame d'Orval was one of Europe's most powerful until its destruction in the religious wars and again during the French Revolution in 1793. The abbey became famous for its beer, whose label shows a fish with a ring in its mouth. This recalls the legend of the abbey's foundation by Countess Mathilda of Tuscany, in thanksgiving after a trout miraculously recovered her wedding ring from a stream. Today, the public can visit the Romanesque-Gothic ruins of the old 12th- and 13th-century monastery church as well as a museum and a herb garden.

㉘ Arlon

57 km (35 miles) E of Bouillon.
Road Map E4. 🚉 28,350. 🚌
ℹ️ Rue des Faubourgs 2; (063) 216360. 🌐 **ot-arlon.be**

The capital of the Belgian Province of Luxembourg, Arlon developed as a trading centre called Orolaunum in Roman times, and claims to be one of the oldest towns in Belgium. Many Roman remains have survived, including the **Tour Romaine**, a tower in the Grand Place, and vestiges of 4th-century Roman baths. The town's **Musée**

Archéologique contains artifacts from Gallo-Roman times and jewellery and pottery from the Merovingian period. The adjacent **Musée Gaspar** celebrates the Gaspar family of Arlon, including the animal sculptor Jean-Marie Gaspar (1861–1931). Its masterpiece is a 16th-century Fisenne retable.
Arlon's Knipchen hill, site of the Église St-Donat, has views that extend over Belgium, Luxembourg and France.

🏛 **Musée Archéologique**
R des Martyrs 13. **Tel** (063) 212849.
Open 9am–noon, 1–5:30pm Tue–Sat; 1:30–5:30pm Sun & public holidays.
Closed 1, 2 & 11 Nov, Christmas. 🚫 📷 🌐 **ial.be.**

🏛 **Musée Gaspar**
R des Martyrs 16. **Tel** (063) 600654.
Open 9:30am–noon and 1–5:30pm Tue–Sat; Apr–Sept: 1:30–5:30pm Sun.
🚫 🌐 **ial.be.**

㉙ Bastogne

40 km (25 miles) N of Arlon.
Road Map E4. 🚉 15,130. 🚌
ℹ️ Place McAuliffe 60; (061) 212711.
🌐 **paysdebastogne.be**

Best known as a focal point of the Battle of the Bulge, Bastogne was also a thriving stronghold in medieval times, as witnessed by the Porte de Trèves, the remnant of the 14th-century city walls. Close by, the Église St-Pierre has a 12th-century tower and a 15th-century Flamboyant-Gothic nave with a painted vaulting dating from 1536. The Battle of the Bulge is remembered primarily on Mardasson Hill, 2 km (1 mile) to the northeast of Bastogne, where a star-shaped American Memorial lists the various American units that fought in the battle, and offers extensive panoramic views from the parapet. The site also includes the **Bastogne War Museum**, a comprehensive museum of the battle.

Battle monument at Bastogne

🏛 **Bastogne War Museum**
Colline de Mardasson. **Tel** (061) 210220. **Open** Tue–Sun. 🚫 📷 🚫
🌐 **bastognewarmuseum.be**

The Ardennes Offensive

Also known as the Battle of the Bulge, the Ardennes Offensive was a surprise counter-attack mounted by the German army during the bitterly cold winter of 1944–5. Allied forces advancing towards Germany had liberated Belgium that September. Beginning on 16 December 1944, German tank divisions led by General von Rundstedt, attempted to punch through the Allied lines across the snow-covered Ardennes in an attempt to reach the Meuse and then advance north to retake Brussels and Antwerp. They managed to push back US and British forces, creating a frontline in the shape of a bulge.

Locator Map
■ Battle of the Bulge

Counter-Offensive of January 1945

When called upon to surrender in Bastogne, US Brigadier-General McAuliffe defiantly responded, "Nuts!" General Patton's army then rescued Bastogne, and the Allied forces eventually pushed the Germans back by the end of January 1945. It had been the largest land battle of World War II, involving more than a million men and 1,000 tanks.

The battlefront of 16 December, from which the German offensive began, is also called the Siegfried Line.

Dinant and the River Meuse marked the most westerly point of the German advance. This is commemorated by a monument at the Rocher Bayard, just south of the town.

0 kilometres 5
0 miles 5

Key
■ German army
■ British army
■ US army
— Battlefront 16 Dec 1944
--- Battlefront 25 Dec 1944
••• International border

At La Roche-en-Ardenne, the Musée de la Bataille des Ardennes underlines the human dimension with figures of uniformed combatants from both sides.

The Bastogne War Museum is built in a star shape, like the American Memorial close by.

㉖ Château-Fort de Bouillon

Standing on a rocky plinth overlooking a loop in the River Semois, the Château-Fort de Bouillon is of ancient origin and is first mentioned in AD 988. The fortress was a vital stronghold in the borderlands with France, on a route often taken by invaders. It was home of the pious knight Godefroid until he left for the First Crusade (1096–99). Bouillon was still an important bastion in 1676, when it fell into the hands of Louis XIV of France, who commissioned upgrades from his architect Vauban. The castle survived its 15th siege in 1815 and finally ceased its military role in 1853. It is now for the most part unfurnished, but provides a fascinating insight into castle architecture and magnificent views of the valley.

★ Tour d'Autriche
Winding stairs lead to the top of the Austria Tower, a key vantage point. Built in 1551, it was named after George of Austria, one of the prince-bishops of Liège.

Bell Tower
Housed in a projecting machicolation, the bell was used to ring out watch-changes and orders. Cast in silver alloy in 1563, it originally came from a chapel and sounds for nearly one minute when struck.

KEY

① **Vauban's three-slit loopholes** gave defenders a broad field of fire.

② **Gun Batteries**

③ **The clocktower** was redesigned by Vauban.

④ **A portcullis** could be lowered to block the passage beyond.

★ Cour d'Honneur
The fort's main quadrangle once served as a parade ground. Today, it features owls, eagles and vultures and is also the setting for a spectacular falconry show.

Godefroid de Bouillon

Bouillon castle was once owned by the celebrated crusader knight Godefroid (1060–1100), Duke of Lower Lorraine. In 1095, Peter the Hermit, a French preacher, whipped the local populace into a ferment over Muslim occupation of the Holy Land. Godefroid took up the cause and joined the First Crusade, selling his castle to the prince-bishop of Liège to obtain money for the expedition. In 1099, his troops were the first to enter Jerusalem and Godefroid was offered the crown of the Kingdom of Jerusalem. He refused to accept it on religious grounds, preferring instead to be called Defender of the Holy Sepulchre. He died in Jerusalem a year later.

Godefroid de Bouillon

VISITORS' CHECKLIST

Practical Information
Esplanade Godefroid de Bouillon, Bouillon. **Road Map** D4.
Tel (061) 464202. **Open** Jul–Aug: 10am–6:30pm daily; Apr–Jun & Sep: 10am–6pm Mon–Fri, 10am–6:30pm Sat & Sun; Mar, Oct & Nov: 10am–5pm daily; Dec & Feb: 1–5pm Mon–Fri, 10am–5pm Sat & Sun; Jan: 10am–5pm Sat & Sun. 🅿 🚻 Falconry Show: Mar–mid Nov: 11:30am, 2pm & 3:30pm daily. 🆆 **bouillon-initiative.be**

Transport
🚌

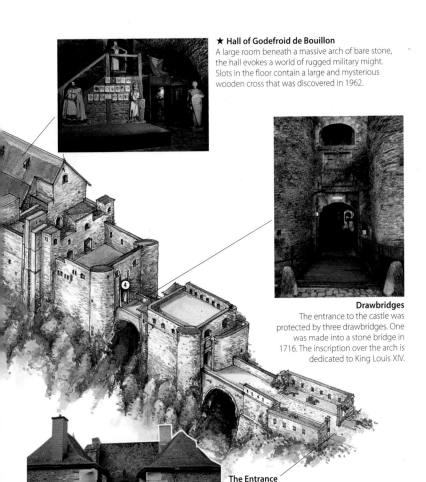

★ Hall of Godefroid de Bouillon

A large room beneath a massive arch of bare stone, the hall evokes a world of rugged military might. Slots in the floor contain a large and mysterious wooden cross that was discovered in 1962.

Drawbridges

The entrance to the castle was protected by three drawbridges. One was made into a stone bridge in 1716. The inscription over the arch is dedicated to King Louis XIV.

The Entrance

There is only one point of access to this fortress – through a narrow arch in the outer castle, flanked by guardrooms. This is now the site of the ticket office, shop and visitors' information office.

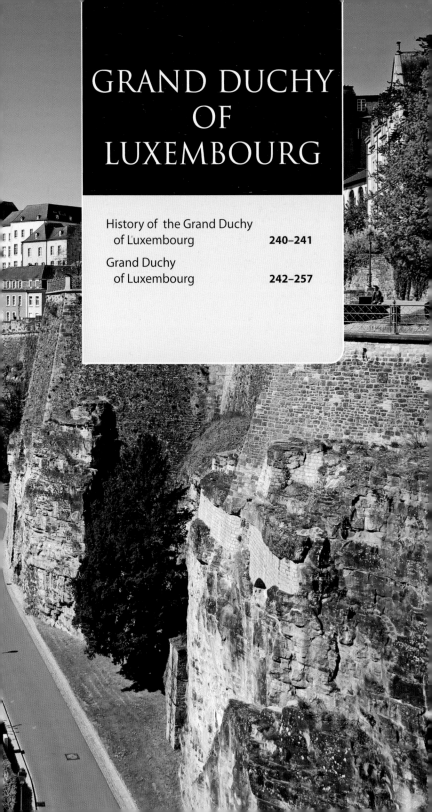

GRAND DUCHY OF LUXEMBOURG

History of the Grand Duchy of Luxembourg

The Grand Duchy of Luxembourg has been a sovereign nation since the 1830s. However, it has a far older history, much of which it shares with Belgium. Over the years, the Duchy's borders have swelled and contracted with the fortunes of war, and, until 1839, included the Belgian Province of Luxembourg. The country's history is very much a dynastic one: a succession of counts, dukes and grand dukes has led up to the present day, with Grand Duke Henri as the current head of state.

Early History

When the Romans came to the Luxembourg region in 54 BC, they found it occupied by a prosperous iron-working tribe called the Treveri who had settled near the Moselle valley, some 600 years earlier. The Franks muscled into this borderland area at the decline of the Roman Empire (5th century), introducing a Germanic language that would become Lëtzebuergesch, the country's national language. In the 6th century, the Franks also introduced Christianity.

After Charlemagne's death in 814, the Frankish Empire divided in two: Luxembourg was assigned to Lotharingia (Lorraine). Luxembourg's ruling dynasty was founded by Siegfried of Lorraine (c.922–98), Count of Ardennes and a vassal of the Holy Roman Empire. In 963, he acquired the castle of Lucilinburhuc on the Bock, a rocky outcrop on which Luxembourg City now stands. This stronghold, fortified over the years into a formidable bastion, became the hub of a small state, strategically placed between the Low Countries, Germany and France. Siegfried is sometimes cited as the first Count of Luxembourg, but others give this distinction to his descendant Conrad I (r.1059–86).

Three of their line became Holy Roman Emperor, beginning with Henry VII in 1312. In 1354, the state was made a Duchy within the Holy Roman Empire. Wenceslas I (r.1353–83), the first duke, added Brabant and Limburg (modern central and eastern Belgium) to his territory.

Philip the Good, Duke of Burgundy (1396–1467) by van der Weyden

Burgundy and Spain

In 1419, Wenceslas II passed away without a male heir. Conflict erupted between rival claimants and was only resolved by a treaty that handed the Duchy to Philip the Good, Duke of Burgundy, who ruled over much of the Low Countries. Philip took power in 1443 and for the next four centuries Luxembourg, like Belgium, was ruled by the dukes of Burgundy; after Mary of Burgundy's marriage to Maximilian, it was ruled by the Habsburg sovereigns of Spain and Austria. However, the Prussians, the Electors of Brandenburg and the related Orange-Nassau family also held a claim to Luxembourg.

In pursuit of his claim to the Spanish Netherlands, King Louis XIV of France invaded in 1684 and ruled Luxembourg until 1698. During this time, Louis's energetic military engineer Vauban reshaped the fortifications of Luxembourg City. The French returned in 1794, when their Revolutionary Army swept through the state, ending the Austrian rule.

A Grand Duchy

The final defeat of Napoleon in 1815 placed the future of Luxembourg in the hands of the victorious allies at the Congress of Vienna. As both the Netherlands and Prussia had claims to Luxembourg, the solution was a compromise. As in Belgium, William I of Orange, King of the Netherlands, was appointed ruler, and Luxembourg was made a Grand Duchy, with territory that included today's Province of Luxembourg in Belgium. The Grand Duchy also became a member of the German Confederation, a union of states set up to replace the Holy Roman

Timeline

962 First Holy Roman Emperor crowned

963 The first castle on the Rocher du Bock, Luxembourg City, is built by Siegfried of Lorraine

1059 Conrad I becomes the count of Luxembourg

Seal of Conrad I

1312 Count Henry VII is elected Holy Roman Emperor, but dies in 1313

1354 The Duchy of Luxembourg is created, with Wenceslas I as the first duke

1419 Rival claimants to the Duchy battle for power

1443 Philip the Good of Burgundy steps in to take over Luxembourg

| 900 | 1040 | 1180 | 1320 | 1460 |

◄ La Corniche and Grund, Luxembourg

Luxembourg City's vast fortress at the peak of its formidable glory around 1858

Empire. The mighty fortress of Luxembourg City was garrisoned by the Prussians.

After the Belgian Revolution in 1830, William I lost control of Belgium; this included, under the 1839 Treaty of London, the French-speaking, western (Belgian) half of Luxembourg. He retained the eastern part, and the Grand Duchy now assumed its modern shape. The Dutch kings William (Guillaume) I, II and III remained grand dukes of Luxembourg until 1890. The collapse of the Germanic Confederation in 1867 led to an international crisis over Prussia's claim to Luxembourg, but war was averted by the Second Treaty of London, under which

European leaders at the Congress of Vienna on 9 June 1815

the states agreed to guarantee Luxembourg's independence and neutrality. The Prussians left Luxembourg City and their fortress was dismantled. In the last decades of the 19th century, Luxembourg began to prosper by exploiting its high-quality steel, produced in the south of the country.

Autonomy and Occupation

In 1890, William III died without a male heir. In the Netherlands, his daughter Wilhelmina could succeed, but in Luxembourg, under the ancient Salic Law of the Franks, women were not allowed to inherit the throne. Instead, a relative, Duke Adolphe of Nassau-Weilburg, became grand duke, founding the present dynastic line. Salic Law was abandoned by his son, William IV, who passed on the title to his eldest daughter Marie-Adélaïde, who became Grand Duchess in 1912. Despite its neutral status, Luxembourg was invaded and occupied by the Germans during World War I. After the end of the war, in 1919, Marie-Adélaïde abdicated in favour of her sister Charlotte, who ruled as Grand Duchess

until 1964. During her reign, neutral Luxembourg was again overrun by the Germans, and in 1942 was formally annexed to Germany. Conscription, forced labour and other oppression inspired a determined campaign of resistance. In the bitter winter of 1944–5, Luxembourg was the scene of the devastating Ardennes Offensive (see p235).

Founder of the EU

Luxembourg is a keen advocate of international cooperation. In 1950, it formed part of the Benelux Customs Union and in 1957, it was one of the six founding nations of the European Economic Community, which evolved into the European Union. Today, Luxembourg City is the location for various EU institutions, including the European Court of Justice and the European Court of Auditors. In 1964, Grand Duchess Charlotte abdicated in favour of her son Jean, who had married Princess Joséphine-Charlotte of Belgium, thus linking the two nations. In 2000, Grand Duke Jean in turn abdicated in favour of his son Henri.

1618–48 The Thirty Years' War

1714 Luxembourg is assigned to Austria

1839 The Grand Duchy attains its current size

1940–45 Germany occupies Luxembourg a second time

2000 Grand Duke Henri succeeds his father

2006 Musée d'Art Moderne Grand-Duc Jean opens

| 1600 | 1740 | 1880 | 2020 |

1684–97 Louis XIV of France rules the Duchy; Vauban fortifies Luxembourg City

1795–1814 Luxembourg is ruled by Revolutionary France

1815–40 The Grand Duchy is ruled by William I, King of the Netherlands

1914–18 Germany occupies Luxembourg

1957 Luxembourg is one of the founder nations of the EEC

Grand Duke Henri

Exploring the Grand Duchy of Luxembourg

The Grand Duchy of Luxembourg measures only 80 km (50 miles) from top to bottom. Its capital, Luxembourg City, is in the southern sector, where the bulk of the population is settled. Called the Gutland (Good Land), the south is also the main farming region. The old industrial heartland of the southwest, the centre of the iron and steel industries, is known as Minette, or the Red Lands for the ore-tinted colour of the soil. The north, called the Eisléck or Oesling, is dominated by the wooded hills of the Ardennes and is more sparsely populated. The famously beautiful landscape of Little Switzerland is in the east. There are four main rivers: the Sûre, which crosses the Ardennes; the Alzette, which flows through Luxembourg City; the Moselle, which forms the southeastern border with Germany, and provides a fertile valley for Luxembourg's vineyards; and the Our, which marks the rest of the German border.

Extensive vineyards at the wine making commune of Remich, on the banks of River Moselle

```
0 kilometres        10
0 miles             10
```

Sights at a Glance

Villages, Towns and Cities
1 *Luxembourg City pp244–49*
2 Fond-de-Gras
4 Mondorf-les-Bains
6 Larochette
8 Echternach
9 Diekirch
12 Clervaux
13 Wiltz
14 Esch-sur-Sûre
15 Rindschleiden

Castles and Châteaux
10 Vianden
11 Château de Bourscheid
16 Vallée des Sept Châteaux

Museums
3 Musée National des Mines de Fer

Tours
7 *A Tour of Petite Suisse Luxembourgeoise p254*

Areas of Natural Beauty
5 Luxembourg's Moselle Valley

For hotels and restaurants see p271 and p292–3

Liège

Weiswampach

Troisvierges

Asselborn

Troine

CLERVAUX 12

Ma

Hosi

N12

Eschweiler

WILTZ 13

Oes

N15

CHÂTEAU
BOURSCHE

Lultzhausen

14

ESCH-SUR-
SÛRE

Welsch

Arsdorf

N27

15 RINDSCHLEIDEN

Martelange

N23

Rambrouch   Wahl

GRAND DUCHY

N23 N12

Uselda

Redange

N24

Beckerich

16

VALLÉE DES SEPT CHÂT

Hollenfe

Gaichel   Septfontaines

Ansem

CR105

Koerich

N4

Cape

Arlon,
Namur

A6

CR1

Clémency

N5

Pétange

Bascharage

A13

Sanem

N1

2 FOND-DE-GRAS

Differdange   Esch-sur-
Alzette

MUSÉE NATIONAL D
MINES DE F

Statue of Grand Duke William II in the serene lamplit Place Guillame II in Luxembourg City

Key

━━ Motorway

═ ═ Motorway under construction

━━ Major road

━━ Secondary road

═ ═ Minor road

━▸━ Main railway

━━ International border

Getting Around

The southern parts of the country, including Luxembourg City, are well served by motorways, with links to Brussels, central Germany and eastern France. Destinations in the north can be accessed rapidly by a mixture of motorways and secondary roads. The railways follow a similar pattern, with better coverage in the south. One line, with just two branches, serves the north, running between Luxembourg City and Troisvierges (and on to Liège). Bus services complement the railways, filling in the gaps to places not accessible by the train network.

For keys to symbols *see back flap*

● Luxembourg City

Bustling, elegant Luxembourg City is the largest urban centre in the country. Its main draw, La Vieille Ville (The Old Town), is perched high on an escarpment over the rivers Alzette and Pétrusse which flow through verdant ravines below. This historic centre is bound by cliffs that once made the city an easily defensible stronghold. The three Villes Basses (Lower Towns) – Grund, Clausen and Pfaffenthal – hug the eastern side of the Old Town. A munitions explosion in 1554 damaged the town, and the stately web of streets and squares seen here today was built during the 18th and 19th centuries. In 1867, the city was demilitarized and most of its ramparts were demolished. Only the casemates survived – dank gunnery compartments and tunnels carved into the rocks, which are a strange contrast to the charm of the city above.

🏛 Palais Grand-Ducal
Rue du Marché-aux-Herbes 17.
ℹ 222809 (tourist office).
Open mid-Jul–Aug: Thu–Tue. 🧴
🕐 4pm. 🅦 **monarchie.lu**

The official residence of the grand duke of Luxembourg, the Palais Grand-Ducal occupies the site of the old medieval town hall. The earliest part dates from 1573, when it was built as the residence of the governor of Luxembourg. This section includes the Flemish Renaissance façade. The palace was extended in the 18th century, and in 1890 it became the winter residence of the grand dukes. In summer, guided tours take visitors around the sumptuous interior, where the ceremonial rooms are lit by chandeliers and decorated with tapestries, stucco, carved wood panelling and wall paintings. The **Chamber of Deputies** stands to the right of the palace and was built in 1859 in Neo-Gothic style.

Arched doorway leading into the city's Cathédrale Notre-Dame

🏛 Cathédrale Notre-Dame
Rue Notre Dame. **Open** 10am–noon & 2–5:30pm daily. 🅦 **cathol.lu**

A curious patchwork of history and styles, Luxembourg's main cathedral, with its dainty 20th-century twin spires, is one of the most eye-catching landmarks of the city. Inside, the nave is early 17th-century and has an ornate Renaissance gallery beneath the organ loft. A gallery on the left of the nave is reserved for the royal family. This central part was extended in the 1930s in a derivative Art Deco style, and the choir is a Neo-Gothic addition of the same era.

The apse holds the church's most famed treasure – a 17th-century wooden statue of the Madonna and Child known as the **Consolatrix Afflictorum**. Crowned and dressed in elaborate robes, the Madonna is the object of veneration and pilgrimage, and the focus of the Octave festival (see p39).

The crypt contains the vault of the grand ducal family and a 17th-century tomb, depicting the entombment of Christ, with seven attendants, created for the remains of the heroic Jean l'Aveugle (1296–1346), Count of Luxembourg and King of Bohemia. He lost his sight as an adult, but still took to the field with France against the English at the Battle of Crécy, and was killed.

🏛 Casemates de Pétrusse
Place de la Constitution. **Open** school holidays: 11am–4pm. 🧴 🕐

Located underground, the casemates are a set of dark rooms carved out of the sandstone rockface by the Spanish in the 1640s, to provide gun emplacements overlooking the valley. In 1684, they were developed further by the military engineer Vauban for Louis XIV, and again in the 18th century by the Austrians. Sealed after 1867, they were rediscovered in 1933.

River Alzette wending its way through the Lower Town, a view from the city's medieval ramparts

For hotels and restaurants see p271 and pp292–93

Glass façade of the Musée d'Histoire de la Ville de Luxembourg

🏛 Musée d'Histoire de la Ville de Luxembourg

14 Rue du St-Esprit. **Tel** 47964500. **Open** 10am–6pm Tue–Sun, 10am–8pm Thu. 🅿 ♿ 🏠
w mhvl.lu

The history of Luxembourg is revealed in this sleek, ultra-modern museum ingeniously converted from four townhouses dating from the 17th to 19th centuries. Modern interactive display techniques combine with artifacts and informational panels to narrate the story of the city. An added attraction is the view from the huge glass panoramic lift that rises through all six of the museum's levels, gliding past 1,000 years of history.

🏛 Musée National d'Histoire et d'Art

Marché-aux-Poissons. **Tel** 479330-1. **Open** 10am–6pm Tue–Sun, 10am–8pm Thu. 🚼 (free 5–8pm Thu). 🖥 🏠 **w** mnha.lu

A group of elegant townhouses and a monolithic modern block combine to form the intriguing Musée National d'Histoire et d'Art. The historical section of the museum covers the history of Luxembourg from prehistoric to medieval times, and includes numerous Gallo-Roman treasures from archaeological finds: coins, mosaics, sculpture, jewellery and domestic wares. There are also decorative and fine arts, paintings from the Middle Ages to modern times and work by artists from all over Europe, including watercolours of the city by landscape painter JMW Turner (1775–1851).

🏰 The Bock

Montée de Clausen. **Open** Mar–Oct: 10am–5pm daily. 🚼 📷
The city's original castle was built on the Rocher du Bock. In AD 963, it was captured and reinforced by Siegfried of Lorraine, and became the key stronghold of the city for centuries. Between 1737 and 1746, the Austrians excavated soft sandstone beneath the castle, creating a network of galleries, staircases and tunnels over a distance of 23 km (14 miles). These casemates included gun emplacements for 50 canons, munitions stores, workshops, stables and kitchens; sufficient for a garrison of 1,200 men. They were part of a programme of reinforcements that made the city almost impregnable – or what French military engineer Lazare Carnot (1753–1823) termed the Gilbraltar of the North. The casements were also used as bomb shelters for 35,000 people during World War II. Tours take visitors around a small portion of the tunnels. The **Archaeological Crypt** presents the excavated remains of the Bock castle.

Luxembourg City

① Palais Grand-Ducal
② Cathédrale Notre-Dame
③ Casemates de Pétrusse
④ Musée d'Histoire de la Ville de Luxembourg
⑤ Musée National d'Histoire et d'Art
⑥ The Bock
⑦ Villa Vauban
⑧ Kirchberg
⑨ Centre Européen
⑩ Cour de Justice
⑪ Musée d'Art Moderne Grand-Duc Jean
⑫ Musée Draï Eechelen

0 metres	500
0 yards	500

Key

⬛ Street-by-Street pp246–7

For keys to symbols see back flap

Street-by-Street: The Old Town

With its cliffs and deep river valleys, La Vieille Ville (The Old Town) has one of the most remarkable locations in any capital city. Although vestiges remain of the mighty military fortifications, which once defended the city in concentric rings, it is the refined elegance of 18th- and 19th-century urban building that predominates, with the Palais Grand-Ducal as the centrepiece. Two of the city's best museums are also found here. But the highlights of the area are the spectacular views, notably from the Place de la Constitution, the Plateau du St-Esprit and the Chemin de la Corniche.

Place Guillaume II
The city's largest square is named after Grand Duke William II (r.1840–49), whose equestrian statue stands in the centre. The 19th-century Neo-Classical Hôtel de Ville lines the entire southern side of the square, which is also known as the Knuedler.

Gëlle Fra
The Monument of Remembrance, in the Place de la Constitution, is a statue on a tall granite obelisk. It commemorates soldiers who served in World War I.

Cathédrale Notre-Dame
Central to the public life of the nation, Cathédrale Notre-Dame was originally a Jesuit church, consecrated in 1621. It became a cathedral when the Grand Duchy was awarded its own bishopric in 1870. The ornately carved gallery forming the organ loft dates from the 17th century.

The Plateau du St-Esprit is a spur of rock fortified in the 1680s. After sensitive modernization, it became the site of the Cité Judiciaire, headquarters of the country's justice system.

For hotels and restaurants see p271 and pp292–3

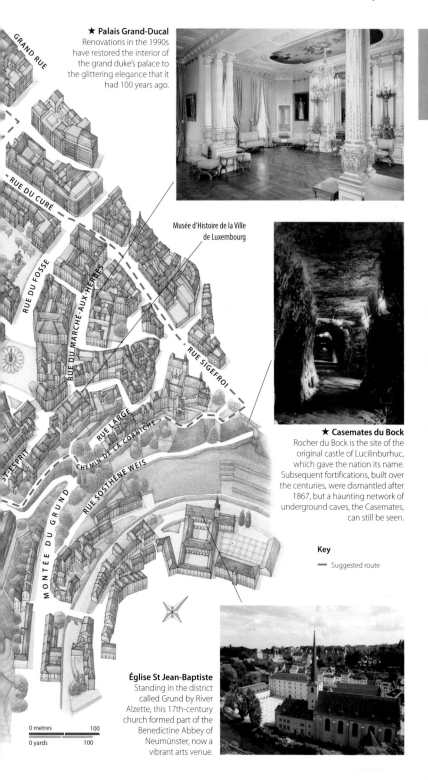

★ **Palais Grand-Ducal**
Renovations in the 1990s have restored the interior of the grand duke's palace to the glittering elegance that it had 100 years ago.

GRAND RUE

RUE DU CURÉ

Musée d'Histoire de la Ville de Luxembourg

RUE DU FOSSE

RUE DU MARCHÉ-AUX-HERBES

RUE SIGEFROI

RUE LARGE

CHEMIN DE LA CORNICHE

ST-ESPRIT

RUE SOSTHÈNE WEIS

MONTÉE DU GRUND

★ **Casemates du Bock**
Rocher du Bock is the site of the original castle of Lucilinburhuc, which gave the nation its name. Subsequent fortifications, built over the centuries, were dismantled after 1867, but a haunting network of underground caves, the Casemates, can still be seen.

Key

— Suggested route

Église St Jean-Baptiste
Standing in the district called Grund by River Alzette, this 17th-century church formed part of the Benedictine Abbey of Neumünster, now a vibrant arts venue.

0 metres   100
0 yards   100

Exploring Luxembourg City

Northeast of the city centre lies the hill of Kirchberg where modern tower blocks house many of the major European institutions that make Luxembourg the third capital of the European Union. There is much here to interest enthusiasts of modern architecture, and some cultural treasures as well. This includes Luxembourg's prestigious modern art museum, set in a sensational cluster of glass prisms and sweeping curves. Just below it, facing the Old Town, is an evocative fortress called Dräi Eechelen, one of many that once ringed the city. Another, the Villa Vauban, stood westwards. Now the home of a fine municipal art collection, its military past is remembered only in its name.

The elegant Villa Vauban set in the calm environs of the city park

🏛 Villa Vauban

Avenue Émile Reuter 18.
Tel 47964900. **Open** 10am–6pm Mon, Wed, Thu, Sat & Sun, 10am–9pm Tue & Fri. 🅿 🆆 villavauban.lu

In the 1680s, the great French military engineer Vauban built a set of outlying fortresses to protect the approaches to Luxembourg City. One of these was located on the western side of the Old Town. Today, this site is occupied by the 19th-century Villa Vauban. A grand residence built between 1871 and 1873, the villa once belonged to the family of the politician, entrepreneur and philanthropist Jean-Pierre Pescatore (1793–1855). For many years, it housed a public art museum displaying his impressive collection as well as other bequests to the city. After a five-year programme of renovations and extension, the museum is now known as Villa Vauban – Musée d'Art de la Ville de Luxembourg. Its collection of some 300 paintings consists mainly of Dutch, Flemish, French, German and Italian art dating from between the 17th and 19th centuries. It includes work by Jan Steen, Anthony van Dyck, Canaletto, Eugène Delacroix and Gustave Courbet. The museum's setting is also a pleasure – it has its own gardens and is surrounded by an extensive municipal park.

Kirchberg

Marché-aux-Poissons. **Tel** 479330-1.
Open 10am–6pm Tue–Sun. 🅿 🖥 📷
At the eastern end of the Pont Grande Duchesse Charlotte (built 1966) lies the raised plateau of Kirchberg where a host of administrative, financial and cultural buildings are concentrated into a strip some 3 km (2 miles) long. Kirchberg was developed as the centre for Luxembourg's European institutions. In recent years, however, a broader vision has overtaken these bureaucratic beginnings and the area has become the focus of a number of exciting architectural projects for financial institutions and the arts. These include the dramatically futuristic MUDAM building and the impressive concert hall of the Philharmonie Luxembourg, a delicately columned drum designed by the award-winning French architect Christian de Portzamparc.

Kirchberg's eastern end, with its concentration of international banks, includes strikingly innovative architecture, such as the HypoVereinsbank Luxembourg, designed by the American architect Richard Meier, and has his signature white cladding. Kirchberg is also remarkable for its Central Park, which contains the largest sports arena in the country. Dotted around this district are public sculptures by international artists such as Henry Moore, Jean Dubuffet, Frank Stella and Richard Serra.

🏛 Centre Européen

Montée de Clausen. 🆆 lcto.lu
A number of major European institutions stand at the western end of Kirchberg. These include the Court of Justice of the European Union (Cour de Justice) and the **European Court of Auditors**. There are also the **European Investment Bank**, designed by Denys Lasdun, architect of the National Theatre in London, and the **Secretariat of the European Parliament**, which operates from the towers, designed by Spanish architect Ricardo Bofill, on either side of Avenue John F Kennedy. The tallest of these structures is the **Alcide de Gasperi Building** or Tower Building, which is part of the European Parliament's

The European Union's Cour de Justice on the Kirchberg plateau

The futuristic glass forms of the Musée d'Art Moderne Grand-Duc Jean

Congress and Conference Centre. The **National Library**, to the west of the Philharmonie, was founded in the late 18th century and will take up residence in a new purpose-built home in the Kirschberg area in 2015. To the south is the curious, cantilevered **Hemicycle**. Completed in 1979, it was used for plenary sessions of the European Parliament and now serves as a conference centre.

🏛 Cour de Justice
Boulevard Konrad Adenauer.
🌐 **perraultarchitecte.com**

One of the most impressive buildings in Kirchberg has always been the Cour de Justice – Court of Justice of the European Union. This classically proportioned, yet uncompromisingly modern structure of dark-brown steel is raised on a broad plinth, suggesting the full force of orderly law. Designed by a Belgian-Luxembourg partnership, it was completed in 1970. The Court has the task of ensuring that EU law is correctly interpreted and applied across all the member states – a huge task that has become even greater with the recent enlargement of the EU to 28 member states.

The original building has been renovated and extended to create an even more impressive effect. Following designs by French architect Dominique Perrault (b.1953), it has been completely surrounded by a giant square frame on pillars, complemented by two additional towers, and all covered in bronzed sheeting.

🏛 Musée d'Art Moderne Grand-Duc Jean (MUDAM)
Park Draï Eechelen, Kirchberg.
Tel 453785-1. **Open** 11am–8pm Wed–Fri, 11am–6pm Sat–Mon & public hols.
🖼 ♿ ▣ 🎬 🌐 **mudam.lu**

Abbreviated to MUDAM, this modern art museum is the country's most prized architectural statement: a stunning glass and sandstone edifice designed by Leoh Ming Pei, the Chinese-American architect best known for his ingenious glass pyramids at the Louvre in Paris. MUDAM first opened its doors in 2006. The exhilarating spaces on three levels inside, are used for temporary exhibitions, where artists are invited to interact with the unique opportunities offered by the varying shapes and light provided by the architecture. MUDAM's growing permanent collection of paintings, photography, film, video art and installations, is also exhibited in rotation at the museum. It includes work by well-known names such as Gilbert & George, Richard Long, Cy Twombly and Grayson Perry.

🏛 Dräi Eechelen
Park Dräi Eechelen 5, Kirchberg. **Tel** 264 335. 🚏 🌐 **m3e.public.lu**

The Three Acorns (Dräi Eechelen in Lëtzebuergesch, Trois Glands in French) is the nickname given to Fort Thüngen, because of the acorn symbols that crown each of its three round towers. Although it looks more like a Renaissance fortress, this curious bastion, with its arrow-shaped ground plan, was built by the Austrians in 1732–3; a century later, it was upgraded by the Prussians. After the destruction of the city's fortifications in 1867, the fort was all but buried and forgotten. However, its historic and architectural value was reassessed and it has now been restored and turned into the fortress museum of military and national history, with particular focus on Vauban's contribution to Luxembourg City's fortifications. The fort forms part of the **Vauban Circuit**, a 4-km (3-mile) long walk that loops between Kirchberg and the eastern side of the Old Town.

Stalwart towers of the Dräi Eechelen, defending the approaches to the city

Panoramic view of the village of Esch-sur-Sûre, Luxembourg ▶

❷ Fond-de-Gras

Administration, Place du Marché 1, Pétange; 20 km (12 mile) SW of Luxembourg City. **Road Map** E5. **Tel** 26504124. 🚉 **Open** May–Sep: 12:30–7pm Sun & public holidays; summer holidays: Thu. 🅿 ▢ **W** fond-de-gras.lu

Known as Le Pays des Terres Rouges (The Red Lands), the southwestern part of the Grand Duchy forms the old industrial heartlands, centre of the iron-and-steel manufacturing. Located here, close to the borders with Belgium and France, is the **Parc Industriel et Ferroviaire du Fond-de-Gras** (Industrial and Railway Park of Fond-de-Gras), a collection of industrial heritage attractions that provides a fascinating insight into bygone days.

Fond-de-Gras is based around an old railway depot. Steam and diesel trains make a 20-minute journey from here to Pétange under the title Train 1900. There is an industry-themed **Musée de Plein Air** (Open Air Museum), with miners' houses, workshops and heavy industrial equipment. A narrow-gauge mine train, *minièresbunn*, travels underground through a disused iron-ore mine to **Lasauvage**, a preserved iron-founding and mining village. Also of interest here is a nature reserve located in a former open-cast pit.

❸ Musée National des Mines de Fer

Carreau de la Mine Walert, Rumelange; 17 km (11 miles) S of Luxembourg City. **Road Map** F5. **Tel** 565688. 🚉 **Open** Apr–Jun & Sep: 2–6pm Thu–Sun; Jul & Aug: 2–6pm Tue–Sun; Oct–Mar: 2:30pm 2nd Sun of month. 🅿 🅲 🅗 **W** mnm.lu

This museum takes visitors underground into the galleries from which ore was extracted for iron-smelting for nearly 200 years, until the 1980s. Guided tours travel into the mine by train. Visitors are then free to wander the galleries and see the collection of massive mining machines. Exhibits reveal the arduous nature of mining, and how this evolved over time.

The soaring façade of the Église St-Michel at Mondorf-les-Bains

Environs

Bettembourg, 8 km (5 miles) to the north, has an activity park and zoo for children. **Parc Merveilleux** offers moving models of classic fairytales, as well as a mini-train, mini-cars, mini-golf and playgrounds.

🅿 **Parc Merveilleux** Route de Mondorf. **Tel** 5110481. **Open** late Mar–mid-Oct. 🅿 🅗 ▢ **W** parc-merveilleux.lu

❹ Mondorf-les-Bains

15 km (9 miles) SE of Luxembourg City. **Road Map** F5. 🚶 4,900. 🚌 **i** Avenue des Bains 26–28; 23667575. **W** mondorf-les-bains.lu

A pretty town on the border, Mondorf-les-Bains is the Grand Duchy's only spa centre. Supplied with naturally hot waters that emerge from the ground at 24°C (75°F), Mondorf has been attracting visitors since the 1820s. The mineral-rich water is said to

benefit those suffering from liver and digestive complaints and rheumatism. The spa installations in the park setting of the **Domaine Thermal** include open-air and indoor pools, saunas, Turkish baths, a fitness centre, massage and a variety of special treatments. Mondorf also has a gambling centre, **Casino 2000**, established in 1983. The town's most interesting church is the pink **Église St-Michel** (built 1764–66), whose interior has stucco work, *trompe-l'oeil* paintings in the apse and a lavish polychrome pulpit.

🅱 **Domaine Thermal** Avenue des Bains. **Tel** 23666666. **Open** daily. 🅿 🅗 🅲 ▢ **W** montdorf.lu

❺ Luxembourg's Moselle Valley

Road Map F5. 🚌 Remich: **i** Esplanade; 26747874. Grevenmacher: Route du Vin 10; 758275. Wellenstein: Heenegässel; 23699858. **W** visitmoselle.lu

The broad River Moselle forms the southeastern border of Luxembourg with Germany. Flowing north from its source in Alsace in France, it enters Luxembourg at the village of **Schengen**, then runs for a distance of 42 km (26 miles) to **Wasserbillig** before turning east into Germany and joining the River Rhine at Koblenz. In Luxembourg, the Moselle valley is known above all for its vineyards, producing mainly white wine. Various vineyards and producers on the Route du

Extensive vineyards of the Moselle Luxembourgeoise, Grevenmacher

The market town of Larochette, huddled in a verdant glen formed by the River Ernz Blanche

Vin (Wine Road) along the river offer wine tastings and tours, for instance at **Remich**, Wormeldange, **Grevenmacher** and the wine cooperatives of **Wellenstein**. Just north of Wellenstein, among the wineries of Bech-Kleinmacher, is a charming wine and folklore museum, the **Musée A Possen**. This has furnished rooms in a set of 400-year-old wine-making buildings and includes wine tasting among its draws. The town of Ehnen, in the commune of Wormeldange, is the site of the **Musée National du Vin**, which explains wine-making processes, again with tastings.

The wine-growing village of Schengen is where the Schengen Agreement was signed in 1985 by European ministers, loosening the border controls between participating countries.

Cruises offer an agreeable way to see the extensive Moselle Luxembourgeoise. The cruise-boat **Princesse Marie-Astrid** runs a daily schedule between varying destinations – with return trips by coach – from late March to late September. Details are available from the Grevenmacher tourist office.

Musée A Possen
Keeseschgaessel 2, Bech-Kleinmacher. **Tel** 23697353. **Open** Easter–Oct: 11am–6pm Tue–Sun.
musee-possen.lu

Musée National du Vin
Route du Vin 115, Ehnen. **Tel** 760026. **Open** Apr–Oct: Tue–Sun.

❻ Larochette

20 km (12 miles) N of Luxembourg City. **RoadMap** F4. 2,130. Chemin J.A. Zinnen 33; 83703042. **larochette.eu.**

A pleasant market town in the valley of River Ernz Blanche, Larochette has more than 800 years of history, centring upon its castle set on a rocky sandstone crag that dominates the town. This location gave the town its name: Larochette is French for The Small Rock. In German, the town is Fels (Rock). Extensive ruins of the 11th–16th-century **Château de Larochette**, destroyed by fire in 1565, cover the top of the crag. Located here is Palais des Hombourg, the medieval palace of two noble sisters who married brothers from the House of Homburg in 1338–45. Restoration of the castle has begun with the now complete Maison de Créhange, an impressive evocation of a 14th-century fortified residence named after a family that inhabited this part of the castle. Looping out from the town are some 30 km (18 miles) of walking paths.

Château de Larochette
Tel 837497. **Open** Easter–Oct: 10am–6pm daily.

The Wines of Luxembourg

Appreciated by wine enthusiasts for their dry, fresh flavours, Luxembourg wines have little of the cloying fruitiness sometimes associated with northern white wines. The Romans are said to have brought wine grapes to the Moselle valley, and the local grape variety Elbling may date right back to that era. The vines grow in a string of 28 towns and villages lining the left bank of the river between Schengen and Wasserbillig. Slopes here are sunny and the climate is cool, favouring white wine grapes. The main varieties are Rivaner, Auxerrois Blanc, Elbling, Riesling, Pinot Blanc and Pinot Gris. Chardonnay and Gewürztraminer also make an appearance. Pinot Noir is grown to make rosé and a small amount of red wine. A sizeable proportion of the harvest is used to make the sparkling wine Crémant Luxembourgeois, and there are three types of sweet wines: *vin de glace, vin de paille* and *vendanges tardives*. Some 80 per cent of the total white wine production is consumed in Belgium, and much of the rest is sent to Germany to be made into *sekt* (sparkling wine).

Barrels stacked in a wine cellar of the Moselle valley

❼ A Tour of Petite Suisse Luxembourgeoise

Aptly called Petite Suisse (Little Switzerland), this segment of the Germano-Luxembourg Nature Park has steep, twisting valleys made intimate by woodlands, rushing streams and dramatic rock formations. Tours take a scenic route to Beaufort castle and to the Ernz Noire valley via Müllerthal village. Müllerthal is also used to refer to Petite Suisse Luxembourgeoise as a whole. Stop-off points along the way give access to signposted paths that go deeper into the landscape.

③ Berdorf

A centre for rock-climbing, the area around Berdorf village has numerous marked paths for walkers. Rising above a plateau, the spire-cum-watertower of Berdorf's church is a noted landmark.

② Gorge du Loup

A walk close to Echternach leads to this Wolf Gorge, with its cleft between two towering walls of rock. Steps lead up to a spectacular viewpoint.

④ Predigstuhl

Named for its shape, the Predigstuhl (Pulpit) is one of many strange rock formations in the region.

① Echternach

This old abbey town is the main urban centre in the region, as well as a hub for activity holidays.

⑤ Werschrumschluff

Close to the Predigstuhl, the Werschrumschluff is an immense rock crevice, just wide enough for a walker to pass through.

Key

━━━ Tour route
━━━ Other Road

0 km 1
0 miles 1

⑥ Beaufort

Extensive ruins of a 12th–16th-century castle, in a wooded valley, stand ready to be explored. The village of Beaufort is noted for its blackcurrant liqueur, Cassero.

Tips for Drivers

Starting point: Echternach.
Length: About 35 km (22 miles).
Duration of drive: Allow half a day, but a whole day if on foot.
Driving conditions: Roads are narrow and winding, but have good surfaces and signposts.
Where to stay and eat: Echternach is the main centre, but there are options at Berdorf, Beaufort and Müllerthal.
Visitors' information:
Ⓦ mullerthal.lu
Ⓦ echternach.lu
Ⓦ berdorf-tourist.lu
Ⓦ visitluxembourg.com

⑦ Müllerthal

The Schiessentümpel bridge and its triple waterfall are set amid woodland. This is a famous beauty spot in the valley of Ernz Noire, which is often referred to as the Müllerthal.

❽ Echternach

35 km (22 miles) NE of Luxembourg City. **Road Map** F4. 🚶 5,350. 🚌
ℹ️ Parvis de la Basilique 9–10; 720230.
🎼 International Classical Music Festival (May–Jun and Sep).
🌐 echternach-tourist.lu

Capital of Luxembourg's Little Switzerland, Echternach is also the country's oldest town. An abbey was founded here in AD 698 by St Willibrord, a Yorkshire missionary monk who was said to cure chorea (or St Vitus's Dance), a disease of the nervous system. This is believed to be the reason for the curious motion of the participants in Echternach's dance parade, the Sprangprëssessioun *(see p39)*. The town is dominated by the massive abbey, which dates mainly from its makeover in austere Classical style in 1727–31. Until its closure in 1794 by the French Revolutionary Army, it was a Benedictine monastery of great influence, noted for its illuminated manuscripts produced during the Middle Ages. These can be seen at the **Musée de l'Abbaye**, laid out in the cellars of the old Abbot's Palace. The crypt of the accompanying **Basilique St-Willibrord** contains the sarcophagus of the saint, as well as 11th-century frescoes. The town's centrepiece, the **Place du Marché**, is an ensemble of traditional buildings, some old, some reconstructed, including the Gothic 15th-century law courts, the **Dënzelt**.

🏛️ **Musée de l'Abbaye**
Parvis de la Basilique 11. **Tel** 727472.
Open daily. **Closed** Nov–Feb. 📷
🌐 willibrord.lu

❾ Diekirch

21 km (13 miles) NW of Echternach.
Road Map F4. 🚶 6,730. 🚉 🚌
ℹ️ Place de la Libération 3; 803023.
🌐 tourisme.diekirch.lu

Located on the River Sûre, Diekirch is an attractive base from which to explore the surrounding area. The town was badly damaged during the Ardennes Offensive *(see p235)*, a subject that is covered by the

Echternach's Place du Marché, with cobbled streets and old buildings

National Museum of Military History, through photographs and film, various artifacts and lifesize dioramas. The museum also covers the history of Luxembourg's army. The **Conservatoire National de Véhicules Historiques**, a veteran car museum, displays changing exhibits mounted by collectors and includes bikes, fire engines – even children's cars. It shares premises with the **Museum of the Diekirch Brewery**; Diekirch is a famous brand of beer. Also of note is Église St-Laurent, a Gothic and Romanesque church built over the site of a Roman villa and containing Roman and early medieval sarcophagi.

🏛️ **National Museum of Military History**
Bamertal 10. **Tel** 808908. **Open** Tue–Sun. **Closed** Carnival Sun. 📷
🌐 mnhm.lu

🏛️ **Conservatoire National de Véhicules Historiques**
Rue de Stavelot 20-22. **Tel** 26800468.
Open 10am–6pm Tue–Sun. 📷
🌐 visitluxembourg.com

❿ Vianden

22 km (14 miles) NW of Echternach.
Road Map F4. 🚶 1,900. 🚌
ℹ️ Rue du Vieux Marché 1A; 834257.
🌐 tourist-info-vianden.lu

This little town of Vianden, on the River Our, is famous for the large medieval **Château de Vianden** that is perched over the town on a rocky outcrop. This château was the seat of the counts of Vianden and the Orange-Nassau family, until it was given to the state by Grand Duke Jean in 1977. The building dates mainly from the 12th and 13th centuries and has Romanesque and Gothic structures.

Vianden also has a charming **Musée d'Histoire de la Ville de Vianden**, with rustic furniture, domestic artifacts, clothing and dolls. The Gothic abbey church, **Église des Trinitaires**, dating mainly from 1250, has a double nave with Baroque flourishes and a tranquil cloister. Also of interest is **Maison de Victor Hugo**, which recalls the author's stay here in 1871. Luxembourg's only *télésiège* (chairlift) rises 220 m (720 ft) from Rue du Sanitorium and offers views over the town and castle.

🏰 **Château de Vianden**
Open daily. 📷 🌐 castle-vianden.lu

🏛️ **Musée d'Histoire de la Ville de Vianden**
96-98 Grande-rue. **Tel** 834591.
Open Easter–Oct: 11am–5pm Tue–Sun. 📷

The Château de Vianden towering over the eponymous riverside town

For hotels and restaurants see p271 and pp292–3

⓫ Château de Bourscheid

11 km (7 miles) W of Vianden. **Road Map** F4. 🚌 **ℹ** Buurschtermillen, Bourscheid-Moulin; 990570. **Open** Apr–Oct: 9:30am–6pm daily; Nov–Mar: 11am–4pm daily. 🚗 🔲 🏠 **W** chateau.bourscheid.lu

Now largely reconstructed from ruins, the Château de Bourscheid is an evocative example of a medieval walled fortress. Building began in about AD 1000, and it was then ruled by the lords of Bourscheid for more than 400 years, from 1095 to 1512. Set 150 m (492 ft) above a dramatic loop of the River Sûre, the castle offers fine views from the ramparts. The current ring wall, with its eight towers, was built between 1350 and 1384, along with the step-gabled **Stolzemburger House** in the lower part of the castle. This now contains a small museum of archaeological finds. The gateway giving access to the upper and lower castle was completed in 1477. Decline set in after 1512, following the death of the last Bourscheid – the ruins were bought by the state in 1972.

Environs
The N27 follows a scenic route along the River Sûre. The **Upper Valley** runs from Ettelbruck, via Bourscheid, for some 70 km (43 miles) almost to the Belgian border.

The sturdy towers and ramparts of Château de Bourscheid

⓬ Clervaux

16 km (10 miles) N of Bourscheid. **Road Map** F4. 🚗 4,815. 🚊 🚌 **ℹ** Grand Rue 11; 920072. **W** destination-clervaux.lu

Located on a loop in the River Clerve in the Germano-Luxembourg Nature Reserve, Clervaux lies at the heart of the forested Ardennes region known as Oesling in northern Luxembourg. At the centre of the town is a whitewashed château of medieval origins, which has been much altered over the centuries. It contains three permanent exhibitions. The first is a collection of photographs known as **The Family of Man**. Then there are the **Musée de la Maquette**, with models of 22 castles in Luxembourg, and **Musée de la**

Bataille des Ardennes or Battle of the Bulge Museum. The tower of the Neo-Romanesque church of the **Abbaye Bénédictine de St-Maurice et de St-Maur**, founded in 1910, crests a hill outside the town. The austere interior of the church is bathed in light from fine stained glass and contains an exhibition on monastic life. The abbey is internationally famed for its choir, which specializes in Gregorian chant.

🏛 **The Family of Man**
Château de Clervaux. **Tel** 929657. **Open** Mar–Dec: noon–6pm Wed–Sun. 🚗 ♿ 🔲 **W** steichencollections.lu

🏛 **Musée de la Maquette and Musée de la Bataille des Ardennes**
Château de Clervaux. **Tel** 26910695. **Open** Mar–Dec.

⓭ Wiltz

11 km (7 miles) NW of Bourscheid. **Road Map** E4. 🚗 6,400. 🚊 🚌 **ℹ** Château; 957444. 🎭 Open-air Festival of Theatre and Music (Jul). **W** tourisme.wiltz.lu

This town is a good base for touring the local Ardennes. The lower part of the town runs along both banks of the River Wiltz, while the upper town shares higher ground with an impressive château. This former residence of the counts of Wiltz is in the Renaissance style. Its stables contain the agreeable **Musée National d'Art Brassicole et de la Tannerie**, which is devoted to beer-brewing, with a small section

The Family of Man Project

The American photographer Edward Steichen (1879–1973) was born in Luxembourg. He became famous during the 1920s, and after World War II was Director of Photography at the Museum of Modern Art in New York. In 1951, he invited submissions for a collection of photographs that would record the unique and universal qualities of mankind. From some two million submissions, he chose 503, by 273 photographers from 68 countries, and assembled them under 37 themes – work, family, birth, war, faith and so on. The Family of Man was first exhibited in 1955 and toured the world to great acclaim. In 1964, the US government gave it to the Grand Duchy of Luxembourg in accordance with Steichen's wishes. Since 1994, the collection has been at the Château de Clervaux, and it is now listed by UNESCO on its Memory of the World register.

Edward Steichen, pictured in 1955

on leather-tanning. Both trades are historically associated with Wiltz. The museum also has its own micro-brewery and a traditional-style bar and *bistrot* called **Café Jhang Primus**. Wiltz is also well known for its Open-air Festival of Theatre and Music (*see p39*).

🏛 Musée National d'Art Brassicole et de la Tannerie

Château de Wiltz. **Tel** 957444. **Open** Jul – Aug: 10am–6pm daily; Jan–Jun & Sep–Dec: 9am–noon & 2–5pm Mon–Fri, 10am–noon Sat. 🅿 🄰 🄸

ⓓ Esch-sur-Sûre

10 km (6 miles) S of Wiltz. **Road Map** E4. 🏠 2,480. 🚌 🛈 Rue de l'Eglise 14; 26889541. 🌐 **esch-sur-sure.lu**

This village is famous above all for its spectacular setting, on an oxbow loop of the River Sûre that virtually performs a complete circle around it. Concentric rings of streets and slate-roofed houses cluster at the foot of a jagged outcrop of rock and the ruins of the castle that line the ridge. The castle dates back to AD 927 and remained in use until the French Revolutionary Army destroyed it in 1795. West of Esch-sur-Sûre, the river is dammed, creating a serpentine lake that is popular for water sports. There are many marked footpaths for walkers.

Fairytale flourishes on the handsome castle of Schoenfels

ⓔ Rindschleiden

8 km (5 miles) S of Esch-sur-Sûre. **Road Map** E4. 🛈 889358. 🌐 **wahl.lu**

The village of Rindschleiden is best known for a little whitewashed church built originally as a chapel in Romanesque style in the 10th century, and later extended. During the 15th and 16th centuries, 170 sq metres (1,830 sq ft) of the vaults and walls inside were painted with delicate murals depicting saints. The church was dedicated in the 16th century to Willibrord, saint of Echternach (*see p255*). Close by is a spring which the saint is said to have divined with his rod – this is the focus of an annual Whitsunday pilgrimage.

ⓕ Vallée des Sept Châteaux

20 km (12 miles) SE of Rindschleiden. **Road Map** F4. 🛈 Hôtel de Ville; 3250231. 🌐 **letzebuergwest.lu**

From Mersch, the River Eisch can be followed westwards for 37 km (23 miles), on the CR 105, to Gaichel, on the Belgian border. This stretch is the Vallée des Sept Châteaux (Valley of the Seven Castles). A footpath, the **Sentier des Sept Châteaux**, also follows the valley. The restored medieval castle at Mersch is now the site of the town hall and tourist office. The second castle is at **Schoenfels**, on CR 102, by the River Mamer. This is a tall medieval keep revamped in the 19th century. **Ansembourg** has two castles. The one above the village is of 12th-century origin, and has been home of the counts Marchant d'Ansembourg since the 17th century. The other, in the valley, is a fine 17th-century Renaissance château with numerous cone-roofed turrets. The medieval-looking **Château de Hollenfels** dates mainly from the 18th century and serves as a youth hostel. **Septfontaines** sits beneath the impressive ruin of a 13th–15th century castle, and **Koerich**, lying south of the route, has another imposing ruin of a medieval castle, as well as a fine Baroque church.

Rustic beauty of the riverside landscape at Esch-sur-Sûre

TRAVELLERS'
NEEDS

WHERE TO STAY

Tourist and traveller accommodation in Belgium and Luxembourg is extremely well organized. High professional standards abound, from the top five-star and boutique hotels to budget options and bed-and-breakfast stays. There are a number of competitively-priced, efficient business hotels, where location is more important than style; plenty of small, luxurious, family-run townhouse hotels, designed to pamper guests; and also a growing set of delightful rural bed-and-breakfasts, full of rustic charm. With a little research, most travellers will find that they are spoilt for choice.

Waiting area of Martin's Klooster *(see p268)*, a top-range hotel in Leuven

Hotels

There are hotels to satisfy every taste, from individual historic homes to sleek, top-notch international establishments, with every facility imaginable and prices to match. Hotels are closely regulated to meet high industry standards.

At the upper end, there are a number of familiar chains such as **Conrad Hilton**, **Marriott** and **Radisson**. Many good, mid-range hotels are affiliated to the **Best Western** group. The group **Logis de France**, specializing in comfortable country hotels, crosses the border with its selection of Logis in Belgium and Luxembourg. The **Accor Group** has hotels at every price level, from the basic Formule 1 chain (offering out-of-centre rooms with shared bathroom facilities), to Etap, Ibis, Mercure, Novotel and the very chic Sofitel chain at the top. All are efficient, clean and offer good value for money. The **InterContinental** hotels group,

similarly, has the brands Express, Crowne Plaza and Holiday Inn.

There are also numerous individual hotels, often taking pride in being family-run, and paying attention to service.

Hotel Gradings

Hotels in Belgium and Luxembourg are judged according to Benelux standards, and the regional licensing authority issues a blue permit shield bearing the number of stars (one to five) that a hotel has been awarded. The star system rates hotels according to their facilities, the quality of their welcome and helpfulness of the staff, the decor, the tranquillity of the rooms and even the price. However, membership to this scheme is voluntary and there may be top-range hotels that are not graded. In general, one- and two-star hotels are basic.

Room Rates

Hotels at the top end of the scale offer high standards of comfort as well as convenience and their prices reflect this – rates in excess of €350 per night for a double room are not unusual. In larger cities, they are designed primarily for corporate clients, which means that during weekends and holiday periods, rates can be attractive. Moderately priced hotels charge between €100 and €150 per night, while bed-and-breakfast prices are usually between €50 and €100. Rates vary according to the season.

In general, the low season extends from November to March, with exceptions during Christmas, New Year, as well as Easter and other holiday weekends. The high season is over the summer holidays, from early July to the end of August.

Taxes and Charges

Room taxes and sales taxes are usually included in the cost of a room, so the price quoted should be the total. In the centre of busy cities, there may be a charge for using the hotel car park.

How to Book

Rooms are available in Belgium and Luxembourg at most times of the year, but you should book in advance to ensure that you get the place you want.

While you can usually book directly with hotels, either on their websites or over the phone, the most efficient way to book a room is by using the services offered by Internet booking websites such as **Booking.com** and **Hotels.com**; all offer instant online bookings, often at rates far below those quoted by the

A visitor at the reservation desk of Hotel De Orangerie *(see p267)*, Bruges

◄ Exterior of restaurant Amadeus, well-known for its spare ribs

Chic, well-equipped room in the Grand Hotel Cravat (see p271), Luxembourg City

hotels themselves. The **Visit Brussels** tourist office and website offers a reservation service, as does the **Luxembourg City Tourist Office**. Likewise, many local tourist offices will reserve accommodation for visitors. **Airbnb.com** lists private homes that are for rent.

Hotel Facilities

Most hotels above the budget or one-star category have rooms with ensuite bathroom facilities. A television comes with virtually every room across the price range. These usually have a range of European channels provided by a cable link. Phone calls using the landlines in hotel rooms can be very expensive. Many hotels have tea- and coffee-making facilities in the rooms. They may also have minibars, with a range of alcoholic drinks, mixers, fruit juice and mineral water, as well as some Belgian beer; prices should be supplied and are not always exorbitant. Many of the top city hotels, and some leading country hotels, have fitness and spa facilities, including saunas and gymnasiums, but only a handful have swimming pools, which are more common in the countryside.

Breakfast

It is important to establish whether breakfast is included in the price of the room; where it is not, guests may find that this is an expensive additional cost. Breakfast may be a simple Continental one with a choice of croissants and other pastries, bread rolls, jam and butter, and tea or coffee.

Breakfast plate from a buffet, with pastries and fruit

A full buffet breakfast will offer cereals, cold meats, sliced cheese, boiled eggs, yoghurt, fruit juices, fresh fruit and more.

Some hotel-restaurants focus on gourmet food, just as some rural bed-and-breakfasts take special care to serve local produce, plus home-made jams, breads and pastries.

Half Board

An increasing number of gourmet hotel-restaurants – particularly those in a rural setting – offer excellent value half-board packages. These include a daily meal at the hotel's restaurant and allow visitors to sample a wide range of outstanding local cuisine.

Internet Information

Most hotels and many bed-and-breakfasts provide a Wi-Fi Internet connection, and this is often free of charge. All major hotels, many of the smaller ones, and some bed-and-breakfast establishments, have their own websites. Check **hotels.com** for more information on hotels.

Disabled Travellers

Hotels in Luxembourg and Belgium take the needs of disabled travellers seriously. Most have rooms designed for wheelchair-bound guests. It is worth remembering, however, that many hotels are in historic buildings and may not be suitable (many do not have lifts). Most hotels allow the visually handicapped to bring a guide-dog on the premises. It is essential to ask in advance about the facilities available. **Bruxelles Pour Tous** and the **Access-Able Travel Source** have some listings.

The four-star La Butte aux Bois (see p268), set amid sprawling lawns in Lanaken

Antwerp's Hilton, a landmark with an ornate 19th-century façade *(see p268)*

Travelling with Children

Children are welcome in just about every hotel in Belgium and Luxembourg. Indeed, many hotels make a concerted effort to cater to the needs of those travelling with children. Most allow one or two children under the age of 12 to stay in their parents' room without extra charge, or for a small supplement. Some hotels extend this to travellers under the age of 16, or even under 18.

Bed-and-Breakfasts

A pleasant alternative to staying in a small hotel, B&Bs are essentially rooms in private houses. The style of accommodation varies considerably, from the mundane to the truly special. For instance, some may be in historic homes, close to a city centre or set in the countryside, with antique furniture and high standards of comfort. Many are run more like mini-hotels, with owners who are careful to provide a high level of professional service in such details as the quality of linen and breakfast. Tourist offices can supply lists of B&B accommodation. Visitors can also check **Bed & Brussels** for more information.

Hoevetoerisme and Chambres d'Hôtes

There is little to distinguish chambres d'hôtes (guest rooms) from B&Bs, but usually the former denotes something a little more special – perhaps a warm welcome in a beautiful farmhouse, a manor house or a historic building. In the Flanders region, many farm B&Bs belong to the movement known as hoevetoerisme (farmstead tourism), under the umbrella federation **Vlaamse Federatie voor Hoeve- en Plattelandstoerisme**. Its equivalent in Wallonia is **Fédération des Gîtes de Wallonie**, which, like its Flemish counterpart, also covers self-catering holiday cottages, or gîtes.

Apartment-Hotels

A number of city hotels offer apartments rather than rooms. For instance, the **Citadines** company has two "apart-hotels" in Brussels. The rooms may be suites, with a sitting area as well as kitchen facilities, though the hotel may also have a breakfast room for guests. Reception services can be as minimal as collecting the key, registering and paying. Apartment-hotels are designed for guests staying a number of days, if not weeks, but some are happy to offer accommodation for one night only. They can be very useful for families on a longer visit.

Youth and Budget Accommodation

There are youth hostels in most major towns and cities. These tend to have excellent modern facilities, reasonably priced food and the chance of more privacy than is usually associated with hostel stays. Accommodation may be in double or single rooms, or in dormitories. Although called youth hostels, there is in fact no age limit for guests. Flanders, Wallonia and Luxembourg each have their own youth hotel association. Members of **Hostelling International**, or an equivalent approved national organization, will find the rates less expensive than non-members.

There are also numerous hostel-like budget hotels, particularly in popular tourist cities such as Brussels and Bruges. Called logements pour jeunes or jeugdlogies, they are specially geared and styled for young people, and may offer a more charcterful (not to say hit-and-miss) experience than official hostels.

Gay and Lesbian Accommodation

There are no specifically gay or lesbian hotels, but same-sex couples should have few problems finding welcoming accommodation. **Tels Quels** is a good source of information for Brussels, and there are websites for Antwerp and Bruges. **Rosa Lëtzebuerg** is the main LGBT association in Luxembourg. The website provides information about LGBT events and activities, as well as listings for places of interest in and around Luxembourg. The **Navigaytor** website includes Belgium in its worldwide listings.

The stately Ter Brughe *(see p267)*, a budget hotel in Bruges

Self-Catering and Gîtes

Belgium and Luxembourg also have a range of self-catering properties for rent. Many of these are located in the countryside and follow a pattern similar to that of the French *gîtes* – self-catering holiday cottages.

Local tourist offices usually provide detailed information for their areas. Vlaamse Federatie voor Hoeve- en Plattelandstoerisme and the Fédération des Gîtes de Wallonie have listings. **Ardennes-Étape** has more than 500 holiday homes to let; and the company **Maisons de Vacances** has chalets in the Hautes Fagnes region.

Pand, an upscale boutique hotel in central Bruges *(see p267)*

Recommended Hotels

The hotels featured in this guide have been selected across a wide price range for their excellent facilities, outstanding location and good value. Historic hotels are often centuries-old buildings, renovated castles and old stately mansions. Modern lodgings have comfortable, standard amenities, while "design" refers to the most fashionable of stylish hotels. Other hotels encompass all price levels, ranging from basic "value" options to luxury ones. The B&B category is used for guesthouses, which usually include breakfast, but check the description to be sure.

For the pick of the very best, look out for hotels featuring the DK Choice symbol. These establishments have been highlighted in recognition of an exceptional feature – a stunning location, notable history, fine food or an inviting atmosphere.

DIRECTORY

Hotels

Accor Group
🌐 accorhotels.com

Best Western
🌐 bestwestern.be

Conrad Hilton
🌐 conradhotels3.
hilton.com

InterContinental
🌐 ihg.com

Logis de France
🌐 logis.be

Marriott
🌐 marriott.com

Radisson
🌐 radissonblu.com

How to Book

Airbnb
🌐 airbnb.com

Booking.com
🌐 booking.com

Hotels.com
🌐 hotels.com

Luxembourg City Tourist Office
30 Place Guillaume II,
Luxembourg City.
Tel 222809.
🌐 lcto.lu

Visit Brussels
Rue Royale 2-4 and
Hôtel de Ville,
1000 BRU.
Tel (02) 5138940.
🌐 visitbrussels.be

Disabled Travellers

Access-Able Travel Source
🌐 access-able.com

Bruxelles Pour Tous
🌐 bruxellespourtous.be

Bed-and-Breakfasts

Bed & Brussels
Rue Kindermans 9,
1050 BRU.
Tel (02) 6460737.
🌐 bnb-brussels.be

Hoevetoerisme and Chambres d'Hôtes

Fédération des Gîtes de Wallonie
Ave Prince de Liège 1/21,
Jambes (Namur).
Tel (081) 311800.
🌐 gitesdewallonie.be

Vlaamse Federatie voor Hoeve- en Plattelandstoerisme
Diestsevest 40,
Leuven.
Tel (016) 286035.
🌐 logereninvlaan
derenvakantieland.be

Apartment-Hotels

Citadines
🌐 citadines.com

Youth and Budget Accommodation

Flanders
Vlaamse JeugdHerbergen,
Beatrijslaan 72,
Antwerp.
Tel (03) 2327218.
🌐 jeugdherbergen.be

Hostelling International
Fretherne Road, Welwyn
Garden City, Herts,
AL8 6RD, England.
Tel (01707) 324170 (UK).
🌐 hihostels.com

Luxembourg
Centrale des Auberges
de Jeunesse
Luxembourgeoises,
Rue du Fort Olisy 2,
Luxembourg City.
Tel 262766200.
🌐 youthhostels.lu

Wallonia
Les Auberges de Jeunesse
de Wallonie, Rue de la
Sablonnière 28, 1000 BRU.
Tel (02) 2195676.
🌐 lesaubergesd
ejeunesse.be

Gay and Lesbian Accommodation

Antwerp
🌐 antwerp.gaycities.
com

Bruges
🌐 j-h.be

Navigaytor
🌐 navigaytor.net

Rosa Lëtzebuerg
Rue des Romains 60,
Luxembourg City.
Tel 26190018.
🌐 gay.lu

Tels Quels
Rue du Marché au
Charbon 81, 1000 BRU.
Tel (02) 5124587.
🌐 telsquels.be

Self-Catering and Gîtes

Ardennes-Étape
Ster 3b, Stavelot.
Tel (080) 292400.
🌐 ardennes-etape.com

Maisons de Vacances
Chemin du Raideu 21,
Xhoffraix-Malmedy.
Tel (080) 799016.
🌐 maisons-
de-vacances.be

Camping and Chalet Parks

Outdoor life is the principal attraction for a number of visitors to Belgium and Luxembourg. They spend summer vacations at the seaside or take hiking, kayaking or cycling trips among the forested hills and rivers of the Ardennes. Camping and caravanning also offer a chance to live close to nature and are remarkably economic ways of holidaying. To meet these needs, both countries offer a great number of campsites – there are more than 500 in Belgium and 120 in Luxembourg.

Types of Campsites

In both countries, campsites vary from rural farm sites, where simplicity is a virtue, to large holiday camps with swimming pools, sports facilities, bicycles for hire, fishing rights and archery. The latter also offer restaurants, cafés, shops, games arcades and evening entertainment. Some campsites have chalets, caravans and pre-installed tents for hire, so all visitors need to do is pitch up and enjoy.

Campsites in Belgium and Luxembourg are ranked into five categories, from one star to five star. One star indicates minimum facilities: drinking water, cold showers, flush toilets and power points. Three stars indicate hot showers, sports facilities and a shop. The five-star camps will in addition have a restaurant, children's playground and a wider range of facilities. Most campsites are ranked as one or two star. Often, it is not a question of facilities, but of the location. Websites offer good, sometimes visual, information on campsites. In a one- or two-star site, a family of four with a tent or caravan can expect to pay about €15–25 per night. There are also a few naturist campsites.

Camping Organizations

In Belgium, there are two camping authorities – the **Flanders Camping Federation**, and a parallel organization in Wallonia called **Fédération des Campings de Wallonie**. In Luxembourg, the organization is named **Camprilux**. These embrace all forms of camping, from tents to caravans and motorhomes (or camping cars). Their websites provide detailed information. Listings of campsites are also available through the various regional tourist offices (*see p323*) and the local ones. A useful and comprehensive list of campsites is available on the **Eurocampings** website. This includes a database on campsites that cater to disabled people. The main umbrella organization is the **FICC** (Fédération Internationale de Camping et de Caravanning), based in Brussels. This also covers motorhomes. The FICC issues the **Camping Card International** (CCI), which bestows a number of club advantages on its holders, including discounts of up to 25 per cent at certain listed campsites.

Booking and Arriving

Campsites in popular areas, such as on the Belgian coast, may be booked up months in advance for the high season of July and August. It is therefore necessary to phone or email ahead to reserve a site. In general, campers can arrive any time after 2pm and are expected to vacate the site and check out by midday.

Independent Camping

Wild or free camping is the term used for pitching a tent wherever a camper chooses. When practised outside official commercial campsites, this activity is frowned upon in Belgium and Luxembourg. The

Campers by the River Sûre in the forested Ardennes of Luxembourg

A slice of Switzerland, Durbuy Adventure's welcoming Chalet Suisse

argument is that there are plenty of cheap campsites, so there is no excuse to fail to use these and threaten to despoil and pollute the countryside. However, there is nothing to stop travellers from camping on private land with the permission of the landowner. Wild camping or wilding for motorhomes and camper vans faces official disapproval for similar reasons: most campsites accept motorhomes and there are also dedicated *aires* (parks), some with basic facilities, which allow overnight stays for a small fee. Police may fine motorhome owners who halt overnight illegally.

Trekkers' Huts

Many campsites across the region offer what are known as trekkers' huts or hikers' huts. These are designed especially for walkers using long-distance paths and for cyclists. Such accommodation permits them to travel without carrying camping equipment. In Flanders, these huts are called *trekkershutten*, while in Wallonia, they are known as *cabanes des randonneurs* or *cabanes pour routards* and in Luxembourg, *Wanderhütten*. The huts can be reserved in advance. In Wallonia, campsite listings show fixed accommodation (bungalows, chalets, tents, caravans) for rent, which can be used for a similar purpose. **Trekkershutten** lists hikers' huts and their websites.

Caravan and Motorhome Sites

The majority of campsites also accept caravans and motorhomes. Any campsite with one star or more will have electrical hook-ups. Listings will show the degree to which each campsite is geared towards caravans and motorhomes, as opposed to tents. A few sites are reserved exclusively for motorhomes.

Chalet Parks and Adventure Camps

Some campsites offer small chalets, also called bungalows or cottages. This is particularly the case in Luxembourg, which has **Europacamping Nommerlayen** near Larochette. There are also a few fully-fledged holiday resorts based around chalet accommodation, set in the countryside. These offer a range of sporting and outdoor facilities, including swimming pools, cycle paths, tennis courts, fitness centres and sauna suites, as well as restaurants and entertainment. The best known of these belong to **CenterParcs**, which has parks across northern Europe. Belgium has two: De Vossemeren and Erperheide, both in the Province of Limburg. Also in Limburg is the chalet park **Molenheide**. There are other centres that focus on more rugged outdoor challenges, such as pot-holing, quadbiking, rock-climbing, and kayak rafting. **Durbuy Adventure** in the Ardennes offers its guests Indian tepees, wooden tree-cabins, igloo tents and residential caravans.

DIRECTORY

Camping Organizations

Camping Card International
w campingcard
international.com

Camprilux
p/a Camping Auf Kengert
7633, Medernach.
w camping.lu

Eurocampings
w eurocampings.nl

FICC
Rue Belliard 20, 1040 BRU.
Tel (02) 5138782.
w ficc.org

Flanders Camping Federation
w camping.be

Fédération des Campings de Wallonie
Rue André Feher 5,
B-6900 Marche-en-Famenne.
Tel (84) 460352.
w camping belgique.be

Trekkers' Huts

Trekkershutten
w trekkershutten.nl

Chalet Parks and Adventure Camps

CenterParcs
Tel (070) 224900.
w centerparcs.be

CenterParks De
Vossemeren:
Elzen 145, Lommel.
Tel (011) 548200.

CenterParks Erperheide:
Erperheidestraat 2, Peer.
Tel (011) 616263.

Durbuy Adventure
Rue de Rome 1, Durbuy.
Tel (086) 212815.
w durbuyadventure.be

Europacamping Nommerlayen
Rue Nommerlayen,
Nommern, Luxembourg.
Tel 878078..
w nommerlayen-ec.lu

Molenheide
Molenheidestraat 7,
Houthalen-Helchteren.
Tel (011) 521044.
w molenheide.be

Where to Stay

Brussels

CENTRAL BRUSSELS:
Grande Cloche €
Historic Map 1 C4
Place Rouppe 10, 1000
Tel *(02) 512 6140*
W hotelgrandecloche.com
This beautifully renovated
19th-century townhouse has
comfortable, spacious rooms.
Breakfast is included.

CENTRAL BRUSSELS:
9Hotel Central €
Modern Map 2 E3
Rue des Colonies 10, 1000
Tel *(02) 504 9910*
W le9hotel.com
Located near the Royal Palace,
this hotel offers bright rooms
with exposed brickwork in a
historic Belgian townhouse.
Breakfast is included.

CENTRAL BRUSSELS:
Le Châtelain €€
Luxury Map 2 D5
Rue de Châtelain 17, 1000
Tel *(02) 646 0055*
W le-chatelain.be
Five-star hotel that prides itself on
traditional hospitality. The large
rooms are all soundproofed and
have well-appointed bathrooms.

CENTRAL BRUSSELS:
Le Dixseptieme €€
Historic Map 2 D3
Rue de la Madeleine 25, 1000
Tel *(02) 517 1717*
W ledixseptieme.be
The former home of a 17th-
century Spanish ambassador,
Le Dixseptieme combines
historic features with modern
decor and facilites.

CENTRAL BRUSSELS:
The Hotel Brussels €€
Luxury Map 2 E5
Blvd de Waterloo 38, 1000
Tel *(02) 504 1111*
W thehotel-brussels.be
Rooms are spacious, many with
superb city views, at this five-star
hotel with top-notch facilities.
The lobby boasts a frieze of the
Grand Place.

CENTRAL BRUSSELS:
Matignon €€
Value Map 1 C2
Rue de la Bourse 8–12, 1000
Tel *(02) 511 0888*
W hotelmatignon.be
This small but exquisite hotel has
simple, thoughtfully decorated
rooms. Price includes breakfast.

CENTRAL BRUSSELS:
Queen Anne Hotel €€
Modern Map 1 B3
Blvd Emile Jacqmain 110, 1000
Tel *(02) 217 1600*
W queen-anne.be
Located at the heart of the city, this
characterful option is good value,
with breakfast included.

CENTRAL BRUSSELS:
Le Quinze €€
Value Map 2 D3
Grand Place 15, 1000
Tel *(02) 511 0956*
W hotel-le-quinze-grand-place.be
There are 15 simple rooms at this
hotel; seven of them offer views
of the Grand Place. Friendly staff.

CENTRAL BRUSSELS: Scandic
Grand Place €€
Luxury Map 2 D2
Rue d'Arenberg 18, 1000
Tel *(02) 548 1811*
W scandichotels.com
The upmarket Scandic Grand
Place has sumptuous rooms, a
popular bar and restaurant and
a sauna and fitness room.

CENTRAL BRUSSELS:
Stanhope €€€
Luxury Map 2 F4
Rue du Commerce 9, 1000
Tel *(02) 506 9111*
W stanhope.be
Housed in three converted
townhouses, Stanhope has
elegant rooms, a beautiful interior
garden and a gourmet restaurant.

DK Choice

CENTRAL BRUSSELS:
Steigenberger Wiltcher's €€€
Luxury Map 2 D3
Avenue Louise 71, 1050
Tel *(02) 542 4242*
W steigenberger.com
Located on exclusive Avenue
Louise, the magnificent 19th-
century façade and largest
selection of suites in Brussels
give this hotel a unique charm.
It combines stylish interiors and
high-class comforts with
proximity to some of the city's
must-see destinations.

GREATER BRUSSELS:
Bloom Hotel €
Modern
Rue Royal 250, 11210
Tel *(02) 220 6611*
W hotelbloom.com
Adjacent to the Botanical Gardens,
this spacious hotel offers
individually designed rooms.

GREATER BRUSSELS: Kasteel
Gravenhof €€
Historic
Alsembergsesteenweg 676,
1653 Dworp
Tel *(02) 380 4499*
W gravenhof.be
The luxurious rooms have period
furnishings at this stately 1649
castle hotel amid rolling parkland.

GREATER BRUSSELS: Monty €€
Design Map 4 F3
Brand Whitlock Boulevard 101, 1200
Tel *(02) 734 5636*
W monty-hotel.be
The contemporary rooms have
lavish bathrooms in this 1930s
townhouse. Breakfast included.

GREATER BRUSSELS: Manos
Stephanie €€€
Luxury Map 2 D5
Chaussée de Charleroi, 28, 1050
Tel *(02) 539 02 50*
W manosstephanie.com
Chic hotel in a converted town-
house. The large rooms have an-
tique fixtures. Breakfast included.

West & East Flanders

BRUGES: Alegria €
B&B Map B1
St-Jakobsstraat 34, 8000 Bruges
Tel *(050) 330937*
W alegria-hotel.com
This charming family-run guest-
house has individually styled
rooms; some face the garden.

Breakfast area at the luxurious
Manos Stephanie, Brussels

BRUGES: Goezeput
€
Historic   Map B1
Goezeputstraat 29, 8000
Tel *(050) 342694*
W hotelgoezeput.be
Converted 18th-century monastery. Some rooms feature original wooden floors and roof beams.

BRUGES: Ter Brughe
€
Value   Map B1
Oost-Gistelhof 2, 8000
Tel *(050) 340324*
W hotelterbrughe.com
Great canal views and a large outdoor patio feature at this 16th-century house. Breakfast included.

BRUGES: Côté Canal
€€
B&B   Map B1
Hertsbergestraat 8-10, 8000
Tel *0475 457707*
W bruges-bedandbreakfast.be
In an 18th-century townhouse, this B&B has two suites with old-world charm but modern facilities.

BRUGES: Prinsenhof
€€
Historic   Map B1
Ontvangersstraat 9, 8000
Tel *(050) 342690*
W prinsenhof.com
Set amid lovely grounds, this 15th-century building offers modern rooms. Serves excellent breakfast.

BRUGES:
Hotel de Orangerie
€€€
Luxury   Map B1
Kartuizerinnenstraat 10, 8000
Tel *(050) 341649*
W hotelorangerie.be
Waterfront hotel in a 15th-century convent with splendid rooms. Common areas boast antiques.

BRUGES: Pand
€€€
Historic   Map B1
Pandreitje 16, 8000
Tel *(050) 340666*
W pandhotel.com
Historic charm is combined with modern, designer touches at this 18th-century mansion.

DAMME: Hoeve de Steenoven
€
B&B   Map B1
Damse Vaart Zuid 24, 8340 Oostkerke
Tel *(050) 501362*
W hoevedesteenoven.be
This *hoevetoerisme* B&B offers four rustic rooms with buffet breakfast. Ideal base for biking or walking.

DE HAAN: Romantik Manoir Carpe Diem
€€
Luxury   Map A1
Prins Karellaan 12, 8421
Tel *(059) 233220*
W manoircarpediem.com
A charming hotel with elegant rooms, a garden and a swimming pool. Breakfast is included.

Elegantly furnished suite in Manoir du Dragon, Knokke-Heist

DENDERMONDE:
Cosy Cottage
€
B&B   Map C2
Oude Eegene 38, 9200
Tel *(052) 428443*
W cosycottage.be
This classy B&B a short distance from Dendermonde serves superb complimentary breakfast.

GHENT: Ghent River Hotel
€€
Historic   Map B2
Waaistraat 5, 9000
Tel *(09) 266 10 10*
W ghent-river-hotel.be
Overlooking the river Leie, the only hotel in Ghent that is reached by boat is an elegant combination of two historic buildings – a Renaissance house and an old cotton factory dating back to 1857.

GHENT: Sandton Grand Hotel Reylof
€€€
Luxury   Map B2
Hoogstraat 36, 9000
Tel *(09) 235 40 70*
W sandton.eu
One of the few hotels in the city with a swimming pool. Most rooms come with balconies offering fine views.

GHENT: De Waterzooi
€€
B&B   Map B2
Sint-Veerleplein 2, 9000
Tel *(04) 7543 61 11*
W dewaterzooi.be
This lovely 18th-century place has only two rooms. Both are gorgeous, especially the split-level Phara suite. Booking well in advance is advisable.

KEMMEL: Hostellerie Kemmelberg
€
Luxury   Map A2
Kemmelbergweg 34, 8950
Tel *(057) 452160*
W kemmelberg.be
Rooms are comfortable and well-furnished, some with balconies. The hotel is located close to World War I Battlefields.

DK Choice
KNOKKE-HEIST:
Manoir du Dragon
€€€
Luxury   Map B1
Albertlaan 73, 8300
Tel *(050) 630580*
W manoirdudragon.be
Located on a golf course, this manor has all the elegance of a premier seaside resort. Many rooms are spacious suites with windows looking out onto the extensive gardens. A delicious gastronomic breakfast is included in the room price.

KORTRIJK: Parkhotel Kortrijk
€
Luxury   Map A2
Stationsplein 2, 8500
Tel *(056) 220303*
W kemmelberg.be
An urgan oasis, Parkhotel Kotrijk has refined rooms, a spa and a swimming pool.

POPERINGE: L'Hotel Recour
€€
Luxury   Map A2
Guido Gezellestraat 7, 8970
Tel *(057) 338838*
W pegasusrecour.be
There is a wide range of rooms at this impressive 1879 step-gabled brick manor in a shady park.

VEURNE: t Kasteel en 't Koetshuys
€
B&B   Map A2
Lindedreef 5-7, 8630
Tel *(057) 33 57 25*
W kasteelenkoetshuys.be
The big rooms are decorated with antique furniture at this family-run B&B with a garden.

YPRES: La Porte Cochère
€
B&B   Map A2
Patersstraat 22, 8900
Tel *(047) 7379505*
W laportecochere.com
This aristocratic house, close to the major attractions, has large, beautifully decorated rooms.

For more information on types of hotels *see pages260–63*

Antwerp, Flemish Brabant & Limburg

ANTWERP: Postiljon
Value   €
                                    Map C1
Blauwmoezelstraat 6, 2000
Tel *(03) 231 7575*
w hotelpostiljon.be
Smart, comfortable rooms, some
with shared bathrooms. Ask for
one with a view of the cathedral.

ANTWERP: Antwerp Hilton
Historic   €€
                                    Map C1
Groenplaats 32, 2000
Tel *(03) 204 1212*
w hilton.com
An architectural landmark, this
hotel occupies part of the former
Grand Bazar store. Large rooms.

ANTWERP: Banks
Design   €€
                                    Map C1
Steenhouwersvest 55, 2000
Tel *(03) 232 40 02*
w hotelbanks.be
Large, bright rooms feature cosy,
wonderful beds at this hotel. There
is a glorious rooftop terrace.

ANTWERP: Firean
Luxury   €€
                                    Map C1
Karel Oomsstraat 6, 2018
Tel *(03) 237 0260*
w hotelfirean.com
This early 20th-century Art
Deco mansion has crystal chan-
deliers in the lounge, antique
furnishings in rooms, and a
pretty, secluded garden.

ANTWERP: Hotel les Nuits
Modern   €€
                                    Map C1
Lange Gasthuisstraat 12, 2000
Tel *(03) 225 0204*
w hotellesnuits.be
Located within walking distance
of the cathedral and main square,
this hotel offers characterful rooms.

ANTWERP: t' Sandt
Historic   €€
                                    Map C1
Zand 13–19, 2000
Tel *(03) 232 9390*
w hotel-sandt.be
The city's first customs duty office
was in this mid-17th-century
Neo-Rococo building. It is now a
charming hotel with individually
decorated rooms and apartments.

ANTWERP: De Witte
Lelie   €€€
Luxury   Map C1
Keizerstraat 16–18, 2000
Tel *(03) 226 1966*
w dewittelelie.be
The elegant, well-equipped
rooms afford great city views in
these three converted 17th-
century canal houses. Free Wi-Fi.

A stylish room with simple interiors in
Martin's Klooster, Leuven

DIEST: De Franse Kroon
B&B   €
                                    Map D2
Leuvensestraat 26, 3290
Tel *(013) 314540*
w defransekroon.be
A 19th-century coaching inn is
the atmospheric setting for this
lovely hotel. Breakfast included.

LANAKEN: La Butte aux Bois
Luxury   €€€
                                    Map E2
Paalsteenlaan 90, 3620
Tel *(089) 739770*
w labutteauxbois.be
This country estate, originally built
for a knight, has elegant rooms
and superb dining options. There
is a spa too, and an indoor pool.

DK Choice

LEUVEN: Martin's Klooster
Luxury   €€€
                                    Map D2
Onze-Lieve-Vrouwstraat 18, 3000
Tel *(016) 213141*
w martinshotels.com
In a beautifully renovated 16th-
century former monastery, this
hotel has spacious, stylish rooms
and suites, each with plenty of
character and modern comforts.
Peace and calm pervade the
public areas. Located within
easy reach of the city's sights.

LIER: Hof van Aragon
Value   €
                                    Map C1
Aragonstraat 6, 2500
Tel *(03) 4910800*
w hva.be
Located in a quiet canal-side
street, this simple hotel offers
comfortable, well-presented
rooms. It has a lovely garden.

MAASEIK: Aldeneikerhof
Historic   €
                                    Map E1
Hamontweg 103, 3680
Tel *(089) 566777*
w aldeneikerhof.be
East of the town, this four-storey
19th-century residence offers
cycling trips with packed lunches.

MECHELEN: Ve
Design   €
                                    Map C2
Vismarkt 14, 2800
Tel *(015) 200755*
w hotelve.be
Minimalism meets comfort at this
stylish hotel in a converted 1920s
fish-smoking factory.

TONGEREN: Kasteelhoeve
De Tornaco   €
Historic   Map E2
Romeinse Kassei 5, 3840
Voort-Borgloon
Tel *(012) 672600*
w detornaco.be
On the site of an old Roman inn,
this rambling collection of farm
buildings offers spacious and
comfortable rooms.

TURNHOUT:
Priorij Corsendonk   €€
Historic   Map D1
Corsendonk 5, 2360 Oud-Turnhout
Tel *(014) 462800*
w priorij-corsendonk.be
Located 15 km (9 miles) from
Turnhout, this 17th-century
priory is surrounded by gardens.
Rooms are spread over several
annexes and have a monastic air.

Western Wallonia

ATH: Le Parc
Value   €
                                    Map B3
Rue de l'Esplanade 12, 7800
Tel *(068) 285485*
w hotelduparcath.com
Rooms are basic, comfortable and
quiet at this small family hotel in a
townhouse opposite a park.

CHARLEROI: Le Mayence
Modern   €
                                    Map C3
Rue du Parc 53, 6000
Tel *(071) 201000*
w lemayence.be
This apart-hotel in a converted
townhouse offers comfortable
rooms with kitchenettes.

DK Choice

CHIMAY: Hostellerie
du Gahy   €
Value   Map C4
Rue du Gahy 2, 6590
Momignies
Tel *(060) 511093*
w legahy.com
In a deeply tranquil countryside
setting, west of the village of
Chimay, this large stone
farmhouse has a large indoor
swimming pool. It also has a
well-regarded restaurant
specializing in local cuisine.
Breakfast is included.

For key to prices *see page 266*

ECAUSSINNES-LALAING:
Le Manoir du Capitaine €
Historic   Map C3
Chemin de Boulouffe 1, 7181 Feluy
Tel *(067) 874540*
W manoirducapitaine.com
Luxurious suites are located in a
collection of 19th-century brick
buildings that were once a
brewery and later a stud farm.

MONS: St. James €
Design   Map C3
Place de Flandre 8, 7000
Tel *(065) 724824*
W hotelstjames.be
St. James offers contemporary
rooms with high-quality fittings
in a smartly renovated 18th-
century building.

THUIN: Le Relais de la
Haute Sambre €
Value   Map C3
Rue Fontaine Pépin 12, 6540 Lobbes
Tel *(071) 597969*
W rhs.be
In a charming rural setting in a
large park with a pond, this hotel
offers basic, comfortable rooms.
Breakfast is served on the terrace
in good weather. Bike rentals
are available.

TOURNAI: Hotel Cathedrale €
Modern   Map B3
Place St-Pierre 2, 7500
Tel *(069) 250000*
W hotelcathedrale.be
Hotel Cathedrale has spacious,
comfortable rooms and an
excellent on-site restaurant.
It also offers bike rental.

Central Wallonia

ANNEVOIE: Moulin des Ramiers €
Historic   Map D3
Rue Basse 31, 5332 Crupet
Tel *(083) 690240*
W moulindesramiers.be
Housed in a converted millhouse
complex dating from the 17th
century, this hotel offers elegant
rooms with antique touches.

DK Choice

DINANT: Auberge-Grill
le Freyr €
Modern   Map D3
*Chaussée des Alpinistes 22, 5500
Anseremme*
Tel *(082) 222575*
W lefreyr.be
Wonderful hotel-restaurant
7 km (4 miles) south of Dinant,
in an authentic chalet-style
building. Rooms occupy a
stable-like extension overlooking the garden. Half-board
is included in the price for some
rooms. The restaurant prides
itself on traditional cooking and
seasonal ingredients.

FLOREFFE: Le Castel €
B&B   Map D3
*Rue du Chapitre 10, 5070
Fosses-la-Ville*
Tel *(071) 711812*
W lecastel.be
Located 9 km (6 miles) from
Floreffe, this 19th-century
mansion has modern, stylish
rooms, a garden and terrace and
an outdoor pool.

HAN-SUR-LESSE: Grenier
des Grottes €
Modern   Map D4
Rue des Chasseurs Ardennais 1, 5580
Tel *(084) 377237*
W cocoonhotels.be
Rooms are large and equipped
with all comforts. There is a
restaurant, garden and a health
centre with sauna and Jacuzzi.
Breakfast is included.

HEER-SUR-MEUSE: Castel les
Sorbiers €€€
Historic   Map E4
Rue des Sorbiers 241, 5543
Tel *(082) 643111*
W castellessorbiers.be
A majestic manor surrounded by
woodland and gardens on the
banks of the river Meuse. There's a
bar, restaurant and a magnificent
terrace overlooking the river.
Breakfast is included.

LAVAUX-STE-ANNE: Lemmonier €
Modern   Map D4
Rue Baronne Lemonnier 82, 5580
Tel *(084) 388883*
W lemonnier.be
Rooms are comfortable and stylish
at this celebrated hotel-restaurant
in a tranquil, countrified setting.

NAMUR: Beauregard €
Modern   Map D3
Avenue Baron de Moreau 1, 5000
Tel *(081) 230028*
W hotelbeauregard.be
Overlooking the River Meuse, this
hotel has smart, good-size rooms;
those in the front have balconies.

NAMUR: Chateau de Namur €€€
Luxury   Map D3
Avenue de l'Ermitage 1, 5000
Tel *(081) 729900*
W chateaudenamur.com
This early 20th-century château
with views of the Meuse valley
has pastel-painted, modern rooms.

NIVELLES: Ferme de Grambais €
Value   Map C3
*Chaussée de Braine-le-Comte 102,
1400*
Tel *(067) 874420*
W fermedegrambais.be
Rooms are spacious with simple
decor at this converted farm-
house. Superb on-site restaurant.

PHILLIPEVILLE: La Côte d'Or €
B&B   Map C3
Rue de la Gendarmerie 1, 5600
Tel *(071) 668145*
W lacotedor.com
Some rooms have four-poster
beds at this family-run B&B. The
restaurant offers superb cooking.

ROCHEFORT: La Martinette €
B&B   Map D4
Rue Louis Banneux 65, 5580
Tel *(04) 97924349*
W martinette.be
On a hill, this *belle-époque* mansion
has fine views. There is also a gîte
with a kitchen, dining and sitting
room. Breakfast is included.

DK Choice

ROCHEFORT: La Malle
Poste €€€
Luxury   Map D4
Rue de Behogne 46, 5580
Tel *(084) 210986*
W malleposte.net
In a beautiful 17th-century coaching inn, this sumptuous hotel has
suites with beamed ceilings,
flagstone floors and four-poster
beds, while the double rooms are
simpler. There is also a swimming
pool, sauna and a poultry
garden. Superb breakfast.

The historic La Malle Poste, Rochefort, with well-manicured gardens

For more information on types of hotels *see pages 260–63*

The Auberge du Moulin Hideux, in the heart of the Semois River Valley

Eastern Wallonia

ARLON: Château du Pont d'Oye
Historic   €   **Map** E4
*Rue du Pont d'Oye 1, 6720
Habay-La-Neuve*
Tel *(063) 420130*
🌐 chateaudupontdoye.be
This beautiful red-brick château dating back to 1652 is set among beech forests. The charming rooms are individually styled and include several majestic suites.

BASTOGNE: Château de Strainchamps
Historic   €   **Map** E4
Rue des Vennes 29, Strainchamps, 6637 Fauvillers
Tel *(063) 600812*
🌐 chateaudestrainchamps.com
Situated 15 km (9 miles) south of Bastogne, this early 18th-century grand country residence has simple, but comfortable rooms.

BOUILLON: Hotel de la Poste
Historic   €   **Map** D4
Place St-Arnould 1, 683
Tel *(061) 465151*
🌐 hotelposte.be
Dating back to 1730, this establishment took on its present form in the 19th century. It builds on a tradition of outstanding hospitality. There's a renowned Michelin-starred restaurant. Breakfast is included.

BOUILLON: Panorama
Luxury   €   **Map** D4
Rue au-dessus de la Ville 25, 6830
Tel *(061) 466138*
🌐 panoramahotel.be
The panoramic terrace offers breathtaking views of Bouillon and the Semois River at this family-run hotel-restaurant. Rooms are spacious and well-presented; some have Jacuzzis. Breakfast is included.

DK Choice

BOUILLON: Auberge du Moulin Hideux
Luxury   €€€   **Map** D4
*Route de Dohan 1, 6831
Noirefontaine*
Tel *(061) 467015*
🌐 moulinhideux.be
This converted 18th-century mill offers high levels of comfort and elegance. Extras include a tennis court, an indoor swimming pool as well as a renowned restaurant which is among the best in the area. Located 7 km (4 miles) east of Bouillon.

CHAUDFONTAINE: Château des Thermes
Historic   €€   **Map** E3
Rue Hauster 9, 4050
Tel *(04) 3678067*
🌐 chateaudesthermes.be
Set in a wooded park, this grand 18th-century mansion offers luxurious, well-appointed rooms and a full spa.

DURBUY: Le Victoria
B&B   €   **Map** E3
Rue des Récollectines 4, 6940
Tel *(086) 212300*
🌐 hotelvictoria.be
Occupying an old townhouse, this guesthouse blends contemporary furnishings with exposed beams and subtle antique touches. There's an excellent restaurant on site.

FLORENVILLE: Domaine du Vieux Château
Value   €   **Map** E4
Place du Moulin 7, 6823 Villers-Devant-Orval
Tel *(061) 320271*
🌐 hotel-du-vieux-chateau.be
A good base for mountain biking and canoeing, this pleasant hotel in converted farm buildings has cosily rustic rooms. There's a private fishing area.

HUY: Hotel du Fort
Modern   €   **Map** D3
Chaussée Napoléon 5-9, 4500
Tel *(085) 212403*
🌐 hoteldufort.be
This simple hotel has been run by the same family since 1957. The on-site restaurant serves traditional French-Belgian dishes.

HUY: Château de Vierset
Historic   €€   **Map** D3
*Rue la Coulée 1, 4577
Vierset-Barse*
Tel *(085) 410170*
🌐 chateaudevierset.be
Elegant *chambres d'hôtes* rooms are set around a courtyard at this 18th-century château.

LIÈGE: Hors Château
Historic   €   **Map** E2
Rue Hors Château 62, 4000
Tel *(04) 2506068*
🌐 hors-chateau.be
Located in the centre of the Coeur Historique, this hotel has small but stylish rooms with modern decor.

LIÈGE: Château de Limont
Luxury   €€   **Map** E2
*Rue du Château 34, 4357
Limont-Donceel*
Tel *(019) 544000*
🌐 chateaulimont.be
All the rooms at this handsome 18th-century château-farm located 15 km (9 miles) south-west of Liege have lovely views of the garden.

MALMEDY: Hotel Saint Géréon
B&B   €   **Map** F3
Place Saint Géréon 7-8, 4960
Tel *(080) 330677*
🌐 saintgereon.be
The rustic exterior contrasts with modern interiors at this welcoming family-run B&B with bright rooms.

MALMEDY: La Forge
Value   €   **Map** F3
Rue Devant les Religieuses 31, 4960
Tel *(080) 799595*
🌐 hotel-la-forge.be
La Forge has simple but comfortable rooms, including large family rooms. The café-bar specializes in local beers.

MALMEDY: L'Esprit Sain
Value   €   **Map** F3
Chemin Rue 46, 4960
Tel *(080) 330314*
🌐 espritsain.be
In the centre of Malmedy, this quiet hotel has eleven modern rooms. Breakfast is included.

For key to prices *see page 266*

SPA: La Vigie €
B&B Map E3
*Avenue Professeur Henrijean
129, 4900*
Tel *(087) 773497*
W lavigie.be
This typical Ardennes stone and
half-timbered mansion from
1902 is set in a tranquil park and
is a ten-minute walk from the
village of Spa. Beautiful rooms.

SPA: Manoir de Lébioles €€€
Luxury Map E3
*Domaine de Lébioles,
4900 Spa*
Tel *(087) 791900*
W manoirdelebioles.com
Built between 1905 and 1910, this
stylish manor was briefly owned
by a Belgian princess. It has a
superb gourmet restaurant.

STAVELOT: Dufays €
Design Map E3
Rue Neuve 115, 4970
Tel *(080) 548008*
W bbb-dufays.be
In a stone-built house dating
from the late 18th century, this
hotel has stylish renovated
rooms. Each room has a different
theme: African, Chinese, 1001
Nights, the 1930s, etc.

**STAVELOT:
Le Val d'Amblève** €€
Modern Map E3
Route de Malmedy 7, 4970
Tel *(080) 281440*
W levaldambleve.be
An architectural delight, this hotel
blends modern with traditional
styles. A great option for families.
Package deals are also available
for business travellers.

Grand Duchy of Luxembourg

BERDORF: Le Bisdorff €€
Luxury Map F4
An der Heesbech 39, 6551
Tel *790208*
W hotel-bisdorff.lu
This charming hotel is
surrounded by a shaded garden.
Handsome rooms have an old-
fashioned charm. There is also
a playground for children, and
guided walks for guests.

BOURSCHEID: Hotel du Moulin €
Historic Map F4
Buurschtermillen 1, 9164
Tel *990015*
W dumoulin.lu
Occupying a large millhouse
that dates back to 1714, this
delightful hotel stands at the
foot of the castle of Bourscheid.

CLERVAUX: Koener €
Modern Map F4
Grand-Rue 14, 9701
Tel *921002*
W hotelkoener.lu
In the heart of Clervaux, this
hotel has been run by the Koener
family since 1886. It has a full spa
with a swimming pool and a
brasserie restaurant on site.
Delicious breakfast.

ECHTERNACH: Eden au Lac €€
Luxury Map F4
Oam Nonnesees, 6474
Tel *728283*
W edenaulac.lu
This modern five-star hotel is
geared to activity holidays and
families. It has a wellness centre
and bike hire.

**EISCHEN: Domaine de la
Gaichel** €€
Value Map E4
Maison 5, 8469 Gaichel-Eischen
Tel *390129*
W lagaichel.lu
Exquisitely designed rooms are
offered at this establishment,
along with excellent French
cuisine in the brasserie and the
fine-dining restaurant.

**ESCH-SUR-SURE: Hotel
de la Sure** €
Value Map E4
Rue du Pont 1, 9650 Esch-sur-Sûre
Tel *839110*
W hotel-de-la-sure.lu
Rooms are stylish and vary in
size at this family-run hotel just
below the castle ruins.

**LUXEMBOURG CITY: Hotel
Francais** €€
Modern Map F5
Place d'Armes 14, 1136
Tel *474534*
W hotelfrancais.lu
Hotel Francais has basic,
comfortable rooms. A buffet
breakfast is included.

**LUXEMBOURG CITY: Grand
Hotel Cravat** €€€
Historic Map F5
Boulevard Roosevelt 29, 2450
Tel *221975*
W hotelcravat.lu
Dating back more than 100 years,
this atmospheric hotel in the city
centre provides a high level of
comfort. It has 1960s-style decor.

LUXEMBOURG CITY: Le Royal €€€€
Luxury Map F5
Boulevard Royal 12, 2449
Tel *2416161*
W leroyal.com
A grand hotel near the Old Town,
Le Royal has deluxe rooms, a
fitness centre, spa and pool.

**LUXEMBOURG CITY: Sofitel
Luxembourg Europe** €€€
Luxury Map F5
Rue du Fort Niedergrünewald 4, 2015
Tel *437761*
W sofitel.com
This hotel offers plush rooms and
two superb restaurants.

**MONDORF LES BAINS: Mondorf
Domaine les Bains** €€
Luxury Map F4
Avenue des Bains BP52, 5601
Tel *23666666*
W mondorf.lu
Guests have full access to the spa
at this hotel in the grounds of
Luxembourg's largest hot springs.

DK Choice

REMICH: Hotel des Vignes €
Modern Map F5
Rue de Montdorf 29, 5552
Tel *23699149*
W hotel-vignes.lu
A haven for wine enthusiasts set
amid vineyards with river views.
Rooms have all modern
comforts; some have terraces.
The restaurant serves exquisite
French and Luxembourgeois
cuisine, and fine local wines.

VIANDEN: Auberge du Château €
Value Map F4
Grand-Rue 74-80, 9401
Tel *834574*
W auberge-du-chateau.lu
In a handsome townhouse, this
family-run hotel near the castle
has beautiful rooms.

**WILTZ: Hotel aux Anciennes
Tanneries** €€
Design Map E4
Rue Joseph Simon 42a, 9550
Tel *957599*
W auxanciennestanneries.com
A leather tannery has been
transformed into a stylish hotel
with individually designed rooms.

A selection of fine wines in the dining room
of the Grand Hotel Cravat, Luxembourg City

For more information on types of hotels *see pages 260–63*

WHERE TO EAT AND DRINK

Belgium offers some of the best food in the world, at restaurants of all price categories. Belgians take pride in a flavourful cuisine that is carefully prepared with fresh, local and seasonal produce. Visitors will find that it is best to be wary of eateries that openly court tourists rather than cater to the local clientele. Luxembourg's cuisine exhibits not just the skill of French cooking, but also has its own range of robust dishes. As in Belgium, establishments that cook and serve fine food are treated with respect and win loyal customers.

Enjoying drinks, snacks and sunshine at a pavement café

What to Eat Where

It is possible to eat just about any kind of food anywhere in Belgium and Luxembourg. Each region, however, has its *produits du terroir* or *streekproducten* (local specialities), which change with the season.

The coast, for instance, is the best place to eat seafood, while game is a speciality of the Ardennes, particularly in winter, and hop shoots are a springtime treat in Western Flanders. Eel is best savoured at Donkmeer, near Ghent, while Ghent itself is the true home of the creamy chicken or fish *waterzooi*. The most delicious strawberries are found at Wépion, on the River Meuse. Geraardsbergen is the place for *mattentaart* pastries and Dinant for *flamiche* leek tarts.

When in Arlon, visitors should drink a maitrank apéritif, but jenever in Hasselt and pékèt gin in Liège. Luxembourg has its famed Moselle wines *(see p253)*, however, excellent wines are also produced in the Hageland region of Vlaams Brabant. Beers too are brewed to high standards in all quarters. Locally-produced brews, such as Boeteling, which celebrates Veurne's annual Procession of the Penitents, are also highly recommended. Some restaurants, such as Brasserie Erasmus in Bruges *(see p283)*, specialize in dishes cooked with beer.

How to Choose a Restaurant

Hotels and tourist offices often willingly suggest good local restaurants. Most eateries display menus outside, and visitors can get an idea of prices beforehand. Avoid tourist-trap places where menus are posted in multiple languages by the door. Good restaurants will be full of people eating happily, not waiting to be served.

It is also possible to eat well in brasseries and cafés. Here, it is often best to choose mainstream fare such as *steak-frites* or *moules*, rather than more elaborate dishes that might tax the establishment's equipment and personnel. Meals can range from €10–20 for a simple brasserie meal to more than €100 for a full three-course dinner in a top restaurant.

Cuisines on the Menu

The food of Belgium and Luxembourg is solidly North European and an expression of what the land produces. North African cuisine is available in the outlying districts of the larger cities, and the well-cooked *tagines*, couscous and pastry-based *briks* are good value. Food from Congo, Rwanda and Senegal is a speciality of the Matonge district in Ixelles. Italian and Chinese restaurants are fairly ubiquitous, and there are also some Portuguese, Spanish, Greek, Turkish, South American, Thai and Indonesian establishments. Indian restaurants are often upmarket and relatively rare. Japanese food also tends to be expensive but is generally of a high quality.

It wasn't long ago when French was the standard language of food across the region. In Flanders, now, it is more usual to see menus in Dutch, sometimes with a French translation. Many restaurants also provide English translations or even separate English menus. Staff can usually explain, or failing that, the menu reader *(see p277)* and phrase book *(see pp340–44)* will be useful.

Art Nouveau decor in Brussels's highly regarded Comme Chez Soi *(see p281)*

Restaurants on Place Guillaume II in Luxembourg City

Vegetarians

Despite a marked increase in vegetarian eating, Belgium and Luxembourg are not generally oriented towards vegetarians and dedicated restaurants are rare. Many menus will, however, include at least one vegetarian dish for each course, or allow a vegetarian starter (or two) as the main course. Vegans might have a harder time. Some health-food shops have cafés and staff that may be able to advise about local vegetarian and vegan-friendly restaurants.

Eating on a Budget

Good, reasonably-priced food can be found at many cafés. There are also plenty of fast-food outlets, such as the burger chain Quick. Many delicatessens offer a sandwich-making service, plus a range of sophisticated cold foods (to be eaten with plastic forks), that are good for picnics. The Belgian chain, Le Pain Quotidien (Het Dagelijks Brood in Dutch) serves upmarket sandwiches and salads to eat at shared pine tables. The special lunch menus offered by many of the best restaurants can be a real bargain.

The classic Belgian street food is a cornet of freshly fried *frites* or *frieten* (chips) from one of the many street-side vans or shed-like outlets called variously as *friteries* or *kots à frites* (*frituurs* or *frietkoten* in Dutch). They will also provide mayonnaise (the traditional accompaniment), plus a range of extra foods that include meatballs, fishcakes, *carbonnades flamandes (see p275)* and *fricadelles* (sausages in batter), all at very reasonable prices. The chips, however, are an inexpensive meal in themselves, and can be second to none.

Tipping and Taxes

Prices on restaurant menus usually include service charges (often 16 per cent). It is, therefore, not necessary to add a tip, unless service has been exceptional. In that case, a small cash tip of perhaps €2–5 is acceptable.

Children

Restaurants in Belgium and Luxembourg are usually willing to receive children, although some upmarket establishments may be too formal for the very young. It is acceptable for children to bring their comics, colouring books and games along to entertain themselves during long meals. Many restaurants have children's menus that offer reduced-price dishes that are likely to appeal to younger palates. In addition, highchairs are generally available on request in most establishments.

Smoking

Establishments in Belgium and Luxembourg strictly forbid smoking inside premises where food is served. This rule is not enforced on terrace areas.

Street food, Belgian style

Recommended Restaurants

The restaurants featured in this guide have been selected for their good food, value, location, atmosphere or a combination of these. A wide range of Belgium and Luxembourg's dining scene has been included, from cafés, pubs and bistros to the broad selection of Michelin-starred restaurants.

Take special note of the venues marked as DK Choice. These restaurants have been highlighted in recognition of an exceptional feature – exquisite food, an inviting atmosphere, an unusual setting or simply great value. Most of these are hugely popular among local residents and visitors, so be sure to enquire regarding reservations or you may face a wait for a table.

Dining room of the Michelin-starred Magis, in Tongeren, overlooking a garden *(see p288)*

The Flavours of Belgium

Most Belgians are passionate about food and standards are very high. The many first-class bakers, greengrocers, fishmongers, butchers and *pâtissiers*, including Belgium's noted chocolatiers, are held in high public esteem, alongside the top chefs and restaurateurs. Restaurant cooking in Wallonia and Flanders is, respectively, French and Dutch in character. Belgian diners appreciate hearty traditional fare, which depends on good ingredients cooked well. Moroccan, Italian, Spanish, Chinese and Indian restaurants add variety to the mix.

Belgian chocolates

Bunches of white asparagus, a seasonal early-summer treat

The North Sea

No place in Belgium is more than a three-hour drive from the coast, and consequently, fresh seafood plays a central role in Belgian cuisine. On the coast, as well as in the fish restaurants of the major cities, a wide variety of the best fish – sole, cod, turbot, skate, hake and monkfish – is always on the menu, either simply grilled, fried in butter or swathed in a well-judged sauce. Huge platters of *fruits de mer*, or mixed seafood, are also widely available in restaurants all over Belgium.

A uniquely Belgian fish dish that is well worth seeking out is *anguilles au vert* (*paling in't groen* in Dutch), which consists of large chunks of eel cooked with a mass of finely chopped, fresh green herbs.

Pasture and Woodland

Northern Belgium and the hills of the south are home to herds of cattle. The Herve Region produces most of Belgium's mostly French-style soft, or semi-soft, cows-milk cheeses. Quality beef is the stock-in-trade of any Belgian butcher, and *steak-frites* (steak and chips) is a classic dish on bistro menus. Belgians are so confident

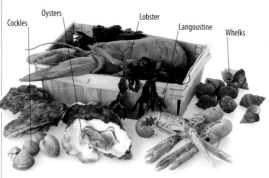

A selection of fine quality North Sea seafood

Oysters Cockles Lobster Langoustine Whelks

Local Dishes and Specialities

Although Belgian chefs produce some of the world's most complex and sophisticated cooking, many of Belgium's greatest classic dishes are relatively simple, striking a healthy balance between nourishment and pleasure. Fine examples include steaming platefuls of *moules-frites* and warming stews such as *carbonnade flamande* and *waterzooi*, which is made with either fish or chicken. These dishes might be labelled comfort food; however, the quality of the ingredients and the skill put into cooking such dishes in Belgium invariably turns such homely fare into a feast. An unusual conserve to look out for at the breakfast, or cheese, table is *sirop de Liège*, a soft spreading fruit paste made of concentrated pears, apples, plums and apricots.

Fruit used in *sirop de Liège*

Moules-frites are mussels steamed with onion and white wine, and served with chips (fries) and mayonnaise.

Fish restaurant in the elegant Galéries St-Hubert in Brussels

about their beef that they are happy to eat it raw, either in *steak américaine* (steak tartare) or on toast as the snack, *toast cannibale*.

Pork products include the noted Ardennes ham, patés and sausages. In autumn and winter, game such as wild boar, pheasant and venison is served, often in a rich fruity sauce. Quail, guinea fowl, pigeon and rabbit are also popular.

The Vegetable Patch

Not long ago, most Belgian householders filled their gardens with tightly-packed rows of top-class vegetables such as beans, leeks, carrots, lettuces, asparagus, potatoes and onions. This tradition may be waning, but the same quest for quality lives on in commercial market-gardens.

In the 1840s, Belgian farmers created *chicon* (*witloof* in Dutch) by forcing the roots of the chicorée lettuce. It is now one of Belgium's most widely used vegetables. The most popular vegetable must be the potato, in the form of chips

Freshly made waffles at a street stall, a familiar sight in Belgium

(French fries). These *frites* (*friet* in Dutch), served with a dollop of mayonnaise, are a favourite street food.

The Pâtissier

No Belgian community is without a pâtisserie selling superlative tarts, cakes and biscuits, and many *pâtissiers* double-up as chocolatiers. *Gaufres* (waffles) are also a a great sweet treat, sold at specialist shops and street stalls or made at home on festive occasions. Belgian bakers also make a range of dry, buttery biscuits, such as the spicy *speculoos*, which are associated with Christmas.

BELGIAN CHEESE

Bouquet des Moines Mild and gooey, with a white rind, this cheese is from Herve.

Chimay Made by the Trappist Abbey here, this is a semi-soft cheese with an orange rind.

Herve and Limburger These are both soft, pungent cheeses with washed rinds.

Maredsous This is a family of St-Paulin-style, semi-soft abbey cheeses.

Passendale This light, semi-soft cheese with tiny holes is from Western Flanders.

Remoudou A strong-smelling Herve cheese, this has a red-brown washed rind.

Carbonnade flamande combines beef cooked in Belgian beer with a touch of sugar in a hearty casserole.

Waterzooi is a classic stew from Ghent with either fish or chicken and vegetables, poached in a creamy broth.

Flamiche aux poireaux is leeks fried in butter, whisked with cream and eggs and baked in a pastry shell.

The Flavours of Luxembourg

The traditional food of Luxembourg is a blend of French and German influences, but more recently it has also absorbed elements of the cuisines of Portuguese and Italian immigrants. As elsewhere in Europe, young chefs are experimenting with innovative takes on traditional dishes, as well as introducing new ingredients and flavours from around the world. As a result, you may have to make a conscious effort to experience genuine Lëtzebuergesch cooking – but it is still out there, in pubs and country bistros, at roadside snack bars, and at all the big annual festivals.

Plums

Honest Fare

It has been said that the food of Luxembourg is "French cuisine in German quantities". This is sometimes viewed as rather dismissive, but, for diners, it is simply the best of both worlds. Local produce is of excellent quality, and the standard of restaurant cooking very high, as might be expected from a land with one of the world's highest per capita incomes. Rather

Grocer's shop selling a range of fresh local and international produce

Pork, cured and preserved in a variety of hams and sausages

like their Belgian neighbours, Luxembourgers have scant regard for over-fussy cuisine. They enjoy familiar, family cooking, which more clearly reveals Germanic influences, such as robust platters of roast pork or sausage with *sauerkraut*, followed by a plum tart. When out and about, they might snack on a sausage and roll – particularly a small, spicy *Thüringer* or a *Lëtzebuerger Grillwurscht* – from a street vendor.

Fish Cuisine

Despite being landlocked, Luxembourg is only 300 km (186 miles) from the sea, and fish plays a major role on menus, with mussels being especially popular. However, freshwater fish such as trout and pike abound in rivers and lakes, and are traditional favourites. Crayfish are also part of the national diet, but demand has now outstripped local supply, so they may very well be imported.

Luxembourg Dishes and Specialities

Luxembourg's signature dishes are grounded in traditional produce. The landscape and climate favour robust farming – grains, root crops and pig-rearing – as well as fruit orchards. There are numerous potato-based dishes, including *Gromperenzopp* (potato and leek soup) and *Gromperekichelcher* (potato cakes). Pork is made into countless types of cured ham and sausage. Buckwheat dumplings, or *Stäerzelen*, are eaten with cream and bacon. In winter, rich game dishes are popular, while in spring, the favourite is *Brennesselszopp*, a delicate soup made with young nettle tips. Moselle vineyards serve dishes cooked with wine, such as *F'rell am Reisleck*, trout in Riesling sauce. Another speciality is *friture de la Moselle* – small freshwater fish, deep-fried in a light batter.

Buckwheat

Judd mat Gaardebounen, a smoked collar of pork served with broad beans in cream sauce, is the national dish.

Reading the Menu

It is worth avoiding tourist restaurants that display menus in English, but many of the best eateries supply translations of their dishes, or have staff on hand who can translate for customers. Belgian cooking is modelled on French cuisine, so those who are familiar with common culinary terms will have little problem with menus in Brussels and Wallonia, or even in Luxembourg. In Flanders, menus are often in Dutch, but someone can usually provide an explanation. The list below covers dishes typical of both countries, as well as words commonly seen on menus.

North Sea mussels

Signage offering a fixed-price menu, often very good value

French/Wallonia

Anguilles au vert Eel in a thick green sauce of fresh herbs, particularly chervil.
Asperges à la flamande Boiled white asparagus with chopped hard-boiled egg.
Carbonnade flamande Rich beef stew with beer.
Chicon Belgian endive (chicory). *Chicons au gratin* are wrapped in ham and cooked in cheese sauce.
Coucou de Malines Mechelen cuckoo. A type of chicken, often braised with beer and *chicons*.
Crevettes grises Tiny but tasty North Sea shrimps.
Croque monsieur Toasted cheese and ham sandwich.
Escavèche Fish cooked in a herb-flavoured stock.
Faisan à la brabançonne Pheasant baked with chicon.
Flamiche aupoireaux Quiche-like leek tart.
Frites Chips/fries.
Jets d'houblon Hop shoots in a creamy sauce.

Moules Mussels.
Plateau de fruits de mer Platter of mixed seafood.
Salade liègeoise Warm potato, bacon, and green bean or frisée lettuce salad.
Steak à l'américaine Minced raw steak (tartare).

Dutch/Flanders

Aardappelen Potatoes.
Asperges op vlaamse wijze see *Asperges à la flamande.*
Boterham Sandwich.
Friet/frietjes Chips/fries.
Garnaalkroketten Deep-fried shrimp croquettes.
Gentse hutsepot Meat stew with winter vegetables.
Karbonaden see *Carbonnades flamandes.*
Konijn Rabbit.
Kreeft Lobster.
Mechelse koekkoek see *Coucou de Malines.*
Noordsee vissoep Thick soup of North Sea fish.
Op zijn Brussels In Brussels style: with *chicons* or beer.
Paling in't groen see *Anguilles au vert.*
Pannekoek Pancake.
Sint-Jacobsoesters/schelpen Scallops.

Stoemp Potato mashed with chopped vegetables or meat.
Tonijn Tuna.
Vlaamse stoverij see *Carbonnades flamandes.*
Waterzooi Chicken or fish poached in a creamy broth.
Wild Game.
Witloof see *Chicon.*
Zalm Salmon.

Luxembourg

Brennesselszopp Soup made with nettle tips.
F'rell am Reisleck Trout in Riesling wine sauce.
Friture de la Moselle Deep-fried freshwater fish.
Gromperekichelcher Deep-fried potato cake, with onions and parsley.
Gromperenzopp Potato soup with leeks.
Judd mat Gaardebounen *see opposite page.*
Kriibsen crayfish.
Lëtzebuerger Grillwurscht Small spicy sausage, also known as *Thüringer.*
Quetscheflued Plum tart.
Sauerkraut Shredded, pickled cabbage.
Stäerzelen Buckwheat dumplings.

Dining outside at a fish restaurant near the Grand Place in Brussels

Belgian Beer

Belgium makes more beers, and in a greater mix of styles and flavours, than any other country in the world. The nation's breweries produce over 400 different beers, and even small bars will stock at least 20 varieties. The Belgian citizen drinks on average 100 litres (200 pints) a year. Even the cheerful peasants in Brueghel the Elder's 16th-century medieval village scenes would have been drinking beer from the local brewery, as most small towns and communities have produced their own beer since the 11th century. By 1900, there were some 3,000 private breweries throughout Belgium. Today, more than 100 still operate, with experts agreeing that even large industrial concerns produce beer of a fine quality.

Detail from *The Wedding Dance* by Pieter Brueghel the Elder

Chimay label with authentic Trappist mark

Label for Westmalle Trappist beer

Trappist Beers

The most revered of refreshments, Belgium's Trappist beers have been highly rated since the Middle Ages when monks began brewing them. The drink originated in Roman times when Belgium was Gallia Belgica, a province of Gaul. Beer was a private domestic product until the monasteries took over and introduced hops to the process. Today's production is still controlled solely by the five Trappist monasteries, although the brewers are mostly laymen. Trappist beers are characterized by their rich, yeasty flavour. They are very strong, ranging from 6.2 to 11 per cent in alcohol content by volume. Perhaps the most famous of the five brands is Chimay, brewed in Belgium's largest monastic brewery in Hainaut. This delicate but potent bottled beer has three different strengths, and is best kept for many years before drinking. The strongest Trappist beer is Westvleteren, from Ieper.

Chimay served in its correct glass

Lambic Beers

The unique family of lambic beers has been made for centuries in the Senne valley around Brussels. The beers are brewed by allowing the yeasts present in the air to ferment the beer, rather than by adding yeasts separately to the water and grain mix. Containers of unfermented wort (water, wheat and barley) are left under a half-open roof in the brewery and fermented by airborne yeasts that are specific to this region of Belgium. Unlike the sterility of many breweries, lambic cellars are officially exempt from EU hygiene regulations, and deliberately left dusty and uncleaned in order for the necessary fungi to thrive. Matured in untreated wooden casks for up to five years, the lambic is deliciously sour to drink, with a strength of 5 per cent alcohol.

Young and old lambic beers are blended to produce the variant gueuze. A tiny bead, distinctive champagne mousse and a toasty, slightly acidic flavour are its characteristics. Bars and restaurants lay down their gueuze for up to two years before it is drunk.

Lambic cherry beer

Brewer sampling beer from the vat at a brewery in Anderlecht, a suburb of Brussels

Speciality Belgian Beers

Duvel

Chimay

Brugse Tripel

De Verboden Vrucht

Kwak

Speciality beers are common in Belgium, where the huge variety of brands includes unusual tastes and flavours. For a characterful amber ale, Kwak is a good choice. Fruit beers are a Brussels speciality but are available throughout the country. The most popular, kriek, is traditionally made with bitter cherries grown in the Brussels suburb of Schaerbeek. Picked annually, these cherries are added to the lambic and allowed to macerate, or steep. The distinctive almond tang comes from the cherry stone. Raspberries are used to make a framboise beer, or frambozen.

Fruit beer mat of Chapeau brewery

Strong beers are also extremely popular. These include the pilseners De Verboden Vrucht (The Forbidden Fruit) and Duvel (Devil). Leffe Radieuse holds 8.2 per cent alcohol by volume, while at 10.5 per cent, Hainaut's Bush beer ranks among the strongest. The bestsellers, Jupiler and Stella Artois, are also good-quality beers.

The façade of a beer emporium in Brussels

Blanche Beers

Hoegaarden

Belgium's refreshing wheat beers are known as *blanche*, or white beers, because of the cloudy sediment that forms when they ferment. Sour, crisp and light, they are relatively low in alcohol at 5 per cent. *Blanche* is produced in the Brabant town of of Hoegaarden, after which the best-known *blanche* brand is named. Many people now serve them with a slice of lemon to add to the refreshing taste, especially on warm summer evenings.

How to Drink Belgian Beer

There are no snobbish distinctions made in Belgium between bottled and casked beer. Some of the most prestigious brews are served in bottles, and, as with casks, bottles are often laid down to mature. However, the choice of drinking glass is a vital part of the beer-drinking ritual. Many beers must be drunk in a particular glass, which the barman will usually supply. These range from goblets to long thin drinking tubes. Beers are often served with a complementary snack – cream cheese on rye bread and radishes are a popular accompaniment.

The traditional drinkers' snack of *fromage blanc* on rye bread

Where to Eat and Drink

Brussels

CENTRAL BRUSSELS: Arcadi €
International   **Map** 2 D2
Rue d'Arenberg 1B, 1000
Tel *(02) 511 3343*
Arcadi is renowned for what are arguably the best quiches in the city. The salmon and broccoli filling is the most popular. It has excellent cakes as well.

**CENTRAL BRUSSELS:
Bier Circus** €
Belgian   **Map** 2 D3
Rue de l'Enseignement 57, 1000
Tel *(02) 218 0034*
Delicious, wholesome dishes are served here, but the real highlight is the extensive beer menu. Many dishes are cooked in beer. Try the beer-and-beef stew.

**CENTRAL BRUSSELS:
Brasserie Houtsiplou** €
Belgian   **Map** 1 C4
Place Rouppe 9, 1000
Tel *(02) 511 3816*
Mouth-watering classics and burgers and fries are the draw in this relaxed brasserie. There is also a good choice of local beers and vegetarian options.

CENTRAL BRUSSELS: Le Cap €
Belgian   **Map** 1 C3
Place de la Vieille Halle aux Blés 28, 1000
Tel *(02) 512 9342*
A popular meeting place for locals, with daily specials alongside a superb selection of old- and new-world wines. The Flemish-style beef chop and the Ghent chicken stew (*waterzooi*) are a must-try.

**CENTRAL BRUSSELS:
Delirium** €
Café   **Map** 2 D3
Impasse de La Fidélité 4A, 1000
Tel *(02) 514 4434*
Beautiful and cosy, this subterranean tourist magnet is a great spot for a beer or glass of wine. It claims to serve over 2,000 beers. These can be enjoyed with an array of meats or cheeses. .

**CENTRAL BRUSSELS: L'Entree
des Artistes** €
French/Belgian   **Map** 2 D4
Place du Grand Sablon 42, 1000
Tel *(02) 502 3161*
This brasserie has a great selection of classic dishes, including house steak tartare and *chicons au gratin* (gratin of endives with cheese). It is great for late-night snacks as it is open daily till midnight.

**CENTRAL BRUSSELS: La Mer
du Nord**
Seafood   €
          Map 1 C2
Rue St Catherine 45, 1000
Tel *(02) 513 1192*
A hugely popular fishbar, La Mer du Nord offers oysters, calamares, *maatjes* (pickled herring), mussels and other fresh seafood delights. Enjoy your meal with a glass of wine at one of the stand-up tables.

**CENTRAL BRUSSELS:
The Monk** €
Café   **Map** 1 C2
Rue Sainte-Catherine 42, 1000
Tel *(02) 511 75 11*
This atmospheric brown bar serves up an amazing beer selection and other Brussels delicacies plus excellent pasta dishes in a magnificent and typical Brussels setting. There are regular live music performances.

**CENTRAL BRUSSELS: A la
Mort Subite** €
Café   **Map** 2 D2
Rue Montagne aux Herbes Potagères 7, 1000
Tel *(02) 513 1318*
The former haunt of Brussels' favourite singer, Jacques Brel, this cavernous Art Deco wonder is where the Mort Subite brand originated. The menu offers tasty sandwiches, salads and omelettes.

**CENTRAL BRUSSELS:
Nüetnigenough** €
Belgian   **Map** 1 C3
Rue du Lombard 25, 1000
Tel *(02) 513 7884*
The extensive menu at this welcoming brasserie includes tasty tapas, beef stew, rabbit saddle in gueuze beer sauce and

Ghent-style meatballs.Small and cosy, it is often packed with people. Great choice of beers.

**CENTRAL BRUSSELS:
Den Teepot** €
Vegetarian   **Map** 1 B2
Rue des Chartreux 66, 1000
Tel *(02) 511 9402*   **Closed** *Sun; dinner*
Located above its sister health-food shop, this is one of the best places for vegetarian food in the city. Many of the dishes feature beans and pulses. Open for lunch only from noon till 2pm.

**CENTRAL BRUSSELS: Het
Warm Water** €
Café   **Map** 1 C5
Rue des Renards 25, 1000
Tel *(02) 513 9159*   **Closed** *Mon–Wed*
This pleasant little Flemish café does not really have a menu. Instead, they serve a different vegetarian dish and soup daily. Unwind with a glass of gueuze, a Belgian beer, and some great cake.

**CENTRAL BRUSSELS: Le Wine
Bar des Marolles** €
French   **Map** 1 C5
Rue Haute 198, 1000
Tel *(02) 503 6250*
Attractively set in a 17th-century house in the heart of Marolles, this restaurant has a less formal atmosphere than other places in historic buildings in Brussels. The bistro menu changes regularly.

Classy decor at L'Entree des Artistes, a French-Belgian restaurant in Brussels

Elegant *belle époque* dining hall of Belga Queen, Brussels

CENTRAL BRUSSELS: Aux Armes de Bruxelles €€
Seafood **Map** 2 D2
Rue des Bouchers 13, 1000
Tel *(02) 511 5550*
This is one of the favourite former haunts of Brussels' most famous chanteur, Jacques Brel. The lobster and mussels are recommended.

CENTRAL BRUSSELS: Belga Queen €€
Belgian **Map** 2 D2
Rue Fossé aux Loups 32, 1000
Tel *(02) 217 2187*
The chic Belga Queen, located in a cavernous *belle époque* building, offers exquisitely presented dishes. A special beer and tasting menu is available.

CENTRAL BRUSSELS: La Belle Maraichere €€
Belgian **Map** 1 C2
Place Ste-Catherine 11, 1000
Tel *(02) 512 9759* **Closed** *Wed & Thu*
This fine restaurant has two set menus that offer a choice of dishes such as goose liver terrine and pan-fried beef tenderloin. Warm, bistro-like atmosphere.

CENTRAL BRUSSELS: Big Mama €€
Belgian **Map** 1 C2
Place de la Vieille Halle aux Blés 41, 1000
Tel *(02) 513 3659*
There is a four-course set menu at this cosy restaurant, as well as a separate kids' menu. Try the fried scampi with garlic, *vol-au-vent* with chicken and fries and the crème brûlée for dessert.

CENTRAL BRUSSELS: Chez Léon €€
Belgian **Map** 2 D2
Rue des Bouchers 18, 1000
Tel *(02) 511 1415*
Founded in 1893, this is a stalwart of traditional Belgian culinary

standards. There are several versions of the classic *moules et frite*. Excellent kids' menu.

CENTRAL BRUSSELS: Falstaff €€
Café **Map** 1 C3
Rue Henri Maus 19, 1000
Tel *(02) 511 8789*
A must-visit for its beautiful Art Nouveau interior and Neo-Classical detailing, Falstaff serves food ranging from sandwiches, salads and croquettes to omelettes and steaks.

CENTRAL BRUSSELS: In 't Spinnekopke €€
Belgian **Map** 1 B2
Place du Jardin aux Fleurs 1, 1000
Tel *(02) 511 8695* **Closed** *Sat: lunch & Sun*
Housed in an intimate former 18th-century coaching inn, "In the Spider's Head" has an extensive range of strong, unusual local brews. Several dishes on the menu are cooked in beer.

CENTRAL BRUSSELS: Kwint €€
Belgian **Map** 2 D3
Mont des Arts 1, 1000
Tel *(02) 505 9595*
Designed by leading Belgian conceptual artist Arne Quinze and adorned with his art, the dazzling Kwint adds exquisite flavours to traditional Belgian cuisine and specializes in truffles and *foie gras*.

CENTRAL BRUSSELS: Les Petits Oignons €€
French/Belgian **Map** 2 D4
Rue de la Régence 25, 1000
Tel *(02) 511 7615*
The family-friendly Les Petis Oignons offer delectable French and Belgian brasserie-style cuisine. The fried goose liver with caramelized onions is particularly recommended.

CENTRAL BRUSSELS: Pin Pon €€
Belgian **Map** 1 C5
Place du Jeu de Balle 62, 1000
Tel *(02) 540 8999*
In a former fire station, this smart but relaxed restaurant offers modern interpretations of classic Belgian cuisine. Ask for a rooftop table to enjoy the great views over Jeu de Balle.

CENTRAL BRUSSELS: Au Vieux Saint-Martin €€
Modern European **Map** 2 D4
Place du Grand Sablon 38, 1000
Tel *(02) 512 6476*
This modern eatery is also a gallery for contemporary artists, with art displayed on the walls. The food is made from the freshest ingredients. Try the *filet americain*.

CENTRAL BRUSSELS: Alexandre €€€
French **Map** 1 C4
Rue du Midi 164, 1000
Tel *(02) 502 4055* **Closed** *Sun & Mon*
Inventive seasonal French fare served in a refined atmosphere. The three-course set menu is excellent value. There are only a few tables, so reserve ahead over the weekend.

DK Choice

CENTRAL BRUSSELS: Comme Chez Soi €€€
Fine Dining **Map** 1 C4
Place Rouppe 23, 1000
Tel *(02) 512 2921* **Closed** *Sun, Mon, Tue lunch & Wed lunch*
A front runner for the city's best restaurant, Comme Chez Soi has two Michelin stars. The menu changes seven times a year and features seasonal produce. Finish off with the dessert trilogy. There is also a lounge area featuring a bar and leather couches. Book ahead.

For more information on types of restaurants *see pages 272–3*

CENTRAL BRUSSELS: L'Ecallier du Palais Royal €€€
Seafood **Map** 2 D4
Rue Bodenbroek 18, 1000
Tel *(02) 512 8751*
This restaurant in a lovely 17th-century mansion serves top-notch seafood and fish dishes. It has an excellent range of high-quality oysters and a superb wine list.

CENTRAL BRUSSELS: L'Esprit de Sel Brasserie €€€
Belgian **Map** 3 B4
Place Jourdan 52–54, 1000
Tel *(02) 230 6040*
Soft wood and velvet decor sets the ambience at this brasserie. The beef stewed in Belgian beer is a speciality. The menu also includes other hearty dishes of lamb, *waterzooi* (stew) and *cassoulet*. There's a good selection of beer and wine.

CENTRAL BRUSSELS: L'Estrille du Vieux Bruxelles €€€
Belgian **Map** 2 D4
Rue de Rollebeek 7, 1000
Tel *(02) 512 5857* **Closed** *Wed & Sun*
La Tribune Poétique (Poetry Collective) once held their meetings at this old establishment with a venerable literary history. It specializes in traditional, beer-soaked cuisine, with savoury dishes of lamb and shrimp, as well as steaks. Decadent desserts.

CENTRAL BRUSSELS: L'Idiot du Village €€€
Modern European **Map** 1 C4
Rue Notre-Seigneur 19, 1000
Tel *(02) 502 5582* **Closed** *Sat & Sun*
The "Village Idiot" is reportedly a favourite with Belgian royalty. The menu offers mouthwatering concoctions such as *escalope* of hot *foie gras*, pepper and vanilla, and braised artichokes with bacon and basil.

CENTRAL BRUSSELS: Sea Grill €€€
Seafood **Map** 2 D2
Rue Fosse aux Loups 47, 1000
Tel *(02) 212 0800* **Closed** *Sat & Sun*
Located within the Radisson Blu hotel, this superb fish restaurant has a number of set menus of tempting dishes, particularly at lunchtime. There are exquisite desserts and a great wine list too.

CENTRAL BRUSSELS: Vismet €€€
Seafood **Map** 1 C2
Place Sainte-Catherine 23, 1000
Tel *(02) 218 8545* **Closed** *Sun & Mon*
Fine seafood as well as other meat dishes are prepared in the big open kitchen for an appreciative crowd. Reservations are usually needed.

Stylish interiors of the atmospheric La Quincaillerie, Brussels

GREATER BRUSSELS: Café Belga €
Café
Place Flagey 18, 1050
Tel *(02) 640 3508*
Light meals and great coffee are served at this Art Deco café with a bohemian feel.

GREATER BRUSSELS: Le Rubis €
Cambodian **Map** 4 E4
Avenue de Terveuren 22, 1040
Tel *(02) 733 0549* **Closed** *Sat & Sun*
Enjoy lightly spiced, aromatic Cambodian dishes such as king prawns with lemongrass and chicken with herbs and coconut milk amid a splendid collection of Khmer art.

GREATER BRUSSELS: Tout Près, Tout Prêt €
Lunch
Chaussée de Boondael 413, 1050
Tel *(02) 640 8080* **Closed** *Sun*
Located between the twin universities of the ULB and VUB, this no-frills sandwich bar is popular with the student crowd. It offers quick, innovative snacks.

GREATER BRUSSELS: Brasserie Georges €€
French
Avenue Churchill 259, 1180
Tel *(02) 347 2100*
Try the rack of lamb with garlic and rosemary at this gorgeous Parisian-style seafood brasserie with a shellfish stall at its entrance. Waiters offer attentive service.

GREATER BRUSSELS: Les Foudres €€
French
Eugène Cattoirstraat 14, 1050
Tel *(02) 647 3636*
One of Brussels' most spectacular restaurants is set in an old wine cellar. During the summer

months diners can also enjoy a delicious dinner in the adjacent garden and orchard.

GREATER BRUSSELS: Bon-Bon €€€
Fine Dining
Avenue de Tervueren 453, 1150
Tel *(02) 346 6615* **Closed** *Sat, Sun & Mon: lunch*
With two Michelin stars but friendlier prices than some of the other places with that honour in Brussels, Bin-Bon has three-, five- and seven-course menus. The wine is as good as the food.

GREATER BRUSSELS: Brasserie La Paix €€€
Belgian
Rue Ropsy Chaudron 49, 1070
Tel *(02) 523 0958*
Run by the same family for more than three decades, this Michelin-starred restaurant offers terrific food to suit all tastes and pockets. The meat dishes are superb.

GREATER BRUSSELS: Chalet de la Forêt €€€
Fine Dining
Drève de Lorraine 43, 1180
Tel *(02) 374 5416*
This first-class, two-Michelin-starred restaurant places an emphasis on the best seasonal and local ingredients and fine wines. The fish is recommended.

GREATER BRUSSELS: Mercedes House €€€
Modern European
Bodenbroekstraat 22-24, 1000
Tel *(02) 400 4250*
Dine on contemporary, inventive fare, including superb steaks and seafood in this spacious setting. The beautiful bar offers a wide range of wines and champagnes.

GREATER BRUSSELS: La Quincaillerie €€€
Belgian
Rue du Page 45, 1050
Tel *(02) 533 9833*
The steaks are excellent here, and the seafood counter is one of the best in Brussels. All desserts are made by the in-house chef patissier. The 1900s hardware store setting makes for great decor.

GREATER BRUSSELS: Rouge Tomate €€€
Modern European
Avenue Louise 190, 1050
Tel *(02) 647 7044* **Closed** *Sat: lunch; Sun*
Rouge Tomate prides itself on the quality of ingredients used. The seasonal menu features contemporary cuisine made with local produce.

GREATER BRUSSELS:
La Truffe Noire €€€
Fine Dining
Boulevard de la Cambre 12, 1050
Tel *(02) 640 4422* **Closed** *Sat: lunch & Sun*
This elegant Michelin-starred restaurant serves extravagantly prepared, mouthwatering food. The menu includes Périgord truffle cooked in a *porto jus*, and warm duck *foie gras* with honey-roasted carrots.

GREATER BRUSSELS:
De Zinneke €€
Belgian
Place de la Patrie 26, 1030
Tel *(02) 245 032*
At this slow-food sanctuary the chef cooks 69 recipes with mussels, accompanied by home-made fries. There are also other local dishes in the Belgian bistro tradition, with a fresh twist on the classics.

West & East Flanders

BLANKENBERGE: Oesterput €€
Seafood **Map** A1
Wenduinse Steenweg 16, 8370
Tel *(050) 411035* **Closed** *Mon & Tue*
Located by the harbour entrance, Oesterput has live lobster tanks that impart the ambience of a fish market. Dine on the large outdoor terrace during fine weather. An excellent wine list complements the food.

BRUGES: Café Vlissinghe €
Café **Map** B1
Blekerstraat 2, 8000
Tel *(050) 343737* **Closed** *Mon & Tue*
The medieval Vlissinghe dates back to 1515 and is the city's oldest hostellery. The menu features tempting appetizers, salads and other dishes, accompanied by excellent beers. Beautiful beer garden.

DK Choice

BRUGES: Den Huzaar €
Flemish **Map** B1
Vlamingstraat 36, 8000
Tel *(050) 333797*
This charming bistro is a firm favourite with locals and visitors alike for its hearty old-school Flemish cooking. Traditional dishes such as *veal ragout* (veal cuts in a creamy sauce with herbs and vegetables) are given a touch of class and a dash of inventiveness. Be sure to try the superb stew of pork cheeks.

BRUGES: Lotus €
Vegetarian **Map** B1
Wapenmakersstraat 5, 8000
Tel *(050) 331078* **Closed** *Sat & Sun; dinner*
There are usually just two options on the menu at this café, but they come in a choice of three sizes and include bulgur, salad, quiche and sautéed leeks.

BRUGES: De Republiek €
Café **Map** B1
St Jacobsstraat 36, 8000
Tel *(050) 734764*
Part of a cinema and theatre complex, this medium-sized brown café is popular with students and artists. The menu includes many vegetarian dishes as well as an array of cocktails.

BRUGES: Books and Brunch €€
Vegan **Map** B1
Garenmarkt 30, 8000
Tel *(050) 709079*
Enjoy a tasty vegetarian or vegan brunch, salad or sandwiches while browsing through the selection of books lining the shelves at this colourful, cosy café and second-hand book store.

BRUGES: Café Craenenburg €€
Café **Map** B1
Markt 16, 8000
Tel *(050) 333402*
Situated northwest of Grote Markt, Café Craenenburg is a little away from the typically touristy bars, and has a more local clientele. The menu includes salads, sandwiches, Flemish stews, pancakes and waffles, enjoyed inside or on the outdoor terrrace.

BRUGES: Cafédraal €€
Belgian **Map** B1
Zilverstraat 38, 8000
Tel *(050) 340845* **Closed** *Sun*
In a delightful medieval setting, Cafédraal is one of the most attractive restaurants in Bruges. The creative dishes are based around meat and shellfish. There is also a daily lunch *formule*.

BRUGES: De Stove €€
Belgian **Map** B1
Kleine Sint-Amandsstraat 4, 8000
Tel *(050) 337835* **Closed** *Mon–Sat: lunch; Wed & Thu*
The *foie gras* at this intimate restaurant with its handful of tables is exceptional; as is the fresh North Sea fish, supplied daily – particularly the breaded cod in butter sauce.

BRUGES: Den Dijver €€€
French/Belgian **Map** B1
Dijver 5, 8000
Tel *(050) 336069* **Closed** *Sun & Mon*
This stylish restaurant offers three-, four- or five-course set menus, in addition to a sophisticated à la carte selection of dishes made with local ingredients. Signatures include Chateaubriand and *entrecôte*.

BRUGES: Duc De Bourgogne €€€
Seafood **Map** B1
Huidenvettersplein 12, 8000
Tel *(050) 332038*
Overlooking a canal in the historical city centre, the Duc is always busy, so reserve a table well in advance. *Bouillabaisse* made with local sea fish is the house speciality.

Chic interiors of Mercedes House, a high-end restaurant in Greater Brussels

For more information on types of restaurants *see pages 272–3*

Quirky decor resembling a medieval butcher's hall at Groot Vleeshuis, Ghent

BRUGES: Den Gouden Harynck
Seafood €€€
Map B1
Groeninge 25, 8000
Tel (050) 337637 **Closed** Sun & Mon
Located in a 17th-century building in the museum district, this charming restaurant is run by chef Philippe Serruys and his wife. The sea bass with coarse sea salt and rosemary for two people is a must-try.

BRUGES: Park Restaurant
Belgian €€€
Map B1
Minderbroedersstraat 1, 8000
Tel (0497) 801872 **Closed** lunch; dinner: Mon & Thu
Run by two brothers, Axel and Frédéric Bruggeman, the cuisine here is authentic Belgian. Try the cod fillet in white sauce, shrimps, samphire and potato soufflé or the Belgian beef fillet in red wine sauce with gratin dauphinoise and vegetables.

BRUGES: De Visscherie
Seafood €€€
Map B1
Vismarkt 8, 8000
Tel (050) 330212 **Closed** Tue & Wed
The house's signature dish is the seafood platter, but any of the turbot variations are also worth trying at this popular haunt overlooking the centuries-old Vismarkt (fish market). Reserve a table in advance.

DAMME: Siphon
Flemish €€
Map B1
Damse Vaart-Oost 1, 8340 Oostkerke
Tel (050) 620202 **Closed** Sat & Sun
Siphon has been run by the same family for three generations and serves exquisite Flemish food. The seafood dishes such as paling in 't groen (eel in a green herb sauce) and peeled shrimps are superb, so are the game dishes in winter.

DE PANNE: Hostellerie Le Fox
Fine Dining €€€
Map A2
Walckierstraat 2, 8660 De Panne
Tel (058) 412855 **Closed** Mon & Tue
The focus is on seafood at this Michelin-starred hotel-restaurant with classic wood-panelled elegance, folded linen, silver, and fresh flowers. Try the tasting menu featuring grilled turbot and fresh duck liver.

DENDERMONDE: 't Truffeltje
Fusion €€€
Map C2
Bogaerdstraat 20, 9200
Tel (052) 224590 **Closed** Sat: lunch; Sun: dinner; Mon & Tue
This spacious Michelin-starred restaurant is housed in an old but modernized mansion. The menu features French-style cuisine with Belgian and Asian influences and changes monthly. Dim sum with truffles and langoustine are a signature dish.

DONKMEER: Palinghuis De Nieuwe Pluim
Seafood €€
Map C2
Brielstraat 9, 9290 Berlare-Overmere
Tel (09) 3678070 **Closed** Mon & Tue
Donkmeer, a set of lakes near Berlare, is the perfect place to try eel. Occupying a chalet-like house with a lovely terrace, this restaurant overlooking the lake has earned a reputation for its preparation of this local speciality.

GERARDSBERGEN: 't Grof Zout
French/Belgian €€€
Map B2
Gasthuisstraat 20, 9500
Tel (054) 423546 **Closed** Mon & Tue; Sat: lunch; Sun: dinner
The patron-chef uses an interesting selection of ingredients – guinea fowl, pigeon, sea bass, fennel and bulgar wheat – to whip up exquisite French-Belgian

dishes. In an elegant building that used to be a mirror factory, this is a charming restaurant.

GHENT: Chez Leontine
Belgian €
Map B2
Groentenmarkt 10–11, 9000
Tel (09) 225 0680 **Closed** Mon–Wed
A friendly little spot where visitors can savour fresh Flemish specialities, some of which are made with beer. There is also a beer and gin house. The rustic setting with its four separate dining areas enhances the unique atmosphere.

GHENT: De Frietketel
Fries €
Map B2
Papegaaistraat 89, 9000
Tel (09) 329 4022 **Closed** Sat; Sun: lunch
Widely regarded as the place that serves the best frites in Belgium, this chip shop is a Ghent legend. There is often a queue for the delicious burgers and fries.

GHENT: Groot Vleeshuis
Belgian €
Map B2
Groentenmarkt 7, 9000
Tel (09) 233 2324 **Closed** Mon
This medieval butcher's hall makes a spectacular setting for a meaty lunchtime sandwich or the even meatier tourist formule. The gentse waterzooi (fish or chicken stew) is highly recommended.

GHENT: 't Oud Clooster
Belgian €
Map B2
Zwartezusterstraat 5, 9000
Tel (09) 233 7802 **Closed** Sun: lunch
If you are seeking quality local food at low prices, this popular restaurant offers authentic Flemish cuisine in a cosy warm atmosphere.

GHENT: De Planck
Belgian €
Map B2
Ter Platen, 9000
Tel (0478) 769 416
Situated in the student district, this wonderfully atmospheric pub converted from a ship is well known for its impressive selection of beers and tasty snacks and steaks. There is an outside terrace.

GHENT: Brasserie Pakhuis
Belgian €€
Map B2
Schuurkenstraat 4, 9000
Tel (09) 223 5555 **Closed** Sun
The menu features seafood platters and Flemish favourites at this ultra-hip, renovated 19th-century warehouse. Oak and marble tables are set among exposed giant cast-iron pillars.

GHENT: Carte Blanche €€
French/Belgian   **Map** B2
Martelaarslaan 321, 9000
Tel *(09) 223 2808*
Set menus of contemporary and classic dishes are offered at this fine restaurant. Food is served by the owner in a friendly and informal atmosphere.

GHENT: Keizershof €€
Belgian   **Map** B2
Vrijdagmarkt 47, 9000
Tel *(09) 223 4446*   **Closed** *Sun & Mon*
Located in a narrow, 17th-century building on the busy market square, Keizershof serves Belgian staples and salads. Try the beef carpaccio or home-made shrimp croquettes. Paintings by local artists adorn the walls.

GHENT: Coeur D'artichaut €€€
European   **Map** B2
Onderbergen 6, 9000
Tel *(09) 225 3318*   **Closed** *Sun & Mon*
There are classic European dishes with a creative twist and an impressive Sunday brunch at this fine-dining restaurant in an impressive mansion. The menu changes every month. Groups of 6–12 diners can book the private Chef's Table.

DK Choice

GHENT: Georges IV €€€
Seafood   **Map** B2
Donkersteeg 23–27, 9000
Tel *(09) 225 1918*   **Closed** *Mon & Tue*
A Ghent institution, this friendly, family-run restaurant is renowned for its delectable seafood. Oysters, crab, mussels, lobster and fish are the primary attraction here. Try the baked mussels with garlic, eel in herb sauce or the *bouillabaisse*.

GHENT: Jan Van Den Bon €€€
Fusion   **Map** B2
Koning Leopold II-laan 43, 9000
Tel *(09) 221 9085*   **Closed** *Sat: lunch; Sun & Mon*
The outstanding Michelin-starred food features flavours from around the world. Both tasting and à la carte menus are available. The extensive wine list includes both regional and international wines.

GHENT: Valentijn €€€
French   **Map** B2
Rodekoningstraat 1, 9000
Tel *(09) 225 0429*   **Closed** *lunch; Thu; Sun: dinner*
Offering a superb four-course menu that is very popular with locals, this restaurant prides itself on using the freshest ingredients.

GHENT: Volta €€€
Seafood   **Map** B2
Nieuwe Wandeling 2b, 9000
Tel *(09) 342 0500*   **Closed** *Sun*
An uber-cool converted turbine hall just outside the city centre is home to one of Ghent's finest restaurants. The superb menu is especially imaginative in its fish and seafood dishes.

GHENT: Vrijmoed €€€
Belgian   **Map** B2
Vlaanderenstraat 22, 9000
Tel *(09) 279 9977*   **Closed** *Sat, Sun & Mon: lunch*
Popular with Ghent's young set, this contemporary Michelin-starred eatery offers excellent set menus. Unusually, there is also a decent range of vegetarian dishes.

KEMMEL: In De Wulf €€€
Belgian   **Map** A2
Wulvestraat 1, 8950 Heuvelland-Dranouter
Tel *(057) 445567* **Closed** *lunch: Mon–Thu & Sat; dinner: Mon & Tue*
A restorative retreat after visiting the battlefields. Dishes are made from natural, seasonal ingredients from both land and sea.

KNOKKE-HEIST: Bartholomeus €€€
Seafood   **Map** B1
Zeedijk 267, 8301 Knokke-Heist
Tel *(050) 517576*   **Closed** *Tue–Thu*
Set on the sea dyke of Heist, this Michelin-starred restaurant is best known for its seafood. The cooking is inventive and dishes are carefully prepared to extract the best flavours from ingredients.

KNOKKE-HEIST: Delys €€€
French   **Map** B1
Dumortierlaan 76, 8300
Tel *(050) 613111*   **Closed** *Mon & Tue (except public holidays)*
A popular venue with gourmets, this fine, family-run restaurant

serves delicious French classics such as *filet meunière* and grilled steaks. Truffles and crispy sweetbreads are a speciality.

KNOKKE-HEIST: Sel Gris €€€
Seafood   **Map** B1
Zeedijk 314, 8301 Duinbergen
Tel *(050) 514937*   **Closed** *Wed & Thu*
An excellent seafront restaurant with a Michelin-starred chef, Sel Gris serves delectable dishes of turbot, sole, plaice, mackerel, skate, scallops, lobster and other North Sea fish.

KORTRIJK: Saint-Christophe €€€
French   **Map** B2
Minister Tacklaan 5, 8500 Kortrijk
Tel *(056) 200337*   **Closed** *Mon; Sun & Tue: dinner*
Saint-Christopher serves outstanding classic cuisine. Highly recommended are the Breton lobster and the tuna with lemon broth. The fixed-price menus are good value. Ask for a table on the garden terrace during summer.

LAARNE: Restaurant Kasteel Van Laarne
Fine Dining   €€€   **Map** B2
Eekhoekstraat 7, 9270 Laarne
Tel *(09) 2307178*   **Closed** *Mon & Tue; Thu & Sun: dinner*
Located in a set of pretty outbuildings at the wonderful medieval castle of Laarne, this prestigious restaurant offers a French-Belgian menu that is a gastronomic *tour de force*.

LISSEWEGE: Hof Ter Doest €€€
French/Belgian   **Map** B1
Ter Doeststraat 4, 8380 Lissewege
Tel *(050) 544082*   **Closed** *Tue: dinner*
This large 17th-century farm-house, stands on the tranquil green opposite a medieval barn. It serves refined seafood and game dishes prepared along traditional lines.

Minimalist decor at the Michelin-starred Vrijmoed, Ghent

For more information on types of restaurants *see pages 272–3*

OOSTENDE: Fort Napoleon €€
French/Belgian   Map A1
Vuurtorenweg, 8400
Tel *(059) 332160* **Closed** *Mon & Tue*
Built in 1811, this old Napoleonic
fortress provides an unusual
setting for high-class French
and Belgian cuisine. A bistro
section serves lighter meals.

OOSTENDE: Ostend Queen €€€
Seafood   Map A1
Monacoplein, 8400
Tel *(059) 445610* **Closed** *Tue & Wed*
On the top floor of the seafront
kursaal (casino), this large and
stunning restaurant sources the
best quality fish and seafood as
well as seasonal produce for its
tasty, inventive dishes.

OUDENAARDE: Bistro 't Veer €
Belgian   Map B2
Berchemweg 191, 9700
Tel *(055) 302588* **Closed** *Thu*
Straightforward, delicious Belgian
classics are prepared with care.
Scampi's 't Veer and Angus beef
entrecôte are the specialities.

OUDENAARDE: Hof Van Cleve €€€
Belgian   Map B2
Riemegemstraat 1, 9770 Kruishoutem
Tel *(09) 3835848*
This three-star Michelin restaurant
is located in a pretty collection
of farm buildings, surrounded by
tranquil countryside. There are a
range of hot and cold starters to
choose from as well as many
vegetarian options.

POPERINGE: 't Hommelhof €€
Belgian   Map A2
Watouplein 17, 8978 Watou
Tel *(057) 388024* **Closed** *Wed;
Mon, Tue & Thu: dinner*
Cooking with beer is the focus of
this friendly hostelry. Dishes such
as rabbit stew, ham, beer and
cheese soup, and even desserts,
are prepared using specialist
local beers.

ST-NIKLAAS: Kok O Vin €€
French/Belgian   Map C1
Heidebaan 46, 9100
Tel *(03) 7668661* **Closed** *Tue &
Wed*
In a restored suburban villa east
of the town, this modern
restaurant offers a French-Belgian
menu, comprising dishes made
with seasonal ingredients.

VEURNE: De Plakker €
French/Flemish   Map A2
Grote Markt 14, 8630
Tel *(058) 315120* **Closed** *Thu, Fri
lunch*
Head here for generous Flemish
and French cuisine, accompanied
by a good range of beers. Try the

Flemish stew in winter or large
salads in summer. There is outside
decking for alfresco dining.

YPRES: Pacific Eiland €€
French/Belgian   Map A2
Island 2, 8900
Tel *(057) 200528* **Closed** *Mon:
dinner; Tue*
In an idyliic setting, this modern,
spacious eatery is on a small
island that can be reached via a
bridge. It serves inventive French
and Belgian fare prepared using
local as well as seasonal produce.

YRES: Hostellerie St-Nicolas €€€
French/Belgian   Map A2
Veurnseweg 532, 8906 Elverdinge
Tel *(057) 200622* **Closed** *Sun & Mon*
This first-class restaurant boasts
two Michelin stars. Try Chef
Franky Vanderhaeghe's
degustation menu comprising of
ten beautifully presented dishes.

Antwerp, Flemish Brabant & Limburg

ALDEN BIESEN: Het Vlierhof €€
Flemish   Map E2
Hasseltsestraat 57a, 3740 Bilzen
Tel *(089) 414418* **Closed** *Mon–Wed;
Sat: lunch*
Much of the superb local food
served at this gastronomic
restaurant is made from produce
from the restaurant's own organic
vegetable garden. There's also a
terrific selection of wines.

ANTWERP: Amadeus €
Belgian   Map C1
Sint-Paulusplaats 20, 2000
Tel *(049) 309 3329*
Set in a former glass-factory, this
restaurant is a mecca for lovers
of spare ribs. The Art Nouveau
interior, with glasswork and
wooden carvings, creates a
traditional brasserie atmosphere.

**ANTWERP: Brasserie
Appelmans** €
French   Map C1
Papenstraatje 1, 2950
Tel *(03) 226 2022*
Excellent brasserie fare, such as
big salads, delicious pasta and
risotto, juicy burgers and steaks
are served at this eatery, which
also has its own absinthe bar.

ANTWERP: Ciro's €
Belgian   Map C1
Amerikalei 6, 2000
Tel *(03) 238 1147* **Closed** *Mon*
Ciro's serves the best steaks in
Antwerp in a cosy interior. Don't
miss the house speciality, steak
Ciro's. The beef stew and *vol-
au-vent* are also worth trying.
Book ahead.

**ANTWERP: L'Epicerie
Du Cirque** €€
French/Belgian   Map C1
Volkstraat 23, 2000
Tel *(03) 238 0571* **Closed** *Sun & Mon*
Excellent old-school-style French-
Belgian food is served in contem-
porary bistro-like surroundings.
The small size of the venue adds
to its charm. Reserve ahead.

ANTWERP: Hippodroom €€
Mediterranean   Map C1
Leopold De Waelplaats 10, 2000
Tel *(03) 248 5252* **Closed** *Sun & Mon*
Set in an early 20th-century
building, this restaurant offers a
menu of seasonal dishes wtih an
oriental twist, using fresh local
ingredients. The fish options
are particularly recommended.

ANTWERP: InVINcible €€
Seafood   Map C1
Haarstraat 9, 2000
Tel *(03) 231 3207* **Closed** *Sat & Sun*
Many of the items on the menu
here are based on the morning's
catch from the North Sea. The
open kitchen allows diners to see
the chefs at work.

The elegantl retro-style dining area at the popular De Kleine Zavel, Antwerp

ANTWERP: De Kleine Zavel €€
Gastro Bar   Map C1
Stoofstraat 2, 2000
Tel *(03) 231 9691* **Closed** *Mon & Tue*
The innovative fare at De Kleine
Zavel has made it popular with
visitors and locals alike. A modern
version of the classic *vol-au-vent*
is among the tasty options.

ANTWERP: Le Zoute Zoen €€
French   Map C1
Zirkstraat 17, 2000
Tel *(03) 226 9220* **Closed** *Mon;
Sat: lunch*
Visit this restaurant for the good-
value set menu or try the à la
carte dishes such as tenderloin of
Belgian blue steak, *vol-au-vent*
and vegetarian options.

ANTWERP: Dome €€€
French   Map C1
Grotehondstraat 2, 2018
Tel *(03) 239 9003* **Closed** *Sun & Mon*
Michelin-starred preparations are
served in a lovely Art Nouveau
building. Enjoy creative, modern
French fare accompanied by one
of the best wine lists in the city.

ANTWERP: Het Gebaar €€€
Modern European   Map C1
Leopoldstraat 24, 2000
Tel *(03) 232 3710* **Closed** *Sun &
Mon dinner*
This Michelin-starred restaurant is
run by renowned chef Roger van
Damme. The location in the
Botanical Gardens is one of the
city's most attractive.

ANTWERP: Kommilfoo €€€
French/Belgian   Map C1
Vlaamsekaai 17, 2000
Tel *(03) 237 3000* **Closed** *Sat: lunch,
Sun & Mon*
An outstanding Michelin-starred
restaurant. The à la carte menu
features fried scampi and seared
turbot rolls. For a real bargain, opt
for the four-course set menu.

ANTWERP: Pazzo €€€
Italian/Japanese   Map C1
Oude Leeuwenrui 12, 2000
Tel *(03) 232 8682* **Closed** *Sat & Sun*
Stir-fries, tempuras and risottos are
served in this converted ware-
house. Wines by the glass com-
plement the variety of tapenades.

ANTWERP: Het Pomphuis €€€
Fusion   Map C1
Droogdok, Siberiastraat 7, 2030
Tel *(03) 770 8625*
This Pacific Rim bistro is in line
with the city's penchant for
industrial resto-bar conversions.
It has a long wine list to go with
dishes such as grilled tuna with
risotto croquettes and beef tenderloin with fries and bearnaise sauce.

Classy industrial decor at Het Pomphuis, an upmarket restaurant in Antwerp

ANTWERP: Rooden Hoed €€€
Belgian   Map C1
Oude Koornmarkt 25, 2000
Tel *(03) 289 0909* **Closed** *Mon*
Dating back to 1750, this is the
oldest and one of the most famed
restaurants in Antwerp. Mussels
and meat dishes predominate.

ANTWERP: T Fornuis €€€
Fine Dining   Map C1
Reyndersstraat 24, 2000
Tel *(03) 233 6270* **Closed** *Sat & Sun*
Chef Johan Segers visits the tables
in person to present the food to
diners at this Michelin-starred
restaurant. Try the beef tartare
with vodka or the eel in cream
sauce. Superb beers.

DK Choice

ANTWERP: T Zilte €€€
Belgian   Map C1
Hanzestedenplaats 5, 2000
Tel *(03) 283 4040* **Closed** *Sat &
Sun*
On the top floor of the Museum
aan de Stroom (MAS), this
gastronomic restaurant with
two Michelin stars offers
modern dishes, with superb
wines and terrific city views.

DIEST: De Groene Munt €€€
French   Map D2
Veemarkt 2, 3290
Tel *(013) 666833* **Closed** *Tue & Wed*
Located in the heart of Diest, this
intimate, cosy eatery boasts
classic English decor. It serves
French gastronomic cuisine made
with seasonal produce.

HALLE: Les Eleveurs €€€
French/Belgian   Map C2
Suikerkaai 1A, 1500
Tel *(02) 3611340* **Closed** *Sun (except
lunch 1st in month) & Mon*
The original purpose of these
charming buildings by a canal
was to breed Brabantine Draught

horses. They are now the location
of this hotel-restaurant famous
for superb French-Belgian food.

HASSELT: 't Kleine Genoegen €€€
Flemish   Map E2
Raamstraat 3, 3500
Tel *(011) 225703* **Closed** *Sun & Mon*
The menu at this family-run place
features seasonal *streek producten*
(regional produce) such as cherries,
rhubarb and rabbit. Try the shrimp
croquettes and Rossini beef fillet.

HASSELT: De Kwizien €€
Modern Belgian   Map E2
Jeneverplein, 3500
Tel *(011) 242344* **Closed** *Tue &
Wed; Sat: lunch*
The innovative cuisine for which
this restaurant is famed is
prepared with a creative flourish
in the open kitchen. There are
two- to five-course menus.

LEUVEN: Café De Blauwe Schuit €
Bistro   Map D2
Vismarkt 16, 3000
Tel *(016) 220570*
In a 19th-century building,
decorated with disparate
memorabilia, this popular café-
style pub has a tree-shaded
terrace. It serves a large selection
of freshly made dishes.

LEUVEN: De Blauwe Maan €€€
French/Belgian   Map D2
Mechelsestraat 22, 3000
Tel *(016) 299747* **Closed** *Sun & Mon;
Wed: dinner*
This popular modern eatery has
daily-changing dishes and fixed-
price, good-value lunch menus.

LIER: Numerus Clausus €€€
French   Map C1
Keldermansstraat 2, 2500
Tel *(03) 4805162* **Closed** *Sun &
Mon; Sat: lunch*
Refined French cuisine is prepared
by chef Steven Persyn using local
seasonal ingredients. Book ahead.

For more information on types of restaurants *see pages 272–3*

MECHELEN: Café Belge €
Belgian Map C2
Grote Markt 9, 2800
Tel *(015) 637266* **Closed** *Mon*
This bustling, friendly bistro serves a typical Belgian menu and offers good views of the Grote Markt.

ST-TRUIDEN: Aen de Kerck van Melveren €€€
French Map D2
St-Godfriedstraat 15-21, 3800
Tel *(011) 683965* **Closed** *Mon & Tue; Sat: lunch; Sun: dinner*
Located 3 km (2 miles) northeast of St-Truiden, this 16th-century red-brick farmhouse has a beautiful garden. It serves classic French cuisine, with special attention to exquisite presentation.

ST-TRUIDEN: De Fakkels €€€
French Map D2
Hasseltsesteenweg 61, 3800
Tel *(011) 687634* **Closed** *Mon–Wed & Sat: lunch; Sun: dinner*
Set in an elegant townhouse with an inviting lounge, the cuisine here is contemporary, varies with the seasons and is paired with excellent wines. In fine weather you can dine in the garden.

TIENEN: De Refugie €€
French/Belgian Map D2
Kapucijnenstraat 75, 3300
Tel *(016) 824532* **Closed** *Tue & Wed*
This charming restaurant is run by an expert owner-chef. The dining room is modern, but the lovely panelling and antique touches give it an intimate atmosphere. The menu changes according to the season. Extensive wine list.

DK Choice

TONGEREN: De Pelgrim €
Belgian Map E2
Brouwersstraat 9, 3700
Tel *(012) 2626266*
In a town steeped in history, De Pelgrim is suitably located on the cobbled Brouwersstraat (Brewers' Street). This fine old pub occupies a red-brick, step-gabled 1642 building with a traditional interior of exposed beams and wooden furniture. It serves excellent beer, and pub food ranging from snacks to spare ribs.

TONGEREN: Magis €€€
French Map E2
Hemelingenstraat 23, 3700
Tel *(012) 743464* **Closed** *Tue & Wed*
Once owned by the Teutonic knights, this grand mansion has been given a very modern makeover and is now a Michelin-starred gastronomic French restaurant.

For key to prices *see page 280*

TURNHOUT: Cucinamarangon €€€
Italian Map D1
Patersstraat 9, 2300
Tel *(014) 424381* **Closed** *Sun & Mon*
Savour refined northern Italian cuisine in a theatrical setting. The seafood is very good, as are the carpaccio, risotto, pasta and other classic main dishes with a twist. There are good-value fixed-price menus.

Western Wallonia

ATH: Viandes Etc €€
Belgian Map B3
Place du Maché aux Toiles 5-7, 7800
Tel *(068) 445977* **Closed** *Wed; Tue & Sun: dinner*
"Meats etc" sets the scene for dedicated non-vegetarian cooking that stays true to local produce and is inventive. Dishes include croquettes with shrimp and horse sirloin sautéed with garlic.

ATTRE: Le Vieux Chaudron €€
French Map B3
Avenue du Château 14, 7941 Attre
Tel *(068) 454279* **Closed** *Wed; Sun–Fri: dinner*
This long-established family-run restaurant is set in a charming 14th-century stone-and-brick house. It is primarily a lunch spot, and offers well-prepared Belgian and French dishes.

BINCHE: Le Bercha €€
French Map C3
Route de Mons 763, 7130 Bray
Tel *(064) 369107* **Closed** *Mon & Tue; Sun: dinner*
The French-style cooking in this family-run restaurant is *cuisine du terroir* (based on local produce and traditions). There's an outdoor terrace.

Traditional interiors of De Pelgrim, a well-known pub in Tongeren

CHARLEROI: La Bouche des Goûts €€
French Map C3
Rue Vauban 14, 6000 Charleroi
Tel *(071) 701747* **Closed** *Mon*
Enjoy authentic French cuisine at this family-run restaurant with a rustic decor. All dishes are home-cooked and include *foie gras*, duck breast and chocolate fondant.

CHARLEROI: La Tête de Boeuf €€
French/Belgian Map C3
Place de l'Abattoir 5, 6000
Tel *(071) 48 7764* **Closed** *Sun*
As the name suggests, this is a meat-eater's paradise, with steaks, *jambonneau* (knuckle of ham) and a range of offal-based dishes to choose from. There are fish and seafood classics on the menu too.

CHARLEROI: Les 3 P'tits Bouchons €€€
Contemporary French Map C3
Avenue Paul Pastur 378, 6032
Tel *(071) 325519* **Closed** *Sat & Sun*
Co-founded by sommelier Roland Kempinaire and chef Yoshida Shunshuke; serves superb dishes prepared using fresh produce. Impressive wine list.

DK Choice

CHIMAY: Chez Edgard Et Madeleine €€
Belgian Map C4
Rue du Lac 35, 6460 Chimay
Tel *(060) 211071* **Closed** *Sun: dinner & Mon*
Set beside the Lac de Virelles, 3 km (2 miles) east of Chimay, this wonderful spot dates from 1910. Wood-panelling and crisp white linen reflect well on the outsanding cooking, which is *à l'ancienne* (old style). The menu includes lake trout and seafood, plus seasonal game such as hare and partridge. Great wine list and plenty of Chimay beer.

LA LOUVIERE: Les Gourmands Disent €€
Belgian Map C3
Rue Sylvain Guyaux 8, 7100
Tel *(064) 284095* **Closed** *Mon, Tue; Sat: lunch*
The emphasis is on fresh market produce at this gastronomic restaurant. Try the *foie gras* with caramelized chicory or snails in garlic butter.

LESSINES: Le Tramasure €€
Belgian Map B2
Porte d'Ogy 3, 7860
Tel *(068) 33 50 82* **Closed** *Mon, Tue & Sun; Wed & Thu: dinner*
With plenty of old-world charm, this lovely eatery specializes in

cuisine du terroir and features snails, duck, rabbit, tripe sausages, Belgian endives and seafood.

MONS: Brasserie Les Enfants Gâtés €€
Mediterranean   Map C3
Rue de Bertaimant 40, 7000
Tel (065) 975964   Closed Mon, Sun: dinner
Considered by many to be the best restaurant in Mons, Les Enfants Gâtés has a tavern-like setting. The top-notch gourmet cooking is southern French in style, with Mediterranean touches.

THUIN: Au Bief Du Moulin €€€
Belgian   Map C3
Rue Vandervelde 290, 6534 Gozée
Tel (071) 516074   Closed Mon & Tue
Popular for its good-quality home-made fare, the prices at this restaurant, notably for the set menus, are very reasonable. There is outdoor seating and a children's playground.

TOURNAI: L'Ecurie D'Ennetieres €
Belgian   Map B3
Ruelle d'Ennetières 7, 7500
Tel (069) 215689   Closed Mon
This refreshingly traditional brasserie serves mouthwatering Belgian dishes including scampi, filet américain, façon tartare, steak, horse meat and jambonneau.

TOURNAI: Le Giverny €€€
French   Map B3
6 Quai Marché au Poisson, 7500
Tel (069) 224464   Closed Mon, Tue: dinner, Sat: lunch, Sun: dinner
Exquisite French cuisine made with seasonal produce is served in an elegant setting with spectacular views. Book ahead.

Central Wallonia

ANNEVOIE: Jardin D'en Bas €€
Belgian   Map D3
Rue d'en Bas 1, 5537
Tel (082) 613706   Closed Tue & Wed
In a lovely 17th-century house decorated in period style, this family-run restaurant offers home-cooked food made using only local produce.

DINANT: La Broche €€
Fusion   Map D3
Rue Grande 22, 5500
Tel (082) 228281   Closed Tue
The cooking is grounded in French cuisine, but has some Asian touches at this comfortable, modern restaurant decorated with old photographs behind a 19th-century shopfront façade.

Outdoor seating in the lovely garden of Jardin De Fiorine, Dinant

DINANT: Jardin De Fiorine €€€
French   Map D3
Rue Georges Cousot 3, 5500
Tel (082) 227474   Closed Wed & Thu; Sun: dinner
A large modernized maison de maître of 1885 is the setting for light French gourmet cooking and cuisine du terroir at Jardine De Fiorine. There is a specially designed menu for children called "An Introduction to Gastronomy".

FLOREFFE: Mas Des Cigales €
Provencale   Map D3
Rue Ferdinand Francot 8, 5150
Tel (081) 444847   Closed Mon & Tue; Sun: dinner; Sat: lunch
Lunch is the main focus of the kitchen, with dishes such as beef carpaccio with parmesan, accompanied by superb wines. The dining room features Provençale decor in warm colours.

LA HULPE: Côté Jardin €
Bistro   Map C2
Rue de Genval 14, 1310
Tel (02) 6530113   Closed Sat: lunch, Sun: dinner, Mon
A small, family-run restaurant with tables set out in the garden during summer, Côté Jardin serves salads with shrimp or smoked duck, scampi and steaks.

LOUVAIN-LA-NEUVE: La Baita €€
Italian   Map D2
Drève du Golf 3, 1348
Tel (010) 451165   Closed Mon; Sun: dinner
This eatery is a tranquil setting for fine Italian and French cooking. Classics include pasta, carpaccio, seafood, veal and chicken. Reasonably priced plats du jour (dishes of the day) are available.

MAREDSOUS: La Fermette €€€
French   Map D3
Rue du Château-Ferme 30, 5522 Falaën
Tel (082) 688668   Closed Wed & Thu
High-quality French cuisine is served to its many dedicated patrons in this farmhouse

restaurant. A platter of Falaën cheeses rounds off meals. There is a lovely rural garden.

NAMUR: Le Père Gourmandin €€
Organic   Map D3
Rue du Président 8, 5000
Tel (081) 229008   Closed Sun; Mon–Fri: dinner
This tea room and organic kitchen specializes in great local cuisine. Try a gourmet platter.

NAMUR: Cuisinémoi €€€
French   Map D3
Rue Notre Dame 44, 5000
Tel (081) 229181   Closed Sun & Mon; Sat: lunch
Creative French-style cuisine made with fresh produce is served at this gourmet Michelin-starred restaurant at the foot of Namur's Citadelle. It has an elegant, bright dining room.

NAMUR: La Petite Fugue €€€
Contemporary French   Map D3
Place Chanoine Descamps 5, 5000
Tel (081) 231320
Enjoy innovative cooking at this restaurant housed in a 17th-century building, with soft lighting. Try the foie gras.

NAMUR: La Plage D'amee €€€
French   Map D3
Rue des Peupliers 2, 5100 Jambes
Tel (081) 309339 Closed Sun: dinner, Mon
The focus is on fish and seafood at this stylish restaurant with a balcony hanging over the river. The interior is spacious and airy.

NIVELLES: Le Champenois €€€
French   Map C3
Rue des Brasseurs 14, 1400 Nivelles
Tel (067) 213500   Closed Wed; Sat: lunch; Sun: dinner
Delicious, sumptuously presented French cuisine is served at this upmarket gastronomic restaurant in a picturesque old quarter of the town. Service is impeccable.

For more information on types of restaurants see pages 272–3

Typical grilled meats, such as pork skewers, served in many restaurants in Wallonia

ROCHEFORT: Restaurant La Couleur Basilic   €€
Mediterranean   **Map** D4
Rue de Behogne 43, 5580
Tel *(084) 468536*   **Closed** *Tue & Wed*
This small restaurant serves a full range of classic dishes such as lobster, grilled beef and lasagna. It has a terrace for eating outside in summer.

WALCOURT: Hostellerie Dispa   €€€
Fine Dining   **Map** C3
Rue du Jardinet 5-7, 5650
Tel *(071) 611423*   **Closed** *Tue, Wed & Sun*
A hotel as well as a highly respected restaurant, the Hostellerie Dispa occupies a grand mansion dating from around 1900. The menu features elaborate French cuisine. There is a special menu for kids.

WATERLOO: La Sucrerie   €€€
French   **Map** C2
Chaussée de Tervuren 198, 1410
Tel *(02) 3521815*   **Closed** *Sat & Sun: lunch*
With vaulted ceilings from the original 1836 sugar factory, the atmosphere here is both majestic and cosy. The modern French cuisine revisits regional recipes and there is an extensive wine list.

WAVRE: La Table Des Templiers   €€€
Belgian   **Map** D2
Chemin du Temple 10, 1300
Tel *(010) 881350*   **Closed** *Sat & Sun*
This fine restaurant was a classic Brabant courtyard farm in the 17th-century. The wide-ranging gastronomic menu is based on seasonal produce. Dishes such as langoustine tartare, fried sirloin beef and seared duck liver make it a popular draw.

Eastern Wallonia

ARLON: L'eau A La Bouche   €€€
French   **Map** E4
Route de Luxembourg 317, 6700
Tel *(063) 233705*   **Closed** *Tue: dinner, Wed*
Housed in a grand, comfortable villa, this delightful, elegant restaurant is run by a husband-and-wife team. The cooking is elaborate French haute cuisine.

BASTOGNE: Wagon-Restaurant Leo   €€
Belgian   **Map** E4
Rue du Vivier 6, 6600
Tel *(061) 211441*   **Closed** *Mon*
This is a glitzy and fun brasserie with retro decor and a wagon-frontage. The wide-ranging menu offers a variety of traditional Belgian dishes, from meatballs and chips to lobster and shrimp.

BOUILLON: La Vieille Ardenne   €
Belgian   **Map** D4
Grande-Rue 9, 6830
Tel *(061) 466277*   **Closed** *Wed*
Set in a 16th-century house in the heart of the town, this restaurant serves tasty cuisine keeping to local produce and traditions such as trout, and game in season. The speciality is meat and fish cooked on a *pierrade* (stone grill).

CHAUDFONTAINE: Le Long Du Bief   €€
Game   **Map** E3
Le Long du Bief, Rue Hauster 5, 4051
Tel *(04) 3679127*   **Closed** *Mon & Tue*
This family-run eatery is located along a tranquil river. Specialities on the menu include grilled meat, beef, duck and other seasonal produce.

DURBUY: Le Fou Du Roy   €€
French   **Map** E3
Rue Comte d'Ursel 4, 6940
Tel *(086) 210868*   **Closed** *Mon & Tue*
The food at this intimate restaurant packed with bric-a-brac is supremely good French cooking with Mediterranean touches – duck breast, rack of lamb and gnocchi and grilled wild shrimp.

DURBUY: La Gargouille   €€
Belgian   **Map** E3
Rue Rowé de Remouleu 20, 6941 Heyd
Tel *(086) 499210*   **Closed** *Tue–Thu*
The menu here is based on local and seasonal produce. Dishes are prepared with imagination and flair and served in fantastically decorated dining areas. There is an excellent Sunday brunch.

FOURNEAU ST-MICHEL: Auberge Du Prevost   €
Belgian   **Map** E4
Fourneau St-Michel, 6870 St-Hubert
Tel *(084) 444811*   **Closed** *Mon, Tue*
This half-timbered 18th-century tavern in the Wallonia Village Museum provides a rustic setting for a full menu of fine traditional Belgian cuisine in either the brasserie or restaurant.

HOTTON: Les Pieds Dans Le Plat   €€€
French   **Map** E3
Rue du Centre 3, 6990 Marenne
Tel *(084) 321792*   **Closed** *Mon & Tue; Wed & Thu: dinner*
An old village school has been imaginatively transformed into a set of rustic dining rooms, with a veranda and garden. The seasonal French cuisine is succulent and delectable.

LIÈGE: Le Paris-Brest   €
Fusion   **Map** E2
Rue des Anglais 18, 4000
Tel *(04) 2234711*   **Closed** *Sat & Sun*
Enjoy well-made regional dishes here, including *boulets à la liégeoise*, a dish of meatballs sweetened with currants and a sauce made with *sirop de Liège*, a Belgian jelly-like spread. There is also more exotic fusion cuisine.

LIÈGE: Restaurant-Café Lequet   €
Bistro   **Map** E2
Quai sur Meuse 17, 4000
Tel *(04) 2222134*   **Closed** *Tue, Sun: dinner*
This classic and folksy Liège brasserie is famous for its mouthwatering *boulettes à la liégeoise*, served with thick *frites* and salad. Other traditional dishes are also available.

LIÈGE: La Charbonnade   €€
Steak House   **Map** E2
Rue Roture 5, 4020
Tel *(04) 3431172*
In a cosy, rustic setting in the historic district of Outremeuse, this restaurant specializes in steaks, grilled meats and meat platters you can grill yourself on hot coals at your table.

LIÈGE: Frédéric Maquin   €€
French   **Map** E2
Rue des Guillemins 47, 4000
Tel *(04) 2534184*   **Closed** *Mon, Tue, Sat: lunch*
The brilliant owner-chef Frédéric Maquin has built up a formidable reputation for his high-end gastronomic fare. The menu features superb dishes made with fresh market produce and changes seasonally. There is an extensive wine list.

LIÈGE: Le Sélys €€€
French Map E2
Mont Saint Martin 9–11, 4000
Tel *(04) 2676804* **Closed** *Sun, Mon*
Occupying the ground floor of the former Sélys Longchamps townhouse, this Michelin-starred restaurant combines creative, fine French cuisine using local Liège produce with remarkable decor, including frescoes and chinoiserie. There is a terrace for dining in good weather.

LIMBOURG: Le Casino €€€
French Map E2
Avenue Reine Astrid 7, 4831
Tel *(087) 762374* **Closed** *Mon, Tue, Sat: lunch*
Located in the heart of the medieval town of Limbourg, this family-run restaurant offers French cuisine prepared with fresh market produce, carefully selected by the chef himself. There is also the option to have some dishes to take away.

MALMEDY: Cyrano €€€
French Map F3
Rue de la Gare 23, 4950 Waimes
Tel *(080) 679989* **Closed** *Mon, Sat: lunch*
Inventive cuisine prepared from recipes inspired by the French region of Périgord (Dordogne) is the speciality of this modern hotel-restaurant. The menu includes dishes of truffles, *foie gras*, duck confit and goat cheese

MARCHIN: Arabelle Meirlaen €€€
Belgian Map D3
Chemin de Bertrandfontaine 7, 4570
Tel *(085) 255555* **Closed** *Sun eve– Tue; Wed–Sat: lunch*
This small, charming restaurant is run by Michelin-starred chef Arabelle Meirlaen. Her modern cooking makes use of local produce and even wild herbs and is exquisitely presented. There's terrace dining under vast shady sails in fine weather.

MODAVE: La Roseraie €€€
French Map E3
Route de Limet 80, 4577
Tel *(085) 411360* **Closed** *Mon–Wed*
Serving first-rate *cuisine française* since 1982, the menus at this tranquil restaurant in an elegant 1920s villa with a garden reflect the changing seasons. The delectable dishes include lamb chops and shrimp croquettes.

REDU: La Gourmandine €€
French/Belgian Map D4
Rue de St-Hubert 16, 6890
Tel *(061) 656390* **Closed** *Wed & Thu*
La Gourmandine offers classic French and traditional regional fare, such as *jambonneau*, as well as lighter meals like goat cheese salad and omelettes.

SPA: Source De Barisart €€
Belgian Map E3
Route de Barisart 295, 4900
Tel *(087) 770988* **Closed** *Tue & Wed*
In a lovely woodland setting, this large chalet-like restaurant has both seafood and game fixed-price menus. The *fondue bourguignonne* (beef fondue) is particularly recommended.

DK Choice

SPA: Art De Vivre €€€
Fusion Map E3
Avenue Reine Astrid 53, 4900
Tel *(087) 770444* **Closed** *Mon, Tue: lunch*
This grand 19th-century mansion offers lessons in the "art of living" through its inspired cooking. The choice of food is driven by the restaurant's creative chef-patron. The menu features seasonal produce, such as asparagus, and other ingredients not always found on Belgian menus. Modern decor with teak decking around a fountain makes a relaxed setting for summer dining.

STAVELOT: Val D'ambleve €€€
French Map E3
Route de Malmedy 7, 4970
Tel *(080) 281440* **Closed** *Mon*
Housed in a building dating from the 1930s, this restaurant has a conservatory-style *jardin d'hiver* (winter garden). The kitchen serves light, seasonal meals.

ST-HUBERT: Le Cor De Chasse €€
Belgian Map E4
Avenue Nestor Martin 3, 6870
Tel *(061) 611644* **Closed** *Tue*
This hotel-restaurant is a good place to savour game dishes during the hunting season. There are superb recipes of quail, rabbit and trout throughout the year.

ST-HUBERT: Auberge Du Grandgousier €€€
French Map E4
Rue du Staplisse 6, 6870 Mirwart
Tel *(084) 366293* **Closed** *Tue & Wed*
Dishes such as steak tartare with black olive tapenade, langoustines on skewers and monkfish medallions are among the high-quality dishes here. The restaurant is housed in a typical Ardennes, half-timbered hostelry that has retained its rustic charm.

THEUX: Le Pied de la Fagne €€€
Belgian/French Map E3
Pied de la Fagne 10, 4910
Tel *(087) 542 799* **Closed** *Tue & Wed*
Just 8 km (5 miles) outside Theux in a delightfully rustic setting, this restaurant is strong on regional, Ardennes-influenced cooking, with an emphasis on seasonal game-based dishes.

VERVIERS: Au Clair Obscur €€
Belgian Map E3
Place Albert 1er 5, 4800
Tel *(087) 232221* **Closed** *Sun & Mon*
The emphasis here is on creative cuisine prepared using local and seasonal ingredients. Dine under parasols on the tranquil terrace on sunny days.

VERVIERS: Le Coin des Saveurs €€€
Modern Belgian Map E3
Avenue de Spa 28, 4800
Tel *(087) 232360* **Closed** *Mon, Tue, Sat: lunch*
This elegant restaurant is known for its use of top-quality seasonal ingredients and a contemporary approach to classic Belgian fare. Try the *menu découverte* (tasting menu) which changes regularly but may include such dishes as squid cubes with tomato jam and sea bass fillet with crumble carbonara.

Simple interiors of Art De Vivre, a restaurant that serves fusion cuisine

For more information on types of restaurants *see pages 272–3*

Picturesque view of Mathes, located on the banks of River Moselle, Ahn-Wormeldange

Grand Duchy of Luxembourg

AHN-WORMELDANGE:
Mathes €€€
French **Map** F5
Route du Vin 37, 5401
Tel 760106 **Closed** *Mon & Tue*
The Moselle Luxembourgeoise has a famous fish dish called *friture de la Moselle* – small river fish deep-fried in batter. Mathes is one of the best place to try it, along with other specialities such as a salad of sautéed squid and risotto with prawns.

CLERVAUX: Les Ecuries
Du Parc €
International **Map** F4
Rue du Parc 4, 9708
Tel 920364 **Closed** *Mon*
This rustic restaurant has been beautifully converted out of stables once belonging to the counts of Clervaux. The speciality is meat – horse steak, cooked ham, veal and beef brochette.

CLERVAUX:
Restaurant-Brasserie K €€€
French **Map** F4
Rue de Stavelot 2, 9964 Huldange
Tel 979056-1 **Closed** *Mon*
Contemporary French-style cuisine is served in this restaurant located in Burrigplatz, widely considered to be the highest point in Luxembourg. There is also a brasserie with lower prices.

ECHTERNACH: Au Vieux
Moulin €€€
French **Map** F4
Lauterborn 6, 6562
Tel 720068-1 **Closed** *Mon*
Situated on the site of a former millhouse 3 km (2 miles) south-west of Echternach, this pretty hotel-restaurant serves elegantly presented French cuisine. There are seasonal fixed-price menus.

ESCH-SUR-ALZETTE: Favaro €€€
Italian **Map** F5
Rue des Remparts 19, 4303
Tel 542723 **Closed** *Mon;
Sat: lunch; Sun: dinner*
Delectable *haute cuisine Italienne* draws customers to the Michelin-starred Favaro. Behind the striking brick-red façade, chef Renato Favaro gives inventive twists to classic Italian food.

FRISANGE: Léa Linster €€€
French **Map** F5
Route de Luxembourg 17, 5752
Tel 23668411
Excellent French cuisine is prepared by the Michelin-starred chef after whom the restaurant is named. Enjoy dining in a peaceful rural setting or the modern dining room suffused with white.

LAROCHETTE: La Distillerie €
Luxembourgeoise **Map** F4
Rue du Château 8, 6162 Bourglinster
Tel 7878781 **Closed** *Mon & Tue*
This Michelin-starred restaurant housed in the Château de Bourglinster serves beautifully presented gourmet dishes such as flank steak with artichokes and chanterelles and veal carpaccio with heirloom tomatoes.

LUXEMBOURG CITY: Um
Dierfgen €
Luxembourgeoise **Map** F5
Côte d'Eich 6, 1450
Tel 226141 **Closed** *Sun & Mon:
dinner*
The kitchen of this rustic, traditional-style inn with wooden tables specializes in *cuisine Luxembourgeoise*. Plenty of hearty pork dishes and other grilled meats are available.

LUXEMBOURG CITY:
L'Annexe €€
French **Map** F5
Rue du St-Esprit 7, 1475
Tel 26262507 **Closed** *Sat: lunch,
Sun*
The good-value dishes at this modern restaurant are brasserie-style, with crayfish risotto, salads, *tagines* and steak tartare on the menu. There is a large terrace.

LUXEMBOURG CITY:
Il Cherubino €€
Italian **Map** F5
Rue de Turi, 3378 Livange
Tel 26522626
The cuisine and wine of Apulia, in Italy, is the main culinary thrust of this excellent restaurant. The decor is classic Italian.

LUXEMBOURG CITY:
Come Prima €€
Italian **Map** F5
Rue de l'Eau, 1449
Tel 241724 **Closed** *Sun*
The menu at this cosy restaurant with bare-brick walls and soft lighting features traditional dishes such as seafood spaghetti, grilled beef fillet and fried scampi.

LUXEMBOURG CITY: Mousel's
Cantine €€
Luxembourgeoise **Map** F5
Montée de Clausen 46, 1343
Tel 470198 **Closed** *Sun; Sat: lunch*
This warm and welcoming brasserie is linked to the Mousel brewery that has been producing beer in Clausen since 1825. Enjoy beer with dishes such as grilled steak, duck breast with orange and shrimp cocktail.

LUXEMBOURG CITY:
Bouquet Garni €€€
French **Map** F5
Rue de l'Eau 32, 1449
Tel 26200620 **Closed** *Sat: lunch,
Sun*
Smart and sophisticated, Bouquet Garni occupies an 18th-century building. The Michelin-starred fare includes dishes such as Scottish salmon with herbs and roasted lobster served with ginger and basil.

LUXEMBOURG CITY:
Clairefontaine €€€
French **Map** F5
Place de Clairefontaine 9, 1946
Tel 462211 **Closed** *Sat & Sun*
Enjoy top-notch fine dining at this exquisite Michelin-starred restaurant near Place Guillaume II.

The excellent five-course set menu of creative modern cuisine is a gastronomic experience not to be missed. There is an outdoor terrace for alfresco dining.

LUXEMBOURG CITY:
Mosconi   €€€
Italian   **Map** F5
Rue Münster 13, 2160
Tel *546994*   **Closed** *Sun & Mon*
Considered to be the best place for Italian food in the city, this riverside restaurant has earned a Michelin star for its exquisite culinary creations. Diners can expect divine pastas, including an eight-course pasta tasting menu, and plenty of truffles.

LUXEMBOURG CITY:
Le Plëss   €€€
French   **Map** F5
Place d'Armes 18, 1136
Tel *274737411*
Located in the Hotel Place d'Armes, this stylish modern brasserie offers exquisite French cuisine with Luxembourgeois twists, such as excellent beef tartare served with fresh herbs, as well as beef carpaccio.

LUXEMBOURG CITY: Restaurant
Essenza @ Apoteca   €€€
Fusion   **Map** F5
Rue de la Boucherie 12, 1247
Tel *267377-1*   **Closed** *Sun;*
Sat: lunch
A medieval building has been transformed into an attractive contemporary restaurant. The cooking is French with strong Asian and Italian accents, and a good selection of wines. For a treat, try the Imperial Mixed Fish Platter featuring tuna in sesame seeds, king prawns, sea bass and sword fish.

LUXEMBOURG CITY: Le Sud   €€€
French   **Map** F5
Rives de Clausen, 1123
Tel *26478750*   **Closed** *Mon,*
Sat: lunch, Sun: dinner
Conveniently located near to Luxembourg's main tourist attractions, Le Sud is a high-end French and Luxembourgeois restaurant. Diners can enjoy fabulous panoramic views across the city from the terrace, which is accessible by a glass lift, or eat in the elegant yet cosy ground-level restaurant. The menu at Le Sud is relatively compact and each dish is beautifully prepared.

MERTERT: Joel Schaeffer   €€€
Luxembourgeoise   **Map** F4
Rue Haute 1, 6680
Tel *26714080*   **Closed** *Mon;*
Sun: dinner
The young chef Joël Schaeffer creates beautiful French dishes in this restaurant housed in a historic building. Try the black pudding ravioli with onion confit from a selection of seasonally-changing dishes, or one of the tasting menus. The fixed lunchtime menu changes weekly and offers good value for money.

MONDORF-LES-BAINS:
De Jangeli   €€€
French   **Map** F5
Rue du Dr E Feltgen, 5601
Tel *23666525* **Closed** *Mon, Tue; Wed,*
Thu & Sat: lunch
This is the main restaurant of the Domaine des Thermes, the town's primary spa centre. Dishes served in the flamboyant dining room include rack of lamb with thyme and hazelnuts, and lobster with chanterelles among others.

DK Choice

PETANGE: Letzebuerger
Kaschthaus   €€
Luxembourgeoise   **Map** E5
Route Rue de Bettembourg 4,
3333 Hellange
Tel *265664*   **Closed** *Tue & Wed*
Owned by Luxembourg's star chef Léa Linster, this is a more casual and less expensive option than her flagship restaurant in nearby Frisange. It has the look of a rustic tavern with a delightful rear terrace. The traditional Luxembourgeois cuisine is absolutely first-rate and in keeping with Linster's attention to culinary detail.

PETITE SUISSE: Parmentier   €€
Luxembourgeoise   **Map** F4
Rue de la Gare 7, 6117 Junglinster
Tel *787168*   **Closed** *Tue*
Head to this family-friendly hotel-restaurant dating from 1904 to enjoy good-quality bistro-style food from a choice of menus, including gourmet and children's options. There is also a sleek wine bar specializing in Luxembourg wines. Service is warm and attentive.

VIANDEN: Auberge Aal
Veinen Beim Hunn   €€
Luxembourgeoise   **Map** F4
Grand-Rue 114, 9411
Tel *834368*   **Closed** *Tue*
This popular village inn, located in a former locksmiths building at the foot of the Château de Vianden, serves traditional local food, notably delicious steaks grilled over an open fire. Try the rib-eye steaks or the brochette of veal and beef.

Roast rack of lamb topped with herbs, a popular dish in Belgium

For more information on types of restaurants *see pages 272– 3*

SHOPPING IN BELGIUM

Belgians love to shop. They use the French term for window shopping with good reason: *lécher les vitrines* literally means licking the windows. This urge is satisfied by a host of excellent shops in every town and city, ranging from highly competitive supermarkets to the most exclusive boutiques. High streets remain vibrant as Belgians enjoy the choice, service and expertise of individual traders. Merchandise of all kinds is available and although it is not cheap, wise shoppers will find it can be good value for money.

Rue Neuve, the longest pedestrian shopping street in Brussels

Opening Hours

Shops are open between 10am and 6pm from Monday to Saturday. Many open at 9am and some stay open until 7 or 8pm, especially if they close for an hour at lunchtime. Food shops and supermarkets have longer hours, from 9am to 8pm. Most supermarkets and shops close on Sundays, although many pâtisseries are open on Sunday mornings.

Where to Shop

Most towns are built around a central square – the Grand Place or Grote Markt – which used to be the focus of trade, guilds and the town administration in medieval times. Today, these squares have weekly markets and many of the best shops. Larger towns and cities have pedestrianized shopping streets or covered malls at their centre. Large supermarkets selling clothes, electrical goods, hardware and CDs tend to be on the outskirts, where they can provide parking. **Delhaize**, **Carrefour** (which now also owns the GB brand), **Cora** and **Colruyt** are the big supermarket chains. Roads leading into towns may be lined with large-scale commercial enterprises – car showrooms, hardware superstores, garden centres and fashion outlets. The Maasmechelen "fashion village" *(see p172)* is a purpose-built, discount-driven shoppers' paradise.

Markets

Towns usually host markets once or twice a week, often in the main square. They sell fruit, vegetables, meat, cheese and local food products as well as clothes, textiles, shoes, household goods, flowers and craft products. The largest market, La Batte, is a sprawling, mixed, Sunday market along the northern bank of the River Meuse in Liège. Many towns also have regular or occasional antique or flea markets (the distinction is often blurred). The largest of these is held on Sunday mornings in Tongeren *(see p173)*. Christmas markets, decorated with lights and selling all sorts of festive fare, are held in December, from before the Feast of St Nicolas on 6 December to 24 December.

Shoppers thronging a display of fresh wares at a town market

How to Pay

Most high-street shops accept payment by credit or debit card. Most market stalls will only accept cash. However, smaller enterprises are not keen on taking payment with the large-denomination notes, which include the 200-euro and the 500-euro notes.

VAT Refunds

Those who live outside the EU can reclaim the Value Added Tax (TVA in French, BTW in Dutch) for any single transaction to the value of over 125 euros. VAT stands at 21 per cent of the purchase price. Shops that have a Tax-free Shopping logo can provide a Tax-free Shopping Cheque on request (customers will need to show their passport). The purchased items and the documentation are stamped at the airport customs before check in, after which the refund can be collected at the Europe Tax-free Shopping desk. Detailed information is available from the main VAT refund agents **Global Blue** and **Premier Tax Free**.

Clothes Sizes

The EU is in the process of introducing a new set of standardized clothes sizes. At present, however, there are different sizing systems in operation. Some manufacturers even use "vanity sizes", marking larger clothes with smaller sizes to flatter customers. The best advice is for customers to get themselves measured, and certainly to try all clothes on in the shop before making a purchase.

Chocolate and Chocolatiers

High-quality Belgian chocolate is famous all over the world for three reasons. Firstly, Belgian chocolatiers insist on top-quality ingredients, starting with the chocolate itself. This has a high density of cocoa-solids and cocoa-butter, which evaporates on the tongue, giving the flavour a cool and silky lift. Secondly, the Belgians (Jean Neuhaus, in 1912, to be precise) pioneered filled chocolates or pralines. These are made with a variety of fillings including hazelnut cream, fresh cream, marzipan, liqueur and assorted fruit pastes. Lastly, Belgian chocolatiers invented the famous white chocolate, a luxury confection of cocoa-butter and milk.

Large-scale manufacturers for leading brands strictly maintain high standards, and their products are exported all over the world.

Filled chocolates or pralines were originally named for their combination of chocolate and hazelnut cream known as *praline*.

Chocolate Manufacturers

The best-known brands are Corné Port-Royal, Neuhaus, Leonidas and Godiva. They have numerous outlets and sell slabs of chocolates as well as pre-packed boxes of pralines. In Belgium, such boxes are remarkably good value, given their very high quality. A large 750-g (26-oz) box will typically cost about 25–50 euros. Cream-filled chocolates have a limited shelf-life, but will keep fresh for three weeks in cool conditions.

Specialist Chocolatiers

There are many small, specialist chocolatiers creating their own products, especially in the cities and popular towns. A number of pâtissiers run a sideline in handmade chocolates as well. There are also some other good, large-scale manufacturers, whose products reach the supermarkets. These include Guylian, who make pralines in the shape of sea creatures; and Galler, famous for their Langues de Chat brand with artwork by the comic-strip artist Philippe Geluck. Côte d'Or is a brand that produces delicious mini-bars called Mignonnette.

A shop displaying assorted Belgian chocolates

Customers can make their selection from the cabinet, and individual chocolates are picked out by the white-gloved shop assistants, placed in a box, weighed and beautifully wrapped in paper and ribbon.

Displays of chocolate in shops radiate an atmosphere of opulence. They are also incomparable for the sheer variety of shapes and choice of flavours.

Brands of Belgian beer on sale at a specialist beer shop, Bruges

Fashion

Belgian fashion has become a force to be reckoned with since the 1980s, when a group of designers, the Antwerp Six, rose to fame. Among them were Dries van Noten, **Ann Demeulemeester** and **Walter van Beirendonck**. Although each is very different, they all developed a novel urban look, which was sometimes anarchic and controversial, and sometimes demurely chic.

Led by the famous school of fashion at the Royal Academy of Fine Arts, Antwerp is a key player in international fashion and a good place to shop. Dries van Noten has an outlet at **Het Modepaleis**. The shop called **Louis** carries the work of many top designers including Raf Simons and Martin Margiela. Likewise, **Verso** has Kris Van Assche and Dirk Schönberger, as well as international brands. Boutiques are also seen in Kammenstraat, Nationalestraat, Kloosterstraat and Schuttershofstraat. **Coccodrillo** is best for shoes.

Leading designers also have shops in other cities, most notably in Brussels (see p90). **Annemie Verbeke** has an outlet in Brussels, and **Olivier Strelli** has branches in 11 towns and cities in Belgium.

Children's Clothes

Belgians produce some very attractive clothes for children. These are available from specialist high-street shops, such as **Filou & Friends**, as well as department stores such as **Inno** (which has branches in 11 towns and cities) and even the major supermarkets.

Diamonds

Antwerp is the global capital for diamonds – the Jewish Quarter near Centraal Station, is where 70 per cent of the world's diamonds are cut and polished. Retail outlets at Pelikaanstraat and neighbouring streets offer diamonds at prices that are 15–30 per cent lower than prices in the high streets of other European cities. A good place to start is **Diamondland**, the largest diamond shop in the city. Bruges claims to have been a pioneer in diamond cutting and polishing in the 15th century.

Belgian Lace

Lace (see pp30–31) has been a traditional product of Belgium since the 16th century. Handmade lace is expensive. It is available at specialist outlets such as **Manufacture Belge de Dentelles** in Brussels as well as **The Little Lace Shop** and **Kantcentrum** (see p120) in Bruges – both cities long associated with lace-making. The tradition of handmade lace has been dramatically undercut by machine-made lace, particularly from the Far East, and is also available for sale in outlets in Belgium. It is therefore important to insist on a certificate of authenticity.

Beer

It is well worth bringing home some bottles of Belgian beer (see pp278–9). There are at least 400 different beers to choose from, and a huge number of brands. Specialist beer shops such as **The Bottle Shop** and the **Brugse Bierpaleis** in Bruges, and a number of others in Brussels (see p91) offer the best. Supermarkets carry a large stock of many top brands, at the best prices.

Jenever

Belgium produces more than 270 types of this high-quality gin (see p170), including fruit-flavoured *jenever*, Liège *pékèt*, straight *jenever* and associated spirits such as *brandewijn* and *corenwijn*. Some are still sold in traditional ceramic bottles that make intriguing gifts for aficionados of fine spirits. Belgian *jenever* is a gin to be drunk pure and on its own, not with a mixer or even as a chaser. To taste the full range before buying, it is best to go to an authentic specialist bar such as **De Vagant** in Antwerp or **'t Dreupelkot** in Ghent.

Biscuits and Patisserie

Belgium has simply fabulous pâtisseries. Every town has several top-class specialist pâtissiers producing sumptuous chocolate cakes, glazed fruit tarts and a range of simpler tarts based on almonds and *crème pâtissière*. Turnover is high and competition fierce. Therefore, tarts and cakes are remarkably good value for money. Belgium also has a fine

Clothes, purses and tablecloths trimmed with fine Belgian lace

tradition of butter-based biscuits such as crumbly *sablés*, delicately thin and crispy *pain d'amandes* (or *amandelbroodje*) and spicy *speculoos*. The most famous specialist biscuit-maker of Brussels is **Dandoy**. A good, distinctively packaged brand that is available in supermarkets is **Jules Destrooper**.

Comic Books

Brussels, with the comic-strip museum, the Centre Belge de la Bande Dessinée *(see p66)*, cites itself as the comic book capital. However, many cities in Belgium claim this title and specialist comic strip bookshops, with a range of titles, are found in all urban centres.

View of the Belgian Comic Strip Center in Brussels

Tintin Merchandise

Apart from the books, Tintin merchandise includes games, figurines, clothes, key rings and mugs. The brand is very carefully protected and official merchandise is tasteful and made to high standards. There is an official **La Boutique Tintin** in Brussels *(see p91)* and plenty of outlets that sell Tintin items among other stock.

Glass and Leather

The **Cristallerie du Val Saint Lambert** at Seraing, near Liège, has been making fine glass since 1826. Its products, mainly blown, cut and engraved clear and coloured glass, are highly sought after. The factory is now open to the public during demonstrations. The best high-quality leather handbags and suitcases are found at shops of **Delvaux**, a Brussels-based firm with branches in major cities.

DIRECTORY

Where to Shop

Carrefour
🆆 carrefour.eu

Colruyt
🆆 colruyt.be

Cora
🆆 cora.be

Delhaize
🆆 delhaize.be

VAT Refunds

Global Blue
🆆 globalblue.com

Premier Tax Free
🆆 premiertaxwfree.com

Chocolate and Chocolatiers

Corné Port-Royal
🆆 corneportroyal.be

Côte d'Or
🆆 cotedor.com

Galler
🆆 galler.com

Godiva
🆆 godivachocolates.eu

Guylian
🆆 guylian.be

Leonidas
🆆 leonidas.com

Neuhaus
🆆 neuhaus.be

Fashion

Ann Demeulemeester
Leopold de Waelplaats, Antwerp. 🆆 anndemeuleumeester.be

Annemie Verbeke
Rue A. Dansaertstreet 64, 1000 BRU. 🆆 annemieverbeke.be

Coccodrillo
Schuttershofstraat 9, Antwerp. 🆆 coccodrillo.be

DVS
Schuttershofstraat 9. **Tel** (04) 88492814. 🆆 waltervanbeirendonck.be

Het Modepaleis
Nationalestraat 16, Antwerp. 🆆 driesvannoten.be

Labels Inc
Aalmoezenierstraat 3a, Antwerp. **Tel** (03) 232 6056. 🆆 labelsinc.be

Louis
Lombardenvest 2, Antwerp. **Tel** (03) 2329872.

Olivier Strelli
Ave de la Couronne 556, Brussels. **Tel** (02) 8527749. 🆆 strelli.be

Verso
Lange Gasthuisstraat 9, Antwerp. **Tel** (03) 2269 292. 🆆 verso.be

Children's Clothes

Filou & Friends
🆆 filoufriends.com

Inno
🆆 inno.be

Diamonds

Diamondland
Appelmansstraat 33a, Antwerp. **Tel** (03) 3690780.

Belgian Lace

Kantcentrum
Balstraat 16, Bruges. 🆆 kantcentrum.com

The Little Lace Shop
Wijngaardstraat 32, Bruges.

Manufacture Belge de Dentelles
6-8 Galerie de la Reine, 1000 BRU. **Tel** (02) 5114477. 🆆 mbd.be

Beer

The Bottle Shop
Wollestraat 13, Bruges. **Tel** (050) 349980. 🆆 thebottleshop.be

Brugse Bierpaleis
Katelijnestraat 25, Bruges. **Tel** (050) 343161.

Jenever

't Dreupelkot
Groentenmarkt 12, Ghent. **Tel** (09) 2242120. 🆆 dreupelkot.be

De Vagant
Reyndersstraat 25, Antwerp. **Tel** (03) 2331538. 🆆 devagant.be

Biscuits and Patisserie

Dandoy
R au Beurre 31, 1000 BRU. **Tel** (02) 5402702. 🆆 maisondandoy.com

Jules Destrooper
Gravestraats 5, 8647 Ghent. 🆆 destrooper.com

Tintin Merchandise

La Boutique Tintin
Rue de la Colline 13. **Tel** (02) 5145152. 🆆 boutique.tintin.com

Glass and Leather

Cristallerie du Val Saint Lambert
Rue du Val 245, Seraing. **Tel** (04) 3373200. 🆆 val-saint-lambert.com

Delvaux
🆆 delvaux.com

ENTERTAINMENT IN BELGIUM

In an understated manner, Belgium has a thriving cultural life, showcasing top-quality international and regional performers in all fields. The country has produced major talent, particularly in modern dance, film and in the contemporary arts scene. On a more communal level, town squares and parks host a variety of concerts, usually during summer, for the benefit of local citizens. It is also for their entertainment that most Belgian bars encourage musicians, while clubs and dance halls provide venues for more interactive fun. Among more traditional attractions are the many vibrant carnivals, whose colourful pageants involve all levels of the society.

Listings

Free listings for all forms of entertainment are available at the tourist offices, or in shops, hotels and bars. *Agenda* is one such trilingual magazine. *The Bulletin* has a purely online presence (www.xpats.com) and provides news, reviews and listings. Likewise, leading newspapers (*see p321*) also carry event listings.

There are several useful websites, notably xPats, **Net Events** and **Visit Belgium**, site of the Belgian tourist office in the USA and Canada. Cinema listings can be found online at **Cinebel** and **Cinenews**. Jazz details are available at **Jazz in Belgium**, while rock and pop concert information is given at the **Music in Belgium** site. Club and disco listings can be found at Noctis and **Dance Vibes**.

Opera

Belgium has four major opera houses – in Antwerp, Brussels, Ghent and Liège. The Opera Ballet Vlaanderen (*see p139*) and La Monnaie in Brussels (*see p92*) are both sumptuously elegant in the traditional 18th-century style. Ghent and Antwerp mount performances by the Flemish company, **Opera Ballet Vlaanderen**, while Liège is the home of the **Opéra Royal de Wallonie**. Operas also take place in the main theatres of Charleroi, Mons and Namur.

Ballet and Dance

Contemporary dance is strong in Belgium and has had a huge international impact. Among its leaders is Anna Teresa de Keersmaeker and her Rosas company (*see p92*). **Charleroi/Danses** is the company of the Centre Chorégraphique de la Communauté Française Wallonie-Bruxelles. Directed by Michèle Anne de Mey and others, it performs at Les Écuries in Charleroi, and at La Raffinerie in Brussels. The world-renowned **Royal Ballet of Flanders** is estab-lished in Antwerp, but performs across Belgium and internationally. Dance performances feature in most theatres and concert venues around the country.

Classical Music

Very high standards of music are maintained by Belgium's leading music schools, such as the **Conservatoire Royal de Musique** in Brussels and the **Conservatoire Royal de Liège**. The capital has several important concert halls (*see p92*), but all major cities have their equivalents. One to look out for is the extremely modern **Concertgebouw** in Bruges. The Salle Philharmonique de Liège, former concert hall of the Conservatoire, is now operated by the **Philharmonic Orchestra of Liège**. Concerts are also held at the splendid Art Deco **Le Forum**. Classical and other types of music are performed at both **Koningin Elisabethzaal**

A spirited performance of the popular classical *Swan Lake* ballet by the Royal Ballet of Flanders

Jazz troupe jamming on stage during a jazz festival outside Brussels

and the modern multi-purpose **deSingel** in Antwerp. Likewise, it is featured at key venues in smaller cities such as the **Palais des Beaux Arts** in Charleroi.

The biggest music event in Belgium is the **Festival of Flanders** (June–December). Classical concerts, plus ballet and opera, are performed in historic houses, churches and halls. The **Festival de Wallonie** (June–October) is the southern equivalent of this event.

Rock, Pop and World Music

Belgium is in the middle of the European tour map for top international artists, rock, pop and world music bands. Fans cross borders to take advantage of cheap tickets and better venues. The biggest concerts take place in Brussels (*see pp92–3*) or at the **Lotto Arena** (Sportspaleis) in Antwerp and some at local venues such as Hasselt's **Muziekodroom**.

Belgium's summer outdoor rock festivals also attract great international attention. They frontline with the current top international acts, and, cost-wise, are considered a bargain. The best known is **Rock Werchter**, which takes place close to Leuven in early July. The mid-July **Dour Festival**, near Mons, is making a name for its techno-oriented fare. In June, **Couleur Café** brings the best of African and South American music to the heart of Brussels. **Pukkelpop** takes place in Hasselt in late August and attracts impressive line-ups. Bruges holds the respected but low-key Cactusfestival (*see p37*) as well as **Moods!**, a low-cost series of concerts held in July and August. Fans of contemporary French singer-songwriters attend the **Francofolies de Spa** in July.

Jazz

Belgium's lively jazz scene features home-grown talent playing in European, New Orleans, contemporary and fusion styles. The great jazz guitarist Django Reinhardt (1910–53) was born here, and so was Toots Thielemans (b.1922), hailed as the world's best jazz harmonica player.

In Antwerp, the **Jazzcafé Hopper** and **De Muze**, an easy-going place with live jazz every night, are excellent. Antwerp's highly respected biennial festival, the **Jazz Middelheim**, has attracted top international names since 1969. Equally star-studded is the annual countrywide **Skoda Jazz Festival**, from October to December. Brussels holds an annual Jazz Marathon (*see p92*). In Ghent, a must-visit is the Art Nouveau **Damberd Jazz Café**, which has live music on Tuesdays. The folksy **Hotsy Totsy** café is also popular. Bruges's **De Werf** is an eagerly attended jazz venue.

Cinema

The film industry in Belgium is quite active, with noted directors whose works win international attention and awards. These include Jaco van Dormael (*Toto the Hero*, 1991; *The Eighth Day*, 1996), Rémy

Belvaux (*Man Bites Dog*, 1992), Alain Berliner (*Ma Vie en Rose*, 1997), Luc and Jean-Pierre Dardenne (*Rosetta*, 1999), Dominique Deruddere (*Everybody's Famous!*, 2000), Nic Balthazar (*BenX*, 2007) and Gérard Corbiau (*Farinelli*, 1999). Actors Jean-Claude Van Damme and Audrey Hepburn were born in Brussels.

Most international films shown are, of course, usually in their original versions. If neither dubbed nor subtitled, they are listed as VO (*version originale*) or OV (*originele versie*). "VO st-bil" or "OV Fr/NL ot" indicate a subtitled version. There are cinemas of all kinds, from small enterprises to huge multiplexes. Belgium also hosts small, specialist film festivals, with the Flanders Film Festival (*see p38*) in Ghent being the best known.

Theatre

There are plenty of fine theatres in Belgium, with most plays staged in either French or Dutch. Many theatres feature mixed programmes of theatre, dance and music. The **Bruges Stadsschouwburg** hosts a blend of theatre, dance and concerts, while the **Antwerp Stadsschouwburg** is dominated by musicals. The **Bourla Schouwburg**, also in Antwerp, maintains a fine programme of plays performed mainly by its Toneelhuis repertory company. Antwerp's multi-purpose concert hall deSingel also runs a highly respected theatre programme. Other noted theatres include **Théâtre Royal de Mons** and **Théâtre de Namur**. The capital also has many venues of note for theatre (*see p93*).

Bright lights and energetic crowds at the Pukkelpop rock festival in Hasselt

Mixed Arts and Music Festivals

The **Europalia** festival is a biennial, countrywide event, focussing on a specific theme, usually the culture of a chosen foreign partner-country. Lasting four months, it presents an ambitious programme of fine music, cinema, dance, theatre and literary events. Belgium's most warm-spirited annual festival is De Gentse Feesten *(see p36)*, a centuries-old celebration where performers, buskers, rock groups and jazz bands compete for the attention of a lively crowd. The Fêtes de Wallonie *(see p38)* is an equally eclectic mix.

Parades and Local Festivals

Pageants and parades fill the streets of towns and cities across Belgium throughout the year. There are several famous carnival parades marking Lent, most notably at Binche and Stavelot, as well as costumed religious processions *(see pp36–9)* at Bruges, Mechelen, Tournai, Dendermonde, Mons, Veurne and a number of other cities across the country, each with its own distinctive flavour. Belgian towns also have local fairs – sometimes called *kermesse* or *kermis*. These are generally celebrated with a parade, a fun fair and several assorted musical events.

Antwerp's energetic nightlife at the upbeat Petrol Club

Casinos

There are several casinos in Belgium, where visitors can play roulette, blackjack, stud poker, slot machines and so on. The most famous are the **Casino Knokke** and the **Casino Oostende**, but there are others at Namur, Blankenberge and Middelkerke. Associated originally with spa towns, Flemish casinos still carry the name Kursaal (Cure Hall). Spa itself has **Casino de Spa**, while the capital city has **Grand Casino Brussels**. Most establishments have a relaxed atmosphere with a smart-casual dress code. Many also welcome guests who arrive simply to relax at the bar in the early hours.

Clubs and Discos

Antwerp has an international reputation for its spirited club-life. Clubbers from across the country flock to the **Café d'Anvers**, a former church located in Antwerp's red light district, that was turned into a house club in 1991. **Petrol Club** blends hip-hop, electro and rock on its big nights on Fridays and Saturdays. **Red and Blue** is a famous gay club in the city. The Latin-American oriented **Café Local** is also worth a visit. Ghent's most famous nightspot is **Culture Club**. Lier has a reputation for nightlife that far exceeds the town's size, attracting clubbers from countries across the borders and the Netherlands in particular. Its most famous clubs are **Illusion** and **La Rocca**. Bruges has a lively but mercurial clubbing scene – it is best to ask at the tourist office or at a youth hostel for the current popular spots. There are many other clubs and discos, with listings on the Noctis site *(see p93)*.

Colourful costumes at a traditional festival parade in Brussels's Grand Place

DIRECTORY

Listings

Cinebel
w cinebel.be

Cinenews
w cinenews.be

Dance Vibes
w dancevibes.be

Jazz in Belgium
w jazzinbelgium.com

Music in Belgium
w musicinbelgium.net

Net Events
w netevents.org

Visit Belgium
w visitbelgium.com

Opera Houses

Opera Ballet Vlaanderen
Van Ertbornstraat 8, Antwerp.
Schouwburgstraat 3, Ghent. **Tel** (070) 220202.
w operaballet.be

Opéra Royal de Wallonie
Place de l'Opéra, Liège.
Tel (04) 2214722.
w operaliege.be

Ballet and Dance

Charleroi/Danses
Les Ecuries, Blvd Pierre Mayence 65c, Charleroi.
Tel (071) 311212.
w charleroi-danses.be

Royal Ballet of Flanders
Kattendijkdok-Westkaai 16, Antwerp.
Tel (07) 2220202.
w operaballet.be

Classical Music

Concertgebouw
Het Zand 34, Bruges.
Tel (050) 476999 (tickets).
w concertgebouw.be

Conservatoire Royal de Liège
Rue Forgeur 14, Liège.
Tel (04) 2220306.
w crlg.be

Conservatoire Royal de Musique
Rue de la Régence 30, BRU. **Tel** (02) 5110427.
w conservatoire.be

Desingel
Desguinlei 25, Antwerp.
Tel (03) 2482828.
w desingel.be

Festival of Flanders
Vlasmarkt 4, Tongeren.
Tel (012) 235719.
w festival.be

Festival de Wallonie
Rue de l'Armée Grouchy 20, Namur.
Tel (081) 733781.
w festivaldewallonie.be

Le Forum
Rue Pont d'Avroy 14, Liège. **Tel** (04) 2231818.
w leforum.be

Koningin Elisabethzaal
Koningin Astridplein 26, Antwerp.
Tel 0900 00311.
w fccc.be

Palais des Beaux Arts
Place du Manège 1, Charleroi. **Tel** (071) 311212. w pba.be

Philharmonic Orchestra of Liège
Salle Philharmonique, Boulevard Piercot 25, Liège. **Tel** (04) 2200000.
w oprl.be

Jazz

Damberd Jazz Café
Korenmarkt 19, Ghent.
Tel (09) 3295337.

Hotsy Totsy
Hoogstraat 1, Ghent.
Tel (09) 2242012.

Jazz Middelheim
w jazzmiddelheim.be

Jazzcafé Hopper
Leopold de Waelstraat 2, Antwerp.
Tel (03) 2484933.
w cafehopper.be

De Muze
Melkmarkt 15, Antwerp.
Tel (03) 2260126.

Skoda Jazz Festival
w skodajazz.be

De Werf
Werfstraat 108, Bruges.
Tel (050) 330529.
w dewerf.be

Rock, Pop and World music

Couleur Café
w couleurcafe.be

Dour Festival
w dourfestival.eu

Francofolies de Spa
Rue Rogier 2b, Spa.
Tel (070) 660601.
w francofolies.be

Moods!
w moodsbrugge.be

Lotto Arena
Schijnpoortweg 119, Antwerp.
Tel (03) 4004040.
w lotto-arena.be

Muziekodroom
Bootstraat 9, Hasselt.
Tel (011) 231313.
w muziekodroom.be

Pukkelpop
w pukkelpop.be

Rock Werchter
w rockwerchter.be

Theatres

Antwerp Stadsschouwburg
Theaterplein 1, Antwerp.
w stadsschouwburg antwerpen.be

Bourla Schouwburg
Komedieplaats 18, Antwerp.
Tel (03) 2248844.
w toneelhuis.be

Bruges Stadsschouwburg
Vlamingstraat 29, Bruges.
Tel (050) 443060.
w ccbrugge.be

Théâtre de Namur
Place du Théâtre 2, Namur.
Tel (081) 226026.
w theatredenamur.be

Théâtre Royal de Mons
Grand Place 1, Mons.
Tel (065) 395939.
w mons.be

Mixed Arts and Music Festivals

Europalia
Galerie Ravenstein 4, 1000 Bruges.
Tel (02) 5049120.
w europalia.be

Casinos

Casino de Spa
Rue Royale 4, Spa.
Tel (087) 772052.
w casinodespa.be

Casino Knokke
Zeedijk-Albertstrand 509, Knokke-Heist.
Tel (050) 630500.
w grandcasino knokke.be

Casino Oostende
Kursaal-Oosthelling 12, Oostende.
Tel (059) 705111.
w casinooostende.be

Grand Casino Brussels
Boulevard Anspach 30, 1000 BRU. **Tel** (02) 3000100. w viage.be

Clubs and Discos

Café d'Anvers
Verversrui 15, Antwerp.
Tel (03) 2263870.
w cafe-d-anvers.com

Café Local
Walsekaai 25, Antwerp.
Tel (03) 5000367.
w cafelocal.be

Culture Club
Afrikalaan 174, Ghent.
Tel (09) 2770237.
w cultureclub.be

Illusion
Mechelsesteenweg 382, Lier.
Tel (015) 310377.

Petrol Club
D'Herbouvillekaai 25, Antwerp.
Tel (03) 2264963.
w petrolclub.be

Red and Blue
Lange Schipperskapelstraat 11–13, Antwerp.
Tel (03) 2130555.
w redandblue.be

La Rocca
Antwerpsesteenweg 384, Lier.
Tel (03) 4891767.
w larocca.be

SHOPPING AND ENTERTAINMENT IN LUXEMBOURG

Nowhere is the prosperity of Luxembourg more evident than in the elegant shopping streets of Luxembourg City's Old Town. This is echoed on a minor scale in all major towns, where even the bakers, butchers and pharmacies have a refined and cultured quality. Luxembourg City also has an entertainment agenda that matches its rank as an important capital of the European Union. It draws international audiences from Belgium, France and Germany. A number of other towns have also developed reputations for consistently mounting music and arts festivals of impressive stature.

Twice-weekly vegetable market at Place Guillaume II, Luxembourg City

Opening Hours

Shops are open on Monday afternoons, and from 8am to noon and 2 to 6pm between Tuesday and Saturday. Many shops in larger towns stay open during lunch. Most are closed on Sunday.

Where to Shop

In Luxembourg City, the main shopping streets are in the pedestrianized area around the Place d'Armes and Place Guillaume II. These have stylish boutiques selling luxury goods, international fashions and accessories, as well as souvenirs and crafts. For more moderate prices, the streets near the railway station are a good hunting ground. The **Auchan** shopping centre in Kirchberg is a flagship branch of the Europe-wide supermarket chain, and a good place to buy general provisions. There are massive shopping centres dotted around the country, such as the **Centre Commercial Belle Étoile** at Bertrange.

Wine

Luxembourg wine is available throughout the country, but it is worth visiting its place of origin, the Moselle valley (see p252). Poll-Fabaire, specialist in sparkling wine, has showrooms and a shop at **Caves Vinicoles de Wormeldange**. The largest private wine producer is **Bernard-Massard** at Grevenmacher, whose labels include Château de Schengen, Clos des Rochers and Cuvée de l'Ecusson. The stylish **Cep d'Or** is a family-run winery known for its Gewürztraminer and Chardonnay.

Chocolate

The famous 1863-established chocolate maker **Namur**, is headquartered in Luxembourg City. It also specializes in ice cream, pâtisserie and sweets.

Markets

The best-known flea market takes place at the capital's Place d'Armes every second and fourth Saturday. Place Guillaume II has a vegetable market on Wednesday and Saturday. Bright Christmas markets spring up in town squares between 6 December and Christmas Eve.

Entertainment Listings

The Luxembourg City Tourist Office offers an online service, **Agenda**, which publishes a reliable set of listings. Listings can be found at the website of **Luxembourg-ticket.lu**.

Classical Music, Dance and Theatre

The beautiful **Philharmonie Luxembourg**, completed in 2005, offers classical music concerts, chamber music as well as more popular fare. The **Grand Théâtre de la Ville de Luxembourg** is the main venue for touring companies performing opera, ballet and dance. It also mounts theatre productions. The **Luxembourg Festival** of music, opera, theatre and dance in October and November is a joint venture by Philharmonie Luxembourg and the Grand Théâtre de la Ville de Luxembourg. **Théâtre National du Luxembourg** runs plays that often involve actors of international standing. An eclectic mix of performances and exhibitions is shown at the **Centre Culturel de Rencontre Abbaye de Neumünster**. Since 1975, Echternach has held an **International Festival of Music** over May and June, with classical music and jazz, staged at Église St-Pierre-et-St-Paul and the Trifolion auditorium. The **Open-air Festival of Theatre and Music** at Wiltz (weekends

A performance from the Open-air Festival of Theatre and Music, Wiltz

in July) presents a rich and varied programme of music, opera and dance.

Contemporary Music

The main venue for rock and pop in the country is **Rockhal** in Esch-sur-Alzette. Its two-hall complex hosts major international acts. Smaller concerts are held in the capital at **Den Atelier**. The biggest rock festival is the one-day **Rock-A-Field**, held near Roeser, on the last Sunday in June. Its frontline billing has become increasingly impressive over the years. Luxembourg City has music festivals running over much of the year. **Printemps Musical-Festival de Luxembourg** presents a broad mix, from jazz to world music. **Summer in the City** (mid-June to mid-September) offers free open-air jazz and blues

Crowds gathered for the open-air Summer in the City festival

concerts. This includes **Rock um Knuedler** (first Sunday of July), a free rock concert at Place Guillaume II and Place Clairfontaine. The **Blues 'n Jazz Rallye** occurs in mid-July in pubs and on open-air stages in the Grund and Clausen.

Cinema

Films are usually shown in their original language with subtitles. Luxembourg City has two multi-screen cinemas showing the latest international offerings – **Ciné Utopia** and **Utopolis**. Film buffs should look out for the programme of arthouse and classic movies presented by **Cinémathèque de la Ville de Luxembourg**.

Clubs and Discos

The capital has an active night-life, especially the area around the station and the adjacent suburb of Hollerich. However, popular venues are mercurial and seem to close just as soon as they get established. The three-storey **Byblos** offers weekend disco and DJs, and prides itself on its sedate vibe. A mellow venue, popular with the student crowd, is **Melusina**. It has different spaces offering a variety of grooves, and a reasonably priced restaurant as well.

DIRECTORY

Where to Shop

Auchan
Rue Alphonse Weicker, 5
Luxembourg City.
Tel 437 743-1.
W auchan.lu

Centre Commercial Belle Étoile
Route d'Arlon, Bertrange.
Tel 28289002.
W belle-etoile.lu

Wine

Bernard-Massard
Route du Vin, 8,
Grevenmacher.
Tel 750545228.
W bernard-massard.lu

Caves Vinicoles de Wormeldange
Route de Vin 115,
Wormeldange.
Tel 768211.
W vinsmoselle.lu

Cep d'Or
Route du Vin 15,
Hëttermillen.
Tel 768383.
W cepdor.lu

Chocolate

Namur
Rue des Capucins 27,
Luxembourg City.
Tel 223408.
W namur.lu

Entertainment Listings

Agenda
W visitluxembourg.lu

Luxembourgticket.lu
Tel 470895-1.
W luxembourgticket.lu

Classical Music, Dance and Theatre

Centre Culturel de Rencontre Abbaye de Neumünster
Rue Münster 28,
Luxembourg City.
Tel 262 052-1.
W ccrn.lu

Grand Théâtre de la Ville de Luxembourg
Rond-point Schuman 1,
Luxembourg City.
Tel 47963900.
W theater-vdl.lu

International Festival of Music
Echternach.
Tel 727112.
W echternachfestival.lu

Luxembourg Festival
Luxembourg City.
W luxembourg festival.lu

Open-air Festival of Theatre and Music
Tel 958145.
W festivalwiltz.lu

Philharmonie Luxembourg
Place de l'Europe 1,
Luxembourg City.
Tel 26322632.
W philharmonie.lu

Théâtre National du Luxembourg
Route de Longwy 194,
Luxembourg City.
Tel 26441270.
W tnl.lu

Contemporary Music

Blues 'n Jazz Rallye
W bluesjazzrallye.lu

Den Atelier
Rue de Hollerich, 54,
Luxembourg-City.
Tel 495 485-1.
W atelier.lu

Printemps Musical-Festival de Luxembourg
W printempsmusical.lu

Rock-A-Field
Roeser.
W atelier.lu

Rock um Knuedler
W rockumknuedler.lu

Rockhal
Esch-sur-Alzette. **Tel** 245 551. W rockhal.lu

Summer in the City
W summerinthecity.lu

Cinema

Cinémathèque de la Ville de Luxembourg
Place du Théâtre 17,
Luxembourg City.
Tel 291259.
W cinematheque.lu

Ciné Utopia
Ave de la Faïencerie 16,
Luxembourg City. **Tel** 224 611. W utopolis.lu

Utopolis Kirchberg
Avenue JF Kennedy 45,
Luxembourg City.
Tel 429 511-1.
W utopolis.lu

Clubs and Discos

Byblos
Rue du Fort Niepperg 58,
Luxembourg City.
Tel 24873321.
W byblos.lu

Melusina
Rue de la Tour Jacob 145,
Clausen, Luxembourg
City. **Tel** 435922.
W melusina.lu

SPORTS AND OUTDOOR ACTIVITIES

Belgium and Luxembourg are well known for periodically producing a flurry of exceptional sporting talent, such as the cyclist Eddy Merckx or the tennis players Justine Henin, Kim Clijsters and David Goffin. There is a constant level of activity in all fields of sport, especially soccer, water sports, cycling, golf, horse riding and judo. Visitors are always welcome to join in.

Popular holiday activities are cycling, walking, kayaking and windsurfing, as these take full advantage of the hills, rivers, lakes and coastline. Both countries have promoted this by creating an extensive network of paths for the exclusive use of cyclists, walkers and riders, with links to accommodation. Here is a chance not only to get healthy, but also have a holiday.

Cyclists dressed for the part in Belgium

Cycling

As a convenient mode of transport, a leisure pursuit and a major professional sport, cycling is big in Belgium. Consequently, there is no shortage of specialist shops, bike-hire companies or cycle routes. The flat landscape in much of Flanders is ideally suited to touring by bicycle. The Ardennes in Wallonia and Luxembourg present more of a challenge, with specialist circuits for mountain bikes.

A number of long-distance cycling routes cross this region. In Flanders, **LF Routes** (Landelijk Fietsplatform routes) take cycle-friendly paths between strategic destinations. The **RAVel** network consists of five routes that criss-cross Wallonia, and are reserved for bicycles, other non-motorized vehicles and pedestrians. The roads tend to follow disused railway- and tram-lines and canal towpaths. The longest, RAVel 1, goes east to west via Tournai, Mons, Namur and Liège, while RAVel 2 runs north to south via Namur and Dinant. **Rando Vélo** provides information about long-distance cycling

routes. Another useful reference is the cycling promoter, **Pro Vélo**. Luxembourg's equivalent of the RAVel network – **Fédération du Sport Cycliste Luxembourgeois** – has built some 575 km (355 miles) of dedicated cycle paths, and plans to double that length.

Hiking and Rambling

Belgium and Luxembourg offer some of northern Europe's most rewarding walks. The region is crossed by several of the marked transnational **Les Sentiers de Grande Randonnée** (Long-distance Paths). One of these is the GR 5, which links the Netherlands to the Mediterranean via Liège and Luxembourg. Another, the GR AE (Ardennes–Eifel) includes the Semois valley (see pp232–3). GR 56 crosses the Hautes Fagnes (see p227); GR 57 follows the valley of River Ourthe past Durbuy, Hotton and La Roche-en-Ardenne (see p230) into Luxembourg; GR 129 links the rivers Scheldt and Meuse; and GR 12 joins Paris to Amsterdam via Brussels. The RAVel routes in Wallonia are also open to walkers. There are many other circular paths, for instance, around Bouillon (see p234), Rochefort (see p215) and Echternach (see p255): maps are available at the local tourist offices. There are also marked paths for short walks in wood-

land areas such as Nationaal Park Hoge Kempen (see p172), Averbode Bos (see p166) and Forêt de Soignes (see p169).

Luxembourg has a dense network of paths, totalling over 5,000 km (3,100 miles) in length. Many begin at a point accessible by train or car. The popular Müllerthal Trail in Little Switzerland (see p254) has 100 km (62 miles) of interlinked paths.

Marathons

The biggest race in Belgium is **20 km de Bruxelles**, a half-marathon run by some 25,000 participants in May. In the same month, Luxembourg has a full marathon. Known as **The Night Run**, it begins at 6pm and may continue past midnight. This event is coupled with a half-marathon.

Grand Duke Henri of Luxembourg in the Luxembourg City marathon

Canoeists at the launch of a voyage on the River Ambléve, near Coo

Swimming

There are plenty of public swimming pools in Belgium and Luxembourg. In many of these, both men and women are expected to wear bathing caps, usually available at the pool. Lifeguards oversee swimming areas at the coast and hoist flags to indicate swimming conditions: a red flag means bathing is forbidden, a yellow flag calls for extra caution and a green flag means safe conditions. Various lakes also have swimming beaches, such as at the Lacs de l'Eau d'Heure (see p195).

Fishing

There is fishing of all kinds: on the coast, in rivers, lakes and canals. A permit is needed for inland fishing. Details of this are available from the **Service de la Pèche** at the Ministry of the Wallon Region and the **Fédération Sportive des Pêcheurs Francophone de Belgique**. In Luxembourg, permits are issued by local authorities or District Commissariats, with details at tourist offices.

Kayaking and Canoeing

The best-known locations for kayaking and canoeing are on Amblève (see p229), Semois (see p232–3), Lesse (see p215) and Ourthe (see p230). All of these have centres offering equipment and guides. The **Nederlandstalig Kano Verbond**, the **Fédération Francophone de Canoë et Kayak** and the **Fédération Luxembourgeoise de Canoë-Kayak** offer information for novices and experts.

Waterskiing

The lakes and broad rivers of Belgium have numerous waterskiing centres. These include the lakes of Barrage de l'Eau d'Heure and the River Meuse (see p210) near Wépion and Profondeville. A good source of information is the **Fédération Francophone du Ski Nautique Belge**. Its parallel in Luxembourg, for waterskiing on the Moselle (see p253) and various lakes is the **Union Luxembourgeoise de Ski Nautique**.

Windsurfing

The brisk breezes of the coast provide excellent conditions for windsurfing. De Panne, Nieuwpoort, Oostende, De Haan, Zeebrugge and Knokke-Heist (see pp122–3) are all noted windsurfing centres, with surf shops where equipment can be bought or hired. On beaches shared with swimmers, there are separate windsurfing areas

demarcated. Windsurfing is practised on some recreational lakes (see p195) as well. Kite-surfing is also popular on the coast.

Sailing

Coastal sailing focusses on the main ports and marinas at Nieuwpoort, Oostende, Blankenberge and Zeebrugge. There is also dinghy sailing on some of the larger lakes. Sailing federations such as **Fédération Francophone du Yachting Belge (FFYB)** and **Vlaamse Vereniging voor Watersport** provide useful information. Luxembourg likewise has a number of opportunities for sailing, overseen by the **Fédération Luxembourgeoise de Voile**.

Sand Yachting

At low tide, the hard surface of the sand beaches along Belgium's coast provide the perfect conditions for sand yachts – wheeled vehicles with sails. This amusement is centuries old; the great Bruges-born mathematician Simon Stevin (1548–1620), had a 26-person sand yacht with two sails. The modern version was invented in the late 19th century near De Panne, the main centre for the sport. Novices must take a training course, for example, at the **Royal Sand Yacht Club**, to obtain a permit for recreational sand yachting.

Professional Cycling

Belgium ranks among the world's top professional cycling nations. It produced probably the greatest cyclist to date: Eddy Merckx (b.1945), five times winner of the Tour de France and winner of over 140 other titles. Other great names include Rik Van Looy (b.1933) and Roger de Vlaeminck (b.1947). Belgium hosts several of the most important world cycling events, including two of the five one-day classics called the Monuments. Of these, the Ronde van Vlaanderen (see p36) includes the notorious cobbled climb, the Mur de Grammont, while the Liège–Bastogne–Liège takes place in the Ardennes. First held in 1882, the latter is the oldest of the Monuments. Other key events include the Flèche Wallonne in April, and the four-day Tour of Belgium in late May–early June. Zesdaagse Vlaanderen-Gent, the six-day European speed cycling race, is held in late November.

A cyclist speeds to victory

Horse riding through the undulating landscape at Oostduinkerke

Golf

There are several excellent golf courses in Belgium, such as the **Royal Zoute Club** in Knokke. For Wallonia, these are listed by the **Association Francophone de Golf Belge**. The governing body of the sport is the **Royal Belgian Golf Federation**. Luxembourg has six major golf courses, including **Golf-Club Grand-Ducal**, 7 km (4 miles) from the capital city. Information is available from the **Fédération Luxembourgeoise de Golf**.

Tennis

Belgium's two former great tennis stars, Justine Henin and Kim Clijsters, have made this game particularly popular, and there are numerous outdoor and indoor courts throughout the country. The top-ranking Proximus Diamond Games, an international ladies tournament, takes place in Antwerp in February. The umbrella organizations for tennis in Belgium and Luxembourg are the **Fédération Royale Belge de Tennis** and the **Fédération Luxembourgeoise de Tennis** respectively.

Rock-Climbing

The rivers of the Ardennes have carved out some dramatic gorges, with the result that rock-climbing and mountaineering (*alpinisme* in French) present rewarding challenges. The best sites are in the valleys of the rivers Meuse and Ourthe: the **Club Alpin Belge** provides information. Pot-holing, another hill pursuit, is overseen by the **Union Belge de Spéléologie**. In Luxembourg, a permit must be obtained from the Ministry of Environment to climb in the best-known area – Müllerthal, near Berdorf (*see p254*).

Horse Riding and Horse Racing

There is plenty of opportunity for riding in both these countries, with stables scattered all over the region. Many rural B&Bs provide riding facilities, and some can even stable their guests' horses. There is a good network of accommodation linked by routes for riders. This is run by **L'Association Wallonne de Tourisme Equestre**. Other important riding associations are the **Fédération Belge des Sports Equestres**, **Fédération Francophone d'Equitation** and **Fédération Luxembourgeoise de Sports Equestres**.

Horse racing takes place at Oostende – the **Hippodrome Wellington** hosts the Grand Prix Prince Rose in July. The Great Flanders Steeple Chase takes place at Waregem in August. The **Hippodrome de Wallonie** at Mons is also a key racing venue. The **Jockey Club de Belgique** has details.

Railbikes

Old Western comedy films feature wheeled handcars moved by pumping a pivoted double handle. Visitors can now do the same with pedal-powered railbikes (*draisines* in French) on some disused railway lines. These family-sized **Railbikes of the Molignée** can be rented near Maredsous (*see p210*), for circuits of up to 14 km (8 miles). Railbikes are also available at Tessenderlo, near Diest (*see p166–7*).

Skiing

When winter coats the higher parts of the Ardennes with snow, Belgians reach for their skis. There are several centres geared up for this sport. Some have lifts for downhill skiing, but cross-country skiing is the primary pursuit. The main ski areas are in the east and south: around Spa, in the Cantons de l'Est and in the Hautes Fagnes. Tobogganing, snow-shoeing and skidooing are popular at Bastogne, Martelange, Bouillon and St-Hubert. In Luxembourg, cross-country skiing is found in the north, at places such as Weiswampach, Asselborn and Hosingen. **Ardenne Tourisme** has a website with information on snow conditions.

Ice-Skating

During very cold winters, the canals and ponds freeze over, and become ideal for skating. In December, towns such as Brussels, Antwerp and Bruges, create ice rinks in their central squares as part of their Christmas market attractions. Skaters can also go to indoor rinks year-round, for example at Namur, Charleroi or Liège.

Motor-Racing

Formula 1 Grand Prix motor racing takes place at the circuit in **Spa-Francorchamps** (*see p228*). This is considered by many aficionados to be one of the most challenging tracks. The race is held over a weekend in early September.

Football

In Belgium, football is followed with passion. The main clubs are **Anderlecht**, **Club Brugge** and **Standard de Liège**, all of which regularly feature in the upper echelons of European championship competitions. The Diables Rouges (or Rode Duivels), Belgium's national team, has an honourable World Cup record, even if it has not yet captured the top prize. The national stadium is the **Stade Roi Baudouin** at Heysel, in northern Brussels.

DIRECTORY

Cycling

Fédération du Sport Cycliste Luxembourgeois
Route d'Arlon 3, Strassen.
Tel 292317.
w fscl.lu

LF Routes
w routeyou.com

Pro Vélo
Tel (02) 5027355.
w provelo.be

Rando Vélo
w randovelo.org

RAVel
w ravel.wallonie.be

Hiking and Rambling

Les Sentiers de Grande Randonnée
w grsentiers.org

Marathons

20 km de Bruxelles
w 20kmdebruxelles.be

The Night Run
w ing-europe-marathon.lu

Fishing

Fédération Sportive des Pêcheurs Francophone de Belgique
Tel (081) 413491.
w pecheurbelge.be

Service de la Pèche
Ave Gouverneur Bovesse 100, Jambes.
Tel (081) 335900.
w belgium.be/fr/environnement/biodiversite_et_nature/conservation_de_la_nature

Kayaking and Canoeing

Fédération Francophone de Canoë et Kayak
w ffckayak.be

Fédération Luxembourgeoise de Canoë-Kayak
w flck.lu

Nederlandstalig Kano Verbond
w nkv.be

Waterskiing

Fédération Francophone du Ski Nautique Belge
w skinautique.be

Union Luxembourgeoise de Ski Nautique
w lwwf.lu

Sailing

Fédération Francophone du Yachting Belge
Ave du Parc d'Armée 90, Jambes. Tel (081) 304979.
w ffyb.be

Fédération Luxembourgeoise de Voile
w flv.lu

Vlaamse Vereniging voor Watersport
Beatrijslaan 25, Antwerp.
Tel (03) 2196967.
w vvw.be

Sand Yachting

Royal Sand Yacht Club
Dynastielaan 20, De Panne.
Tel (058) 420808.
w rsyc.be

Golf

Association Francophone de Golf Belge
Tel (02) 6790220.
w afgolf.be

Fédération Luxembourgeoise de Golf
Domaine de Belenhaff, Junglinster.
Tel 26782383.
w flgolf.lu

Gold-Club Grand-Ducal
Route de Trèves 1, Senningerberg.
Tel 340 090.
w gcgd.lu

Royal Belgian Golf Federation
Chausée de la Hulpe 110, BRU. Tel (02) 6722389.
w golfbelgium.be

Royal Zoute Club
Caddiespad 14, 8300 Knokke.
Tel (050) 601617.
w zoute.be

Tennis

Fédération Luxembourgeoise de Tennis
Blvd Hubert Clement, Esch-sur-Alzette.
Tel 574 4701.
w flt.lu

Fédération Royale Belge de Tennis
Galerie de la Porte Louise 203/3, 1050 BRU.
Tel (02) 5480304.
w frbt.be

Rock-Climbing

Club Alpin Belge
129, Ave Albert I, Namur.
Tel (081) 234320.
w clubalpin.be

Union Belge de Spéléologie
Ave Arthur Procès 5, Namur. Tel (081) 230009.
w speleoubs.be

Horse Riding and Horse Racing

L'Association Wallonne de Tourism Equestre
Tel (071) 818292.
w awte.be

Fédération Belge des Sports Equestres
Tel (02) 4785056.
w equibel.be

Fédération Francophone d'Equitation
Tel (081) 390640.
w ffe.be

Fédération Luxembourgeoise de Sports Equestres
Tel 484999.
w flse.lu

Hippodrome de Wallonie
w hippodromede wallonie.be

Hippodrome Wellington
Koningin Astridlaan.
Tel (059) 806055.
w oostendekoerse.be

Jockey Club de Belgique
Tel (02) 6727248.
w jockey-club.be

Railbikes

Railbikes of the Molignée
116 Rue de la Molignée, Warnant.
Tel (082) 699 079.
w draisine.be

Skiing

Ardenne Tourisme
Tel (084) 411981.
w infoski.be

Motor-Racing

Spa-Francorchamps
w spa-francor champs.be

Football

Anderlecht
Tel (02) 5294060.
w rsca.be

Club Brugge
Tel (050) 402121.
w clubbrugge.be

Stade Roi Baudouin
Ave du Marathon 135, BRU. Tel (02) 4743943.

Standard de Liège
Tel (04) 2299898.
w standard.be

Belgium and Luxembourg for Children

A great deal of family-oriented socializing and entertainment occurs in both countries. Museums, amusement parks and galleries are organized with families or school parties in mind. There are also a variety of activities such as rides on historic trains and trips on canal boats. Visitors will therefore find it easy to keep children amused in towns and cities. The countryside has its draws in the form of ancient caves and awe-inspiring fortresses. To add to these experiences are the ever-present treats of Belgian chips and waffles.

Thrilling swings and rides at the Walibi theme park near Wavre

Theme Parks

Visiting theme parks seems to be an integral part of childhood in Belgium, and there are parks to suit people of all ages. Some, notably the **Plopsaland** parks, are specifically aimed at the younger crowd. There are branches at De Panne and Coo, and an indoor Plopsaland at Hasselt. Bobbejaanland *(see p160)*, near Turnhout, is a traditional theme park, packed with thrills-and-spills rides. But the most famous Belgian theme park is Walibi *(see p202)*, near Wavre, to the southeast of Brussels. With its broad variety of rides, from roundabouts to state-of-the-art roller coasters and live entertainment shows, Walibi caters to children of all ages. Attached to it is the swimming complex (pools, shoots, tubes) called Aqualibi. There is a similar swimming complex at Océade, part of the Bruparck complex *(see p88)* on the northern outskirts of Brussels. Bruparck also includes a number of other attractions such as Mini-Europe and a huge cinema complex. Close at hand is the Atomium *(see p88)*, always fascinating to children. The Bellewaerde Park *(see p128)*, near Ieper, combines a collection of zoo animals with theme park rides. The **Boudewijn Seapark**, near Bruges, has a dolphinarium and performing sea lions, as well as a roller coaster, pirate ship and other rides.

Zoos and Aquariums

Shoehorned into a small urban space near the Centraal Station and Diamond District, Belgium's famous **Antwerp Zoo** contains a variety of animals and prides itself on its captive breeding programme and conservation work. The zoo also operates the much larger Planckendael Animal Park *(see p161)* near Mechelen. Pairi Daiza *(see p189)* in Hainaut is very child-friendly. Réserve d'Animaux Sauvages at Han-sur-Lesse *(see p215)* is a safari park with large north European animals such as bears, lynx and bison. The **Monde Sauvage Safari** on the River Amblève *(see p229)* has a more Africa-oriented safari. Bouillon's castle *(see pp236–7)* has a famous falconry show. There are two sealife aquariums on the coast: the Noordzeeaquarium *(see p126)* at Oostende and the **National Sealife Marine Park** at Blankenberge, which also has a **Serpentarium**. Liège's well respected Aquarium *(see p222)* is operated by the university's Institute of Zoology.

Museums and Galleries

Many museums and galleries produce printed documentation to make their exhibits more interesting for children, including lists for treasure hunts. Audioguides also help bring the exhibits alive – at the Musée des Instruments de Musique *(see p69)* in Brussels, visitors can listen to the instruments. Demonstrations and costumed characters at the Bokrijk Openluchtmuseum *(see p171)* make this fine collection of historic rural buildings seem almost lived in.

Museums specifically aimed at children include the toy museums, Musée du Jouet *(see p78)* and Speelgoedmuseum *(see p161)*. The Centre Belge de la Bande Dessinée *(see p66)* appeals more to aficionados of the history of the comic-strip form. There are several interactive science museums such as the **Museum of Natural Sciences**, which has moving dinosaur displays and the skeleton of a blue whale. The Parc d'Attractions Scientifiques *(see p193)* offers a host of introductory exhibits on science and technology.

A string puppet of Pinocchio at Mechelen's Speelgoedmuseum

An old steam powered train at Fond-des-Gras

Steam Trains and Tram Rides

Railway engines and tracks have been preserved in many places in Luxembourg and Belgium, and visitors can now enjoy gentle rides into quiet corners of the countryside and into the past. Maldegem's Stoomcentrum (see p141) runs historic steam and diesel trains. Likewise, Mariembourg is the starting point for train trips on the Chemin de Fer des Trois Vallées (see p214). Visitors can also head off down the tracks under their own steam with a railbike (see p306). The Musée du Transport Urbain Bruxellois (see p89) has rides in a historic tram complete with a hooter-blowing conductor, all the way to Tervuren and the Musée Royale de l'Afrique Centrale, which children also enjoy. The industrial museum of Fond-de-Gras (see p252), in southern Luxembourg, operates steam trains along normal-gauge and narrow-gauge rails.

Canal Boats

Bruges and Ghent are great places in which to take children on a canal boat trip. This offers a completely different view of the cities, as visitors glide gently along in the company of ducks and moorhens, passing under bridges and encountering new aromas. The ever-changing scenery is captivating, for adults and children alike.

Castles and War

Setting alive the imagination with tales of sieges and derring-do are the region's many castles (see pp34–5). Bouillon is the most impressive medieval castle, while Beersel (see p168), Jehay (see p224) and Lavaux-Ste-Anne (see p215) could be the backdrops for fairytales. With its thick walls, turrets and crenellations, Gravensteen (see p138) in Ghent also looks the part; it even has an exhibition of instruments of torture. Children will also enjoy tunnelling around the casemates of Luxembourg City. On a more sombre note, older children may find the museum of the former concentration camp at Fort Breendonk (see p160) impressively chilling. Equally, many older children are moved and amazed by the museums, monuments and exhibits marking World War I (see p130–31), especially the museum called In Flanders Fields at Ieper (see pp128).

Belfries and Towers

Offering the chance to see towns and cities from a new angle, Belgium's many belfries are more than just historic monuments. Narrow spiral staircases climb to the parapet, from where there are fine, and sometimes scary, views over the rooftops and of the ant-like activities below. Visitors may hear the carillon tinkle out a tune, or be deafened by the colossal racket of a big bell as the clock strikes the hour.

Caves

The Ardennes region is riddled with caves, which fascinate children. The most famous of these, at Han-sur-Lesse (see p215), can be explored on foot and by boat. There are many others, each with their own magical landscapes of glittering stalactites and still pools (see pp212–13).

Chips and Waffles

In Belgium, deep-fried food is the basis of traditional snacks. The outdoor frietkoten offer cornets of crispy, double-fried chips with some mayonnaise to dunk them into. There are also sweetened waffles from streetside vendors – the traditional snack of fairs and festivals and of summer holidays on the coast. This is the kind of cultural treat that children the world over really relish.

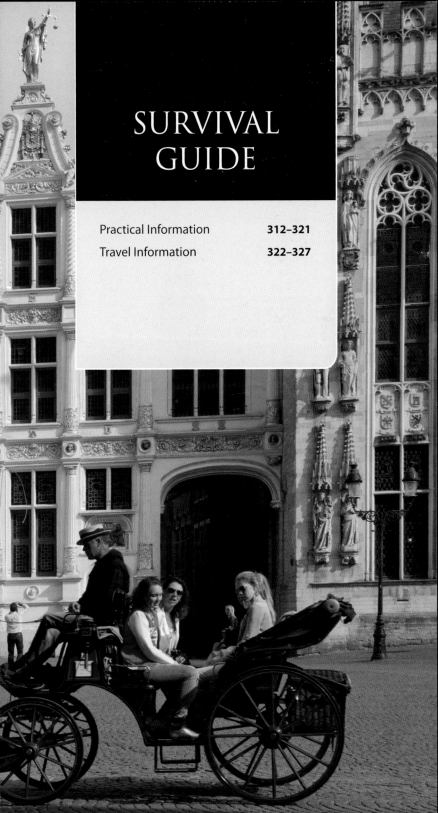

SURVIVAL GUIDE

PRACTICAL INFORMATION

Belgium and Luxembourg are well organized countries, whose people like to see the practicalities of life properly managed in a transparent and efficient manner. Tourism is a major industry in both nations and is actively promoted by the authorities. As a result, tourist offices, both abroad and within the countries, have a wealth of information, much of which is accessible on the Internet. Travel hubs and most towns also have visitor centres. If things go wrong, these centres have helpful, English-speaking people to help sort out problems. However, it is always best to learn a few basic phrases or to take a phrasebook along. In Wallonia, most information is given in French, while in Flanders it is provided in Dutch.

The Grand Place, Brussels, in December

When to Go

Both countries can be visited year-round. However, from April to October there is a better chance of sunshine and mild weather, and towns lay on a host of festivities and outdoor concerts. Summer (June to August) is the height of the tourist season, so all museums, galleries and attractions are open to the fullest schedules. However, Bruges, Belgium's most popular town, has the largst number of vistors in August, when it can get very crowded. From October to March, many of the smaller museums, and the less frequented churches and historic houses, open only at weekends, or may close completely. December has its Christmas markets (see p38) while February and March have carnivals (see p36–9).

What to Pack

Where clothing is concerned, visitors need to think in terms of layers. The average temperatures are 20°C (68°F) in summer and 5°C (41°F) in winter, but the weather is always unpredictable – it is easy to adjust to this by just adding or subtracting a fleece or a cardigan. It is also best to be prepared for wet weather.

Despite Belgium's reputation for cutting-edge fashion, most people dress in a practical, down-to-earth kind of way. Smart-casual would be the dress code for better restaurants and even business meetings and formal occasions. A pair of sturdy walking shoes is recommended to deal with the cobbled streets. Also essential are adaptor plugs for electrical appliances and mosquito repellent for places with open canals, such as Bruges.

Tourist Information

The Belgian authorities, and individual towns and cities, are working hard to promote their country as a holiday destination. They produce copious amounts of promotional material, published both in printed brochures and on the Internet. The degree to which such information is available in English depends to a large extent on how much holiday traffic is expected. Flanders and Wallonia have separate tourist agencies – **Tourism Flanders** and **Belgian Tourist Office**. Abroad, they often have separate offices. Both deal with Brussels,

◀ A horse-drawn carriage in front of the Stadhuis buildings in Burg Square, Brugge

Helpful advice from the Tourist Office in Ghent

although Brussels also has its own agency. The best place to begin looking for information is the Internet. Virtually all towns in Belgium have dedicated websites in the format *www.townname.be* and these generally have links to their tourist offices. Again, almost all towns with any kind of attraction will have a tourist office, often located in the main town square, if not in the town hall itself. Most offices and visitor centres have English-speaking staff. They can provide hotel listings and may even offer to make bookings on a visitor's behalf.

The **Luxembourg Tourist Office** also produces a wealth of visitor information. The Grand Duchy has tourist offices in most locations, which generally follow the format *www.townname.lu* on the Internet.

Visas and Passports

Visitors from countries of the European Union can travel freely to Luxembourg and Belgium provided they have a valid passport or identity card. EU nationals wishing to stay for longer than 90 days should apply for a residence permit at the local town hall within eight days of arrival. Passport-holders from the USA, Canada, Australia, New Zealand and Japan do not require a visa for visits of up to 90 days.

However, regulations may change, so it advisable to check with your local embassy before departure. It is a legal requirement in Belgium to carry identification at all times.

Embassies and Consulates

Belgium has embassies in most capital cities of the world. Queries about visas and other formalities can be addressed to these centres before departure from the home country, although much of this information is available on their official websites. Luxembourg has embassies or consulates in most major countries. Likewise, most nations, including the **UK**, the **USA**, **Canada**, **Australia** and **New Zealand** have embassies in Brussels and Luxembourg.

Customs

Visitors from EU countries travelling to and from Belgium and Luxembourg face almost no restrictions on the quantities of alcohol and tobacco they can carry with them, provided that this is for their personal use. Duty-free goods are available only to nationals of countries outside the EU (such as Canada and the USA). Non-EU visitors can get a tax refund

at the customs desk at the airport on presentation of a completed Tax Free Form and relevant receipts. Local restrictions apply regarding how much visitors can bring into their country of destination.

Travel Safety Advice

Visitors can get up-to-date travel safety information from the **Foreign and Commonwealth Office** in the UK, the **State Department** in the US and the **Department of Foreign Affairs and Trade** in Australia.

Travelling with Children

Belgium and Luxembourg are both family-oriented nations, and children are widely welcomed – provided that they are reasonably well behaved. Restaurants and hotels are accommodating: Belgian children are taken to restaurants from an early age, and soon adopt the gastronomic expertise of their parents.

There are numerous concessions for families, such as reduced-price museum entrance tickets and free public transport for children under the age of six (if accompanied by an adult). Apart from this, there are plenty of attractions and activities to keep children entertained (*see pp308–309*).

It is also easy for parents to get carried away with the variety of beautiful clothes and toys available from the numerous specialist shops in both countries.

Families at the Plopsaland theme park on the Western Flanders coast

Parking spaces for disabled travellers in front of the Palais Royal, Brussels

Facilities for Disabled Travellers

Belgium is full of historic buildings, steps, kerbs, narrow doors and cobbled streets, but little has been done to accommodate people with reduced mobility. The good news is the Belgians are remarkably willing to assist people with disabilities of any kind. Although improvements are being made all the time, facilities for disabled people in hotels, restaurants and public places are far from uniform, so it is wise never to make assumptions about access, and to phone ahead. Local tourist offices can also advise disabled travellers. Various websites provide more detailed information and help, notably those of the **Infopunt Toegankelijk Reizen** (Accessible Travel Info Point) in Flanders, and **Able Travel**. Tourist offices also recommend the services of the **Belgian Red Cross**. **Brussels For All** has web-based information for travellers with reduced mobility. For those travelling in Luxembourg, **Info-Handicap** is the best resource – but its webpages are, at present, in French and German only.

Language

Belgium has two main languages – French (which is spoken in Wallonia in southern Belgium, and in Brussels) and Dutch, which is used in Flanders in northern

Belgium *(see p133)*. In addition, German is the third offical language, used in the Cantons de l'Est. English is widely spoken within the tourist industry, especially in the main holiday-destination cities such as Brussels, Ghent, Bruges and Antwerp. Note that Belgium is not, in practice, a bilingual country. Many Flemish do not speak French, and even more French-speaking Belgians do not speak Dutch. In Flanders, it is generally unwise to communicate in French in the first instance. Visitors who do not speak Dutch are better off trying English – French should be used only as a last resort.

The national language of Luxembourg is Lëtzebuergesch *(see p240)*. However, French and German are both official languages and frequently used across the country. English is also widely spoken.

Time Difference

Belgium and Luxembourg are on Central European Time (CET), which is GMT + 1 (one hour ahead of Greenwich Mean Time). Both nations operate the same daylight saving time over winter, which means that they move their clocks one hour forward in spring (last Sunday in March), and one hour back in autumn (last Sunday in October).

Weights and Measures

Metric to Imperial
1 kilometre (km) = 0.62 miles
1 metre (m) = 3.28 feet (ft)
1 centimetre (cm) = 0.39 inches (in)
1 litre (l) = 1.76 British pints or 2.11 US pints
1 kilogram (kg) = 2.2 pounds (lb)
1 gram (g) = 0.03 ounces (oz)
1°C = 33.8°F
From degrees Celsius to degrees Farenheit, multiply by 1.8 and add 32.

Electricity

The electrical current in both countries is 220 volts AC, and standard European plugs with two round pins are used. British electrical equipment, which runs on 230 volts, operates fine on 220 volts, but requires adaptors for the standard three-pin British plug. These are best bought in the UK or at the airport before arrival, as they are hard to find in Belgium. American equipment, which runs on 120 volts, requires a voltage converter or transformer, although some equipment, such as electric razors, may run on both.

Signboard at the Zwin displaying information in Dutch and French

Specialist equipment on display at the *jenever* museum in Hasselt

Opening Hours

Most shops and businesses in Belgium are open Mondays to Saturdays between 10am and 6pm or 7pm, with some shops closing for an hour at lunch time. The supermarkets are usually open between 9am and 8pm. Opening hours in Luxembourg are similar. However, shops there tend to be open between 8am and noon, and again between 2pm and 6pm, and many are closed on Monday mornings.

Museums and Galleries

The Belgians are often avid collectors, and up and down the country there are numerous small private museums – on bicycles, military insignia, beer labels and so forth – that are essentially extensions of private hobbies. There is also a passion for the more established museums, instilled at an early age through school visits – in fact, in 2008, the Flemish introduced a scheme whereby young people under the age of 26 could visit 23 of the leading museums of Flanders and Brussels for just one euro. Public investment is considerable, with major new museums and galleries being built to the highest standards of presentation and old ones being modernized.

Many museums are closely focussed on local traditions and products, for example hops in Poperinge *(see p129)*, jenever gin in Hasselt *(see p170)* and slate in Bertrix *(see p234)*. Visitors will find that labels are often in one language only (either French or Dutch), but newer museums may have foreign-language audio-guides. Almost all have admission charges, and special deals are sometimes available from the city tourist offices that allow visits to many of the museums for a single, much-reduced price. Opening hours vary, but broadly, most public museums, in both Belgium and Luxembourg, are open between 10am and 5pm, with the majority being closed on Mondays.

Tipping

Tipping is not very common in either Luxembourg or Belgium. A service charge is included in restaurant prices, but customers can leave a small extra tip if service has been particularly good. The service is also included in taxi fares, although rounding up the fare by up to 10 per cent is customary. Ushers who show visitors to their seats in some cinemas will expect a tip of about 50 cents–€1.50 per spectator and doormen €1.25–€2.50.

DIRECTORY

Tourist Information

Belgian Tourist Office: Brussels-Wallonia
w belgiumtheplaceto.be
w belgium-tourism.be
w diplomatie.belgium.be

Luxembourg Tourist Office
w luxembourg.co.uk
w luxembourg.com
w visitluxembourg.com
w lcto.lu

Tourism Flanders
w visitflanders.com

Embassies

Australia
Avenue des Arts 56, 1000 BRU.
Tel (02) 2860500.
w belgium.embassy.gov.au

Canada
Avenue de Tervuren 2, 1040 BRU.
Tel (02) 7410611.
w canadainternational.gc.ca/belgium-belgique

UK
Avenue d'Auderghem 10, 1040 BRU
Tel (02) 2876211.
w gov.uk/government/world/belgium

USA
Boulevard du Régent 27, 1000 BRU.
Tel (02) 8114000.
w belgium.usembassy.gov

New Zealand
Level 7, 9-31 Avenue des Nerviens, 1040 BRU.
Tel (02) 5121040.
w nzembassy.com

Travel Safety Advice

UK
Foreign and Commonwealth Office
w gov.uk/foreign-travel-advice

US
US Department of State
w travel.state.gov

Australia
Department of Foreign Affairs and Trade
w dfat.gov.au
w smartraveller.gov.au

Facilities for Disabled Travellers

Able Travel
w able-travel.com

Belgian Red Cross
Rue de Stalle 96, 1180 BRU. Tel (02) 3713111.
w redcross.be

Belgian Red Cross
Motstraat 40, Mechelen.
Tel (015) 443322.
w rodekruis.be

Brussels For All
w bruxellespourtous.be

Info-Handicap
Tel (02) 3664661, (02) 360885.
w info-handicap.lu
w welcome.lu

Infopunt Toegankelijk Reizen
w accessinfo.be

Personal Security and Health

Belgium and Luxembourg are relatively safe places for visitors and citizens alike. Politeness, honesty and respect for others are cherished and normal levels of vigilance should suffice. As in any well organized society that broadly looks after its citizens, there is a good network of services to deal with unexpected crises. Those unfortunate enough to fall ill will find that the health service in particular is extremely well run, with first-class hospitals and readily available facilities.

Crime

Like in most countries, crime rates tend to be higher in larger cities than in rural areas in Belgium and Luxembourg, though serious crime in the large cities is overall low . In the cities, visitors need to be alert to pickpockets and bag-snatchers, especially in tourist areas and on public transport. Some hotels have reported that smartly-dressed pickpockets have been infiltrating their premises by pretending to be clients, then targeting guests in lifts and other communal spaces. Outside the larger cities, crime is generally not a problem, but it is wise always to be on the alert.

Law Enforcement

Belgium has two integrated levels of police. Major crimes and motorway offences are handled by the **Federal Police**. However, visitors are more likely to encounter the Local Police, who are responsible for law and order in their area. Visitors in the capital can also get in touch with the **Brussels Central Police Station**. In Luxembourg, the main law enforcement agency is the **Grand Ducal Police**.

Victims of theft will need to go to a police station and acquire the necessary paperwork to claim insurance. Police stations in major cities will have someone who speaks English.

A Belgian police officer

Safety Guidelines

Precautions to take in Luxembourg and Belgium are similar to those taken in any city in the Western world. Busy, crowded places, such as stations, public transport, major tourist attractions and markets, are the haunts of opportunist thieves and pickpockets. When parking a car, the doors need to be properly locked and bags or possessions that might be construed as potentially valuable be hidden away. When out sightseeing or shopping on foot in the bigger towns and cities, and when sitting in busy cafés or restaurants, bags and wallets should be firmly secured at all times. On public transport and in crowded places, women should wear handbags with the strap across the shoulder and the clasp facing the body. In hotels, rooms and suitcases need to be locked and it is best to avoid leaving cash or valuables lying around. Rooms often come with a safe; if not, there should be one at reception. It is advisable always to keep two separate sets of money and credit cards in case one set gets lost. Avoid lonely and questionable areas after dark.

Lost Property

The chances of retrieving property are minimal if it was lost in the street. However, Belgians are essentially honest and believe strongly in the inviolable rights of ownership to personal possessions. As a result, property left behind or lost in a restaurant, museum or shop can usually be retrieved. The public transport authorities operate lost-and-found services. For insurance purposes, travellers need to get in touch with the local police station and lodge a report.

Travel and Health Insurance

Under reciprocal agreements, travellers to Belgium and Luxembourg coming from EU countries are entitled to the same subsidized healthcare that local nationals receive, provided they are in possession of an **EHIC** (European Health Insurance Card). British citizens can apply for an EHIC using forms available at post offices or online. Before receiving treatment, EU citizens should make it clear that they have state insurance, or they may end up with a large bill. Patients will usually be asked to pay first and then seek reimbursement from the authorities at home – so it is essential to retain all receipts. While generous, state healthcare subsidies do not cover all problems (such as dental treatment or repatriation) or

Crowded market typical of town squares such as Place d'Armes, Luxembourg

A typical pharmacy in Belgium, doubling as a herbalist

costs, so it is worth taking out full travel insurance, which covers additional risks such as theft or lost property and travel cancellation. Travellers from outside the EU are strongly advised to take out full travel insurance, with medical cover – a serious accident involving hospitalization and repatriation by special air transport can cost tens of thousands of euros.

Doctors, Hospitals and Pharmacies

Belgium and Luxembourg have efficient health services funded by a mixture of state subsidies and national and private insurance. Hospitals are plentiful, modern and well run, and the quality of treatment is generally very good. Guests taken ill at a hotel will be provided details of local doctors by the staff. Whether or not a person has insurance, doctors will expect to settle the bill on the spot, and in cash. Pharmacists are well trained and run their businesses with clinical efficiency. For minor ailments, they should be the first port of call. Pharmacies are generally open Mondays to Fridays from 9am to 6pm, and every district operates a rota system for late-night, weekend and national holiday cover. All pharmacies also display information about where to find the nearest 24-hour chemist.

Emergencies

Police, Ambulance and Fire Services in Belgium and Luxembourg have dedicated nationwide phone numbers.

Visitors can also make use of local knowledge in an emergency as people are quick to step forward and help. Those staying at a hotel can ask staff at the reception for assistance.

Public Toilets

In general, most places with tourist footfall have adequate provision for public toilets. Many of these facilities are meticulously maintained by attendants, who charge a rate for usage. Where no rate is shown, people are expected to leave between 25 and 50 cents. If caught short, it is possible to use the toilet of a bar or café, but one would be expected to return the favour by buying a drink or coffee.

Smoking

In both countries, smoking is officially forbidden in confined public places and on public transport. It is also prohibited in restaurants and large cafés (unless they have a dedicated smoking area, or food represents less than one-third of their business and they have special permission). Smoking may be tolerated in smaller bars. In Luxembourg, there is a complete ban on smoking in cafés, bars and restaurants.

Mosquitoes

In Belgium, mosquitoes can be a problem on warm summer nights. The canals of Bruges and the polders of the north are favoured breeding areas and visitors to these places will need suitable repellants.

Beer Strength

Belgian beer is very good, but also very strong – Trappist and Abbey beers regularly contain 6.5–9.5 per cent alcohol by volume (abv). The beer is usually drunk slowly and in moderate quantities. Drinkers who are used to a beer-strength of 3.5–4 per cent abv will really notice the difference, and may run into trouble if they heedlessly apply their normal quantities of intake to Belgian beer.

Bottles of Belgian beer with labels signalling the alchohol content

Banking and Currency

As befits their status at the heart of the European Union, both geographically and administratively, Belgium and Luxembourg have trustworthy and efficient banking systems, dedicated to businesses as well as individuals. The currency used by both countries, as well as by most of the older member-states of the European Union, is the euro. Cash is easily available through Automated Teller Machines (ATMs) and banks, and most of the essential transactions can be conducted through major credit cards.

Debit and credit cards, accepted at major stores and most hotels

A man collects money at a BNP Paribas Fortis Bank ATM

Banks

Banking hours in Belgium and Luxembourg are generally 9am to 4pm from Monday to Friday. In Belgium, some banks might close for lunch between noon and 2pm. A few branches operate until 4:30pm or 5pm on Fridays, and may open on Saturday mornings. Most banks within the city centre are happy to serve non-clients, and often offer very competitive exchange rates. They are also able to cash travellers' cheques and exchange foreign currency. To do this, the signatory's passport or some other form of photographic identification will be required.

All transactions, especially money transfers, are liable to banking fees, and it is best to check the rates in advance.

ATM Services

Most bank branches have 24-hour cashpoint facilities. Visitors will find that there is often a machine in the lobby used by members of the bank, while a second ATM on the wall outside is available to everyone. ATMs accept a wide range of cards, including those belonging to Maestro and Cirrus. It is advisable to check with the home bank or card-provider whether a card is acceptable abroad. Usually, there is no transaction fee at the ATM itself, but the bank or card-provider at home may have set the exchange rate and will charge a fee.

Foreign Exchange Bureaus

Visitors who are unable to change money at a bank or use a cashpoint machine to obtain euros, may be forced to rely on foreign exchange bureaus (*bureaux de change* in French; *wisselkantoren* in Dutch). These can be found in all cities and travel hubs that regularly receive foreign visitors. They have much longer opening hours than banks, but will often charge a commission of 3–4 per cent, on top of which they may not have as competitive exchange rates. It is worth comparing prices between different bureaus to ensure a good deal.

Credit and Charge Cards

MasterCard and **Visa** cards are widely accepted across the region; more reluctance may be shown towards **Diners Club** and **American Express**. Most hotels accept credit cards to secure reservations and for payment when leaving. Small hotels and bed-and-breakfast accommodation may take only cash. The mode of payment needs to be established before the stay. Again, restaurants are usually happy to take payment by credit card, but it is best to check before ordering if this is not clear. Bars almost always accept only cash payments (no cards).

DIRECTORY

Credit and Charge Cards

American Express
Tel (02) 6762121.
W americanexpress.be

Diners Club
Tel (44) 1244 470928.
W dinersclub.be

MasterCard
Tel 0800 15096.
W mastercard.com/be

Visa
Tel 0800 18397.
W visaeurope.com

Foreign exchange bureau at the Brussels Midi railway station

Currency

The euro replaced the Belgian franc and Luxembourg franc at the beginning of 2002, and, in contrast to some Euro-zone nations, there are few regrets and little nostalgia for the old currencies. The euro currency is a blessing for travellers moving across Euro-zone nations. It is also easy to handle – with notes in denominations from €5 upwards, shoppers are not unduly burdened with excessive notes or change. Those unaccustomed to the euro will discover that 1-, 2- and 5-cent coins (in French, *centimes*) are of little practical value and tend to accumulate. At the other end of the scale, €500 notes are just too valuable for many enterprises as they are subject to counterfeiting; many refuse to take €500 notes at all.

Bank Notes

Euro bank notes have seven denominations. The €5 note (grey in colour) is the smallest, followed by the €10 note (pink), €20 note (blue), €50 note (orange), €100 note (green), €200 note (yellow) and €500 note (purple). All notes show the stars of the European Union.

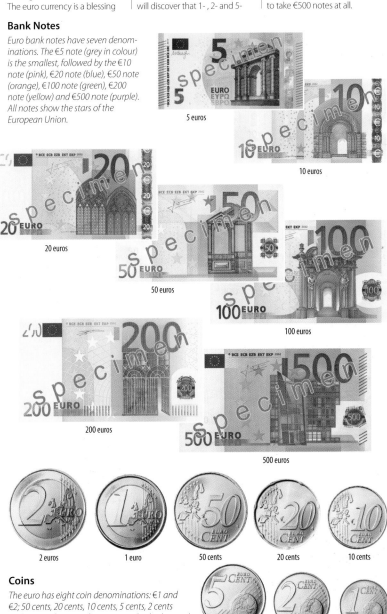

5 euros

10 euros

20 euros

50 euros

100 euros

200 euros

500 euros

2 euros

1 euro

50 cents

20 cents

10 cents

5 cents

2 cents

1 cent

Coins

The euro has eight coin denominations: €1 and €2; 50 cents, 20 cents, 10 cents, 5 cents, 2 cents and 1 cent. The €2 and €1 coins are both silver and golden in colour. The 50-, 20- and 10-cent coins are golden. The 5-, 2- and 1-cent coins are bronze.

Communications and Media

Belgium and Luxembourg have excellent communications links. Both countries are also areas of rapid change: mobile telephones are replacing landlines and public telephones have all but disappeared; email is undermining the postal service; and the Internet has made inroads into newspaper journalism and broadcasting. However, both nations have a conservative streak that battles to maintain traditional services, but they are also keen to grab a front seat in the communications revolution. As a result, both the old and the new media are generally well provided for.

Accessing free Wi-Fi at a café in the Galéries St-Hubert, Brussels

A shop selling mobile phones and SIMs in Belgium

Telephones

Mobile phone networks cover Belgium and Luxembourg effectively. Not all coverage in the region is equal, however, and it is worth checking with the network provider how good the signal will be where you are travelling. It is also a good idea to check with your provider that full roaming services are available – and how much they cost to use.

Mobile networks in Belgium and Luxembourg use the European-standard GSM 900/1800 MHz frequencies, so UK and Australian mobiles work if they have a roaming facility

enabled. North American mobile phones will only operate in Belgium and Luxembourg if they are tri- or quad-band. Roaming charges are being abolished in Europe from June 2017. Until then, to save money and avoid extra charges, visitors can buy a prepaid SIM for a local network provider and pay local rates. Make sure before travelling that your phone is unlocked so that it accepts a SIM card from another network. In Belgium, the main networks are **Proximus**, **Mobistar** and **BASE** and in Luxembourg, **Post**, **Tango** and **Orange**.

Hotels generally charge premium rates to use their landline phones for international calls, making them a very expensive option. There are very few public telephones.

Internet Services

Belgium and Luxembourg have good Internet infrastructures. Most hotels have Wi-Fi. Sometimes guests have to

pay for usage, but often it is included as part of the hotel service, accessed by codes supplied by the hotel reception.

Many restaurants, cafés and bars offer free Wi-Fi. There are a number of free Wi-Fi hotspots in public areas throughout the region, especially in key cities, such as the Grand Place and the Place de Brouckere in Brussels. **Proximus** has a hotspot system for Wi-Fi users in Belgium, while in Luxembourg, free Wi-Fi is available from **Luxembourg City**.

Postal Services

Post offices in Belgium are generally open Monday to Friday from 8:30am or 9am to 4pm or 5pm. Some stay open late on Fridays, and are open

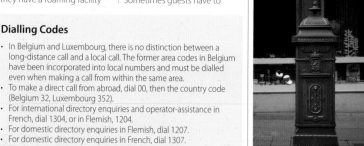

A distinctive traditional red post box in Belgium

Dialling Codes

- In Belgium and Luxembourg, there is no distinction between a long-distance call and a local call. The former area codes in Belgium have been incorporated into local numbers and must be dialled even when making a call from within the same area.
- To make a direct call from abroad, dial 00, then the country code (Belgium 32, Luxembourg 352).
- For international directory enquiries and operator-assistance in French, dial 1304, or in Flemish, 1204.
- For domestic directory enquiries in Flemish, dial 1207.
- For domestic directory enquiries in French, dial 1307.
- For domestic directory enquiries in German, dial 1404.
- For domestic directory enquiries in English, dial 1404.
- For directory enquiries and international operator assistance in Luxembourg, dial 118171 or 11816.

GENERAL INDEX | **337**

Acknowledgments

Dorling Kindersley would like to thank the many people whose help and assistance contributed to the preparation of this book.

Main Contributor
Antony Mason is the author of 70 books on travel, art, geography and history, including DK Top 10 Travel Guide to Brussels, Bruges, Antwerp and Ghent, Cadogan Guide to Brussels and Cadogan Guide to Bruges. He has taught writing at Goldsmiths College, University of London, as a Fellow of the Royal Literary Fund. His long-standing admiration for Belgium dates from 1975.

Additional Contributors
Zoë Hewetson, Philip Lee, Zoë Ross, Sarah Wolff, Timothy Wright, Julia Zyrianova, Emma Jones, Leigh Phillips
Fact Checker Dan Colwell

Proofreader Swati Meherishi

Indexer Kathryn O'Donoghue

Design and Editorial
Publisher Douglas Amrine
List Manager Vivien Antwi
Managing Art Editor Jane Ewart
Project Editor Alastair Laing
Project Designer Kate Leonard, Shahid Mahmood
Senior Cartographic Editor Casper Morris
Managing Art Editor (jackets) Karen Constanti
Jacket Design Tessa Bindloss
Senior DTP Designer Jason Little
Picture Researcher Ellen Root
Production Controller Rita Sinha

Editorial Assistance Fay Franklin

Additional Picture Research
Rhiannon Furbear

DK Picture Library
Romaine Werblow

Additional Photography
Stuti Tiwari Bhatia, Gerard Brown, Demetrio Carrasco, Anthony Cassidy, Jeoff Davis, Paul Kenward, Mathew Kurien, David Murray, Ian O'Leary, Alessandra Santarelli, Jules Selmes, Tony Souter

Additional Illustrations
Gary Cross, Richard Draper, Paul Guest, Robbie Polley, Kevin Robinson

Revisions Team
Ashwin Raju Adimari, Subhadeep Biswas, Claire Baranowski, Dan Colwell, Caroline Elliker, Amy Harrison, Shikha Kulkarni, Jude Ledger, Darren Longley, Sonal Modha, Catherine Palmi, Rada Radojicic, Preeti Singh, Ankita Sharma, Avantika Sukhia, Ajay Verma, Richa Verma, Dora Whitaker, Lesley Williamson

Special Assistance
Dorling Kindersley would like to thank the following: Rym Neffoussi at the Belgian Tourist Office; Serge Moes at the Luxembourg Tourist Office, London; Jean-Claude Conter and Gelz Pit at the Luxembourg National Tourist Office, Luxembourg; Mia Prce at the Musées Royaux des Beaux-Arts de Belgique; Anita Rampall at Tourism Flanders-Brussels, UK

Photography Permission
Dorling Kindersley would like to thank the following for their assistance and kind permission to photograph at their establishments:
Abbaye de Maredsous; Abbaye de Stavelot; Attre Château; Basilica St-Hubert; Bokrijk Openluchtmuseum; Brüsel comic-book store; Brussels Tourism Office; Castle of Jehay; Cathédrale Notre Dame; Cathédrale St-Paul; Centraal Station, Antwerp; Château de Modave; Château des Princes de Chimay; Château-Fort de Bouillon; Comme Chez Soi; Design Museum Gent; Église Ste-Catherine; Église St-Jacques; Église St-Quentin Euro Space Centre, Transinne; Gaasbeek Castle; Grimbergen Abbey Church; Groot Vleeshuis; Grottes de Hotton; Grottes de Lorette; Grottes de Neptune; Hôpital Notre Dame à la Rose; Hotel Eurostars Sablon; Hotel Metropole; Le Falstaff; Le Méridien Hotel, Brussels; Maison de la Metallurgie et de l'Industrie; Memorial Breendonk; Musée d'Ansembourg; Musée de Cire; Musée de l'Art Wallon; Musée de la Bataille des Ardennes; Musée du Circuit de Spa Francorchamps; Musée du Folklore; Musée Groesbeek de Croix; Musée Horta; Musée Provincial des Arts Anciens du Namurois; Musée Royal de l'Armée et d'Histoire Militaire; Musée Tchantchès; Nationaal Jenevermuseum; Noordseeaquarium; Parc du Cinquantenaire; Plantin-Moretus Museum; Rochefort; Rubenshuis; St Christopher's Church, Charleroi; Stadhuis, Antwerp; Stadhuis, Ghent; World War I Museum.

Picture Credits
Key- a - above; b - below/bottom; c - centre; f - far; l - left; r - right; t - top.

Every effort has been made to trace the copyright holders, and we apologize in advance for any unintentional omissions. We would be pleased to add appropriate acknowledgments in any subsequent editions of this publication.

Works of art have been reproduced with the kind permission of the following copyright holders:
Le journal de spirou © dupuis, 1938–2008 28tr; © lucky comics 2008 28br; © moulinsart sa 28tl, 28bc; © marvano – dargaud benelux (daragud-lombard s.a.) 2007 29C; casterman 29 br; © standaard uitgeverij 29bl; © imps sa 29bc; © dacs, london 2009 84tl; the domain of arnheim, 1962, oil on canvas, 146 x 114 cm © charly herscovici, with his kind authorization – c/o sabam-adagp, 2009 74bl; musée horta © 2009 arch. Victor horta, sofam belgium 84tl.

The publisher would like to thank the following for their kind permission to reproduce their photographs:
4Corners: SIME / Gräfenhain Günter 104cl, Cozzi Guido 243tr, SIME / Schmid Reinhard 227cla. **Maarten Vanden Abeele** : 92bl. **akg-images**: 44tc, 44bl, 48tr, 50bc, 51bc, 124tc, Collection Schloß Ambras. / Erich Lessing 240cb, Galleria Naz. di Capodimonte. 30–31c, Kunsthistorisches Museum/Erich Lessing 278tr, Joseph Martin 118c, Musée du Louvre/Erich Lessing 41bc, Musées Royaux d'Art et d'Hist. 49crb. **Alamy Images**: A & J Visage 24clb, Albaimages/Ronald Weir 24cb, Per Andersen 138cl, 164cl, Arco Images/De Meester, J. 217b, Arco Images/Delpho, M. 25clb, Arterra Picture Library 320cla, Arterra Picture Library/Clement Philippe 123bl, 284tl, Authors Image / Nicolas Rung 39cra, Sigitas Baltramaitis 24cl, David A. Barnes 197b, Pat Behnke 153tc, 275tl, Bildagentur-online/McPhoto-Weber 258–9, Bildarchiv Monheim GmbH/Paul M. R. Maeyaert 164bc, BL Images Ltd 59tr, David Boag 25cfrb, Tibor Bognar 32bl, Jacky Chapman 127crb, Choups 4br, 21tr, David Coleman 118tr, CW Images 277cla, D Gee 314tl, David Noble Photography 178–9c, Hasan Dogantürk 62tr, Stuart Forster 287tr, Foto 28 122br, Fotolincs 24bc, Liz Garnett 36bl, Andrew Harrington 25tc, Brian Harris 36cr, hemis.fr/BORGESE Maurizio 22br, Hemis.fr/Rieger Bertrand 123tl, Peter Horree 43cb, 77tr, 121bc, 179crb, 276cra, 277br, Imagebroker 318tr, Imagebroker/Michael Krabs 25bc, ImageState/Martin Ruegner 25cb, ImageState/Pictor International 54cl, 176cl, INSADCO Photography/Martin Bobrovsky 274cl, INTERFOTO/Fine Arts 167crb, INTERFOTO Pressebildagentur 240bc, Eric James 138br, Jon Arnold Images Ltd 33tl, Oliver Knight 95cra, Lebrecht Music and Arts Photo Library 44bc, Lordprice Collection 200bl, magestate Media Partners Limited - Impact Photos/Laurent Grandadam 94tr, Mary Evans Picture Library 45bl, Bruce McGowan 42bl, Melba Photo Agency 34bl, Nature Picture Library/BERNARD CASTELEIN 24fcrb, 25cr, 25fclb, NRT-Travel 130ca, Witry Pascal 25cl, Pictorial Press Ltd 67cb, Picture Contact/Jochem Wijnands 122bl, 306t, PjrFoto/studio 47fcrb, Juergen Ritterbach 2–3br, Robert Estall photo agency/Malcolm Aird 42bc, David Robertson 250–51, 254br, Rough Guides 170br, David Russell 318bl, Stephen Frink Collection/Masa Ushioda 25tr, Stephen Roberts Photography 23t, 276clb, Mark Sunderland 95tl, The London Art Archive/Borch or Terborch, Gerard ter (1617–81) 46clb, The London Art Archive/Delacroix, (Ferdinand Victor) Eugene (1798–1863) 43tr, The London Art Archive/Eyck, Jan van (c.1390–1441) 106tr, The London Art Archive/Jordaens, Jacob (1593–1678) 107br, The London Art Archive/Memling, Hans (c.1433–94) 106bl, The London Art Archive/Weyden, Rogier van der (1399–1464) 106cl, The London Art Archive/Wouters, Rik (1882–1916) 156bl, The Print Collector 49bc, 118bl, 157cr, TNT Magazine 129tl, Rohan Van Twest 275cb, Martyn Vickery 130cl, Wild Places Photography/Chris Howes 35crb, 180, Wilmar Photography 178clb, 182bl, 213bl, Peter M. Wilson 58cl. **Antony Mason**: 140tr. **Antwerp Hilton**: 262tl. **Art De Vivre**: 291bl. **AWL**

Images: Neil Farrin 94cla. © CH Bastin & J Evrard: 169tr. Belga Queen: 281t. Bieres de Chimay S.A: 278cr. The Bridgeman Art Library: Adoration of the Magi, 1624 (oil on panel), Rubens, Peter Paul (1577–1640)/Koninklijk Museum voor Schone Kunsten, Antwerp, Belgium/Giraudon/The Bridgeman Art Library 107cr, Christie's Images, London Peter Paul Rubens (1557–1640) Self Potrait 27tl, Dawn, Brussels, c.1725–30 (lace), Flemish School, (18th century)/Musee Crozatier, Le Puy-en-Velay, France/Giraudon 31br, Flemish citizens, fighting on foot, batter the well armoured and mounted French Knights at the Battle of the Golden Spurs near Courtrai in 1302, c.1900 (colour litho), Bombled, Louis (1862–1927)/Private Collection/Archives Charmet/The Bridgeman Art Library 129br, Interior of a Forge near Huy, Belgium, engraved by Jean-Baptiste Jobard (1792–1861) (tinted litho), Howen, Anton de (1774–1848) (after)/Science Museum, London, UK/The Bridgeman Art Library 50clb, Louis XIV (1638–1715) of France in the costume of The Sun King in the ballet 'La Nuit' c.1665 (litho), French School, (19th century)/Private Collection/Roger-Viollet, Paris/The Bridgeman Art Library 46br, Madonna and Child with Canon Joris van der Paele, 1436 (oil on panel), Eyck, Jan van (c.1390–1441)/Groeningemuseum, Bruges, Belgium/The Bridgeman Art Library 106–107c, 118br, Philip II (1527–98) Crowned by Victory, 1628 (oil on canvas), Rubens, Peter Paul (1577–1640)/Prado, Madrid, Spain, Giraudon/The Bridgeman Art Library 45cb, Pieta, c.1629 (oil on canvas) (detail of 179424), Dyck, Sir Anthony van (1599–1641)/Koninklijk Museum voor Schone Kunsten, Antwerp, Belgium/Giraudon/The Bridgeman Art Library 157br, Portrait of Philip The Good, Duke of Burgundy, and his third wife Isabel of Portugal, 1430 (oil on board), Flemish School, (15th century)/Museum voor Schone Kunsten, Ghent, Belgium, Giraudon/The Bridgeman Art Library 43bc, The Battle of Pavia, 24 February 1525 (tapestry) (detail of 156716), Orley, Bernard van (c.1488–1541) (after)/Museo e Gallerie Nazionale di Capodimonte, Naples, Italy/The Bridgeman Art Library 44crb, The Congress of Vienna, 9th June 1815 (engraving), Anonymous/Museo del Risorgimento, Brescia, Italy/Roger-Viollet, Paris/The Bridgeman Art Library 241clb, The Lacemakers of Ghent, 1913 (oil on canvas), Silbert, Max (b.1871)/Private Collection 31tr, The Ommegance in Brussels on 31st May 1615: detail of the Triumph of Isabella of Spain (1566–1633) 1615 (detail of 69871) (oil on canvas), Alsloot, Denys van (1570–1628)/Victoria & Albert Museum, London, UK/The Bridgeman Art Library 45t, The Raising of the Cross (panel), Rubens, Peter Paul (1577–1640) (attr. to)/Musee Bonnat, Bayonne, France/The Bridgeman Art Library 45bc. Brussels Airlines: 322cla. Corbis: Dave Bartruff 29cb, Tibor Bognar 194br, CORBIS SYGMA/REUTER RAYMOND 304br, Jon Hicks 150clb, Olivier Polet 57b, 295cla, Schlegelmilch 38cla, Stapleton Collection 89crb, Sygma/Sophie Bassouls 28cl, zefa/Eberhard Streichan 51crb. Corbis: Hemis/Richard Soberka 204–205, Patrick Ward 18. Das Fotoarchiv: 316c. De Kleine Zavel: 286br. De Munt La Monnaie: 49tr. De Pelgrim: 288bc. Rudy Denoyette: 140cla. Diamond Land: 23c. Bart van Dijk: 139tr. Dorling Kindersley: Tony Briscoe 293b, Demetrio Carrasco 15tr, 62bl, 67tl, 68tr, 68bc, DACS, London 2009. 84tl, David Murray and Jules Selmes 95br, Paul Kenward 137tl, ian O'Leary 274–75, Rough Guides/Anthony Cassidy 13tc, 14tr, 323tl, Tony Souter 322br, Paul Tait 13br, 14bl, 15bc. Dreamstime.com: Pitchathorn Chitnelawong 148cl, Dinozzaver 149bc, Galinasavina 321tl, Imladris 142br, Ixuskmitl 66tc, Jacob Kooistra 66bl, Karol Kozlowski 90br, Jan Kranendonk 321br, Mikhail Markovskiy 132–33, Borna Mirahmadian 12tl, Martin Molcan 52–3, Mosessin 290tl, Neirfy 10bl, Saaaaa 12br, Jozef Sedmak 11crb, Tacna 142tl, 231tc, 312c, Tigger76 151cra, Travelpeter 11tl, VanderWolfImages 21bl. Duncan Baird Publishers: Alan Williams 151tr, 279br. Durbuy Adventure: 265tl. FLPA: Imagebroker/Anton Luhr 24bl. Paul Garland: 212cla. Getty Images: AFP 23br, AFP/Stringer 123cr, Hervé Gyssels 216, Hans-Peter Merten 238–39, Popperfoto/Haynes Archive 256bl, Staff/AFP/JEAN-LOUP GAUTREAU 27crb. Getty Images: DEA/G. SOSIO/De Agostini Picture Library 179bl, Hulton Archive/Stringer 43br, Hulton Archives 47bc,

Keystone 51tl, Macduff Everton: 270tl, Staff/Pascal Le Segretain 241br, Georgia Glynn Smith: 70bl, Stone/Richard Elliott 38br, The Bridgeman Art Library/English Scho 40. Grand Hotel Cravat: 261tl, 271br. The Granger Collection, New York: 47tc, 47crb. Grottes de Remouchamps: 213cra. Reproduced by permission of The Henry Moore Foundation: 75cr. Hotel De Orangerie: 260br. Hotel Metropole: 94clb. Michael Hurt: 102–103. IMPS S.A.: 29bc. Institut royal du Patrimoine artistique: 30tr, 65tl. iStockphoto.com: Eva Katalin Kondoros 320tr, Jeroen Peys 232clb, Flavio Vallenari 89t, Duncan Walker 41br. Jardin De Fiorine: 289tr. Kasteel Beauvoorde: 128c. Jos L. Knaepen: 299tl. Koninklijk Museum voor Schone Kunsten: 157tc. L'Entree des Artistes: 280br. La Butte aux Bois: 261br. La Malle Poste: 269bl. La Quincaillerie: 282tc. Landcommanderij Alden Biesen: 146b. Le Roy d'Espagne: 94-95c. Lonely Planet Images: Martin Moos 153c, Wayne Walton 232bl. Luxembourg National Tourist Office: 19b, 242cl, 246c, 247tr, 247cr, 248cl, 248tr, 249tl, 249br, 252br, 253br, 302cla, 302br, 303tc. Maagdenhuismuseum : KIK/IRPA", Brussels 152bl. Raf Maes: 299br. Manoir du Dragon: 267tr. Manos Stephanie: 266br. Martin's Klooster: 260cl, 268tc. Mary Evans Picture Library: 107bl, 241t. Mathes: 292tl. Claude Mathon: 105cra. MDD (Museum Dhondt-Dhaenens) : Kris Martin 140br. Mediatoon: Dupuis, 1938–2008 28tr, Lucky Comics 2008 28br, Marvano – Dargaud Benelux (Daragud-Lombard s.a.) - 2007 29c. Moulinsart: Herge 28bc. Musée De L'art Wallon: Musée de l'Art 49tl. Musée de Folklore: Ville de Tournai 188bl. Nationaal Park Hoge Kempen: 14tr. naturepl.com: Bernard Castelein 25bl, Philippe Clement 24fclb. Björn Olievier: 37c. Opera Ballet Vlaanderen: Tom Dhaenens 139cl. petrolclub: Petrolclub/Tom Van Ghent 300tr. Photolibrary: Age fotostock/Charles Bowman 273tl, Age fotostock/Javier Larrea 185tl, Age fotostock/Nils-Johan Norenlind 55tl, age fotostock/P Narayan 117tl, THE BRIDGEMAN ART LIBRARY 8–9, Corbis 176br, Hemis/RIEGER Bertrand 109b, 177bl, Japan Travel Bureau 181b, John Warburton-Lee Photography/Amar Grover 82, Mauritius/Josephine Clasen 295cr, Photononstop/Yvan Travert 56, Dan Porges 24tr, RESO/Diaphor La Phototheque 145b, Tips Italia/Alberto Nardi 35tr, 236br, Tips Italia/Charles Mahaux 20bc, Tips Italia/Christina Jansen 187cr. Photolibrary: Image Source 22tl. Photoshot: Picture Alliance 237cla, World Pictures 20t, 37br. Robbie Polley: 114bc. Private Collection: 42crb, 48cl, 48bl, 48br, 119crb, 209cb. Alain Riviere : 278br. Robert Harding Picture Library: James Emmerson 108, 310–11, Heinz-Dieter Falkenstein 174–5, Gtw 196, Jesus Nicolas Sanchez 144, J. Moreno 162–3. Royal Ballet of Flanders: Johan Persson/Wim Vanlessen en ensemble 298b. Royal Museum of Fine Arts of Belgium, Brussels: 77b. Royal Museums of Fine Arts of Belgium: 74cl, 74bl, 75crb, Photo Cussac 26cl, 48–9c, 72bl, 73tc, 73cr, 76tr, Photo Speltdoorn 26br, 27c, 30cl, Photo Speltdroon 72cl, 76bl, 107tl. Rubenshuis (Rubens House): 155tc, 155cra. Stad Brugge Stedelijke Musea: Groeninge Museum 119cr, Groeningemuseun 42tl, Gruithuis 116br. Standaard Uitgeverij: 29bl. Stoomcentrum Maldegem: 141br. SuperStock: Age Fotostock/Alvaro Leiva 263tc. Marky Tjemmes: 211tc, 233cla. Toerisme Vlaanderen: M. Decleer 125t, D. de Kievith 111t. Tourisme Charleroi: Gina Santin 191tr. Tourisme Namur: OTN/Cederik Leeuw 207tl. Tourist office ville de Tournai: 30bl, 186br. Travel-Images.com: A.Umidova 229cra. Vrijmoed: Heikki Verdurme 285br. www.Dendermonde.be: 143br. www.heuvelland.be: VVV Heuvelland 131cr, 131bc. www.trussel.com: Steve Trussel 223cb. WY: Kris Vlegels 283br.
All other images © Dorling Kindersley. For further information see: www.Dkimages.Com

Cover Picture Credits
Front: Alamy Stock Photo: Alpineguide. Spine: Alamy Stock Photo: Alpineguide.

Special Editions of DK Travel Guides

DK Travel Guides can be purchased in bulk quantities at discounted prices for use in promotions or as premiums. We are also able to offer special editions and personalized jackets, corporate imprints, and excerpts from all of our books, tailored specifically to meet your own needs.

To find out more, please contact:
in the United States specialsales@dk.com
in the UK travelguides@uk.dk.com
in Canada DK Special Sales at specialmarkets@dk.com
in Australia penguincorporatesales@penguinrandomhouse.com.au

Phrase Book

Tips for Pronouncing Dutch

The Dutch language is pronounced in largely the same way as English, although many vowels, particularly double vowels, are pronounced as long sounds. *J* is the equivalent of the English *y*, while *v* is pronounced *f*, and *w* is *v*.

In an Emergency

Help!	**Help!**	help
Stop!	**Stop!**	stop
Call a doctor!	**Haal een dokter!**	haal uhn **dok**-tur
Call the police!	**Roep de politie!**	roop duh poe **leet**-see
Call the fire brigade!	**Roep de brandweer!**	roop duh **brahnt**-vheer
Where is the nearest telephone?	**Waar ist de dichtsbijzijnde telefoon?**	vhaar iss duh **dikst**-baiy-zaiyn-duh-tay-luh-**foan**
Where is the nearest hospital?	**Waar ist het dichtsbijzijnde ziekenhuis?**	vhaar iss het **dikst**-baiy-zaiyn-duh **zee**-kuh-hows

Communication Essentials

Yes	**Ja**	yaa
No	**Nee**	nay
Please	**Alstublieft**	ahls-tew-**bleeft**
Thank you	**Dank u**	dhank-ew
Excuse me	**Pardon**	pahr-**don**
Hello	**Goed dag**	ghoot dahgh
Goodbye	**Tot ziens**	tot zins
Good night	**Slaap lekker**	slap **lek**-kah
morning	**morgen**	**mor**-ghun
afternoon	**middag**	**mid**-dahgh
evening	**avond**	**av**-vohnd
yesterday	**gisteren**	**ghis**-tern
today	**vandaag**	**van**-daagh
tomorrow	**morgen**	**mor**-ghugh
here	**hier**	heer
there	**daar**	daar
What?	**Wat?**	vhat
When?	**Wanneer?**	vhan-**eer**
Why?	**Waarom?**	vhaar-**om**
Where?	**Waar?**	vhaar
How?	**Hoe?**	hoo

Useful Phrases

How are you?	**Hoe gaat het ermee?**	hoo ghaat het er-**may**
Very well, thank you	**Heel goed, dank u**	hayl ghoot, dhank ew
How do you do?	**Hoe maakt u het?**	hoo maakt ew het
See you soon	**Tot ziens**	tot zeens
That's fine	**Prima**	**pree**-mah
Where is/are...?	**Waar is/zijn...?**	vhaar iss/zayn
How far is it to...?	**Hoe ver is het naar...?**	hoo vehr iss het nar
How do I get to...?	**Hoe kom ik naar...?**	hoo kom ik nar
Do you speak English?	**Spreekt u engels?**	spraykt uw **eng**-uhls
I don't understand	**Ik snap het niet**	ik snahp het neet
Could you speak slowly?	**Kunt u langzamer praten?**	kuhnt ew **lahng**-zarmer-praat-tuh
I'm sorry	**Sorry**	sorry

Useful Words

big	**groot**	ghroat
small	**klein**	klaiyn
hot	**warm**	vharm
cold	**koud**	khowt
good	**goed**	ghoot
bad	**slecht**	slekht
enough	**genoeg**	ghuh-**noohkh**
well	**goed**	ghoot

open	**open**	open
closed	**gesloten**	ghuh-**slow**-tuh
left	**links**	links
right	**rechts**	rekhts
straight on	**rechtdoor**	rehkht dohr
near	**dichtbij**	dikht baiy
far	**ver weg**	vehr vhekh
up	**omhoog**	om-**hoakh**
down	**naar beneden**	naar buh **nay**-duh
early	**vroeg**	vrookh
late	**laat**	laat
entrance	**ingang**	**in**-ghang
exit	**uitgang**	**ouht**-ghang
toilet	**wc**	vhay-say
occupied	**bezet**	buh-**zett**
free (vacant)	**vrij**	vraiy
free (no charge)	**gratis**	**ghraah**-tiss

Making a Telephone Call

I'd like to place a long-distance telephone call	**Ik wil graag interlokaal telefoneren**	ik vhil ghraakh **inter**-loh-kaal tay-luh-foh-**neh**-ruh
I'd like to call collect	**Ik wil "collect call" bellen**	ik vhil "collect call" **bel**-luh
I will try again later	**Ik probeer het later nog wel eens**	ik pro-**beer** het laater nokh vhel ayns
Can I leave a message?	**Kunt u een boodschap doorgeven?**	kuhnt ew uhn **boat**-skhahp **dohr**-ghay-vuh
Could you speak up a little please?	**Wilt u wat harder praten?**	vhilt ew vhat **hahr**-der **praat**-ew
Local call	**Lokaal gesprek**	low-**kaahl** ghuh-**sprek**

Shopping

How much does this cost?	**Hoeveel kost dit?**	hoo-**vayl** kost dit
I would like...	**Ik wil graag...**	ik vhil ghraakh
Do you have...?	**Heeft u...?**	hayft ew
I'm just looking	**Ik kijk alleen even**	ik kaiyk alleen **ay**-vuh
Do you take credit cards?	**Neemt u krediet-kaarten aan?**	naymt ew kray-deet kaart-en aan
Do you take travellers' cheques?	**Neemt u reischeques aan?**	naymt ew **raiys**-sheks aan
What time do you open?	**Hoe laat gaat u open?**	hoo laat ghaat ew opuh
you close?	**u dicht?**	ew dikht
This one	**Deze**	**day**-zuh
That one	**Die**	dee
expensive	**duur**	dewr
cheap	**goedkoop**	ghoot-**koap**
size	**maat**	maat
white	**wit**	vhit
black	**zwart**	zvhahrt
red	**rood**	roat
yellow	**geel**	ghayl
green	**groen**	ghroon
blue	**blauw**	blah-ew

Types of Shops

antique shop	**antiekwinkel**	ahn-**teek**-vhin-kul
bakery	**bakkerij**	**bah**-ker-aiy
bookshop	**boekwinkel**	**book**-vhin-kul
butcher	**slagerij**	slaakh-er-aiy
cake shop	**banketbakkerij**	bahnk-**et**-bahk-er-aiy
chemist	**apotheek**	ah-poe-**taiyk**
department store	**warenhuis**	**vhaah**-uh-houws
newsagent	**krantenwinkel**	**krahn**-tuh-vhin-kul
post office	**postkantoor**	**pohst**-kahn-tor
supermarket	**supermarkt**	**sew**-per-mahrkt
travel agent	**reisburo**	**raiys**-bew-roa

Sightseeing

art gallery	**gallerie**	ghaller-ee
bus station	**busstation**	**buhs**-stah-shown
bus ticket	**ticket/biljet**	tik-et/bil-yet

closed on public holidays	op feestdagen gesloten	op fayst-daa-ghuh ghuh-slow-tuh
garden	tuin	touwn
railway station	station	stah-shown
return ticket	heen en terug	hayn-uhn-trug
single journey	enkele reis	eng-kuh-luh raiys
tourist information	dienst voor toerisme	deenst vor tor-is-muh

Staying in a Hotel

Do you have a vacant room?	Zijn er nog kamers vrij?	zaiyn er nokh kaa-mers vray
double room with double bed	een twees persoons-kamer met een twee persoonsbed	uhn tvhay per-soans-ka-mer met uhn tvhay per-soans beht
twin room	een kamer met twee bedden	uhn kaa-mer met tvhay beh-tuh
single room	eenpersoons-kamer	ayn-per-soans kaa-mer
room with a bath/shower	kaamer met bad/douche	kaa-mer met baht/doosh
I have a reservation	Ik heb gereserveerd	ik hehp ghuh-ray-sehr-veert

Eating Out

Have you got a table?	Is er een tafel vrij?	iss ehr uhn tah-fuhl vraiy
I would like to reserve a table	Ik wil een tafel reserveren	ik vhil uhn tah-fel ray sehr-veer-uh
The bill, please	Mag ik afrekenen	muhk ik ahf-ray-kuh-nuh
I am a vegetarian	Ik ben vegetariër	ik ben fay-ghuh-taahr-ee-er
waitress/waiter	serveerster/ober	sehr-veer-ster/oh-ber
menu	de kaart	duh kaahrt
wine list	de wijnkaart	duh vhaiyn-kart
glass	het glass	het ghlahss
bottle	de fles	duh fless
knife	het mes	het mess
fork	de vork	duh fork
spoon	de lepel	duh lay-pul
breakfast	het ontbijt	het ont-baiyt
lunch	de lunch	duh lernsh
dinner	het avondeten	het av-vond-ay-tuh
main course	het hoofdgerecht	het hoaft-ghuh-rekht
starter, first course	het voorgerecht	het vhor-ghuh-rekht
dessert	het nagerecht	het naa-ghuh-rekht
dish of the day	het dagschotel	het dahg-skhoa-tel
bar	het cafe	het kaa-fay
café	het eetcafe	het ayt-kaa-fay
rare	rood	roat
medium	half doorbakken	hahlf door-bah-kuh
well done	gaar	gaar

Numbers

1	een	ayn
2	twee	tvhay
3	drie	dree
4	vier	feer
5	vijf	faiyf
6	zes	zess
7	zeven	zay-vuh
8	acht	ahkht
9	negen	nay-guh
10	tien	teen
11	elf	elf
12	twaalf	tvhaalf
13	dertien	dehr-teen
14	veertien	feer-teen
15	vijftien	faiyf-teen
16	zestien	zess-teen
17	zeventien	zayvuh-teen
18	achtien	ahkh-teen
19	negentien	nay-ghuh-teen
20	twintig	tvhin-tukh
21	eenentwintig	aynuh-tvhin-tukh
30	dertig	dehr-tukh
40	veertig	feer-tukh
50	vijftig	faiyf-tukh
60	zestig	zess-tukh
70	zeventig	zay-vuh-tukh
80	tachtig	tahkh-tukh
90	negentig	nay-guh-tukh
100	honderd	hohn-durt
1000	duizend	douw-zuhnt
1,000,000	miljoen	mill-yoon

Time

one minute	een minuut	uhn meen-ewt
one hour	een uur	uhn ewr
half an hour	een half uur	een hahlf uhr
half past one	half twee	hahlf twee
a day	een dag	uhn dahgh
a week	een week	uhn vhayk
a month	een maand	uhn maant
a year	een jaar	uhn jaar
Monday	Maandag	maan-dahgh
Tuesday	Dinsdag	dins-dahgh
Wednesday	Woensdag	vhoons-dahgh
Thursday	Donderdag	donder-dahgh
Friday	Vrijdag	vraiy-dahgh
Saturday	Zaterdag	zaater-dahgh
Sunday	Zondag	zon-dahgh

Food and Drink

asparagus	asperges	as-puhj
bass	zeebars	see-buhr
beef	rundvlees	ruhnt-flayss
beer	bier	beeh
Brussels sprouts	spruitjes	spruhr-tyuhs
chicken	kip	kip
coffee	koffie	coffee
duck	eend	aynt
fish	vis	fiss
fresh orange juice	verse jus	vehr-suh zjhew
fruit	fruit/vruchten	vroot/vrooh-tuh
garlic	knoflook	knoff-loak
green beans	princesbonen	prins-ess-buh-nun
haricot beans	snijbonen	snee-buh-nun
herring	haring	haa-ring
hot chocolate	chocola	sho-koh-laa
lamb	lamsvlees	lahms-flayss
meat	vlees	flayss
mineral water	mineraalwater	meener-aahl-vhaater
monkfish	lotte/zeeduivel	lot/seeduhvul
oyster	oester	ouhs-tuh
pancake	pannekoek	pah-nuh-kook
pheasant	fazant	fay-zanh
pike	snoek	snook
pork	varkensvlees	vahr-kuhns-flayss
potatoes	aardappels	aard-uppuhls
prawn	garnaal	gar-nall
salmon	zalm	sahlm
sea bream	dorade/zeebrasem	doh-rard/zay-brah-sum
skate	rog	rog
spinach	spinazie	spin-a-jee
tea	thee	tay
trout	forel	foh-ruhl
truffle	truffel	truh-fuhl
tuna	tonijn	toe-naiyn
veal	kalfsvlees	karfs-flayss
venison	ree (bok)	ray (bok)
vegetables	groenten	ghroon-tuh
waffle	wafel	vaff-uhl
water	water	vhaa-ter
wine	wijn	vhaiyn

Tips for Pronouncing French

The Walloons and other French-speaking Belgians may display a throaty, deep accent noticeably different from French spoken in France. The vocabulary, however, is mostly the same as that used in France, with a few notable exceptions, such as the use of *septante* (instead of *soixante-dix*) for seventy.

Consonants at the end of words are mostly silent and not pronounced. *Ch* is pronounced *sh*; *th* is *t*; *w* is *v*; and *r* is rolled gutturally. *Ç* is pronounced *s*.

In an Emergency

Help!	**Au secours!**	oh sek**oor**
Stop!	**Arrêtez!**	aret-**ay**
Call a doctor!	**Appelez un médecin!**	apuh-**lay**uñ med**sañ**
Call the police!	**Appelez la police!**	apuh-**lay** lah pol-ees
Call the fire brigade!	**Appelez les pompiers!**	apuh-lay leh poñ-**peeyay**
Where is the nearest telephone?	**Où est le téléphone le plus proche?**	oo ay luh tehleh**fon** luh ploo **prosh**
nearest hospital?	**l'hôpital le plus proche?**	oo ay l'**opeetal** luh ploo **prosh**
nearest police station?	**commissariat de police le plus proche?**	oo ay luh **kom**-ee-sah-ree-**ah** deh pol-**ees** luh ploo **prosh**

Communication Essentials

Yes	**Oui**	wee
No	**Non**	noñ
Please	**S'il vous plait**	seel voo **play**
Thank you	**Merci**	mer-**see**
Excuse me	**Excusez-moi**	exkoo-**zay** mwah
Hello	**Bonjour**	boñ**zhoor**
Goodbye	**Au revoir**	oh ruh-**vwar**
Good night	**Bonne nuit**	boñ-**nwee**
morning	**le matin**	matañ
afternoon	**l'après-midi**	l'apreh-**meedee**
evening	**le soir**	swah
yesterday	**hier**	eeyehr
today	**aujourd'hui**	oh-zhoor-**dwee**
tomorrow	**demain**	duh**mañ**
here	**ici**	ee-**see**
there	**là-bas**	lah bah
What?	**Quel/quelle?**	kel, kel
When?	**Quand?**	koñ
Why?	**Pourquoi?**	poor-**kwah**
Where?	**Où?**	oo
How?	**Comment?**	kom-**moñ**
Now	**Maintenant**	maynt-**noñ**
Later	**Plus tard**	ploo-**tar**

Useful Phrases

How are you?	**Comment allez vous?**	kom-moñ talay voo
Very well, thank you	**Très bien, merci**	treh byañ, mer-**see**
How do you do?	**Comment ça va?**	kom-moñ sah **vah**
See you soon	**A bientôt**	byañ-toh
That's fine	**Ça va bien**	Sah vah byañ
Where is/are…?	**Où est/sont…?**	ooh ay/soñ
How far is it to…?	**Combien de kilomètres d'ici à…?**	kom-**byañ** duh keelo-**metr** d'ee-**see** ah
Which way to…?	**Quelle est la direction pour…?**	kel ay lah **deer**-ek-**syoñ** poor
Do you speak English?	**Parlez-vous anglais?**	par-**lay** voo -oñg-**lay**
I don't understand	**Je ne comprends pas**	zhuh nuh kom-**proñ** pah
Could you speak slowly?	**Pouvez-vous parler plus lentement?**	Poo-vay voo par-lay ploos **lon**tuh-moñ
I'm sorry	**Excusez-moi**	exkoo-**zay** mwah

Useful Words

big	**grand**	groñ
small	**petit**	puh-**tee**
hot	**chaud**	show
cold	**froid**	frwah
good	**bon**	boñ
bad	**mauvais**	moh-**veh**
enough	**assez**	as**say**
well	**bien**	byañ
open	**ouvert**	oo-**ver**
closed	**fermé**	fer-**meh**
left	**gauche**	gohsh
right	**droite**	drawht
straight on	**tout droit**	too drwah
near	**près**	preh
far	**loin**	lwañ
up	**en haut**	oñ oh
down	**en bas**	oñbah
early	**tôt**	toh
late	**tard**	tar
entrance	**l'entrée**	l'on-**tray**
exit	**la sortie**	sor-**tee**
toilet	**toilette**	twah-let
occupied	**occupé**	o-koo-**pay**
free (vacant)	**libre**	leebr
free (no charge)	**gratuit**	grah-**twee**

Making a Telephone Call

I would like to place a long-distance telephone call	**Je voudrais faire un interurbain**	zhuh voo-**dreh** faire uñ añter-oorbañ
I would like to call collect	**Je voudrais faire un communication PCV**	zhuh voo-**dreh** faire oon kom-oonikah-**syoñ** peh-seh-veh
I will try again later	**Je vais essayer plus tard**	zhuh vay ess-ay-eh ploo tar
Can I leave a message?	**Est-ce que je peux laisser un message?**	es-**keh** zhuh puh les-**say** uñ meh-**sazh**
Hold on	**Ne quittez pas, s'il vous plait**	nuh kee-**tay** pah seel voo **play**
Could you speak up a little please?	**Pouvez-vous parler un peu plus fort?**	poo-**vay** voo par-**lay** uñ puh ploo for
Local call	**Communication local**	komoonikah-**syoñ** low-**kal**

Shopping

How much does this cost?	**C'est combien?**	say kom-**byañ**
I would like….	**Je voudrais**	zhuh voo-**dray**
Do you have…?	**Est-ce que vous avez…?**	es-**kuh** voo zavay
I'm just looking	**Je regarde seulement**	zhuh ruh**gar** suhl-moñ
Do you take credit cards?	**Est-ce que vous acceptez les cartes de crédit?**	es-**kuh** voo zaksept-**ay** leh kart duh kreh-dee
Do you take travellers' cheques?	**Est-ce que vous acceptez les chèques de voyage?**	es-**kuh** voo zak-sept-**ay** lay shek duh vwayazh
What time do you open? you close?	**À quelle heure vous êtes ouvert? vous êtes fermé?**	ah kel urr voo zet oo-**ver** fer-**may**
This one	**Celui-ci**	suhl-wee **see**
That one	**Celui-là**	suhl-wee **lah**
expensive	**cher**	shehr
cheap	**pas cher, bon marché**	pah shehr, boñ mar-shay
size, clothes	**la taille**	tye
colour	**couleur**	kool-**urr**
white	**blanc**	bloñ
black	**noir**	nwahr
red	**rouge**	roozh
yellow	**jaune**	zhownh
green	**vert**	vehr
blue	**bleu**	bluh
orange	**orange**	oroñzh

English	French	Pronunciation
pink	rose	roz
brown	brun	broñ
purple	violet	vee-oh-lay
grey	gris	gree

Types of Shops

English	French	Pronunciation
antiques shop	le magasin d'antiquités	maga-zañ d'oñteekee-tay
bakery	la boulangerie	booloñ-zhuree
bank	la banque	boñk
bookshop	la librairie	lee-brehree
butcher	la boucherie	boo-shehree
cake shop	la pâtisserie	patee-sree
cheese shop	la fromagerie	fromazh-ree
chocolate shop	le chocolatier	shok-oh-lah-tyeh
chip stand	la friterie	free-tuh-ree
chemist	la pharmacie	farmah-see
delicatessen	la charcuterie	shah-koo-tuh-ree
department store	le grand magasin	groñ maga-zañ
fishmonger	la poissonerie	pwasson-ree
gift shop	le magasin de cadeaux	maga-zañ duh kadoh
greengrocer	le marchand des légumes	mar-shoñ duh lay-goom
grocery	l'alimentation	alee-moñta-syoñ
hairdresser	le coiffeur	kwafuhr
market	le marché	marsh ay
newsagent	le magasin de journaux	maga-zañ duh zhoor-no
post office	le bureau de poste	boo-roh duh pohst
supermarket	le supermarché	soo-pehr-marshay
travel agent	l'agence de voyage	l'azhons duh vwayazh

Sightseeing

English	French	Pronunciation
abbey	l'abbaye	labey-ee
airport	l'aeroport	layr-por
art gallery	la galérie d'art	galer-ree dart
bus station	la gare routière	gahr roo-tee-yehr
bus ticket	billet	bee-yay
cathedral	la cathédrale	katay-dral
church	l'église	laygleez
closed on public holidays	fermeture jour ferié	fehrmeh-tur zhoor fehree-ay
garden	le jardin	zhah-dañ
library	la bibliothèque	beebleeo-tek
museum	le musée	moo-zay
railway station	la gare	gahr
tourist office	les informations	layz uñ-for-mah-syoñ
town hall	l'hôtel de ville	lohtel duh vil
train	le train	luh trañ

Staying in a Hotel

English	French	Pronunciation
Do you have a vacant room?	est-ce que vous avez une chambre?	es-kuh voo zavay oon shambr
double room with a double bed	la chambre à deux personnes avec un grand lit	la shambr uh duh per-son uh-vek uñ groñ lee
twin room	la chambre à deux lits	la shambr ah duh lee
single room	la chambre à une personne	la shambr ah oon pehr-son
room with a bath shower	la chambre avec salle de bain une douche	la shambr ah-vek sal duh bañ oon doosh
key	clef	clay
I have a reservation	J'ai fait une réservation	zhay fay oon ray-zehrva-syoñ

Eating Out

English	French	Pronunciation
Have you got a table?	Avez vous une table libre?	avay-voo oon tahbl leebr
I would like to reserve a table	Je voudrais réserver une table	zhuh voo-dray rayzehr-vay oon tahbl
The bill, please	L'addition, s'il vous plait	l'adee-syoñ-seel voo play

English	French	Pronunciation
I am a vegetarian	Je suis végétarien	zhuh swee vezhay-tehryañ
menu	le menu	men-oo
fixed-price menu	le menu à prix fixe	men-oo ah pree feeks
cover charge	le couvert	koo-vehr
wine list	la carte des vins	kart-deh vañ
glass	le verre	vehr
bottle	la bouteille	boo-tay
knife	le couteau	koo-toh
fork	la fourchette	for-shet
spoon	la cuillère	kwee-yehr
breakfast	le petit déjeuner	puh-tee day-zhuh-nay
lunch	le déjeuner	day-zhuh-nay
dinner	le dîner	dee-nay
main course	le grand plat	groñ plah
first course	l'hors d'oeuvres	or duhvr
dessert	le dessert	duh-zehrt
dish of the day	le plat du jour	plah doo joor
drinks	boissons	bwa-ssoñ
bar	le bar	bah
wine bar	le bar à vin	bar ah-van
café	le café	ka-fay
rare	saignant	say-nyoñ
medium	à point	ah pwañ
well done	bien cuit	byañ kwee

Numbers

	French	Pronunciation
0	zero	zeh-roh
1	un/une	uñ, oon
2	deux	duh
3	trois	trwah
4	quatre	katr
5	cinq	sañk
6	six	sees
7	sept	set
8	huit	weet
9	neuf	nerf
10	dix	dees
11	onze	oñz
12	douze	dooz
13	treize	trehz
14	quatorze	katorz
15	quinze	kañz
16	seize	sehz
17	dix-sept	dees-set
18	dix-huit	dees-zweet
19	dix-neuf	dees-znerf
20	vingt	vañ
21	vingt-et-un	vañ tay uhn
30	trente	tront
40	quarante	karoñt
50	cinquante	sañkoñt
60	soixante	swahsoñt
70	soixante-dix septante	swahsoñt dees septoñt
80	quatre-vingt	katr-vañ
90	quatre-vingt-dix/ nonante	katr vañ dees nonoñt
95	quatre-vingt-quinze	katr vañ-kañz
100	cent	soñ
1000	mille	meel
1,000,000	million	miyoñ

Time

English	French	Pronunciation
What is the time?	Quelle heure est-il?	kel uhr ay-teel
one minute	une minute	oon mee-noot
one hour	une heure	oon uhr
half an hour	une demi-heure	oon duh-mee uhr
half past one	une heure et demi	oon uhr ay duh-mee
a day	un jour	uhn zhuhr
a week	une semaine	oon suh-mehn
a month	un mois	uhn mwah
a year	une année	oon annay
Monday	Lundi	luñ-dee
Tuesday	Mardi	mah-dee
Wednesday	Mercredi	mehrkruh-dee
Thursday	Jeudi	zhuh-dee
Friday	Vendredi	voñdruh-dee

Saturday	**Samedi**	sam-**dee**
Sunday	**Dimanche**	dee-**moñsh**

Food and Drink

asparagus	**asperges**	ahs-pehrj
bass	**bar/loup de mer**	bah/loo duh mare
beef	**boeuf**	buhf
beer	**une bière**	byahr
Brussels sprouts	**choux de bruxelles**	shoo duh broocksell
bread	**pain**	pan
butter	**buerre**	burr
chicken	**poulet**	poo-**lay**
chocolate	**chocolat**	shok-oh-lah
cheese	**fromage**	from-**azh**
coffee	**café**	kah-**fay**
draft beer	**bière à la pression**	byahr ah lah pres-**syoñ**
duck	**canard**	kan-**ar**
fish	**poisson**	pwah-**ssoñ**
fruit	**fruits**	frwee
garlic	**ail**	eye
green beans	**haricots verts**	arrykoh vehr
ham	**jambon**	zhañ-**boñ**
haricot beans	**haricots**	arrykoh
herring	**hareng**	ah-**roñ**
hot chocolate	**chocolat chaud**	shok-oh-lah shoh
house wine	**vin maison**	vañ may-sañ
lamb	**agneau**	ah**yoh**
lemonade	**limonade**	lee-moh-nad
lobster	**homard**	oh-ma
meat	**viande**	vee-**yand**
mineral water	**l'eau minérale**	l'oh meenay-ral
monkfish	**lotte**	lot

mustard	**moutarde**	moo-**tard**
orange juice	**jus d'orange**	zhoo doh-ronj
oyster	**huitre**	weetr
pancake	**crêpe**	crayp
pepper	**poivre**	pwavr
pheasant	**faisant**	feh-zoñ
pike	**brochet**	brosh-ay
pork	**porc**	por
potatoes	**pommes de terre**	pom-duh **tehr**
prawn	**crevette**	kreh-vet
red wine	**vin rouge**	vañ **roozh**
salmon	**saumon**	soh-moñ
salt	**sel**	sel
sausage	**saucisse**	soh-**sees**
scallop	**coquille Saint-Jacques**	kok-eel sañ jak
sea bream	**dorade/daurade**	doh-rad
shellfish	**crustacés**	**kroos**-ta-say
skate	**raie**	ray
soup	**potage**	poh-**tahz**
spinach	**épinard**	aypeenar
steak	**bifteck**	beef-**tek**
tea	**thé**	tay
trout	**truite**	trweet
truffle	**truffe**	troof
tuna	**thon**	toñ
veal	**veau**	voh
venison	**cerf/chevreuil**	sairf/shev-rui
vegetables	**légumes**	lay-**goom**
waffle	**gauffre**	gohfr
water	**l'eau**	l'oh
white coffee	**café au lait**	kah-**fay** oh lay
white wine	**vin blanc**	vañ **bloñ**
wine	**vin**	vañ